CERTIFICATE IN BOOKKEEPING AND ACCOUNTS

(MANUAL)

Institute of Certified Bookkeepers

Level III

British Library Cataloguing-in-Publication Data

A catalogue record for this book is available from the British Library.

Published by:

Kaplan Publishing UK
Unit 2 The Business Centre
Molly Millars Lane
Wokingham
RG41 2QZ

ISBN 978-1-78415-569-8

Printed and bound in Great Britain.

CONTENTS

Quality and accuracy are of the utmost importance to us so if you spot an error in any of our products, please send an email to mykaplanreporting@kaplan.com with full details.

Our Quality Co-ordinator will work with our technical team to verify the error and take action to ensure it is corrected in future editions.

INTRODUCTION

HOW TO USE THESE MATERIALS

These Kaplan Publishing learning materials have been carefully designed to make your learning experience as easy as possible and to give you the best chance of success in your ICB assessments.

They contain a number of features to help you in the study process.

The sections on the Syllabus and Study Skills should be read before you commence your studies.

They are designed to familiarise you with the nature and content of the assessment and to give you tips on how best to approach your studies.

STUDY TEXT

This study text has been specially prepared for the ICB qualification.

It is written in a practical and interactive style:

- key terms and concepts are clearly defined
- all topics are illustrated with practical examples with clearly worked solutions
- frequent activities throughout the chapters ensure that what you have learnt is regularly reinforced
- 'pitfalls' and 'assessment tips' help you avoid commonly made mistakes and help you focus on what is required to perform well in your assessment.
- practice workbook activities can be completed at the end of each chapter.

WORKBOOK

The workbook comprises:

Practice activities at the end of each chapter with solutions at the end of the text, to reinforce the work covered in each chapter.

The questions are divided into their relevant chapters and students may either attempt these questions as they work through the textbook, or leave some or all of these until they have completed the textbook as a final revision of what they have studied.

ICONS

The study chapters include the following icons throughout.

They are designed to assist you in your studies by identifying key definitions and the points at which you can test yourself on the knowledge gained.

Definition

These sections explain important areas of Knowledge which must be understood and reproduced in an assessment

Example

The illustrative examples can be used to help develop an understanding of topics before attempting the activity exercises

Activity

These are exercises which give the opportunity to assess your understanding of all the assessment areas.

SYLLABUS

Purpose of Level III Certificate in Bookkeeping and Accounts

The Level III Certificate in Bookkeeping and Accounting covers the preparation of ledger balances, control accounts and reconciliations, adjustments and the preparation of final accounts for non-incorporated businesses or organisations.

On completion of this qualification candidates will be able to carry out the role of an employed or self-employed bookkeeper, be able to reconcile bank statements with the ledgers, produce a VAT return, control the sales and purchases ledgers, post year-end adjustments and produce the final accounts for a sole trader, partnership and not-for-profit organisation in both a manual and a computerised system.

Before commencing the study at this level the candidate should have achieved ICB Level II Certificate in Bookkeeping or its equivalent with another awarding body.

This study text covers all the aspects of manual bookkeeping included in the syllabus.

Computerised Bookkeeping and Accounts for Level III is covered in a separate study text.

Learning objectives

On completion of the Level III Certificate in Bookkeeping and Accounts, the student will be able to:

- Understand the following areas of underpinning knowledge:
  - The importance of adhering to a set of ethical principles
  - How and when to take action to cope with unethical behaviour
  - The concepts of business entity, going concern, historical cost, consistency, prudence and accruals
  - The legal requirements for forming a partnership
  - Different ways of processing VAT for EU and non-EU transactions
  - Alternative VAT systems e.g. VAT margin scheme

- Prepare a bank reconciliation statement
- Understand the purpose and use of control accounts as a checking mechanism
- Account for VAT and prepare a VAT return
- Prepare a ledger account to record the disposal of a fixed asset and to calculate the profit or loss on disposal
- Calculate adjustments to the accounts including:
  - Opening and closing stock
  - Depreciation of fixed assets
  - Accruals and prepayments
  - Provision for doubtful debts
- Prepare the final accounts for a non-incorporated business including processing of adjustments for opening and closing stock, depreciation, accruals, prepayments, provision for doubtful debts in the following areas:
  - Sole trader
  - Partnership
  - Not-for-Profit Organisation

Learning Outcomes and Assessment criteria

The unit consists of five Learning Outcomes which are further broken down into Assessment criteria.

The computerised elements of these learning outcomes are covered in a separate study text.

The Learning Outcomes for both the manual and the computerised elements of Level III, as well as their assessment criteria, are listed below:

Topic 1 – Underpinning knowledge	
Learning Outcome	**Assessment Criteria**
1.1 Understand the importance of adhering to a code of ethical principles	Be able to: • understand the importance of adhering to a set of professional ethics when working with clients, suppliers, colleagues and others with regards to: – integrity and honesty – objectivity – professional competence and due care and diligence – confidentiality – professional behaviour including separating personal duties from business life – adhering to organisational codes of practice and regulations – working within own professional experience, knowledge and expertise
1.2 Understand when and how to take appropriate action to cope with unethical behaviour	Be able to: • identify relevant authorities to whom unethical behaviour, suspected illegal acts or other malpractice should be reported • identify inappropriate client behaviour and how to report it to relevant authorities • explain the procedure which should be followed if it is suspected that an act has been committed which is believed to be unethical, or illegal
1.3 Understand the legal differences between the structures of various types of businesses	Be able to: • understand the nature of liability for sole traders and partners • define the term partnership • identify the characteristics of a partnership agreement • understand the rules that apply in the absence of a partnership agreement • identify the characteristics of not-for-profit organisations and their accounting requirements

<table>
<tr><td>1.4 Understand the main accounting concepts that apply</td><td>Be able to:
• identify and explain the concepts of:
– business entity, going concern, historical cost, consistency, prudence, accruals
• identify the method of producing accounts for those businesses who may declare income under the simpler income tax regime for the simplest small businesses</td></tr>
<tr><td>1.5 Understand the different rules that apply when processing VAT transactions</td><td>Be able to:
• understand that there are different schemes for applying VAT such as:
– annual accounting scheme
– flat rate scheme
– retail scheme
– partial exemption
– VAT margin scheme
Note: questions will not be set testing data entry or completion of VAT returns for such schemes</td></tr>
<tr><td colspan="2">Topic 2 – Reconciliation of accounts and correction of errors</td></tr>
<tr><td>Learning Outcome</td><td>Assessment Criteria</td></tr>
<tr><td>2.1 Reconcile supplier statements</td><td>Be able to:
• reconcile supplier statements with the accounts</td></tr>
<tr><td>2.2 Prepare a bank reconciliation statement.</td><td>In both a manual and computerised system, be able to:
• compare individual items on the bank statement with those in the cash book
• up-date the cash book
• prepare the bank reconciliation statement</td></tr>
<tr><td>2.3 Use control accounts to reconcile sales and purchase ledgers</td><td>In both a manual and computerised system, be able to:
• reconcile sales and purchase ledger control accounts with totals from the subsidiary ledgers to check the accuracy of the ledgers</td></tr>
</table>

2.4 Understand the need to correct errors	Be able to: • understand what to do if the trial balance does not balance • open a suspense account where applicable to account for any imbalance in the trial balance • identify and correct errors, including the correct treatment for VAT, that do not affect the trial balance e.g. omission, commission, principle, original entry, reversal, compensating • prepare and clear the suspense account as appropriate • produce a corrected trial balance • prepare journal entries for the above errors • post relevant corrections in a computerised system
Topic 3 – VAT Returns	
Learning Outcome	**Assessment Criteria**
3.1 Reconcile the VAT account	In both a manual and computerised system, be able to: • reconcile the VAT return figures with the VAT account
3.2 Complete a VAT return	In both a manual and computerised system, be able to: • complete and submit a VAT return (standard and/or cash VAT only)
Topic 4 – Calculate and post adjustments to the ledgers	
Learning Outcome	**Assessment Criteria**
4.1 Calculate depreciation	Be able to: • calculate depreciation on a fixed asset using both straight line and reducing balance method • calculate the original cost price of an asset given net book value and depreciation rates and number of years of depreciation

<table>
<tr><td>4.2 Account for the disposal of fixed assets</td><td>In both a manual and computerised system, be able to:
<ul>
<li>correctly identify the original cost of the asset disposed of</li>
<li>correctly identify and record all disposal costs and revenues in the appropriate accounts</li>
<li>correctly calculate and determine the cumulative depreciation to date on a disposal</li>
<li>prepare the disposal account</li>
<li>determine profit and or loss on sale of the asset</li>
<li>make relevant journal entries to record the disposal</li>
</ul></td></tr>
<tr><td>4.3 Understand the need to allow for adjustments to the accounts</td><td>In both a manual and computerised system, be able to:
<ul>
<li>post entries to the ledgers for the following adjustments:
<ul>
<li>opening and closing stock including valuing stock at the lower of cost and net realisable value</li>
<li>accruals and prepayments including dealing with the relevant entries in the following year</li>
<li>depreciation (straight line and reducing balance)</li>
<li>account for the revaluation of fixed assets</li>
<li>provision for doubtful debts account including
<ul>
<li>identifying the need to provide such a provision</li>
<li>calculating the provision</li>
<li>accounting for both an increase and decrease in the provision</li>
<li>preparing the relevant journal entry</li>
</ul></li>
</ul></li>
</ul></td></tr>
<tr><td colspan="2">Topic 5 – Final accounts of non-incorporated businesses</td></tr>
<tr><td>Learning Outcome</td><td>Assessment Criteria</td></tr>
<tr><td>5.1 Prepare a set of final accounts for a sole trader from a given trial balance</td><td>In both a manual and computerised system, be able to:
<ul>
<li>prepare a trading and profit and loss account from a trial balance to include adjustments</li>
<li>prepare a Balance Sheet showing clearly the main categories of assets and liabilities</li>
<li>close down the revenue accounts at the year end</li>
</ul></td></tr>
</table>

5.2 Prepare a set of final accounts for 'not-for-profit' organisations	In both a manual and computerised system, be able to: • prepare an opening statement of affairs • distinguish between a receipts and payments account and an income and expenditure account • make adjustments for accruals, prepayments, depreciation and the treatment of subscriptions in arrears and advance • prepare the Income and Expenditure account • prepare a Balance Sheet • close down the revenue accounts at the year end • prepare a brief summary of the accounts for the membership
5.3 Prepare a set of final accounts for a partnership	In both a manual and computerised system, be able to: • prepare a trading and profit and loss account and appropriation account from a trial balance to include adjustments • provide for the revaluation of assets and show the effect on the various capital and/or current accounts • prepare relevant partnership accounts: capital accounts and current accounts • prepare a balance sheet showing clearly the main categories of assets and liabilities • close down the revenue accounts at the year end

THE ASSESSMENT

The format of the assessment

The testing of knowledge and skills for the qualification will comprise three online assessments, all of which are taken in the candidate's home or place of work plus one assessment taken at an external ICB centre. All assessments will include testing of the Level III Bookkeeping and Accounts (Computerised) syllabus topics.

Paper BA4: Reconciliations and final accounts of a sole trader

- Home/place of work based assessment to include:
- Underpinning knowledge (5% weighting)
- Reconciliation and correction of errors (customer and supplier reconciliations, bank reconciliation, correction of errors) (15% weighting)
- VAT Returns (15% weighting)
- Posting adjustments including disposal and acquisition of fixed assets (15% weighting)
- Final accounts of a sole trader (20% weighting)
- Production of final accounts of a sole trader with adjustments using a computerised package (30% weighting)

This paper must be sat first.

Paper BA5 – Final accounts of a partnership

Home/place of work based assessment to include:

- Underpinning knowledge (10% weighting)
- Posting adjustments including disposal and acquisition of fixed assets (30% weighting)
- Final accounts of a partnership including the appropriation account and production of partners' current accounts (60% weighting)

Paper BA6 – Final accounts of a not-for-profit organisation

Home/place of work based assessment to include:

- Underpinning knowledge (10% weighting)
- Posting adjustments including the subscriptions account and disposal and acquisition of fixed assets (30% weighting)
- Final accounts of a not-for-profit organisation (60% weighting)

These two papers can be sat in any order.

Paper BA7 – Level III External Assessment

A single assessment to be taken at an ICB assessment centre will be a mixture of multi-choice and data entry questions which will cover all elements of the syllabus.

This assessment is taken last of all.

All assessments must be successfully achieved to gain the full qualification.

Each assessment will generate a separate unit accreditation notification.

STUDY SKILLS

Preparing to study

Devise a study plan

Determine which times of the week you will study.

Split these times into sessions of at least one hour for study of new material. Any shorter periods could be used for revision or practice.

Put the times you plan to study onto a study plan for the weeks from now until the assessment and set yourself targets for each period of study – in your sessions make sure you cover the whole course, activities and the associated questions in the study text and revision kit.

If you are studying more than one unit at a time, try to vary your subjects as this can help to keep you interested and see subjects as part of wider knowledge.

When working through your course, compare your progress with your plan and, if necessary, re-plan your work (perhaps including extra sessions) or, if you are ahead, do some extra revision / practice questions.

Effective studying

Active reading

You are not expected to learn the text by rote, rather, you must understand what you are reading and be able to use it to pass the assessment and develop good practice.

A good technique is to use SQ3Rs – Survey, Question, Read, Recall, Review:

1 **Survey the chapter**

Look at the headings and read the introduction, knowledge, skills and content, so as to get an overview of what the chapter deals with.

2 **Question**

Whilst undertaking the survey ask yourself the questions you hope the chapter will answer for you.

3 Read

Read through the chapter thoroughly working through the activities.

4 Recall

At the end of each section and at the end of the chapter, try to recall the main ideas of the section / chapter without referring to the text. This is best done after short break of a couple of minutes after the reading stage.

5 Review

Check that your recall notes are correct.

You may also find it helpful to re-read the chapter to try and see the topic(s) it deals with as a whole.

Note taking

Taking notes is a useful way of learning, but do not simply copy out the text.

The notes must:

- be in your own words
- be concise
- cover the key points
- be well organised
- be modified as you study further chapters in this text or in related ones.

Trying to summarise a chapter without referring to the text can be a useful way of determining which areas you know and which you don't.

Three ways of taking notes

1 **Summarise the key points of a chapter**

2 **Make linear notes**

A list of headings, subdivided with sub-headings listing the key points.

If you use linear notes, you can use different colours to highlight key points and keep topic areas together.

Use plenty of space to make your notes easy to use.

3 **Try a diagrammatic form**

The most common of which is a mind map.

To make a mind map, put the main heading in the centre of the paper and put a circle around it.

Draw lines radiating from this to the main sub-headings which again have circles around them.

Continue the process from the sub-headings to sub-sub-headings.

Highlighting and underlining

You may find it useful to underline or highlight key points in your study text – but do be selective.

You may also wish to make notes in the margins.

Revision phase

Kaplan has produced material specifically designed for your final assessment preparation for this unit.

These include a bank of revision questions that both test your knowledge and allow you to practice questions similar to those you will face in the assessment.

Further guidance on how to approach the final stage of your studies is given in these materials.

Double entry bookkeeping

1

Introduction

A sound knowledge of double entry underpins many of the learning outcomes and skills required for Level III. A sound understanding of double entry bookkeeping is essential in order to pass this unit: candidates will be tested on this in the assessment and so this must be very familiar ground.

CONTENTS

1 Principles behind double entry bookkeeping

1.1 Introduction

There are two main principles that underlie the process of double entry bookkeeping – these are the dual effect and the separate entity concept.

1.2 The dual effect

Definition

The principle of the dual effect is that each and **every** transaction that a business makes has **two** effects.

For example if a business buys goods for cash then the two effects are that cash has decreased and that the business now has some purchases. The principle of double entry bookkeeping is that each of these effects must be shown in the ledger accounts by a ***debit entry*** in one account and an equal ***credit entry*** in another account.

Each and every transaction that a business undertakes has ***two equal and opposite effects.***

1.3 The separate entity concept

Definition

The separate entity concept (also referred to as the business entity concept – see below) is that the business is a completely separate accounting entity from the owner.

Therefore if the owner pays his personal money into a business bank account this becomes the capital of the business which is owed back to the owner. Similarly if the owner takes money out of the business in the form of drawings then the amount of capital owed to the owner is reduced.

The business itself is a completely separate entity in accounting terms from the owner of the business.

1.4 The accounting equation

At its simplest, the accounting equation simply says that:

Assets = Liabilities

If we treat the owner's capital as a special form of liability then the accounting equation is:

Assets = Liabilities + Capital

Or, rearranging:

Assets – Liabilities = Capital

Profit will increase the proprietor's capital and drawings will reduce it, so that we can write the equation as:

Assets – Liabilities = Capital + Profit – Drawings

1.5 Rules for double entry bookkeeping

There are a number of rules that can help to determine which two accounts are to be debited and credited for a transaction:

- When money is paid out by a business this is a credit entry in the cash or bank account.
- When money is received by a business this is a debit entry in the cash or bank account.
- An asset or an increase in an asset is always recorded on the debit side of its account.
- A liability or an increase in a liability is always recorded on the credit side of its account.
- An expense is recorded as a debit entry in the expense account.
- Income is recorded as a credit entry in the income account.

The Golden Rule

Every debit has an equal and opposite credit.

Ledger account

A debit entry represents	**A credit entry represents**
An increase to an asset	An increase to a liability
A decrease to a liability	A decrease to an asset
An item of expense	An item of income

For increases we can remember this as DEAD CLIC

Ledger account

Debtors	Creditors
Expenses	Liabilities
Assets	Income
Drawings	Capital

2 Accounting Concepts

2.1 Introduction

Accounting Concepts are fundamental principles or assumptions that underpin the preparation of financial statements. Two of these concepts, the going concern concept and the accruals or matching principle, are embedded in current accounting standards.

At this level of study you need an understanding of the following fundamental principles.

- Business Entity
- Going Concern
- Accruals Concept (or Matching Concept)
- Historical Cost
- Consistency
- Prudence

2.2 Business Entity

This concept is based on the principle that the financial information relates solely to the activities of the business, not the activities of its owner(s). Therefore, for accounting purposes, the business and its owner(s) are seen to be two separately identifiable entities.

2.3 Going concern

The going concern concept assumes that a business (or entity) will **continue in operational existence for the foreseeable future**.

This means that the financial statements are drawn up on the assumption that there is no **intention or necessity to liquidate or curtail significantly the scale of operation**.

Circumstances where the going concern assumption would not be justified would include:

(i) where there is a specific intention to liquidate the business in the near future

(ii) where there is a strong possibility that shortage of finance will force the business into liquidation. This may be revealed by preparing a cash flow forecast for the next 12 months where a month-by-month comparison of expected cash inflows and outflows indicates financing requirements that are unlikely to be satisfied by the bank or by outside lenders

(iii) where there is a strong possibility that shortage of finance will result in the sale of a significant part of the business.

In the above circumstances the going concern assumption would not be valid, and the financial statements would be prepared on a basis which takes the likely consequences into account.

In most cases, however, financial statements will be prepared on a going concern basis and the owners of the business will be able to justify the idea that such a basis is valid.

2.4 Accruals concept (Matching concept)

The accruals or matching concept states that costs and revenues should be matched one with the other and dealt with in the accounting period to which they relate.

The starting position should be to use the concept to determine the accounting period in which revenue (i.e. sales) is recognised.

Revenue is usually recognised when it is realised. The realisation of revenue is usually taken to occur on the date of sale rather than on the date when the cash relating to the sale is received.

The efforts of expenditure in the past have led to the revenues accruing now. It is therefore logical to match the costs or expenses of earning revenue with the revenue reported in any particular period. The accounting profit determined in this way is supposed to indicate how efficiently the resources of the business have been utilised.

Although the accruals or matching principle is conceptually simple, it does run into practical difficulties.

For example, expenditure on fixed assets will provide benefits extending over several accounting periods. When a fixed asset is acquired it is necessary to estimate its useful life. The **service potential** of a fixed asset will diminish over its useful life, and this reduction is a cost or expense to be matched against the revenue of each period and is called **depreciation**.

2.5 Historical cost

The historical cost accounting system is a system of accounting in which all transactions are recorded at their original value and are not adjusted for the effects of inflation.

2.6 Consistency

A business should be consistent in its accounting treatment of similar items, both **within** a particular accounting period and **between** one accounting period and the next.

For example, in the case of depreciation of fixed assets, there is more than one accepted accounting treatment. One business may use one method, another business may use another. As far as the consistency concept is concerned, once a business has selected a method, it should use this method consistently for all assets in that class and for all accounting periods. Only in this way can users of financial statements draw meaningful conclusions from reported results. If a business were to change any of its accounting policies (e.g. the basis of depreciation) it must have a good reason for doing so.

2.7 Prudence

Prudence states that revenues and profits are not reported and recognised in the financial statements unless realised. Revenues and profits are not deemed realised until the likelihood of conversion to cash is high. In most cases this means the date of sale. By way of contrast, immediate provision is made for anticipated losses, even if such losses are not yet realised.

An example of the prudence concept is the situation in which a liability has been estimated to be between £500 and £600. Some accountants will make provision for the highest estimate on the grounds of prudence. Modern accounting thought though would make provision for the most likely value, high or low.

3 Double entry – cash/bank transactions

3.1 Introduction

For this revision of double entry bookkeeping we will start with accounting for cash/bank transactions – remember that money paid out is a credit entry in the cash/bank account and money received is a debit entry in the cash/bank account.

Cash/Bank Account	
DEBIT	**CREDIT**
Money in	Money out

Example

Dan Baker decides to set up in business as a sole trader by paying £20,000 into a business bank account. The following transactions are then entered into:

(i) purchase of a van for deliveries by writing a cheque for £5,500;

(ii) purchase of goods for resale by a cheque for £2,000;

(iii) payment of shop rental by standing order for £500;

(iv) sale of goods for £2,500 (paid by cheque by the customer);

(v) Dan withdrew £200 from the bank for his own personal expenses.

State the two effects of each of these transactions and record them in the relevant ledger accounts.

Solution

Money paid into the business bank account by Dan:

- increase in bank;
- capital now owed back to Dan.

Double entry:

- a debit to the bank account as money is coming in
- a credit to the capital account

Bank account

	£		£
Capital	20,000		

Capital account

	£		£
		Bank	20,000

(i) Purchase of a van for deliveries by writing a cheque for £5,500;

- bank decreases
- the business has a fixed asset, the van

Double entry:

- a credit to the bank account as cash is being paid out
- a debit to an asset account, the van account

Bank account

	£		£
Capital	20,000	Van	5,500

Van account

	£		£
Bank	5,500		

(ii) Purchase of goods for resale by a cheque for £2,000

- decrease in the bank balance
- increase in purchases

Double entry:

- a credit to the bank account as money is paid out
- a debit to the purchases account, an expense account

Purchases of stock are always recorded in a purchases account and never in a stock account. The stock account is only dealt with at the end of each accounting period and this will be dealt with in a later chapter.

Bank account

	£		£
Capital	20,000	Van	5,500
		Purchases	2,000

Purchases account

	£		£
Bank	2,000		

(iii) Payment of shop rental by standing order, £500

- decrease in the bank balance
- expense incurred

Double entry:

- a credit to the bank account as money is paid out
- a debit to the rent account, an expense

Bank account

	£		£
Capital	20,000	Van	5,500
		Purchases	2,000
		Rent	500

Rent account

	£		£
Bank	500		

(iv) Sale of goods for £2,500

- the bank balance increases
- sales increase

Double entry:

- a debit to the bank account as money is coming in
- a credit to the sales account, income

Bank account

	£		£
Capital	20,000	Van	5,500
Sales	2,500	Purchases	2,000
		Rent	500

Sales account

	£		£
		Bank	2,500

(v) Dan withdrew £200 from the bank for his own personal expenses

- the bank balance decreases
- drawings increase (money taken out of the business by the owner)

Double entry:

- a credit to the bank account as money is paid out
- a debit to the drawings account

Bank account

	£		£
Capital	20,000	Van	5,500
Sales	2,500	Purchases	2,000
		Rent	500
		Drawings	200

Drawings account

	£		£
Bank	200		

4 Double entry – credit transactions

4.1 Introduction

We will now introduce sales on credit and purchases on credit and the receipt of money from debtors and payment of money to creditors. For the sales and purchases on credit there is no cash increase or decrease therefore the cash/bank account rule cannot be used. Remember though that increase in income (sales) is always a credit entry and an increase in an expense (purchases) is a debit entry.

Example

Dan now makes some further transactions:

(i) purchases are made on credit for £3,000

(ii) sales are made on credit for £4,000

(iii) Dan pays £2,000 to the credit suppliers

(iv) £2,500 is received from the credit customers

(v) Dan returned goods costing £150 to a supplier

(vi) goods were returned by a customer which had cost £200.

State the two effects of each of these transactions and write them up in the appropriate ledger accounts.

Solution

(i) Purchases are made on credit for £3,000

- increase in purchases
- increase in creditors

Double entry:

- a debit entry to the purchases account, an expense
- a credit to the creditors account

Purchases account

	£		£
Bank	2,000		
Creditors	3,000		

Creditors account

	£		£
		Purchases	3,000

(ii) Sales are made on credit for £4,000

- increase in sales
- increase in debtors

Double entry:

- a credit entry to the sales account, income
- a debit entry to the debtors account

Sales account

	£		£
		Bank	2,500
		Debtors	4,000

Debtors account

	£		£
Sales	4,000		

(iii) Dan pays £2,000 to the suppliers

- decrease in the bank account
- decrease in creditors

Double entry:

- a credit entry to the bank account as money is paid out
- a debit entry to creditors as they are reduced

Bank account

	£		£
Capital	20,000	Van	5,500
Sales	2,500	Purchases	2,000
		Rent	500
		Drawings	200
		Creditors	2,000

Creditors account

	£		£
Bank	2,000	Purchases	3,000

(iv) £2,500 is received from the credit customers

- increase in bank
- decrease in debtors

Double entry

- a debit entry in the bank account as money is received
- a credit entry to debtors as they are reduced

Bank account

	£		£
Capital	20,000	Van	5,500
Sales	2,500	Purchases	2,000
Debtors	2,500	Rent	500
		Drawings	200
		Creditors	2,000

Debtors account

	£		£
Sales	4,000	Bank	2,500

(v) Dan returned goods costing £150 to a supplier

- purchases returns increase
- creditors decrease

Double entry

- a debit entry to the creditors account as creditors are now decreasing
- a credit entry to the purchases returns account (the easiest way to remember this entry is that it is the opposite of purchases which are a debit entry)

Creditors account

	£		£
Bank	2,000	Purchases	3,000
Purchases returns	150		

Purchases returns account

	£		£
		Creditors	150

(vi) Goods were returned by a customer which had cost £200

- sales returns increase
- debtors decrease

Double entry:

- a credit entry to the debtors account as debtors are now decreasing
- a debit entry to sales returns (the opposite to sales which is a credit entry)

Debtors account

	£		£
Sales	4,000	Bank	2,500
		Sales returns	200

Sales returns account

	£		£
Debtors	200		

5 Balancing a ledger account

5.1 Introduction

Once all of the transactions for a period have been recorded in the ledger accounts then it is likely that the owner will want to know the answer to questions such as how much cash there is in the bank account or how much has been spent on purchases. This can be found by balancing the ledger accounts.

5.2 Procedure for balancing a ledger account

The following steps should be followed when balancing a ledger account:

Step 1

Total both the debit and credit columns to find the larger total – enter this figure as the total for both the debit and credit columns.

Step 2

For the side that does not add up to this total put in the figure that makes it add up and call it the balance carried down.

Step 3

Enter the balance brought down on the opposite side below the totals.

Example

We will now balance Dan's bank account.

Bank account

	£		£
Capital	20,000	Van	5,500
Sales	2,500	Purchases	2,000
Debtors	2,500	Rent	500
		Drawings	200
		Creditors	2,000

Bank account

	£		£
Capital	20,000	Van	5,500
Sales	2,500	Purchases	2,000
Debtors	2,500	Rent	500
		Drawings	200
		Creditors	2,000
		Balance c/d ***Step 2***	**14,800**
Step 1	**25,000**	***Step 1***	**25,000**
Balance b/d ***Step 3***	**14,800**		

Activity 1

(a) Show by means of ledger accounts how the following transactions would be recorded in the books of Bertie Dooks, a seller of second-hand books:

- (i) paid in cash £5,000 as capital;
- (ii) took the lease of a stall and paid six months' rent – the yearly rental was £300;
- (iii) spent £140 cash on the purchase of books from W Smith;
- (iv) purchased on credit from J Fox books at a cost of £275;
- (v) paid an odd-job man £25 to paint the exterior of the stall and repair a broken lock;
- (vi) put an advertisement in the local paper at a cost of £2;
- (vii) sold three volumes containing The Complete Works of William Shakespeare to a customer for £35 cash;
- (viii) sold a similar set on credit to a local schoolmaster for £3;
- (ix) paid J Fox £175 on account for the amount due to him;
- (x) received £1 from the schoolmaster;
- (xi) purchased cleaning materials at a cost of £2 and paid £3 to a cleaner;
- (xii) took £5 from the business to pay for his own groceries.

(b) Balance off the ledgers, clearly showing balance carried down (c/d) and balance brought down (b/d).

6 Ledger accounting and the trial balance

6.1 Introduction

Definition

A trial balance is the list of the balances on all of the ledger accounts in an organisation's main or general ledger.

6.2 Trial balance

The trial balance will appear as a list of debit balances and credit balances depending upon the type of account. If the double entry has been correctly carried out then the debit balance total should be equal to the credit balance total.

A trial balance lists all of the ledger account balances in the general ledger.

6.3 Preparing the trial balance

When all of the entries have been made in the ledger accounts for a period, the trial balance will then be prepared.

Step 1

Balance off each ledger account and bring down the closing balance.

Step 2

List each balance brought down as either a debit balance or a credit balance.

Step 3

Total the debit balances and the credit balances to see if they are equal.

Example

Given below are the initial transactions for Mr Smith, a sole trader. Enter the transactions in the ledger accounts using a separate account for each debtor and creditor. Produce the trial balance for this sole trader at the end of 12 January 20X1.

On 1 Jan 20X1	Mr Smith put £12,500 into the business bank account.
On 2 Jan 20X1	He bought goods for resale costing £750 on credit from J Oliver. He also bought on the same basis £1,000 worth from K Hardy.
On 3 Jan 20X1	Sold goods for £800 to E Morecombe on credit.
On 5 Jan 20X1	Mr Smith returned £250 worth of goods bought from J Oliver, being substandard goods.
On 6 Jan 20X1	Sold goods on credit to A Wise for £1,000.
On 7 Jan 20X1	Mr Smith withdrew £100 from the bank for his personal use.
On 8 Jan 20X1	Bought a further £1,500 worth of goods from K Hardy, again on credit.
On 9 Jan 20X1	A Wise returned £200 worth of goods sold to him on the 6th
On 10 Jan 20X1	The business paid J Oliver £500 by cheque, and K Hardy £1,000 also by cheque.
On 12 Jan 20X1	Mr Smith banked a cheque for £800 received from E Morecombe.

Solution

Step 1

Enter the transactions into the ledger accounts and then balance off each ledger account. Use a separate ledger account for each debtor and creditor. (Note that in most assessments you will be required to complete the double entry for debtors and creditors in the sales ledger control account and purchase ledger control account as seen in Level II, but for practice we are using the separate accounts.)

Step 2

Balance off each of the ledger accounts as at 12th January.

Capital account

	£		£
		1 Jan Bank	12,500

Sales account

	£		£
		3 Jan E Morecombe	800
12 Jan Balance c/d	1,800	6 Jan A Wise	1,000
	1,800		1,800
		13 Jan Balance b/d	1,800

Purchases account

	£		£
2 Jan J Oliver	750		
2 Jan K Hardy	1,000		
8 Jan K Hardy	1,500	12 Jan Balance c/d	3,250
	3,250		3,250
13 Jan Balance b/d	3,250		

Purchases returns account

	£		£
		5 Jan J Oliver	250

Sales returns account

	£		£
9 Jan A Wise	200		

Drawings account

	£		£
7 Jan Bank	100		

Bank account

		£			£
1 Jan	Capital	12,500	7 Jan	Drawings	100
12 Jan	E Morecombe	800	10 Jan	J Oliver	500
				K Hardy	1,000
			12 Jan	Balance c/d	11,700
		13,300			13,300
13 Jan	Balance b/d	11,700			

Debtor – E Morecombe account

		£			£
3 Jan	Sales	800	12 Jan	Bank	800

Debtor – A Wise account

		£			£
6 Jan	Sales	1,000	9 Jan	Sales returns	200
			12 Jan	Balance c/d	800
		1,000			1,000
13 Jan	Balance b/d	800			

Creditor – J Oliver account

		£			£
5 Jan	Purchases returns	250	2 Jan	Purchases	750
10 Jan	Bank	500			
		750			750

Creditor – K Hardy account

	£		£
10 Jan Bank	1,000	2 Jan Purchases	1,000
12 Jan Balance c/d	1,500	8 Jan Purchases	1,500
	2,500		2,500
		13 Jan Balance b/d	1,500

Note that accounts with only one entry do not need to be balanced as this entry is the final balance on the account.

Step 3

Produce the trial balance by listing each balance brought down as either a debit balance or a credit balance.

Make sure that you use the balance brought down below the total line as the balance to list in the trial balance.

Step 4

Total the debit and credit columns to check that they are equal.

Trial balance as at 12 January 20X1 for Mr Smith

	Debits	*Credits*
	£	£
Capital		12,500
Sales		1,800
Purchases	3,250	
Purchases returns		250
Sales returns	200	
Drawings	100	
Bank	11,700	
Debtor – A Wise	800	
Creditor – K Hardy		1,500
	16,050	16,050

6.4 Purpose of the trial balance

One of the main purposes of a trial balance is to serve as a check on the double entry. If the trial balance does not balance, i.e. the debit and credit totals are not equal then some errors have been made in the double entry. The trial balance can also serve as the basis for preparing an extended trial balance (this is not part of the Level III syllabus) and finally the financial statements of the organisation.

Activity 2

Enter the following details of transactions for the month of May 20X6 into the appropriate books of account. You should also extract a trial balance as at 1 June 20X6. Open a separate ledger account for each debtor and creditor, and also keep separate 'cash' and 'bank' ledger accounts. Balance off each account and prepare a trial balance.

20X6	
1 May	Started in business by paying £6,800 into the bank.
3 May	Bought goods on credit from the following: J Johnson £400; D Nixon £300 and J Agnew £250.
5 May	Cash sales £300.
6 May	Paid rates by cheque £100.
8 May	Paid wages £50 in cash.
9 May	Sold goods on credit: K Homes £300; J Homes £300; B Hood £100.
10 May	Bought goods on credit: J Johnson £800; D Nixon £700.
11 May	Returned goods to J Johnson £150.
15 May	Bought office fixtures £600 by cheque.
18 May	Bought a motor vehicle £3,500 by cheque.
22 May	Goods returned by J Homes £100.
25 May	Paid J Johnson £1,000; D Nixon £500, both by cheque.
26 May	Paid wages £150 by cheque

6.5 Debit or credit balance?

When you are balancing a ledger account it is easy to see which side, debit or credit, the balance brought down is on. However if you were given a list of balances rather than the account itself then it is sometimes difficult to decide which side the balance should be shown in the trial balance, the debit or the credit?

There are some rules to help here:

- assets are debit balances;
- expenses are debit balances;
- liabilities are credit balances;
- income is a credit balance.

6.6 Discounts allowed and received

Another common problem area is determining whether settlement discounts allowed and received are debits or credits.

The double entry for a discount allowed to a customer is:

- debit to the discounts allowed account (an expense account);
- credit to the debtors account (reducing the amount owed by the customer).Therefore the balance on the discounts allowed account is a debit balance. This is an expense of the business as it is the cost to the business of getting the money due into their bank account earlier.

The double entry for a discount received from a supplier is:

- debit to the creditors account (reducing the amount owed to the supplier);
- credit to the discounts received account (a form of sundry income).

Therefore the balance on the discounts received account is a credit balance. This is income as it means that the business has paid less for the goods than originally envisaged although the payment was made earlier.

Activity 3

The following balances have been extracted from the books of Fitzroy at 31 December 20X2:

Prepare a trial balance at 31 December 20X2.

	£	Debit	Credit
Capital on 1 January 20X2	106,149		
Freehold factory at cost	360,000		
Motor vehicles at cost	126,000		
Stocks at 1 January 20X2	37,500		
Debtors	15,600		
Cash in hand	225		
Bank overdraft	82,386		
Creditors	78,900		
Sales	318,000		
Purchases	165,000		
Rent and rates	35,400		
Discounts allowed	6,600		
Insurance	2,850		
Sales returns	10,500		
Purchase returns	6,300		
Loan from bank	240,000		
Sundry expenses	45,960		
Drawings	26,100		
TOTALS			

Activity 4

(1) The rental income account for January is as follows:

Rent Account

	£		£
Balance b/d	1,900	Bank account	7,000
Invoice	2,500		
Invoice	500		
	______		______
	______		______

At the end of the month there is a **debit/credit** balance of **£7,000/4,900/2,100.**

Circle the correct answer.

(2) True or false, to increase a liability a debit entry is made.

True

False

Select the correct answer for question 2.

Circle the correct answer for questions 3, 4, 5, 6 and 7.

(3) When a sole trader uses goods for resale for his own personal use the drawings account is **Debited / Credited** and the purchases account is **Debited / Credited**

(4) When a supplier is paid the bank account is **Debited / Credited** and the supplier account is **Debited / Credited**

(5) When goods are sold to a debtor, the sales account is **Debited / Credited** and the debtor account is **Debited / Credited**

(6) A bank overdraft is a **Debit / Credit** balance.

(7) Discounts received are a **Debit / Credit** balance.

7 Summary

The basic principles of double entry are of great importance for this unit and in particular all students should be able to determine whether a particular balance on an account is a debit or a credit balance in the trial balance.

Answers to chapter activities

Activity 1

Ledger accounts

Cash account

	£		£
Capital account (i)	5,000	Rent (six months) (ii)	150
Sales (vii)	35	Purchases (iii)	140
Debtors (x)	1	Repairs (v)	25
		Advertising (vi)	2
		Creditors (ix)	175
		Cleaning (xi)	5
		Drawings (xii)	5
		Balance c/d	4,534
	5,036		5,036
Balance b/d	4,534		

J Fox – Creditor account

	£		£
Cash (ix)	175	Purchases (iv)	275
Balance c/d	100		
	275		275
		Balance b/d	100

Schoolmaster – Debtor account

	£		£
Sales (viii)	3	Cash (x)	1
		Balance c/d	2
	3		3
Balance b/d	2		

Capital account

	£		£
Balance c/d	5,000	Cash (i)	5,000
	5,000		5,000
		Balance b/d	5,000

Sales account

	£		£
		Cash (vii)	35
Balance c/d	38	Schoolmaster (viii)	3
	38		38
		Balance b/d	38

Purchases account

	£		£
Cash (iii)	140	Balance c/d	415
J Fox (iv)	275		
	415		415
Balance b/d	415		

Rent account

	£		£
Cash (ii)	150	Balance c/d	150
	150		150
Balance b/d	150		

Repairs account

	£		£
Cash (v)	25	Balance c/d	25
	25		25
Balance b/d	25		

Advertising account

	£		£
Cash (vi)	2	Balance c/d	2
	2		2
Balance b/d	2		

Cleaning account

	£		£
Cash (xi)	5	Balance c/d	5
	5		5
Balance b/d	5		

Drawings account

	£		£
Cash (xii)	5	Balance c/d	5
	5		5
Balance b/d	5		

Activity 2

Cash account

	£		£
5 May Sales	300	8 May Wages	50
		31 May Balance c/d	250
	300		300
1 June Balance b/d	250		

Bank account

	£		£
1 May Capital	6,800	6 May Rates	100
		15 May Office fixtures	600
		18 May Motor vehicle	3,500
		25 May J Johnson	1,000
		D Nixon	500
		26 May Wages	150
		31 May Balance c/d	950
	6,800		6,800
1 June Balance b/d	950		

Creditor – J Johnson account

	£		£
11 May Purchase returns	150	3 May Purchases	400
25 May Bank	1,000	10 May Purchases	800
31 May Balance c/d	50		
	1,200		1,200
		1 June Balance b/d	50

Creditor – D Nixon account

	£		£
25 May Bank	500	3 May Purchases	300
31 May Balance c/d	500	10 May Purchases	700
	1,000		1,000
		1 June Balance b/d	500

Creditor – J Agnew account

		£			£
31 May	Balance c/d	250	3 May	Purchases	250
			1 June	Balance b/d	250

Debtor – K Homes account

		£			£
9 May	Sales	300	31 May	Balance c/d	300
		300			300
1 June	Balance b/d	300			

Debtor – J Homes account

		£			£
9 May	Sales	300	22 May	Sales returns	100
			31 May	Balance c/d	200
		300			300
1 June	Balance b/d	200			

Debtor – B Hood account

		£			£
9 May	Sales	100	31 May	Balance c/d	100
1 June	Balance b/d	100			

Capital account

		£			£
31 May	Balance c/d	6,800	1 May	Bank	6,800
			1 June	Balance b/d	6,800

Purchases account

		£			£
3 May	J Johnson	400			
	D Nixon	300			
	J Agnew	250			
10 May	J Johnson	800			
	D Nixon	700	31 May	Balance c/d	2,450
		2,450			2,450
1 June	Balance b/d	2,450			

Sales account

		£			£
			5 May	Cash	300
			9 May	K Homes	300
				J Homes	300
31 May	Balance c/d	1,000		B Hood	100
		1,000			1,000
			1 June	Balance b/d	1,000

Rates account

		£			£
6 May	Bank	100	31 May	Balance c/d	100
1 June	Balance b/d	100			

Wages account

		£			£
8 May	Cash	50			
26 May	Bank	150	31 May	Balance c/d	200
		200			200
1 June	Balance b/d	200			

Purchase returns account

		£			£
31 May	Balance c/d	150	11 May	J Johnson	150
			1 June	Balance b/d	150

Office fixtures account

		£			£
15 May	Bank	600	31 May	Balance c/d	600
1 June	Balance b/d	600			

Motor vehicle account

		£			£
18 May	Bank	3,500	31 May	Balance c/d	3,500
1 June	Balance b/d	3,500			

Sales returns account

		£			£
22 May	J Homes	100	31 May	Balance c/d	100
1 June	Balance b/d	100			

Trial balance as at 31 May 20X6	*Dr* £	*Cr* £
Cash	250	
Bank	950	
J Johnson		50
D Nixon		500
J Agnew		250
K Homes	300	
J Homes	200	
B Hood	100	
Capital		6,800
Purchases	2,450	
Sales		1,000
Rates	100	
Wages	200	
Purchase returns		150
Office fixtures	600	
Motor vehicles	3,500	
Sales returns	100	
	8,750	8,750

Activity 3

Trial balance at 31 December 20X2 of Fitzroy

	Dr	*Cr*
	£	£
Capital on 1 January 20X2		106,149
Freehold factory at cost	360,000	
Motor vehicles at cost	126,000	
Stocks at 1 January 20X2	37,500	
Debtors	15,600	
Cash in hand	225	
Bank overdraft		82,386
Creditors		78,900
Sales		318,000
Purchases	165,000	
Rent and rates	35,400	
Discounts allowed	6,600	
Insurance	2,850	
Sales returns	10,500	
Purchase returns		6,300
Loan from bank		240,000
Sundry expenses	45,960	
Drawings	26,100	
	831,735	831,735

Activity 4

(1) The rental income account for January is as follows:

Rent Account

	£		£
Balance b/d	1,900	Bank account	7,000
Invoice	2,500		
Invoice	500		
Balance c/d	**2,100**		
	7,000		7,000
		Balance b/d	**2,100**

The correct answer is **CREDIT** of **£2,100**

(2) False.

(3) When a sole trader uses goods for resale for his own personal use the drawings account is **Debited** and the purchases account is **Credited**

(4) When a supplier is paid the bank account is **Credited** and the supplier account is **Debited**

(5) When goods are sold to a debtor, the sales account is **Credited** and the debtor account is **Debited**

(6) A bank overdraft is a **Credit** balance.

(7) Discounts received are a **Credit** balance.

8 Test your knowledge

Workbook Activity 5

Musgrave starts in business with capital of £20,000, in the form of cash £15,000 and fixed assets of £5,000.

In the first three days of trading he has the following transactions:

- Purchases stock £4,000 on credit terms, supplier allows one month's credit.
- Sells some stock costing £1,500 for £2,000 and allows the customer a fortnight's credit.
- Purchases a motor vehicle for £6,000 and pays by cheque.

The accounting equation at the start would be:

Assets less Liabilities	=	Capital
£20,000 – £0	=	£20,000

Required:

Restate in values the accounting equation after all the transactions had taken place.

Workbook Activity 6

Heather Simpson notices an amount of £36,000 on the trial balance of her business in an account called 'Capital'. She does not understand what this account represents.

Briefly explain what a capital account represents.

Workbook Activity 7

Tony

Tony started a business selling tapes and CDs. In the first year of trading he entered into the following transactions from his business bank account:

(a) Paid £20,000 into a business bank account.

(b) Made purchases from Debbs for £1,000.

(c) Purchased goods costing £3,000 from Gary.

(d) Paid £200 for insurance.

(e) Bought storage units for £700 cash from Debbs.

(f) Paid £150 for advertising.

(g) Sold goods to Dorothy for £1,500.

(h) Paid the telephone bill of £120.

(i) Sold further goods to Dorothy for £4,000.

(j) Bought stationery for £80.

(k) Withdrew £500 cash for himself.

Required:

Show how these transactions would be written up in Tony's ledger accounts, followed by balancing the accounts.

Workbook Activity 8

Dave

Dave had the following transactions during January 20X3:

1 Introduced £500 cash as capital.

2 Purchased goods on credit from A Ltd worth £200.

3 Paid rent for one month, £20.

4 Paid electricity for one month, £50.

5 Purchased a car for cash, £100.

6 Sold half of the goods on credit to X Ltd for £175.

7 Drew £30 for his own expenses.

8 Sold the remainder of the goods for cash, £210.

Required:

Write up the relevant ledger accounts necessary to record the above transactions.

Workbook Activity 9

Audrey Line

Audrey Line started in business on 1 March, opening a toy shop and paying £6,000 into a business bank account. She made the following transactions during her first six months of trading:

	£
Payment of six months' rent	500
Purchase of shop fittings	600
Purchase of toys on credit	2,000
Payments to toy supplier	1,200
Wages of shop assistant	600
Electricity	250
Telephone	110
Cash sales	3,700
Drawings	1,600

All payments were made by cheque and all stocks had been sold by the end of August.

Required:

Record these transactions in the relevant accounts.

Accounting for sales – summary

Introduction

We have previously studied the double entry bookkeeping for sales and receipts in detail within Level II Certificate in Bookkeeping. It is essential that you have completed and achieved Level II before you commence your studies for Level III.

When studying Level II we concentrated on the basic entries so that the double entry would be clear. It is now time to build on these basic entries and study these transactions again using more realistic material.

CONTENTS

1 The sales day book

The sales day book is a book of prime entry where credit sales are recorded. This example provides us with a recap of the material from our Level II studies.

Example

Given below are three invoices that have been sent out by your organisation today. You are required to record them in the sales day book

INVOICE

A.J. Broom & Company Limited
59 Parkway
Manchester
M2 6EG
Tel: 0161 560 3392

Invoice to:
T J Builder
142/148 Broadway
Oldham
OD7 6LZ

Deliver to:
As above

Invoice no: 69489
Tax point: 28 August 20X3
Sales tax reg no: 625 9911 58
Delivery note no: 68612
Account no: SL21

Code	*Description*	*Quantity*	*VAT rate*	*Unit price*	*Amount excl of VAT*
			%	£	£
874 KL7	Brown Brick Roof Tiles	40	20	43.95	1,758.00
Trade discount 5%					87.90
					1,670.10
VAT					334.02
Total amount payable					2,004.12
A discount of 3% of the full price applies if payment is made within 14 days. No credit note will be issued. Following payment you must ensure you have only recovered the VAT actually paid If you pay within 14 days, the discounted price is:					
Net					1,619.99
VAT					323.99
Total amount payable					1,943.98

Invoice to: McCarthy & Sons Shepherds Moat Manchester M6 9LF **Deliver to:** As above	**INVOICE** **A.J. Broom & Company Limited** 59 Parkway Manchester M2 6EG Tel: 0161 560 3392 Fax: 0161 560 5322 Invoice no: 69490 Tax point: 28 August 20X3 Sales tax reg no: 625 9911 58 Delivery note no: 68610 Account no: SL08

Code	*Description*	*Quantity*	*VAT rate*	*Unit price*	*Amount excl of VAT*
			%	£	£
617 BB8	Red Wall Bricks	400	20	2.10	840.00
294 KT6	Insulation Brick	3	20	149.90	449.70
					1,289.70
Trade discount 4%					51.58
					1,238.12
VAT					247.62
Total amount payable					1,485.74

Invoice to: Trevor Partner Anderson House Bank Street Manchester M1 9FP **Deliver to:** As above	**INVOICE** **A.J. Broom & Company Limited** 59 Parkway Manchester M2 6EG Tel: 0161 560 3392 Fax: 0161 560 5322 Invoice no: 69491 Tax point: 28 August 20X3 Sales tax reg no: 625 9911 58 Delivery note no: 68613 Account no: SL10

Code	*Description*	*Quantity*	*VAT rate*	*Unit price*	*Amount excl of VAT*
			%	£	£
611 TB4	Bathroom Tiles	160	20	5.65	904.00
Trade discount 2%					18.08
					885.92
VAT					177.18
Total amount payable					1,063.10
A discount of 2% of the full price applies if payment is made within 21 days. No credit note will be issued. Following payment you must ensure you have only recovered the VAT actually paid If you pay within 14 days, the discounted price is					
Net					868.20
VAT					173.64
Total amount payable					1,041.84

Solution

SALES DAY BOOK

Date	*Invoice No*	*Customer name*	*Code*	*Total* £	*VAT* £	*Net* £
28/08/X3	69489	T J Builder	SL21	2,004.12	334.02	1,670.10
28/08/X3	69490	McCarthy & Sons	SL08	1,485.74	247.62	1,238.12
28/08/X3	69491	Trevor Partner	SL10	1,063.10	177.18	885.92

2 The analysed sales day book

2.1 Introduction

Many organisations analyse their sales into different groups. This may be analysis by different products or by the geographical area in which the sale is made. If the sales are eventually to be analysed in this manner in the accounting records then they must be analysed in the original book of prime entry, the sales day book.

Example

You work for an organisation that makes sales to five different geographical regions. You are in charge of writing up the sales day book and you have listed out the details of the invoices sent out yesterday, 15 August 20X1. They are given below and must be entered into the sales day book and the totals of each column calculated. The VAT rate in use is 20%.

The invoice details are as follows:

	£
Invoice number 167 – France	
Worldwide News – (Code W5)	
Net total	2,500.00
VAT	500.00
	———
Gross	3,000.00
	———
Invoice number 168 – Spain	
Local News – (Code L1)	
Net total	200.00
VAT	40.00
	———
Gross	240.00
	———
Invoice number 169 – Germany	
The Press Today – (Code P2)	
Net total	300.00
VAT	60.00
	———
Gross	360.00
	———

Invoice number 170 – Spain	
Home Call – (Code H1)	
Net total	200.00
VAT	40.00
	–––––––
Gross	240.00
	–––––––
Invoice number 171 – France	
Tomorrow – (Code T1)	
Net total	100.00
VAT	20.00
	–––––––
Gross	120.00
	–––––––
Invoice number 172 – Russia	
Worldwide News – (Code W5)	
Net total	3,000.00
VAT	600.00
	–––––––
Gross	3,600.00
	–––––––

Solution

SALES DAY BOOK

Date	*Invoice no*	*Customer name*	*Code*	*Total*	*VAT*	*Russia*	*Poland*	*Spain*	*Germany*	*France*
				£	£	£	£	£	£	£
15/08/X1	167	Worldwide News	W5	3,000.00	500.00					2,500.00
	168	Local News	L1	240.00	40.00			200.00		
	169	The Press Today	P2	360.00	60.00				300.00	
	170	Home Call	H1	240.00	40.00			200.00		
	171	Tomorrow	T1	120.00	20.00					100.00
	172	Worldwide News	W5	3,600.00	600.00	3,000.00				
				7,560.00	1,260.00	3,000.00	–	400.00	300.00	2,600.00

When you have totalled the columns you can check your additions by 'cross casting'. If you add together the totals of all of the analysis columns and the VAT column, they should total the figure in the 'Total' column. The terms 'Total' and 'Gross' both mean the amounts inclusive of VAT.

Activity 1

Sweepings Ltd is a wall covering manufacturer. It produces four qualities of wallpaper:

01 – Anaglypta

02 – Supaglypta

03 – Lincrusta

04 – Blown Vinyl

Francis is a sales ledger clerk and he is required to write up the sales day book each week from the batch of sales invoices he receives from the sales department.

He has just received this batch of sales invoices which show the following details. All sales are standard-rated for VAT.

Invoice no	*Date*	*Customer*	*Description*	*Amount (incl VAT)* £
1700	06.09.X1	Gates Stores	Anaglypta, 188 rolls	480.00
1701	06.09.X1	Texas	Blown Vinyl, 235 rolls	1,800.00
1702	07.09.X1	Dickens	Blown Vinyl, 188 rolls	1,440.00
1703	07.09.X1	Hintons DIY	Supaglypta, 470 rolls	1,920.00
1704	08.09.X1	Co-op Stores	Anaglypta, 94 rolls	240.00
1705	08.09.X1	B & Q Stores	Lincrusta, 125 rolls	1,200.00
1706	09.09.X1	Ferris Decor	Supaglypta, 235 rolls	960.00
1707	09.09.X1	Ferris Decor	Blown Vinyl, 94 rolls	720.00
1708	10.09.X1	Homestyle	Lincrusta, 25 rolls	240.00
1709	10.09.X1	Quick Style	Anaglypta, 47 rolls	120.00

Show how this information would appear in the sales day book given below, including the totals of the relevant columns.

Date	*Invoice*	*Customer*	*Total*	*VAT*	*Group 01*	*Group 02*	*Group 03*	*Group 04*
			£	£	£	£	£	£
06.09	1700	Gates Stores	480	80	400			
06.09	1701	Texas	1800	300				1500
07.09	1702	Dickens	1440	240				1200
07.09	1703	Hintons	1920	320		1600		
08.09	1704	Co-op	240	40	200			
08.09	1705	B&Q	1200	200			1000	
09.09	1706	Ferris	960	160		800		
09.09	1707	Ferris	720	120				600
10.09	1708	Homestyle	240	40			200	
10.09	1709	Quinnstyle	120	20	100			
			9120	1520	700	2400	1200	3300

Activity 2

Given below are the totals from the analysed sales day book for an organisation for a week.

Sales day book				
	Gross	*VAT*	*Sales Type 1*	*Sales Type 2*
	£	£	£	£
Totals	8,652.00	1,442.00	4,320.00	2,890.00

You are required to post these totals to the main ledger accounts given below:

SLCA

8652 £	601,80 £

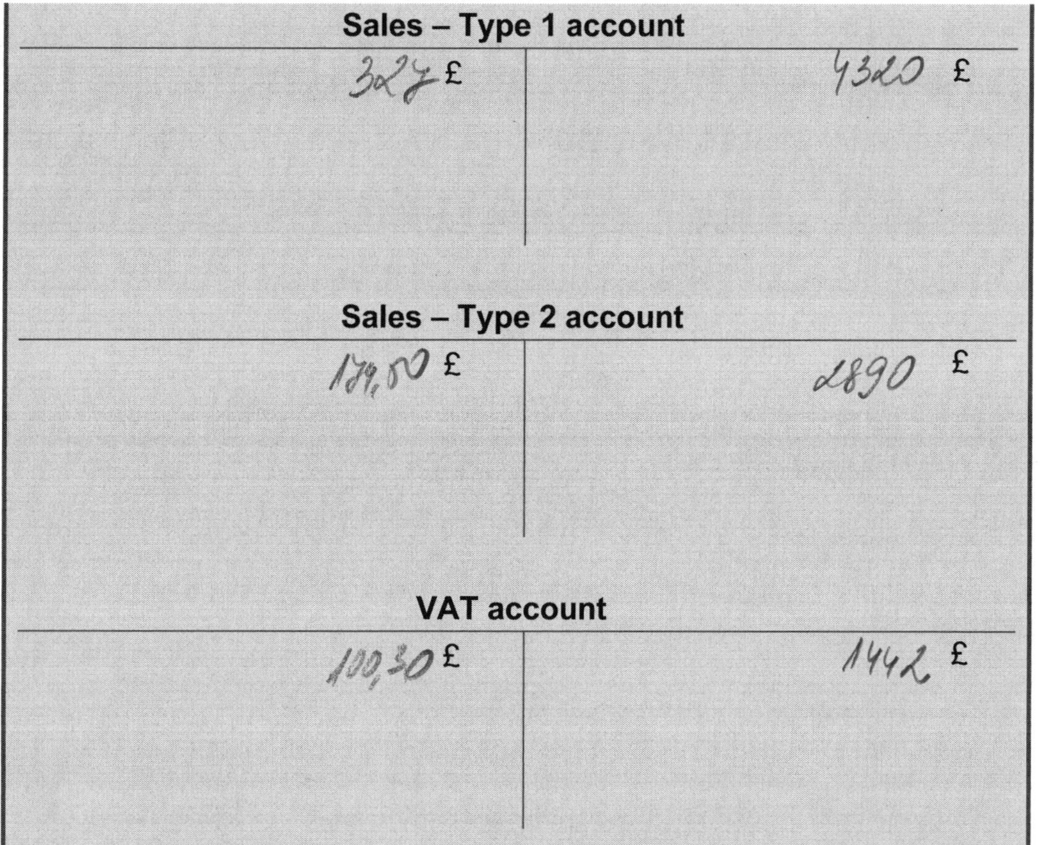

3 The sales returns day book

3.1 Introduction

When goods are returned by customers and credit notes sent out then these credit notes are also recorded in their own book of prime entry, the sales returns day book.

3.2 Sales returns day book

The sales returns day book is effectively the reverse of the sales day book but will have the same entries, the total of the credit note, including VAT, the VAT element and the net amount, excluding the VAT.

Example

Given below are the totals from three credit notes that your organisation has sent out this week, the week ending 21 January 20X4. They are to be recorded in the sales returns day book. VAT is at 20%.

Credit note no:	03556	To: J Slater & Co	Code: SL67
		£	
Goods total		126.45	
VAT		25.29	
Credit note total		151.74	

Credit note no:	03557	To: Paulsons	Code: SL14
		£	
Goods total		58.40	
VAT		11.68	
Credit note total		70.08	

Credit note no:	03558	To: Hudson & Co	Code: SL27
		£	
Goods total		104.57	
VAT		20.91	
Credit note total		125.48	

Solution

Sales returns day book

Date	*Credit note no*	*Customer name*	*Code*	*Total*	*VAT*	*Net*
				£	£	£
21/01/X4	03556	J Slater & Co	SL67	151.74	25.29	126.45
21/01/X4	03557	Paulsons	SL14	70.08	11.68	58.40
21/01/X4	03558	Hudson & Co	SL27	125.48	20.91	104.57

3.3 Analysed sales returns day book

If the business keeps an analysed sales day book then it will also analyse its sales returns day book in exactly the same manner.

Example

In an earlier example we considered the sales day book for an organisation that makes sales to five different geographical regions. The sales returns day book would also be analysed into these geographical regions. The details of two credit notes issued this week are given and are to be written up in the sales returns day book. Today's date is 21 October 20X6. VAT in use is 20%.

Credit note no: 0246 – Poland	To: Russell & Sons	Code: R03
	£	
Goods total	85.60	
VAT	17.12	
	102.72	

Credit note no: 0247 – Germany	To: Cleansafe	Code: C07
	£	
Goods total	126.35	
VAT	25.27	
	151.62	

Solution

Sales returns day book

Date	*Credit*	*Customer*	*Code*	*Total*	*VAT*	*Russia*	*Poland*	*Spain*	*Germany*	*France*
21/10/X6	0246	Russell & Sons	R03	102.72	17.12		85.60			
21/10/X6	0247	Cleansafe	C07	151.62	25.27				126.35	

Activity 3

A business analyses its sales into Product 1 sales and Product 2 sales. During the week ending 14 March 20X4 the following credit notes were sent out to customers.

CN3066	£120.00 plus VAT	–	Product 2, Customer K Lilt, Code L04
CN3067	£16.00 plus VAT	–	Product 1, Customer J Davis, Code D07
CN3068	£38.00 plus VAT	–	Product 1, Customer I Oliver, Code O11
CN3069	£80.00 plus VAT	–	Product 2, Customer D Sharp, Code S02

Enter the credit notes in the analysed sales returns day book given below and total the day book for the week.

Sales returns day book

Date	*Credit note no*	*Customer name*	*Code*	*Total*	*VAT*	*Product 1*	*Product 2*
14.03	CN3066	K. Lilt	L04	£144	£24	£	£120
	CN3067	J Davis	D07	19,20	3,20	16	
	CN3068	I. Oliver	O11	45,60	7,60	38	
	CN3069	D. Sharp.	S02	96	16		80
				304,80	50,80	54	200

Activity 4

Given below are the totals from the analysed sales returns day book for an organisation for a week:

Date	*Customer name*	*Credit note no*	*Code*	*Total*	*VAT*	*Sales Type 1*	*Sales Type 2*
				£	£	£	£
25/09/X2				601.80	100.30	327.00	174.50

Post these totals to the general ledger accounts.

4 Posting to the sales ledger

As well as posting the totals from the books of prime entry to the main ledger accounts each individual invoice and credit note must also be posted to the individual customer's account in the sales ledger. You must remember that the sales ledger is sometimes referred to as the subsidiary (sales) ledger.

Example

Here is an account from the sales ledger of Frosty Limited, a glass manufacturer which specialises in glassware for the catering trade.

Account name:		**Account code:**	
	£		£

You have taken over writing up the sales ledger because the ledger clerk has been ill for several months.

You have gathered together the following information about sales. The customer is a new customer whose name is Arthur Pickering. The account code will be SP05.

Sales invoices/Credit notes

Date	*Invoice/CN number*	*Gross*	*VAT*	*Net*
		£	£	£
02/05/X1	325	598.06	99.67	498.39
03/06/X1	468	243.98	40.66	203.32
15/06/X1	503	115.84	19.30	96.54
16/06/X1	510	49.74	8.29	41.45
25/06/X1	CN048	28.32	4.72	23.60
17/07/X1	604	450.51	75.08	375.43

Solution

Account name: Arthur Pickering **Account code: SP05**

		£			£
02/05/X1	Inv 325	598.06	25/06/X1	CN048	28.32
03/06/X1	Inv 468	243.98			
15/06/X1	Inv 503	115.84			
16/06/X1	Inv 510	49.74			
17/07/X1	Inv 604	450.51			

Remember that sales invoices are always entered on the debit side of the customer's account and credit notes on the credit side of the account.

5 The cash book

5.1 Introduction

One of the most important books used within a business is the cash book. There are various forms of cash book, a 'two column' and a 'three column' cash book

Definition

A cash book is a record of cash receipts and payments that confirms to the double entry system.

5.2 Two column cash book

A proforma two column cash book is shown below.

CASH BOOK							
Date	*Narrative*	*Cash* £	*Bank* £	*Date* £	*Narrative* £	*Cash* £	*Bank* £

Notes:

(a) The left hand side of the cash book represents the debit side – money received.

(b) The right hand side of the cash book represents the credit side – money paid out.

(c) The date column contains the date of the transaction

(d) The narrative column describes the transactions – typically the name of the customer who is paying. It would also contain the sales ledger code of the debtor.

(e) The cash column on the debit side represents cash received, whereas the cash column on the credit side represents cash paid.

(f) The bank column on the debit side represents money received (by cheque or other bank payment) whereas the bank column on the credit side represents money paid (by cheque or other bank payment).

A business may operate a bank current account as a means to settle business transactions. Receipts may be made in the form of a cheque, cash may be deposited into the current account and payment may be made by drawing a cheque against the current account.

To be able to record these bank specific transactions, a separate column must be introduced to the cash book to account for them. This is what leads to the use of a two column cash book; a column for cash transactions and a column for transactions made through the bank current account. Each column represents a separate account, cash account and bank account, each with its own double entry.

As well as being aware of the use of two columns for bank and cash, you should also be aware that a cash book may have additional columns for the purpose of analysing the receipts and payments in terms of sources and types of income and expenditure.

Definition

An analysed cash book is a cash book with additional columns for analysing principal sources and payments for cash.

5.3 Three column cash book

The three-column cashbook incorporates the cash discounts for each relevant entry into a third column, and also includes VAT adjustment columns.

At the end of a certain period of time, when the cashbook is balanced off, the totals from these discount columns would then be transferred to the discount accounts in the general ledger, and the totals from the VAT adjustment columns would be transferred to the VAT account.

Discounts received, and any related VAT adjustment, are entered in the discounts and VAT adjustment columns on the credit side of the cashbook.

Discounts allowed, and any related VAT adjustment, are entered in the discounts and VAT adjustment columns on the debit side of the cashbook.

The discount and VAT adjustment columns are memorandum columns only: they are not balanced and they do not form part of the double entry system.

A proforma three column cash book is shown below.

CASH BOOK

Date	*Narrative*	*Cash* £	*Bank* £	*Discount allowed* £	*VAT Adjustment* £	*Date* £	*Narrative* £	*Cash* £	*Bank* £	*Discount received* £	*VAT Adjustment* £

The purpose of each of the columns is consistent to that of a two column cash book with the addition of the discount and VAT adjustment columns in both the receipts (debit) side and the payments (credit) side. It is important to note that cash books can be in different formats with different numbers of analysis columns.

We will now focus on the cash receipts book. The cash payments book will be reviewed in the chapter that follows.

5.4 The cash receipts book

In order to revise the layout of the cash receipts book consider the following example.

Cash receipts book for the week commencing 15 September 20X4

Date	*Narrative*	*Total*	*VAT*	*SLCA*	*Cash/ cheque sales*	*Discount allowed*
		£	£	£	£	£
15 Sept	Paying-in slip 584	653.90		653.90		
16 Sept	Paying-in slip 585	864.60		864.60		
17 Sept	Paying-in slip 586	954.98	11.24	887.54	56.20	
18 Sept	Paying-in slip 587	559.57		559.57		
19 Sept	Paying-in slip 588	238.18	31.69	48.00	158.49	
		3,271.23	42.93	3,013.61	214.69	

The bankings are a mixture of cash sales and cheques from debtors. The VAT is just the VAT on the cash/cheque sales. There are no discounts.

Check that the three analysis column totals add back to the total column total.

Example

Returning to the cash receipts book, post the totals to the general ledger accounts.

Cash receipts book

Date	*Narrative*	*Total*	*VAT*	*Debtors*	*Cash/ cheque sales*	*Discount allowed*
		£	£	£	£	£
15 Sept	Paying-in slip 584	653.90		653.90		
16 Sept	Paying-in slip 585	864.60		864.60		
17 Sept	Paying-in slip 586	954.98	11.24	887.54	56.20	
18 Sept	Paying-in slip 587	559.57		559.57		
19 Sept	Paying-in slip 588	238.18	31.69	48.00	158.49	
		3,271.23	42.93	3,013.61	214.69	

Solution

The double entry for posting the cash receipts book totals is:

		£	£
DR	Bank account	3,271.23	
CR	VAT account		42.93
	Sales ledger control account		3,013.61
	Sales account		214.69

Bank account

	£		£
Cash receipts book (CRB)	3,271.23		

VAT account

	£		£
		CRB	42.93

Sales ledger control account

	£		£
		CRB	3,013.61

Sales account

	£		£
		CRB	214.69

Note that the description of each transaction is the primary record that it came from, the cash receipts book, shortened to CRB.

Activity 5

The cheques received from customers of Passiflora Products Ltd, a small company which produces herbal remedies and cosmetics and supplies them to shops and beauty parlours, for a week are given below:

Cheques received:

	Paying-in slip/customer	*Amount* £	*Discount allowed* £	*VAT Adjustment* £
01/05/X6	Paying-in slip 609			
	Natural Beauty	11,797.05	176.95	35.39
	Grapeseed	417.30	6.26	1.25
	New Age Remedies	6,379.65	95.69	19.13
	The Aromatherapy Shop	9,130.65	136.96	27.39
03/05/X6	Paying-in slip 610			
	Comfrey Group	5,689.20	85.34	17.06
	Natural Elegance	2,056.89	30.85	6.17
08/05/X6	Paying-in slip 611			
	The Herbalist	8,663.45	129.95	25.99
12/05/X6	Paying-in slip 612			
	Edwards Pharmacy	106.42		
	Healthworks	17,213.94	258.21	51.64
19/05/X6	Paying-in slip 613			
	The Beauty Box	11,195.85	167.94	33.58
	Crystals	54.19		
25/05/X6	Paying-in slip 614			
	The Village Chemist	7,662.55	114.94	22.98
29/05/X6	Paying-in slip 615			
	Brewer Brothers	2,504.61	37.57	7.51
30/05/X6	Paying-in slip 616			
	Lapis Lazuli	112.58		
31/05/X6	Paying-in slip 617			
	Lorelei	5,618.40	84.27	16.85
	Spain & Co, Chemists	197.93		

Required:

(a) Enter the totals for each paying-in slip (including discounts) into the cash receipts book given below.

(b) Total the cash receipts book and post the totals for the month to the general ledger accounts given.

(a) **Cash receipts book**

Date	*Narrative*	*Total*	*VAT*	*SLCA*	*Other*	*Discount*	*VAT Adjustment*
		£	£	£	£	£	£
01/05/x4	609	27724.65		27724.65		415.86	83,16
03/05	610	7746.09		7746.09		116.19	23,23
08/05	611	8663.45		8663.45		129.95	25,99
12/05	612	17320.36		17320.36		258.21	51,64
19/05	613	11250.04		11250.04		167.94	33,58
25/05	614	7662.55		7662.55		114.94	22,98
29/05	615	2504.61		2504.61		37.57	7.51
30/05	616	112.58		112.58			
31/05	617	5816.33		5816.33		84.27	16.85
		88800.66		88800.66		1324.93	264.94

(b) **General ledger**

Sales ledger control account

	£		£
		CRB	88800.66
			1324.93

Discount allowed account

	£		£
CRB	1324.93		

VAT account

	£		£
CRB adj.	264.94		

Activity 6

Given below are the details of paying-in slip 609 from the previous activity, Passiflora Products Ltd. You are required to enter the details in the sales ledger accounts given.

Paying-in slip 609

	Amount	*Discount allowed*	*VAT Adjustment*
	£	£	£
Natural Beauty	11,797.05	176.95	35.39
Grapeseed	417.30	6.26	1.25
New Age Remedies	6,379.65	95.69	19.13
The Aromatherapy Shop	9,130.65	136.96	27.39

Natural Beauty

	£		£
Opening balance	17,335.24		

The Aromatherapy Shop

	£		£
Opening balance	12,663.42		

New Age Remedies

	£		£
Opening balance	6,475.34		

Grapeseed

	£		£
Opening balance	423.56		

Activity 7

Cash book – Debit side

Date	Details	Discount £	VAT Adjustment £	Bank £
30 Nov	Balance b/f			10,472
30 Nov	SMK Ltd	300	60	12,000

(a) What will be the THREE entries in the sales ledger?

Sales Ledger

Account name	Amount £	Debit / Credit
SMK Ltd	12000	CR
CRB . discount	300	CR
CRB . VAT adjustment	60	CR

(b) What will be the FIVE entries in the general ledger?

General Ledger

Account name	Amount £	Debit / Credit
SCLA	12000	CR
Discount	300	Dr
VAT Adjustment	60	Dr
CRB - Discount	300	CR
CRB - VAT Adj	60	CR

6 Document retention policies

6.1 Introduction

Throughout the studies for Level II and Level III we will have seen many documents that businesses produce. It is a legal requirement that all financial documents, and some non-financial documents, must be kept by a business for six years. Therefore it is essential that a business has a secure and organised method of filing such information, to ensure that they can be located easily.

6.2 Reasons for document retention

Documents must be kept for three main reasons:

- in order that they could be inspected by HM Revenue and Customs in a tax inspection;
- in order that they could be inspected by HM Revenue and Customs in a VAT inspection;
- in order that they could be used as evidence in any legal action.

7 Summary

In this chapter we have pulled together into one place all the main documents and double entry for the sales cycle. If you have had any trouble with any of these points, you should refer again to the relevant chapters of the textbook for Level II where the double entry is explained in basic terms. Level III is building on our knowledge from Level II.

Answers to chapter activities

Activity 1

Date	*Invoice*	*Customer*	*Total*	*VAT*	*Group 01*	*Group 02*	*Group 03*	*Group 04*
			£	£	£	£	£	£
06/09/X1	1700	Gates Stores	480.00	80.00	400.00			
06/09/X1	1701	Texas	1,800.00	300.00				1,500.00
07/09/X1	1702	Dickens	1,440.00	240.00				1,200.00
07/09/X1	1703	Hintons DIY	1,920.00	320.00		1,600.00		
08/09/X1	1704	Co-op Stores	240.00	40.00	200.00			
08/09/X1	1705	B & Q Stores	1,200.00	200.00			1,000.00	
09/09/X1	1706	Ferris Decor	960.00	160.00		800.00		
09/09/X1	1707	Ferris Decor	720.00	120.00				600.00
10/09/X1	1708	Homestyle	240.00	40.00			200.00	
10/09/X1	1709	Quick Style	120.00	20.00	100.00			
			9,120.00	1,520.00	700.00	2,400.00	1,200.00	3,300.00

Activity 2

SLCA

	£		£
SDB	8,652.00		

Sales – Type 1 account

	£		£
		SDB	4,320.00

Sales – Type 2 account

	£		£
		SDB	2,890.00

VAT account

	£		£
		SDB	1,442.00

Activity 3

SALES RETURNS DAY BOOK

Date	*Credit note no*	*Customer name*	*Code*	*Total*	*VAT*	*Product 1*	*Product 2*
				£	£	£	£
14/03	3066	K Lilt	L04	144.00	24.00		120.00
14/03	3067	J Davis	D07	19.20	3.20	16.00	
14/03	3068	I Oliver	O11	45.60	7.60	38.00	
14/03	3069	D Sharp	S02	96.00	16.00		80.00
				304.80	50.80	54.00	200.00

Activity 4

Sales ledger control account

	£		£
		SRDB	601.80

Sales returns – Type 1

	£		£
SRDB	327.00		

Sales returns – Type 2

	£		£
SRDB	174.50		

VAT account

	£		£
SRDB	100.30		

Activity 5

(a) Cash receipts book

Date	*Narrative*	*Total* £	*VAT* £	*SLCA* £	*Other* £	*Discount* £	*VAT Adj* £
01/05/X6	609	27,724.65		27,724.65		415.86	83.16
03/05/X6	610	7,746.09		7,746.09		116.19	23.23
08/05/X6	611	8,663.45		8,663.45		129.95	25.99
12/05/X6	612	17,320.36		17,320.36		258.21	51.64
19/05/X6	613	11,250.04		11,250.04		167.94	33.58
25/05/X6	614	7,662.55		7,662.55		114.94	22.98
29/05/X6	615	2,504.61		2,504.61		37.57	7.51
30/05/X6	616	112.58		112.58			
31/05/X6	617	5,816.33		5,816.33		84.27	16.85
		88,800.66	–	88,800.66	–	1,324.93	264.94

(b) General ledger

Sales ledger control account

	£		£
		CRB	88,800.66
		CRB – VAT Adj	1,324.93

Discount allowed account

	£		£
CRB	1,324.93		

VAT account

	£		£
CRB	264.94		

Activity 6

Natural Beauty

	£		£
Opening balance	17,335.24	CRB	11,797.05
		CRB – discount	176.95
		CRB – VAT adjustment	35.39

The Aromatherapy Shop

	£		£
Opening balance	12,663.42	CRB	9,130.65
		CRB – discount	136.96
		CRB – VAT adjustment	27.39

New Age Remedies

	£		£
Opening balance	6,475.34	CRB	6,379.65
		CRB – discount	95.69
		CRB – VAT adjustment	19.13

Grapeseed

	£		£
Opening balance	423.56	CRB	417.30
		CRB – discount	6.26
		CRB – VAT adjustment	1.25

Activity 7

Cashbook – Debit side

Date	Details	Discount £	VAT Adjustment £	Bank £
30 Nov	Balance b/f			10,472
30 Nov	SMK Ltd	300	60	12,000

(a) What will be the THREE entries in the sales ledger?

Sales Ledger

Account name	Amount £	Debit/Credit
SMK Ltd	12,000	Credit
SMK Ltd	300	Credit
SMK Ltd	60	Credit

(b) What will be the THREE entries in the general ledger?

General Ledger

Account name	Amount £	Debit/Credit
SLCA	12,000	Credit
Discount allowed	300	Debit
SLCA	300	Credit
VAT account	60	Debit
SLCA	60	Credit

8 Test your knowledge

 Workbook Activity 8

Your organisation receives a number of cheques from debtors through the post each day and these are listed on the cheque listing. It also makes some cash sales each day which include VAT at the standard rate.

Today's date is 28 April 20X1 and the cash sales today were £240.00 including VAT at 20%. The cheque listing for the day is given below:

Cheque listing 28 April 20X1

Customer	Received	Discount taken	VAT Adj
	£	£	£
G Heilbron	108.45		
L Tessa	110.57	3.31	0.66
J Dent	210.98	6.32	1.26
F Trainer	97.60		
A Winter	105.60	3.16	0.63

An extract from the customer file shows the following:

Customer	*Sales ledger code*
J Dent	SL17
G Heilbron	SL04
L Tessa	SL15
F Trainer	SL21
A Winter	SL09

Required:

(a) Write up the cash receipts book given below; total each of the columns of the cash receipts book and check that they cross cast

(b) Post the totals of the cash receipts book to the general ledger accounts.

(c) Post the individual receipts to the sales ledger.

Cash receipts book								
Narrative	*SL Code*	*Discount* £	*VAT Adj* £	*Cash* £	*Bank* £	*VAT* £	*Cash Sales* £	*SLCA* £
Cash sales				240		40	200	240
G. Heilbron	SL04				108,45			108,45
L. Tessa	SL15	3,31	0,66		110,57			110,57
J. Dent	SL17	6,32	1,26		210,98			210,98
F. Trainer	SL21				97,60			97,60
A. Winter	SL09	3,16	0,63		105,60			105,60
		12,79	2,55	240	633,20	40	200	633,20

Workbook Activity 9

There are 5 receipts to be entered into Longley Ltd's cash receipts book.

Cash receipts

From Irlam Transport – £468.00 (inc VAT)

From Paulson Haulage – £216.00 (inc VAT)

From Mault Motors – £348.00 (inc VAT)

Cheques received from credit customers

From James John Ltd – £579.08 (discount of £24.39 taken, VAT adjustment of £4.78 required)

From Exilm & Co – £456.74 (discount of £19.80 taken, VAT adjustment of £3.96 required)

Required:

Write up the cash receipts book given below; total each of the columns of the cash receipts book and check that they cross cast.

Cash receipts book						
Narrative	*Discount* £	*Cash* £	*Bank* £	*VAT* £	*Cash Sales* £	*SLCA* £
Islam T R.		468		78	390	
Paulson Haulage		216		36	180	
Marlt Motors		348		58	290	
James Jones	24,39		579.08			579.08
Exilm & Co	19,80		456.74			456.74
	44,19	1032	1035,82	172	860	1035,82

Workbook Activity 10

Indicate whether each of the following statements is true or false.

	True/False
Documents can be disposed of as soon as the year end accounts are prepared	False
Documents cannot be inspected by anyone outside the business	False
Documents can be used as legal evidence in any legal actions	True
Businesses must keep an aged debtor analysis as part of their financial documents	False
Businesses do not need to keep copies of invoices	False
Businesses need to keep copies of their bank statements available for inspection	True

Accounting for purchases – summary

3

Introduction

As well as recapping accounting for sales as seen in the previous chapter, we also need to recap on the techniques learned for purchases in Bookkeeping Level II.

CONTENTS

1 The purchases day book

1.1 Introduction

In the purchases day book, the purchase invoices are normally given an internal invoice number and are also recorded under the supplier's purchase ledger code and possibly the type of purchase.

1.2 Authorisation stamp

This is often done by stamping an authorisation stamp or grid stamp onto the invoice once it has been thoroughly checked and the relevant details entered onto the authorisation stamp. A typical example of an authorisation stamp is shown below:

Purchase order no	04618
Invoice no	04821
Cheque no	
Account code	PL06
Checked	L Finn
Date	23/02/X2
GL account	07

1.3 Entries on the authorisation stamp

At this stage of entering the invoice in the purchases day book, it has been checked to the purchase order and the delivery note, therefore the purchase order number is entered onto the authorisation stamp.

The purchase invoice will then be allocated an internal invoice number which will be sequential and therefore the next number after the last invoice entered into the purchases day book.

At this stage the invoice will not necessarily have been authorised for payment, therefore the cheque number will not yet be entered onto the authorisation stamp.

The purchase invoice details such as trade and settlement discounts should have been checked to the supplier's file to ensure that the correct percentages have been used and at this point, the supplier's purchases ledger code can be entered onto the authorisation stamp.

The person checking the invoice should then sign and date the authorisation stamp to show that all details have been checked.

Finally, the general ledger account code should be entered. We have seen that in some businesses a simple three column purchases day book will be used with a total, VAT and net column. In such cases all of the invoices will be classified as 'purchases' and will have the general ledger code for the purchases account.

However, if an analysed purchases day book is used then each analysis column will be for a different type of expense and will have a different general ledger code.

If your organisation does have an authorisation stamp procedure then it is extremely important that the authorisation is correctly filled out when the invoice has been checked. Not only is this evidence that the invoice is correct and is for goods or services that have been received, it also provides vital information for the accurate accounting for this invoice.

Example

Given below are three purchase invoices received and the authorisation stamp for each one. They are to be entered into the purchases day book. Today's date is 25 April 20X1.

INVOICE

Invoice to: Keller Bros Field House Winstead M16 4PT **Deliver to:** Above address	**Anderson Wholesale** Westlife Park Gripton M7 1ZK Tel: 0161 439 2020 Fax: 0161 439 2121 Invoice no: 06447 Tax point: 20 April 20X1 VAT reg no: 432 1679 28 Account no: SL14

Code	*Description*	*Quantity*	*VAT rate*	*Unit price*	*Amount excl of VAT*
			%	£	£
PT417	Grade A Compost	7 tonnes	20	15.80	110.60
					110.60
Trade discount 5%					5.53
					105.07
VAT					21.01
Total amount payable					126.08

Purchase order no	34611
Invoice no	37240
Cheque no	
Account code	PL14
Checked	C Long
Date	25/04/X1
GL account	020

INVOICE

Invoice to:
Keller Bros
Field House
Winstead
M16 4PT

Deliver to:
Above address

Better Gardens Ltd
Broom Nursery
West Lane
Farforth M23 4LL
Tel: 0161 380 4444
Fax: 0161 380 6128

Invoice no: 46114
Tax point: 21 April 20X1
VAT reg no: 611 4947 26
Account no: K03

Code	*Description*	*Quantity*	*VAT rate*	*Unit price*	*Amount excl of VAT*
			%	£	£
B4188	Tulip bulbs	28 dozen	20	1.38	38.64
B3682	Daffodil bulbs	50 dozen	20	1.26	63.00
					101.64
VAT					20.32
Total amount payable					121.96
Deduct discount of 3% if paid within 14 days					
A discount of 3% of the full price applies if payment is made within 14 days. No credit note will be issued. Following payment you must ensure you have only recovered the VAT actually paid If you pay within 14 days, the discounted price is:					
Net					98.59
VAT					19.71
Total amount payable					118.30

Purchase order no	34608
Invoice no	37241
Cheque no	
Account code	PL06
Checked	C Long
Date	25/04/X1
GL account	020

INVOICE					
Invoice to: Keller Bros Field House Winstead M16 4PT **Deliver to:** Above address	**Winterton Partners** **28/32 Coleman Road** **Forest Dene** **M17 3AT** Tel: 0161 224 6760 Fax: 0161 224 6761 Invoice no: 121167 Tax point: 22 April 20X1 VAT reg no: 980 3012 74 Account no: SL44				
Code	*Description*	*Quantity*	*VAT rate*	*Unit price*	*Amount excl of VAT*
			%	£	£
A47BT	Seedlings	120	20	0.76	91.20
					91.20
Trade discount 7%					6.38
					84.82
VAT					16.96
Total amount payable					101.78
A discount of 2% of the full price applies if payment is made within 14 days. No credit note will be issued. Following payment you must ensure you have only recovered the VAT actually paid If you pay within 14 days, the discounted price is:					
Net					83.12
VAT					16.62
Total amount payable					99.74

Purchase order no	34615
Invoice no	37242
Cheque no	
Account code	PL23
Checked	C Long
Date	25/04/X1
GL account	020

Solution

Purchases day book						
Date	*Invoice no*	*Code*	*Supplier*	*Total*	*VAT*	*Net*
				£	£	£
25/04/X1	37240	PL14	Anderson Wholesale	126.08	21.01	105.07
25/04/X1	37241	PL06	Better Gardens Ltd	121.96	20.32	101.64
25/04/X1	37242	PL23	Winterton Partners	101.78	16.96	84.82

Note that the net total is the invoice amount after deducting any trade discount as the trade discount is a definite reduction in the list price of the goods. At this stage any settlement discount is ignored as it will not necessarily have been decided whether or not to take advantage of the settlement discount.

Activity 1

You are a purchases clerk for Robins, a soft drink manufacturer. Here is part of the layout of the purchases day book. VAT is at 20%.

Purchases day book									
Date	*Invoice no*	*Code*	*Supplier*	*Total*	*VAT*	*01*	*02*	*03*	*04*
				£	£	£	£	£	£
10.11.x2	4221	DF2	Drip Farm	120	20	100			
10.11.x2	4222	DN1	Daily news	360	60		300		
10.11.x2	4223		Yellow	180					
10.11x2	4223	SM4	Stand.M.	2400	400				2000
				2880	480	100	300		2000

01 represents purchases of parts or raw materials for manufacture

02 represents advertising expenditure

03 represents entertaining expenditure

04 represents purchases of fixed assets

Here are five documents that are to be written up in the purchases day book on 10.11.X2 as necessary.

Document 1

No: 511 X

SALES INVOICE

Drip Farm
Lover's Lane
Norwich NO56 2EZ

To: Robins Ltd
Softdrink House
Wembley
London
NW16 7SJ

Tax point: 7.11.X2
VAT Reg No: 566 0122 10

Quantity	*Description*	*VAT rate*	*Price/unit*	*Total*
50 litre drum	Apple juice (inferior)	20%	£2/litre	100.00
			VAT	20.00
				120.00

Grid stamp on reverse of invoice

Invoice no	4221
Account code	DF2
Checked	R Robins
Date	9.11.X2
GL account	01

Document 2

Sales Invoice | Inv No: 5177

DAILY NEWS PLC 

Europe Way
Southampton
SO3 3BZ

Tax point 5.11.X2
VAT Reg No: 177 0255 01

To: Robins Ltd
Softdrink House
London
NW16 7SJ

Sale details:

4 line advertisement			£
3 weeks	04.10.X2 @ £100/week		
	11/10.X2	Net price	300.00
	18.10.X2	VAT 20%	60.00
			360.00

Grid stamp on reverse of invoice.

Invoice no	4222
Account code	DN1
Checked	R Robins
Date	9.11.X2
GL account	02

Document 3

RECEIPT

9/11/12

Received with thanks the sum of
£17.50

T W Wang

Document 4

SALES ORDER 562		
BTEB Stores Gateshead		**Robins Ltd** Softdrink House Wembley LONDON NW16 7SJ
Quantity	**Description**	**Price**
20 cases	0.75 bottles of Norfolk apple juice	£2/bottle

Document 5

SALES INVOICE P261

STANDARD MACHINES
Starlight Boulevard, Milton Keynes
MK51 7LY

To: Robins Ltd
Softdrink House
Wembley
LONDON
NW16 7SJ

Tax point: 6.11.X2
VAT Reg No: 127 0356 02

Quantity	*Description*	*VAT*	*Price (£)/unit*
1	Bottling machine	20%	2,000
		VAT	400
			2,400

Grid stamp on reverse of invoice.

Invoice no.	4223
Account code	SM4
Checked	R Robins
Date	9.11.X2
GL account	04

Activity 2

A newsagents shop has received the following invoices. Write them up in the purchases day book using the format provided. The last internal invoice number to be allocated to purchase invoices was 114.

1.1.X1	Northern Electric – invoice	£120 including VAT at 5%
	Northern News – invoice	£230 (no VAT)
2.1.X1	Post Office Ltd – invoice	£117.00 (no VAT)
	Northern Country – invoice	£48 including VAT
3.1.X1	South Gazette – invoice	£360 including VAT

The supplier codes are as follows:

Northern Country (a newspaper)	N1
Northern News (a newspaper)	N2
Northern Gas	N3
Post Office Ltd	P1
South Gazette (a newspaper)	S1

Purchases day book

Date	*Invoice no*	*Code*	*Supplier*	*Total*	*VAT*	*Goods for resale*	*Heat and light*	*Postage and stationery*
				£	£	£	£	£

2 Returns of goods

2.1 Introduction

Returns may be made for various reasons, e.g.

- faulty goods
- excess goods delivered by supplier
- unauthorised goods delivered.

All returned goods must be recorded on a returns outwards note.

2.2 Credit notes

The return should not be recorded until the business receives a credit note from the supplier. This confirms that there is no longer a liability for these goods. A credit note from a supplier is sometimes requested by the organisation issuing a debit note.

The credit note should be checked for accuracy against the returns outwards note. The calculations and extensions on the credit note should also be checked in just the same way as with an invoice.

2.3 Purchases returns day book

When credit notes are received from suppliers they are normally recorded in their own primary record, the purchases returns day book. This has a similar layout to a purchases day book. If the purchases day book is analysed into the different types of purchase that the organisation makes then the purchases returns day book will also be analysed in the same manner.

Example

Today, 5 February 20X5, three credit notes have been passed as being checked. The details of each credit note and the authorisation stamp are given below. The credit note details are to be entered into the purchases returns day book.

From Calderwood & Co	£
Goods total	16.80
VAT	3.36
Credit note total	20.16

Purchase order no	41120
Credit note	C461
Cheque no	–
Account code	053
Checked	J Garry
Date	05/02/X5
GL account	02

From Mellor & Cross	£
Goods total	104.50
Less: Trade discount 10%	10.45
	94.05
VAT	18.81
Credit note total	112.86

Purchase order no	41096
Credit note	C462
Cheque no	–
Account code	259
Checked	J Garry
Date	05/02/X5
GL account	02

From Thompson Bros Ltd	£
Goods total	37.60
Less: Trade discount 5%	1.88
	35.72
VAT	7.14
Credit note total	42.86

Purchase order no	41103
Credit note	C463
Cheque no	–
Account code	360
Checked	J Garry
Date	05/02/X5
GL account	01

Solution

Purchases returns day book

Date	*Credit note no*	*Code*	*Supplier*	*Total* £	*VAT* £	*01* £	*02* £	*03* £	*04* £
05/02/X5	C461	053	Calderwood & Co	20.16	3.36		16.80		
05/02/X5	C462	259	Mellor & Cross	112.86	18.81		94.05		
05/02/X5	C463	360	Thompson Bros Ltd	42.86	7.14	35.72			

Note that it is the credit note total which is entered into the total column and the VAT amount into the VAT column. The amount entered into the analysis columns is the goods total less the trade discount. The analysis column is taken from the general ledger code on the authorisation stamp.

3 Accounting entries in the general ledger

3.1 Introduction

The accounting entries that are to be made in the general ledger are the same as those that have been considered in Bookkeeping Level II and are made from the totals of the columns in the purchases day book and purchases returns day book.

3.2 Analysed purchases day book

If an analysed purchases day book is being used then there will be a debit entry in an individual purchases or expense account for each of the analysis column totals.

Remember that these totals are the net of VAT purchases/expenses totals.

Example

Reproduced below is a purchases day book for the first week of February 20X5. Each column has been totalled and it must be checked that the totals of the analysis columns agree to the 'Total' column. Therefore you should check the following sum:

	£
01	744.37
02	661.23
03	250.45
04	153.72
VAT	338.43
	2,148.20

Purchases day book

Date	*Invoice no*	*Code*	*Supplier*	*Total*	*VAT*	*01*	*02*	*03*	*04*
				£	£	£	£	£	£
20X5									
1 Feb	3569	265	Norweb	151.44	25.24	126.20			
2 Feb	3570	053	Calderwood & Co	98.60			98.60		
3 Feb	3571	259	Mellor & Cross	675.15	112.52		562.63		
4 Feb	3572	360	Thompson Bros Ltd	265.71	44.28	221.43			
5 Feb	3573	023	Cooplin Associates	18.90				18.90	
	3574	056	Heywood Suppliers	277.86	46.31			231.55	
	3575	395	William Leggett	46.33	7.72				38.61
	3576	271	Melville Products	374.29	62.38	311.91			
	3577	301	Quick-Bake	101.79	16.96	84.83			
	3578	311	Roger & Roebuck	138.13	23.02				115.11
				2,148.20	338.43	744.37	661.23	250.45	153.72

The totals of the purchases day book will now be posted to the general ledger accounts.

Solution

Purchase ledger control account

	£		£
		PDB	2,148.20

VAT account

	£		£
PDB	338.43		

Purchases – 01 account

	£		£
PDB	744.37		

Purchases – 02 account

	£		£
PDB	661.23		

Purchases – 03 account

	£		£
PDB	250.45		

Purchases – 04 account

	£		£
PDB	153.72		

3.3 Purchases returns day book

The purchases returns day book is kept in order to record credit notes received by the business. The totals of this must also be posted to the general ledger.

Example

Given below is a purchases returns day book for the week. The totals are to be posted to the general ledger accounts. VAT is at 20%.

Purchases day book									
Date	*Credit note no*	*Code*	*Supplier*	*Total*	*VAT*	*01*	*02*	*03*	*04*
				£	£	£	£	£	£
20X3									
4 May	CN 152	PL21	Julian R Partners	132.00	22.00		110.00		
6 May	CN 153	PL07	S T Trader	81.60	13.60			68.00	
8 May	CN 154	PL10	Ed Associates	70.32	11.72		58.60		
8 May	CN 155	PL03	Warren & Co	107.52	17.92	89.60			
				391.44	65.24	89.60	168.60	68.00	–

Solution

First, check that each of the column totals add back to the total column total:

	£
VAT	65.24
01	89.60
02	168.60
03	68.00
04	–
	391.44

Then post the totals to the general ledger accounts:

Purchases ledger control account

	£		£
Purchases return day book (PRDB)	391.44		

VAT account

	£		£
		PRDB	65.24

Purchases returns – 01

	£		£
		PRDB	89.60

Purchases returns – 02

	£		£
		PRDB	168.60

Purchases returns – 03

	£		£
		PRDB	68.00

If the purchases returns day book is analysed then there will be an account in the general ledger for each different category of purchases returns.

Activity 3

Given below is the purchases day book. You are required to check the total of each analysis column and that the total of each analysis column agrees to the total column, and then to enter the totals in the correct general ledger accounts.

Purchases day book

Date	*Invoice no*	*Code*	*Supplier*	*Total* £	*VAT* £	*Goods for sale* £	*Heat and light* £	*Postage and stationery* £
01.01.X1	115	N2	Northern Electric	120.00	5.71		114.29	
	116	N3	Northern News	230.00		230.00		
02.01.X1	117	P1	Post Office	117.00				117.00
	118	N1	Northern Country	48.00	8.00	40.00		
03.01.X1	119	S1	South Gazette	360.00	60.00	300.00		
				875.00	73.71	570.00	114.29	117.00

4 Accounting entries in the purchases ledger

4.1 Purchases ledger

As well as posting the totals from the books of prime entry to the general ledger accounts, each individual invoice and credit note must also be posted to the individual supplier's account in the purchases ledger (also referred to as the subsidiary (purchases) ledger.

Example

Here is an account from the purchases ledger of Frosty Limited.

Account name: **Code:**

Date	*Transaction*	£	*Date*	*Transaction*	£

We will write up the account for Jones Brothers, account number PJ06. This is a new supplier.

Frosty Limited has only been trading for a short time and is not yet registered for VAT.

Purchase invoices and credit notes

02.5.X1	9268	£638.26
06.6.X1	9369	£594.27
15.6.X1	9402	£368.24
17.6.X1	C Note 413	£58.62
19.6.X1	9568	£268.54

Solution

Account name: Jones Brothers **Account number:** PJ06

Date	*Transaction*	£	*Date*	*Transaction*	£
17.6.X1	Credit note 413	58.62	02.5.X1	Invoice 9268	638.26
			06.6.X1	Invoice 9369	594.27
			15.6.X1	Invoice 9402	368.24
			19.6.X1	Invoice 9568	268.54

Each purchase invoice from the Purchases Day Book must be entered on the credit side of that individual suppliers account in the purchases ledger. Any credit notes recorded in the Purchases Returns Day Book must be recorded on the debit side of the supplier's account. Where there is VAT involved the amount to be recorded for an invoice or credit note is the gross amount or VAT inclusive amount.

5 The impact of value added tax

5.1 Introduction

Having looked at the accounting for purchase invoices and credit notes, we will now move on to consider the accounting for payments to suppliers. First we will consider the impact of VAT in this area.

When writing up the payments side of the cash book VAT must be considered.

Any payments to suppliers or creditors included in the Purchases ledger column need have no analysis for VAT as the VAT on the purchase was recorded in the purchases day book when the invoice was initially received.

However any other payments on which there is VAT must show the gross amount in the Total column, the VAT in the VAT column and the net amount in the relevant expense column.

Example

Peter Craddock is the cashier for a business which manufactures paper from recycled paper. The payments that were made for one week in September are as follows:

15 September	Cheque no 1151 to K Humphrey (credit supplier)	£1,034.67
	Cheque no 1152 to Y Ellis (credit supplier)	£736.45
	Cheque no 1153 to R Phipps (credit supplier)	£354.45
	Standing order for rent	£168.15
	Direct debit to the electricity company	£130.98
		(including VAT of £6.23)

16 September	Cheque no 1154 to L Silton (credit supplier)	£1,092.75
	Cheque no 1155 to the insurance company	£103.18
17 September	Cheque no 1156 to F Grange (credit supplier)	£742.60
	Cheque no 1157 to Hettler Ltd for cash purchases	£504.00 (including VAT at 20%)
18 September	Cheque no 1158 to J Kettle (credit supplier)	£131.89
19 September	BACS payment of wages	£4,150.09
	Cheque no 1159 to Krane Associates for cash purchases	£223.20 (including VAT at 20%)

Enter these transactions into the cash payments book, total the columns and post the totals to the general ledger.

Solution

Date	*Details*	*Cheque no*	*Total* £	*VAT* £	*PLCA* £	*Cash purchases* £	*Rent* £	*Elec-tricity* £	*Wages* £	*Insurance* £
15/9	K Humphrey	1151	1,034.67		1,034.67					
	Y Ellis	1152	736.45		736.45					
	R Phipps	1153	354.45		354.45					
	Rent	SO	168.15				168.15			
	Electricity	DD	130.98	6.23				124.75		
16/9	L Silton	1154	1,092.75		1,092.75					
	Insurance	1155	103.18							103.18
17/9	F Grange	1156	742.60		742.60					
	Hettler Ltd	1157	504.00	84.00		420.00				
18/9	J Kettle	1158	131.89		131.89					
	Wages	BACS	4,150.09						4,150.09	
19/9	Krane Ass	1159	223.20	37.20		186.00				
			9,372.41	127.43	4,092.81	606.00	168.15	124.75	4,150.09	103.18

The analysis column totals should add back to the Total column – this must always be done to check the accuracy of your totalling.

	£
VAT	127.43
Purchases ledger	4,092.81
Cash purchases	606.00
Rent	168.15
Electricity	124.75
Wages	4,150.09
Insurance	103.18
	9,372.41

Purchase ledger control account

		£			£
19/9	CPB	4,092.81			

VAT account

		£			£
19/9	CPB	127.43			

Purchases account

		£			£
19/9	CPB	606.00			

Electricity account

		£			£
19/9	CPB	124.75			

Wages account

		£			£
19/9	CPB	4,150.09			

Rent account

		£			£
19/9	CPB	168.15			

Insurance account

		£			£
19/9	CPB	103.18			

All of the entries in the general ledger accounts are debit entries. The credit entry is the total column of the cash payments book and these individual debit entries form the double entry.

6 Paying supplier statements

6.1 Introduction

A supplier statement shows all the invoices and credit notes that have been received from a particular credit supplier for that month, together with any amounts outstanding from previous months. The statement also details any payments sent to the credit supplier.

When sales to a customer are on a credit basis, it is important that there are procedures in place to ensure that the monies outstanding are received promptly.

In practice most customers do not settle their debt after receiving every invoice, as customers can purchase from their suppliers numerous times within a month. Therefore, payment will tend to be made when a statement has been sent by the supplier detailing all the invoices, credit notes and any payments that have occurred within the month. The information contained on the statement will come from the individual receivable's account within the subsidiary sales ledger.

When these statements are sent out and then received by the customer, the customer should compare them to the account they hold for the supplier in their subsidiary purchases ledger.

Once the statement has been reconciled against the customer's own accounting records, the customer will then pay the amount due.

6.2 Checking supplier statements

Before any payments are made it is important to check that the supplier's statement is correct. Each invoice and credit note should be checked either to the original documentation or to the supplier's account in the purchases ledger.

When the accuracy of the statement has been ascertained then it must be determined exactly which invoices from the statement are to be paid.

Example

Given below is a statement from a supplier together with that supplier's account from the purchases ledger.

To: Scott Brothers 34 Festival Way Oldham OL2 3BD			Nemo Limited Date: 31 August 20X3		
		STATEMENT			
Date	*Transaction*	*Total* £	*Current* £	*30+* £	*60+* £
12 May 20X3	Invoice 2569	92.35			92.35
13 June 20X3	CN 2659	(23.60)			(23.60)
09 July 20X3	Invoice 2701	102.69		102.69	
18 July 20X3	Invoice 2753	133.81		133.81	
02 Aug 20X3	Invoice 2889	56.50	56.50		
10 Aug 20X3	Invoice 2901	230.20	230.20		
28 Aug 20X3	Invoice 3114	243.24	243.24		
	TOTALS	835.19	529.94	236.50	68.75
		May we remind you our credit terms are 30 days			

Nemo Ltd

		£			£
13 June	CN 2659	23.60	12 May	Invoice 2569	92.35
			09 July	Invoice 2701	102.69
			18 July	Invoice 2753	133.81
			02 Aug	Invoice 2889	56.50
			10 Aug	Invoice 2901	203.20
			28 Aug	Invoice 3114	243.24

To check that the supplier's statement is correct prior to paying any amounts, the statement should be carefully checked to the supplier's account in the purchases ledger.

Solution

The invoice dated 10 August is in the purchases ledger at a total of £203.20 whereas it appears on the supplier's statement as £230.20.

The purchase invoice itself should be accessed from the filing system to determine whether the amount is £203.20 or £230.20. If the supplier's statement is incorrect then a polite telephone call should be made or letter sent to the supplier, Nemo Ltd, explaining the problem.

6.3 Which invoices to pay

Once the supplier's statement has been checked for accuracy then it has to be decided which invoices shall be paid. Most organisations will have a policy regarding the payment of supplier's invoices or, alternatively, a fairly senior figure in the business will decide each month which invoices are to be paid.

Example

Using the supplier's statement shown above suppose that payment has been authorised for all amounts that have been outstanding for 30 days or more. What amount should the cheque be made out for?

Solution

	£
60+ days total	68.75
30+ days total	236.50
Cheque amount	305.25

6.4 Using remittance advices

Some suppliers will attach a remittance advice to the bottom of their statement so that the customer can indicate which invoices less credit notes are being paid with this cheque.

This makes it much easier for the business receiving the cheque to know which outstanding invoices are actually being paid.

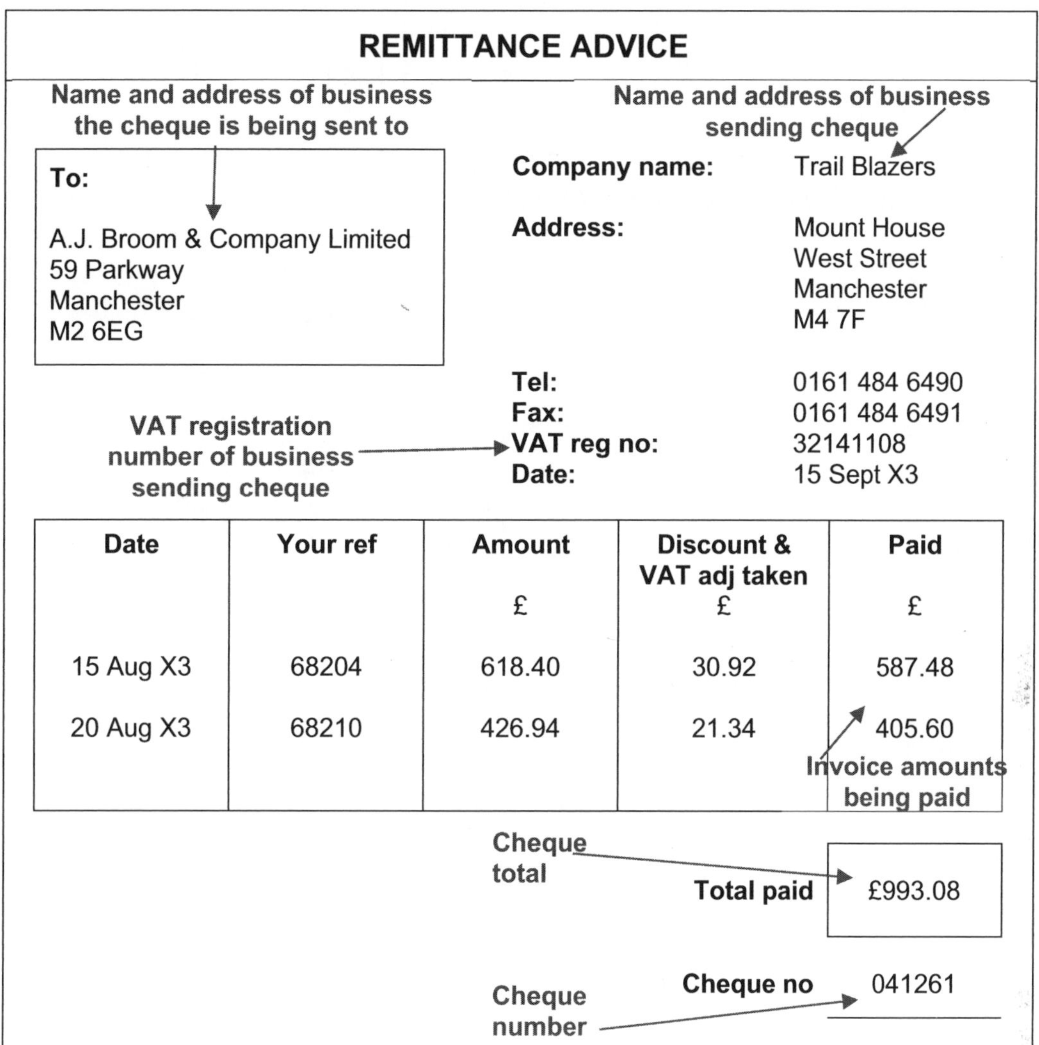

REMITTANCE ADVICE

To:

A.J. Broom & Company Limited
59 Parkway
Manchester
M2 6EG

Company name: Trail Blazers

Address: Mount House, West Street, Manchester, M4 7F

Tel: 0161 484 6490
Fax: 0161 484 6491
VAT reg no: 32141108
Date: 15 Sept X3

Date	Your ref	Amount £	Discount & VAT adj taken £	Paid £
15 Aug X3	68204	618.40	30.92	587.48
20 Aug X3	68210	426.94	21.34	405.60

Total paid £993.08

Cheque no 041261

7 Cash (settlement) discounts

7.1 Introduction

If a business takes advantage of cash discounts on items purchased, the discount is treated as income as it is a benefit to the business i.e. although the invoice is paid earlier, the amount paid is less than the invoice net amount due to the discount.

Cash or settlement discounts, and the necessary VAT adjustment, are recorded in memorandum columns in the cash book. The memorandum columns do not form part of the double entry. They require an entire piece of double entry (see below).

The business must record these settlement discounts and associated VAT adjustments in the cash book. Trade discounts are not recorded in the cash book.

Two extra columns are included in the analysed cash payments book. These should be the two final right hand columns.

Example

The following four payments have been made today, 12 June 20X6:

Cheque no. 22711 B Caro	Purchases ledger code CL13 £339.96 after taking a settlement discount of £14.20 (VAT adjustment of £2.84 required)	
Cheque no.22712 S Wills	Cash purchases of £240.00 inclusive of VAT	
Cheque no. 22713 P P & Co	Purchases ledger code CL22	£116.40
Cheque no. 22714 W Potts	Purchases ledger code CL18	£162.84

The relevant purchases ledger accounts are shown below:

B Caro (CL 13)

	£		£
		PDB Invoice	357.00

W Potts (CL 18)

	£		£
PRDB Credit note	10.00	PDB Invoice	172.84

P P & Co (CL 22)

	£		£
		PDB Invoice	116.40
		PDB Invoice	121.27

In this example we will:

- write up the cash payments book for the day
- total the columns to check that they add back to the total of the Total column
- enter the totals in the general ledger
- write up each individual entry in the purchases ledger.

Solution

Date	*Details*	*Cheque*	*Code*	*Total*	*VAT*	*PLCA*	*Cash purchases*	*Discounts*	*VAT Adj*
				£	£	£	£	£	£
12 Jun	B Caro	22711	CL13	339.96		339.96		14.20	2.84
	S Wills	22712		240.00	40.00		200.00		
	PP&Co	22713	CL22	116.40		116.40			
	W Potts	22714	CL18	162.84		162.84			
				859.20	40.00	619.20	200.00	14.20	2.84

Total Check

	£
Purchases ledger	619.20
Cash purchases	200.00
VAT	40.00
	859.20

Note that the discount received and VAT adjustment columns are not included in the total check as they are simply memorandum columns.

General ledger

Purchase ledger control account

	£		£
CPB	619.20		
CPB – discount	14.20		
CPB – VAT adjustment	2.84		

Purchases account

	£		£
CPB	200.00		

VAT account

	£		£
CPB	40.00	CPB – VAT adjustment	2.84

Discounts received account

	£		£
		CPB	14.20

When posting the cash payments book to the general ledger there are two distinct processes. Firstly enter the totals of each of the analysis columns as debits in their relevant accounts in the general ledger. Then do the double entry for the discounts received (debit the purchase ledger control account and credit the discounts received account) and the VAT adjustment (debit the purchase ledger control account and credit the VAT account).

Purchases ledger

B Caro (CL 13)

		£			£
CPB	Payment	339.96	PDB	Invoice	357.00
CPB	Discount	14.20			
CPB – VAT adjustment		2.84			

Note that the discount and VAT adjustment are entered here as well as the cash payment

W Potts (CL 18)

		£			£
PRDB	Credit note	10.00	PDB	Invoice	172.84
CPB	Payment	162.84			

P P & Co (CL 22)

		£			£
CPB	Payment	116.40	PDB	Invoice	116.40
			PDB	Invoice	121.27

Activity 4

Given below is a completed cash payments book. You are required to:

(a) Total each of the columns and check that the totals add across to the total column.

(b) Post the totals to the general ledger accounts given.

(c) Post the individual creditor entries to the creditors' accounts in the purchases ledger, also given.

Date	*Details*	*Cheque no*	*Code*	*Total* £	*VAT* £	*PLCA* £	*Cash purchases* £	*Wages* £
1/7	G Hobbs	34	PL14	325.46		325.46		
1/7	Purchases	35	GL03	68.40	11.40		57.00	
2/7	Purchases	36	GL03	50.59	8.43		42.16	
3/7	P Taylor	37	PL21	157.83		157.83		
3/7	S Dent	38	PL06	163.58		163.58		
4/7	K Smith	39	GL07	24.56				24.56

Purchase ledger control account

	£		£

Cash purchases account

	£		£

Wages account

	£		£

VAT account

	£		£

Purchases ledger

G Hobbs		PL14
	£	£

P Taylor		PL21
	£	£

S Dent		PL06
	£	£

8 The cash payments book

8.1 Introduction

We considered the difference between a two and three column cash book in the previous chapter. We must be aware that a cash book can be analysed in different ways. We have already reviewed the cash receipts book. We will now review the cash payments book.

A proforma analysed cash payments book is shown below.

CASH PAYMENTS BOOK

Date	*Narrative*	*Reference*	*Total* £	*VAT* £	*PLCA* £	*Cash purchases* £	*Admin* £	*Rent and rates* £	*Discount received* £	*VAT Adjust-ment* £
		TOTALS								

Notes:

(a) The date column contains the date of the transaction.

(b) The narrative column describes the transactions.

(c) The total column contains the total cash paid (including any VAT).

(d) The VAT column contains the VAT on the transaction but not if the VAT has already been entered in the purchases day book. This is a tricky point but is in principle exactly the same as the treatment of VAT that we studied for the cash receipts book.

(e) The PLCA column contains any cash paid that has been paid to a supplier. The total paid including VAT is entered in this column.

(f) The cash purchases column contains cash paid for purchases that are not bought on credit.

(g) We saw with the analysed cash receipts book that nearly all receipts come from debtors or cash sales. In the case of payments, there is a great variety of suppliers who are paid through the cash book; rent and rates, telephone, electricity, marketing, etc. The business will have a separate column for the categories of expense that it wishes to analyse. There may be as many or as little as a business wishes.

(h) The discount received and the VAT adjustment columns are memorandum columns that contain details of any cash/settlement discounts received and the associated VAT adjustment. These discounts and VAT adjustments will need to be entered into the ledger accounts as we saw in the example above.

Activity 5

Cashbook – Credit side

Date	Details	VAT £	Bank £
30 Nov	Motor expenses	40	240
30 Nov	Wages		6,200
30 Nov	HMRC (VAT)		4,750

What will be the FOUR entries in the general ledger?

General Ledger

Account name	Amount £	Debit / Credit
Motor expenses	200	Dt
Wages	6200	Dt
HMRC (VAT)	4750	Dt
VAT	40	Dt

9 Summary

In this chapter we have pulled together into one place all the general documents and double entry for the purchases cycle. If you have had any trouble with any of these points, you should refer again to the Certificate in Bookkeeping Level II (Manual) Study Text where the double entry is explained.

Answers to chapter activities

Activity 1

Purchases day book

Date	Invoice no	Code	Supplier	Total	VAT	01	02	03	04
				£	£	£	£	£	£
10/11/X2	4221	DF2	Drip Farm	120.00	20.00	100.00			
10/11/X2	4222	DN1	Daily News plc	360.00	60.00		300.00		
10/11/X2	4223	SM4	Standard Machines	2,400.00	400.00				2,000.00
				2,880.00	480.00	100.00	300.00	–	2,000.00

Document 3 receipt is not a purchase invoice, it is a receipt for cash paid.

Document 4 is a sales order to supply 20 cases of bottled juice. It is not a purchase invoice so would not appear in the purchases day book.

Activity 2

Purchases day book

Date	Invoice no	Code	Supplier	Total	VAT	Goods for resale	Heat and light	Postage and stationery
				£	£	£	£	£
01.01.X1	115	N2	Northern Electric	120.00	5.71		114.29	
	116	N3	Northern News	230.00	–	230.00		
02.01.X1	117	P1	Post Office Ltd	117.00	–			117.00
	118	N1	Northern Country	48.00	8.00	40.00		
03.01.X1	119	S1	South Gazette	360.00	60.00	300.00		
				875.00	73.71	570.00	114.29	117.00

Activity 3

	£
Goods for resale	570.00
Heat and light	100.00
Postage and stationery	117.00
VAT	88.00
Total	875.00

Purchases (goods for resale)

	£		£
PDB	540.00		

Heat and light

	£		£
PDB	100.00		

Postage and stationery

	£		£
PDB	117.00		

VAT

	£		£
PDB	88.00		

Purchases ledger control account

	£		£
		PDB	875.00

Activity 4

(a) **Cash payments book**

Date	*Details*	*Cheque no*	*Code*	*Total*	*VAT*	*PLCA*	*Cash purchases*	*Wages*
				£	£	£	£	£
1/7	G Hobbs	34	PL14	325.46		325.46		
1/7	Purchases	35	GL03	68.40	11.40		57.00	
2/7	Purchases	36	GL03	50.59	8.43		42.16	
3/7	P Taylor	37	PL21	157.83		157.83		
3/7	S Dent	38	PL06	163.58		163.58		
4/7	K Smith	39	GL07	24.56				24.56
				790.42	19.83	646.87	99.16	24.56

Check that totals add across:

	£
VAT	19.83
Purchases ledger	646.87
Cash purchases	99.16
Wages	24.56
	790.42

(b) **General ledger accounts**

Purchases ledger control account

	£		£
CPB	646.87		

Cash purchases account

	£		£
CPB	99.16		

Wages account

	£		£
CPB	24.56		

VAT account

	£		£
CPB	19.83		

(c) **Purchases ledger**

	G Hobbs		**PL14**
	£		£
CPB	325.46		

	P Taylor		**PL21**
	£		£
CPB	157.83		

	S Dent		**PL06**
	£		£
CPB	163.58		

Activity 5

Cashbook – Credit side

Date	Details	VAT £	Bank £
30 Nov	Motor expenses	40	240
30 Nov	Wages		6,200
30 Nov	HMRC		4,750

What will be the FOUR entries in the general ledger?

General Ledger

Account name	Amount £	Debit / Credit
Motor expenses	200	Debit
VAT	40	Debit
Wages	6,200	Debit
VAT control account	4,750	Debit

9 Test your knowledge

Workbook Activity 6

Given below is the cheque listing for a business for the week ending 12 March.

Cheque payment listing

Supplier	*Code*	*Cheque number*	*Cheque amount* £	*Discount taken* £	*VAT Adj* £
Homer Ltd	PL12	03648	167.69	5.06	1.01
Forker & Co	PL07	03649	178.38	5.38	1.07
Print Associates	PL08	03651	190.45		
ABG Ltd	PL02	03652	219.35	6.62	1.32
G Greg	PL19	03654	67.89		

Cash purchases were made for £342.00 and £200.40.

The cash purchases include VAT at standard rate 20%.

You are required to:

- enter the payments into the cash payments book and total each of the columns
- post the totals to the general ledger accounts given
- post the individual entries to the purchases ledger accounts given.

CASH PAYMENTS BOOK

Date	*Details*	*Code*	*Discount* £	*VAT Adj* £	*Cash* £	*Bank* £	*VAT* £	*PLCA* £	*Cash purchases* £	*Other* £
12/03	Homer	PL12	5,06	1,01		167,69		167,69		
12/03	Forker	PL07	5,38	1,07		178,38		178,38		
12/03	Print	PL08				190,45		190,45		
12/03	ABG	PL02	6,62	1,32		219,35		219,35		
12/03	G Greg	PL19				67,89		67,89		
12/03	Purchg				285		57		342	
12/03	Purch.				167		33,40		200,40	
			17,06	3,40	452	823,76	90,40	823,76	542,40	

1366.16

General ledger

Purchases ledger control account

		£			£
			5/3	Balance b/d	4,136.24

VAT account

		£			£
			5/3	Balance b/d	1,372.56

Purchases account

		£			£
5/3	Balance b/d	20,465.88			

Discounts received account

		£			£
			5/3	Balance b/d	784.56

Purchases ledger

ABG Ltd PL02

		£			£
			5.3	Balance b/d	486.90

Forker & Co PL07

		£			£
			5/3	Balance b/d	503.78

Print Associates PL08

		£			£
			5/3	Balance b/d	229.56

	Homer Ltd			PL12
	£			£
		5/3	Balance b/d	734.90

	G Greg			PL19
	£			£
		5/3	Balance b/d	67.89

Workbook Activity 7

There are 7 payments to be entered into JR Ltd's cash payments book.

Cash payments

To JD & Co – £96.00 (inc VAT at 20%)

To LJ Ltd – £240.00 (inc VAT at 20%)

To MK Plc – £60.00 (inc VAT at 20%)

Cheque payments

To credit supplier TB Ltd – £68.89 (discount of £2.52 taken, VAT adjustment of £0.50 required)

To credit supplier CF Ltd – £156.72 (discount of £3.16 taken, VAT adjustment of £0.63 required)

Electricity – £90.00 (ignore VAT)

Stationery – £84.00 (inc VAT at 20%)

Required:

Write up the cash payments book given below; total each of the columns of the cash payments book and check that they cross cast.

	Cash payments book							
Narrative	Discount £	VAT Adj £	Cash £	Bank £	VAT £	Cash Purchases £	PLCA £	Expenses £
JD & Co			96		16	80		
LJ Ltd			240		40	200		
MM PLC			60		10	50		
TB LTD	2,52	0,50		68,89			68,89	
CF Ltd	3,16	0,63		156,72			156,72	
electricity				90				90
stationary				84	14			70
	5,68	1,13	396	399,61	80	330	225,61	160

Workbook Activity 8

Given below are four invoices received by Nethan Builders that are to be paid today, 18 May 20X1. It is the business policy to take advantage of any settlement discounts possible.

You are required to complete a remittance advice for each payment. The last cheque used was number 200549.

INVOICE

Invoice to:
Nethan Builders
Brecon House
Stamford Road
Manchester
M16 4PL

Building Contract Supplies
Unit 15
Royal Estate
Manchester
M13 2EF
Tel: 0161 562 3041
Fax: 0161 562 3042

Deliver to:
As above

Invoice no: 07742
Tax point: 8 May 20X1
VAT reg no: 776 4983 06

Code	*Description*	*Quantity*	*VAT rate %*	*Unit price £*	*Amount excl of VAT £*
SDGSL6	SDGS Softwood 47 × 225 mm	20.5 m	20	8.30	170.15
					170.15
VAT					34.03
Total amount payable					204.18

A discount of 1.5% of the full price applies if payment is made within 14 days. No credit note will be issued. Following payment you must ensure you have only recovered the VAT actually paid
If you pay within 14 days, the discounted price is:

Net	167.60
VAT	33.52
Total amount payable	201.12

167.60

0,51

INVOICE

Invoice to:
Nethan Builders
Brecon House
Stamford Road
Manchester
M16 4PL

Deliver to:
As above

Jenson Ltd
30 Longfield Park, Kingsway
M45 2TP
Tel: 0161 511 4666
Fax: 0161 511 4777

Invoice no: 47811
Tax point: 5 May 20X1
VAT reg no: 641 3229 45
Purchase order no: 7174

Code	*Description*	*Quantity*	*VAT rate %*	*Unit price* £	*Amount excl of VAT* £
PL432115	Door Lining set 32 × 115 mm	6	20	30.25	181.50
					181.50
Trade discount 15%					27.22
					154.28
VAT					30.85
Total amount payable					185.13
A discount of 3% of the full price applies if payment is made within 10 days. No credit note will be issued. Following payment you must ensure you have only recovered the VAT actually paid If you pay within 14 days, the discounted price is:					
Net					149.65
VAT					29.93
Total amount payable					179.58

INVOICE

Magnum Supplies
140/150 Park Estate
Manchester
M20 6EG
Tel: 0161 561 3202
Fax: 0161 561 3200

Invoice to:
Nethan Builders
Brecon House
Stamford Road
Manchester
M16 4PL

Deliver to:
As above

Invoice no: 077422
Tax point: 11 May 20X1
VAT reg no: 611 4337 90

Code	*Description*	*Quantity*	*VAT rate %*	*Unit price £*	*Amount excl of VAT £*
BH47732	House Bricks – Red	600	20	1.24	744.00
					744.00
Trade discount 15%					111.60
					632.40
VAT					126.48
Total amount payable					758.88

A discount of 2% of the full price applies if payment is made within 10 days. No credit note will be issued. Following payment you must ensure you have only recovered the VAT actually paid
If you pay within 14 days, the discounted price is:

Net	619.75
VAT	123.95
Total amount payable	743.70

INVOICE

Haddow Bros
The White House
Standing Way
Manchester
M13 6FH
Tel: 0161 560 3140
Fax: 0161 560 6140

Invoice to:
Nethan Builders
Brecon House
Stamford Road
Manchester
M16 4PL

Deliver to:
As above

Invoice no: G33940
Tax point: 9 May 20X1
VAT reg no: 460 3559 71

Code	*Description*	*Quantity*	*VAT rate %*	*Unit price £*	*Amount excl of VAT £*
PLY8FE1	Plywood Hardwood 2440 × 1220 mm	24	20	17.80	427.20
					427.20
VAT					85.44
Total amount payable					512.64

A discount of 2% of the full price applies if payment is made within 10 days. No credit note will be issued. Following payment you must ensure you have only recovered the VAT actually paid
If you pay within 10 days, the discounted price is:

Net	418.66
VAT	83.73
Total amount payable	502.39

REMITTANCE ADVICE

To: Building Contract Supplies
Unit 15
Royal Estate
Manchester
M13 2EF

Nethan Builders
Brecon House
Stamford House
Manchester
M16 4PL

Tel: 0161 521 6411
Fax: 0161 530 6412
VAT reg: 471 3860 42
Date:

Date	Invoice no	Amount £	Discount taken and VAT adj £	Paid £
18/05/x1	07742	204.18	2,55 0,51 } 3,06	201,12

Total paid £ 201,12

Cheque no 200550

REMITTANCE ADVICE

To: Jenson Ltd.

Nethan Builders
Brecon House
Stamford House
Manchester
M16 4PL

Tel: 0161 521 6411
Fax: 0161 530 6412
VAT reg: 471 3860 42
Date:

Date	Invoice no	Amount £	Discount taken and VAT adj £	Paid £
18/05/x1	47811	185,13	5,55	179.58

4,63
0,92

Total paid £ 179.58

Cheque no 200551

REMITTANCE ADVICE

To: Magnum Supplies

Nethan Builders
Brecon House
Stamford House
Manchester
M16 4PL

Tel: 0161 521 6411
Fax: 0161 530 6412
VAT reg: 471 3860 42
Date:

Date	Invoice no	Amount £	Discount taken and VAT adj £	Paid £
18/05/x1	077422	758.88	15,18	743,70

Total paid £ 743.70

Cheque no 200552

REMITTANCE ADVICE

To: Haddow Bros

Nethan Builders
Brecon House
Stamford House
Manchester
M16 4PL

Tel: 0161 521 6411
Fax: 0161 530 6412
VAT reg: 471 3860 42
Date:

Date	Invoice no	Amount £	Discount taken and VAT adj £	Paid £
18/05/x1	G-33940	512,64	10,25	502,39

Total paid £ 502,39

Cheque no 200553

Ledger balances and control accounts

Introduction

In this chapter we will be finding the correct ledger account balances by revising balancing off ledger accounts as the basis for drafting an initial trial balance (covered in Bookkeeping Level II and in chapter 1). In particular, we will be looking at ways of ensuring the accuracy of the balances for debtors (sales ledger control account) and creditors (purchases ledger control account).

CONTENTS

1 Balancing ledger accounts

1.1 Introduction

The purpose of maintaining double entry ledger accounts is to provide information about the transactions and financial position of a business. Each type of transaction is gathered together and recorded in the appropriate ledger account, for example all sales are recorded in the sales account. Then at intervals it will be necessary to find the total of each of these types of transactions.

This is done by balancing each ledger account. This has been covered earlier in your studies but is worth revising here, by attempting Activity 1.

Activity 1

You are required to balance off the following ledger accounts:

Sales ledger control account

	£		£
SDB – invoices	5,426.23	CRB	3,226.56
		CRB - VAT adjustment	63.11
		CRB - Discounts allowed	315.57

VAT account

	£		£
PDB	846.72	SDB	1,036.54
CRB – VAT adjustment	63.11		

Sales account

	£		£
		SDB	2,667.45
		SDB	1,853.92

2 Opening balances

2.1 Introduction

If an account has a balance on it at the end of a period then it will have the same balance at the start of the next period. This is known as an opening balance.

2.2 Debit or credit?

The key to determining whether an opening balance on a ledger account is a debit or a credit is to understand the general rules for debit and credit balances. This can be expressed in the assessment either as a journal, or by entering the amount directly onto the ledger account.

2.3 Debit and credit balance rules

Let's revise the mnemonic DEAD/CLIC from chapter 1 which will help you determine if an entry should be made on the debit side or on the credit side of a ledger account.

Ledger account	
DEBIT	**CREDIT**
• Debtors	• Creditors
• Expenses	• Liabilities
• Assets	• Income
• Drawings	• Capital

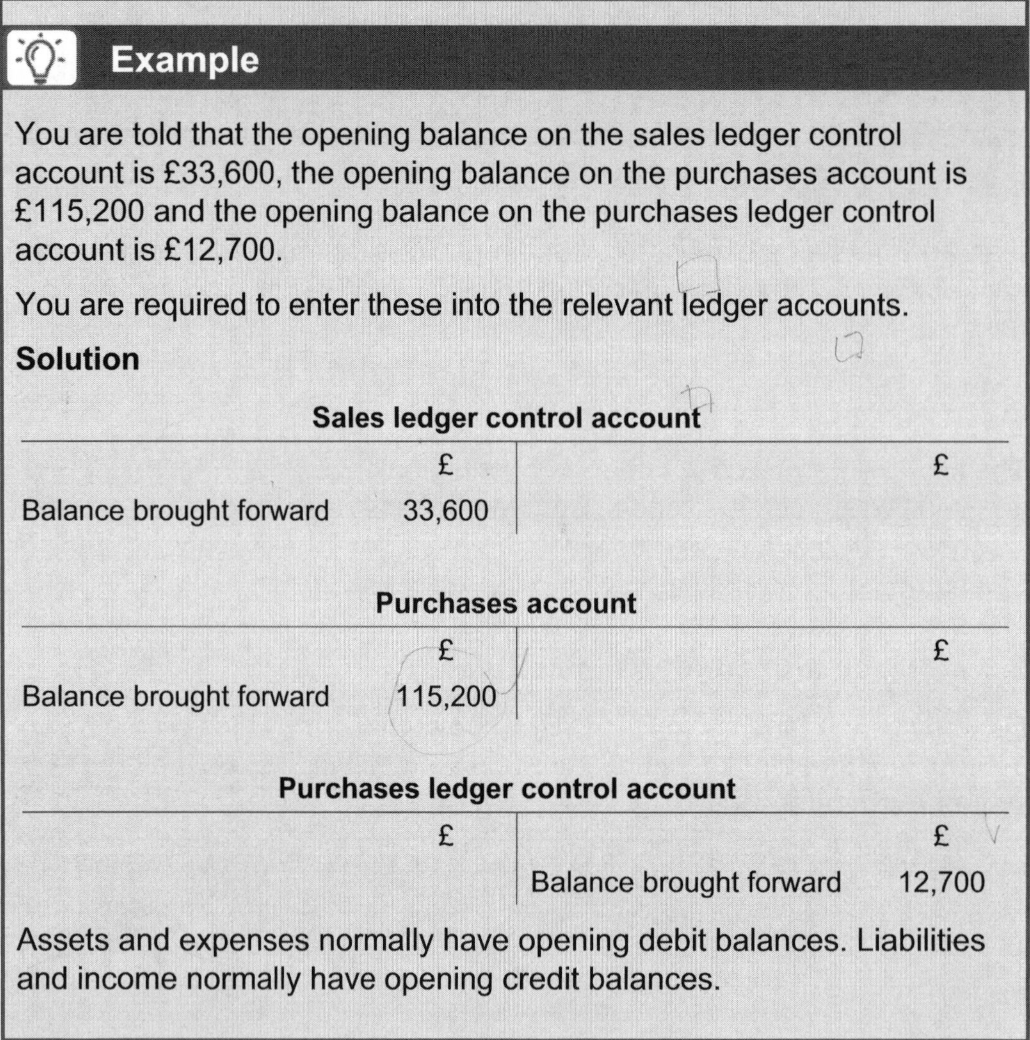

Example

You are told that the opening balance on the sales ledger control account is £33,600, the opening balance on the purchases account is £115,200 and the opening balance on the purchases ledger control account is £12,700.

You are required to enter these into the relevant ledger accounts.

Solution

Sales ledger control account

	£		£
Balance brought forward	33,600		

Purchases account

	£		£
Balance brought forward	115,200		

Purchases ledger control account

	£		£
		Balance brought forward	12,700

Assets and expenses normally have opening debit balances. Liabilities and income normally have opening credit balances.

2.4 Journals

A journal entry is a written instruction to the bookkeeping to enter a double entry into the general ledger accounts. It is shown below in its most basic form, although the journal voucher itself is explained later in this chapter.

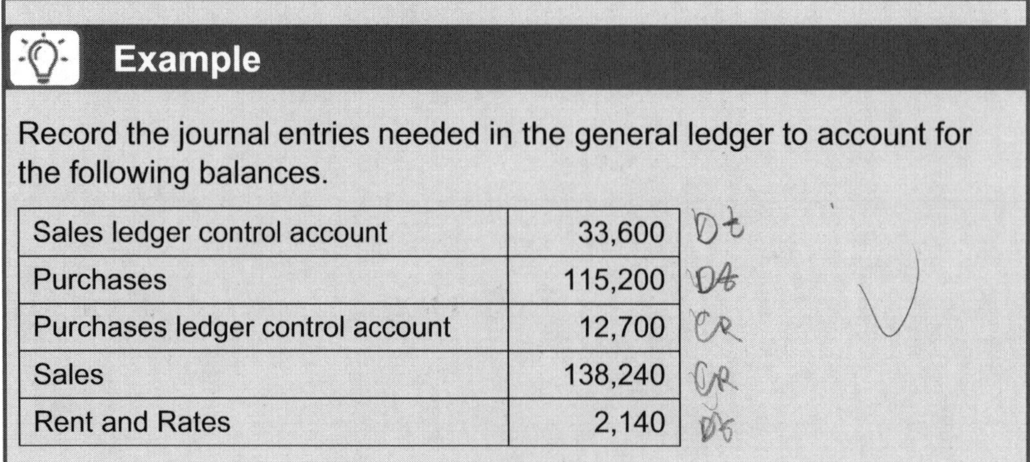

Example

Record the journal entries needed in the general ledger to account for the following balances.

Sales ledger control account	33,600
Purchases	115,200
Purchases ledger control account	12,700
Sales	138,240
Rent and Rates	2,140

Solution

Sales ledger control account	33,600	Debit
Purchases	115,200	Debit
Purchases ledger control account	12,700	Credit
Sales	138,240	Credit
Rent and Rates	2,140	Debit

The total of the debit entries should equal the total of the credit entries.

Activity 2

Would the balances on the following accounts be debit or credit balances?

(a) Sales account

(b) Discounts allowed account

(c) Discounts received account

(d) Wages expense account

Activity 3

The following are the opening balances for a new business. Complete the journal to record these balances.

Account name	Amount £	Debit / Credit
Bank overdraft	6,975	
Cash	275	
VAT payable	2,390	
Motor vehicles	10,500	
Plant and machinery	25,700	
Loan from bank	12,000	
Motor expenses	1,540	
Rent and rates	2,645	
Miscellaneous expenses	725	

Activity 4

The following transactions all occurred on 1 December 20X1 and have been entered into the relevant books of prime entry (given below). However, no entries have yet been made into the ledger system. VAT has been calculated at a rate of 20%.

Purchases day book

Date	*Details*	*Invoice no*	*Total*	*VAT*	*Purchases*	*Stationery*
		£	£	£	£	
20X1						
1 Dec	Bailey Limited	T151	240	40	200	
1 Dec	Byng & Company	10965	960	160	800	
1 Dec	Office Supplies Ltd	34565	336	56		280
1 Dec	O'Connell Frames	FL013	5,040	840	4,200	
	Totals		6,576	1,096	5,200	280

Purchases returns day book

Date	*Details*	*Invoice no*	*Total*	*VAT*	*Purchases returns*	*Stationery*
		£	£	£	£	
20X1						
1 Dec	O'Connell Frames	CO11	2,160	360	1,800	
1 Dec	Office Supplies Ltd	CR192	48	8		40
	Totals		2,208	368	1,800	40

Sales day book

Date	*Details*	*Invoice no*	*Total*	*VAT*	*Sales*
			£	£	£
20X1					
1 Dec	Bentley Brothers	H621	1,680	280	1,400
1 Dec	J & H Limited	H622	4,320	720	3,600
1 Dec	Furniture Galore	H623	4,800	800	4,000
1 Dec	The Sofa Shop	H624	2,640	440	2,200
	Totals		13,440	2,240	11,200

Opening balances

The following are some of the balances in the accounting records and are all relevant to you at the start of the day on 1 December 20X1:

	£
Credit Suppliers	
Bailey Limited	11,750
Byng & Company	1,269
Office Supplies Limited	4,230
O'Connell Frames	423
PLCA	82,006
SLCA	180,312
Purchases	90,563
Sales	301,492
Purchases returns	306
Stationery	642
Discounts received	50
VAT (credit balance)	17,800

Receipts on 1 December 20X1

	Total £
Lili Chang (cash sale including VAT)	528
Bentley Brothers (credit customer)	5,875

Cheque issued

	Total £
Bailey Limited (in full settlement of debt of £819)	799

Task 1

Enter the opening balances listed above into the following accounts, blanks of which are provided on the following pages:

Task 2

Using the data shown above, enter all the relevant transactions into the accounts in the purchases ledger and general ledger. Entries to the sales ledger for debtors are not required.

Task 3

Enter the receipts and payments shown above into the cash book given on the following pages.

Task 4

Transfer any relevant sums from the cash book into the purchases ledger for creditors and general ledger.

Task 5

Balance off all of the accounts and the cash book, showing clearly the balances carried down. The opening cash balance was £3,006. Find the closing balance on the cash book.

Tasks 1, 2, 4 and 5

Purchases ledger

Bailey Limited

	£		£

Byng & Company

	£		£

Office supplies Limited

	£		£

O'Connell Frames

	£		£

General ledger

PLCA

	£		£
01.12	759	Op. bal	82006
01.12	20	01.12	6576
01.12 Returns	2106		
			85555

SLCA

	£		£
Op. bal	180312	01 Dec	5875
01 Dec	13440		
Balance b/d	187877		

Purchases

	£		£
Op. bal	90563		
01 Dec	5200		
Balance b/d	95763		

Sales

	£		£
		Op. bal	301492
		01 Dec	11200
		01 Dec	440
			313132

Purchases returns

	£		£
		Op. bal	306
		01 Dec	1800
			2106

Stationery

	£		£
Op. bal	642	01 Dec	40
01 Dec	280		
	882		

Discounts received

	£		£
		Op. bal.	50
		01 Dec	20
			70

VAT

	£		£
01 Dec	1096	Op. bal	17800
		01 Dec	368
		01 Dec	2240
		01 Dec	88
			19400

Tasks 3, 4 and 5

Cash receipts book

Date	*Narrative*	*Total* £	*VAT* £	*SLCA* £	*Cash sales* £	*Discount allowed* £
01 Dec	Lili Chang	528	88		440	
	Bentley Brothers	5875		5875		
	Baily Limited					20
		6403	88	5875	440	

Cash payments book

Date	*Details*	*Cheque no*	*Code*	*Total* £	*VAT* £	*PLCA* £	*Cash purchases* £	*Other* £	*Discounts received* £
01 Dec	Baily Limited	XX		799		799			20

Cash book b/d - 8610

3 Accounting for debtors

3.1 Sales ledger control account

Within the general ledger the total amount outstanding from debtors is shown in the sales ledger control account.

The totals of credit sales (from the sales day book), returns from customers (from the sales returns day book) and cash received, discounts and any VAT adjustments (from the analysed cash book) are posted to this account. This account therefore shows the total debtors outstanding. It does not give details about individual customers' balances. This is available in the sales ledger for debtors.

However, as both records are compiled from the same sources, the total balances on the customers' individual accounts should equal the outstanding balance on the control account at any time.

3.2 Double entry system

The double entry system operates as follows.

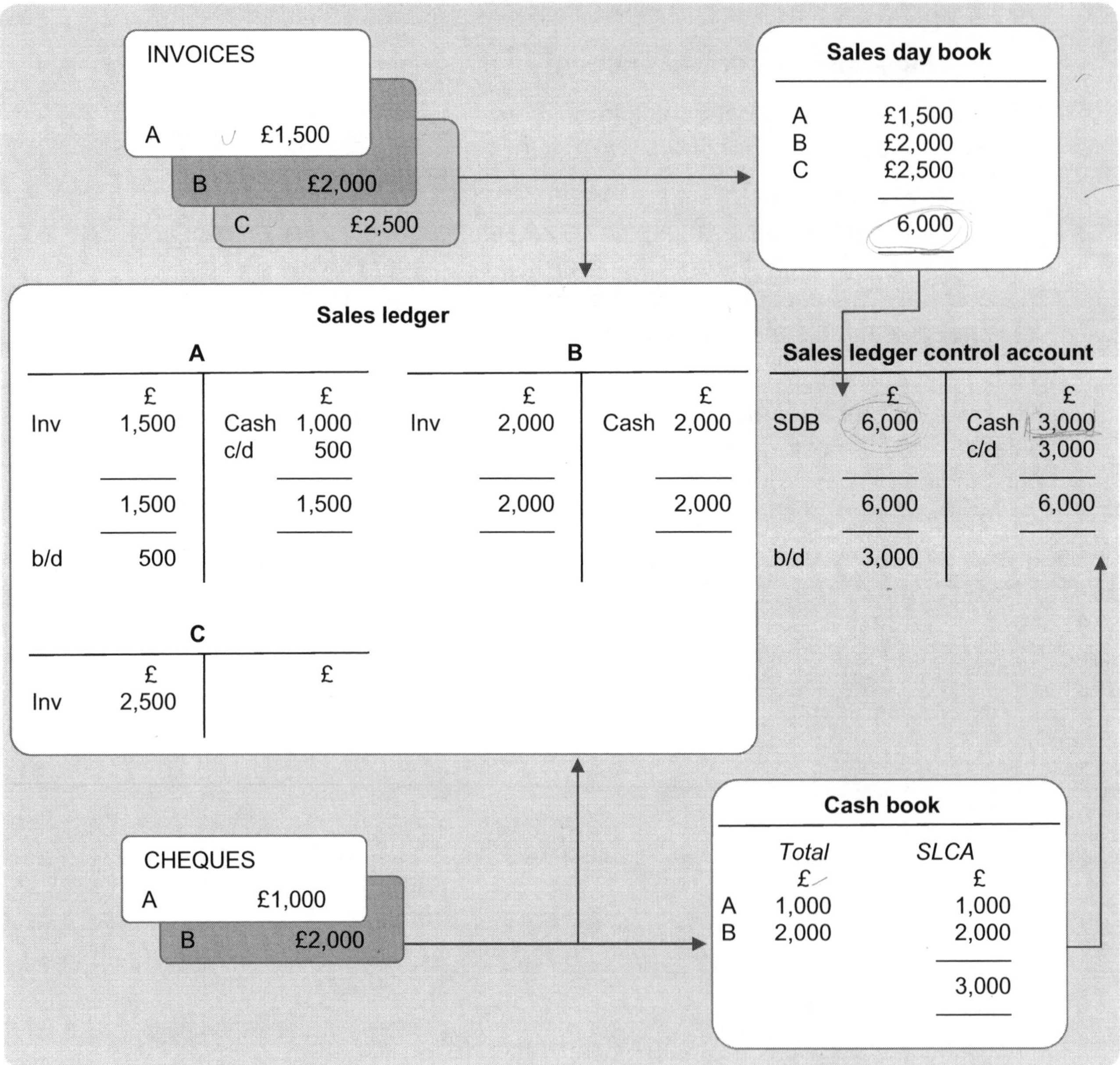

Notice that the remaining balance on the control account (£3,000) is equal to the sum of the remaining balances on the individual debtors' accounts (A £500 + C £2,500).

If all of the accounting entries have been made correctly then the balance on the sales ledger control account should equal the total of the balances on each of the individual debtors' accounts in the sales ledger.

3.3 Proforma sales ledger control account

A sales ledger control account normally appears like this.

Sales ledger control account

	£		£
Balance b/d	X	Returns per sales day book	X
Sales per sales day book	X	* Cash from debtors	X
		* Discounts allowed	X
		* VAT adjustment	X
		Bad debt written off	X
		Contra entry	X
		Balance c/d	X
	X		X
Balance b/d			

* Per cash receipts book

3.4 Bad debts

Definition

A bad debt is a debt which is not likely to be received; it is therefore not prudent for the business to consider this debt as an asset.

3.5 Reasons for bad debts

A business may decide that a debt is bad for a number of reasons:

- customer is in liquidation – no cash will be received
- customer is having difficulty paying although not officially in liquidation
- customer disputes the debt and refuses to pay all or part of it.

3.6 Accounting for bad debts

The business must make an adjustment to write off the bad debt from the customer's account in the sales ledger and to write it off in the general ledger. The double entry in the general ledger is:

DR Bad debt expense

CR Sales ledger control account

Notice that the bad debt becomes an expense of the business. Writing off bad debts decreases the profits made by a business, but is not deducted from sales. The sale was made in the anticipation of receiving the money but, if the debt is not to be received, this does not negate the sale it is just an added expense of the business.

The bad debt must also be written off in the individual debtor's account in the sales ledger by crediting the customer's account as this amount is not going to be received.

When you invoiced the customer you will have recorded the VAT and paid it to HMRC. Once the debt is more than 6 months old and it has been determined that the customer is not going to pay you, you can reclaim that VAT back from HMRC.

DR Bad debt expense	Net amount
DR VAT control account	VAT amount
CR Sales ledger control account	Gross amount

Accounting for bad debts is covered in more detail in a later chapter.

3.7 Contra entries

A further type of adjustment that may be required to sales ledger and purchases ledger control accounts is a contra entry.

3.8 Why a contra entry is required

In some instances a business will be both a debtor and a creditor of another business as it both buys from the business and sells to it. If this is the case then there will be money owed to the business and money owing from it. This can be simplified by making an adjustment known as a contra entry.

Example

James Associates has a customer, X Brothers. X Brothers also sells goods to James Associates. Therefore X Brothers is both a debtor and a creditor of James Associates. The subsidiary ledger accounts of James Associates show the following position:

Sales ledger – debtors

X Brothers

	£		£
Balance b/d	250		

Purchases ledger – creditors

X Brothers

	£		£
		Balance b/d	100

The problem here is that X Brothers owes James Associates £250 and is owed £100 by James Associates. If both parties are in agreement it makes more sense to net these two amounts off and to say that X Brothers owes James Associates just £150. This is achieved in accounting terms by a contra entry.

Solution

Step 1 Take the smaller of the two amounts and debit the purchases ledger account for the creditor and credit the sales ledger account for the debtor with this amount.

Sales ledger – debtors

X Brothers

	£		£
Balance b/d	250	Contra	100

Purchases ledger – creditors

X Brothers

	£		£
Contra	100	Balance b/d	100

Step 2 Balance off the accounts in the subsidiary ledgers.

Sales ledger – debtors

X Brothers

	£		£
Balance b/d	250	Contra	100
		Balance c/d	150
	250		250
Balance b/d	150		

Purchases ledger – creditors

X Brothers

	£		£
Contra	100	Balance b/d	100

This now shows that X Brothers owes £150 to James Associates and is owed nothing by James Associates.

Step 3 The double entry must also be carried out in the general ledger accounts. This is:

DR Purchases ledger control account

CR Sales ledger control account

When a contra entry is made you must remember not just to deal with the entries in the subsidiary ledgers but also to put through the double entry in the general ledger accounts, the sales ledger and purchases ledger control accounts.

3.9 General ledger and sales ledger

We will now return to the relationship between the sales ledger control account in the general ledger and the individual accounts for debtors in the sales ledger.

Example

James has been trading for two months. He has four credit customers. James is not registered for VAT. Here is the day book for the first two months:

Sales day book (SDB)

Date	*Customer*	*Invoice*	£
02.2.X4	Peter Brown	01	50.20
05.2.X4	Ian Smith	02	80.91
07.2.X4	Sid Parsons	03	73.86
23.2.X4	Eva Lane	04	42.30
	Total		247.27
09.3.X4	Ian Smith	05	23.96
15.3.X4	Sid Parsons	06	34.72
20.3.X4	Peter Brown	07	12.60
24.3.X4	Sid Parsons	08	93.25
31.3.X4	Total		164.53

Here is the receipts side of the analysed cash book for March 20X4 (no cash was received from debtors in February).

Cash receipts book (CRB)

Date	*Narrative*	*Total* £	*Cash sales* £	*Sales ledger* £	*Rent* £
01.3.X4	Peter Brown	50.20		50.20	
03.3.X4	Clare Jones	63.80	63.80		
04.3.X4	Molly Dell	110.00			110.00
12.3.X4	Sid Parsons	50.00		50.00	
13.3.X4	Emily Boyd	89.33	89.33		
20.3.X4	Frank Field	92.68	92.68		
25.3.X4	Eva Lane	42.30		42.30	
31.3.X4	Total	498.31	245.81	142.50	110.00

We will write up the sales ledger and the sales ledger control account and compare the balances.

Solution

Sales ledger – debtors

Peter Brown

		£			£
02.2.X4	01	50.20	28.2.X4	c/d	50.20
		50.20			50.20
01.3.X4	b/d	50.20	01.3.X4	Cash	50.20
20.3.X4	07	12.60	31.3.X4	c/d	12.60
		62.80			62.80
01.4.X4	b/d	12.60			

Eva Lane

		£			£
23.2.X4	04	42.30	28.2.X4	c/d	42.30
		42.30			42.30
01.3.X4	b/d	42.30	25.3.X4	Cash	42.30

Sid Parsons

		£			£
07.2.X4	03	73.86	28.2.X4	c/d	73.86
		73.86			73.86
01.3.X4	b/d	73.86	12.3.X4	Cash	50.00
15.3.X4	06	34.72	31.3.X4	c/d	151.83
24 3 X4	08	93.25			
		201.83			201.83
01.4.X4	b/d	151.83			

Ian Smith

		£			£
05.2.X4	02	80.91	28.2.X4	c/d	80.91
		80.91			80.91
01.3.X4	b/d	80.91	31.3.X4	c/d	104.87
09.3.X4	05	23.96			
		104.87			104.87
01.4.X4	b/d	104.87			

Sales ledger control account

		£			£
28.2.X4	SDB	247.27	28.2.X4	c/d	247.27
		247.27			247.27
01.3.X4	b/d	247.27	31.3.X4	CRB	142.50
31.3.X4	SDB	164.53	31.3.X4	c/d	269.30
		411.80			411.80
01.4.X4	b/d	269.30			

Let us compare balances at 31 March 20X4.

Subsidiary ledger – debtors

	£
Peter Brown	12.60
Eva Lane	–
Sid Parsons	151.83
Ian Smith	104.87
	269.30
Sales ledger control account	269.30

As the double entry has been correctly carried out, the total of the balances on the individual debtors' accounts in the sales ledger is equal to the balance on the sales ledger control account.

4 Sales ledger control account reconciliation

4.1 Introduction

Comparing the sales ledger control account balance with the total of the sales ledger accounts is a form of internal control. The reconciliation should be performed on a regular basis by the sales ledger clerk and reviewed and approved by an independent person.

If the total of the balances on the sales ledger do not equal the balance on the sales ledger control account then an error or errors have been made in either the general ledger or sales ledger, and these must be discovered and corrected.

4.2 Journal entries

We saw earlier how a journal can be used to enter opening balances to start a new period of accounts. Journal entries are also used for unusual items that do not appear in the primary records, or for the correction of errors or making of adjustments to ledger accounts.

A typical journal entry to write off a bad debt is shown below:

Sequential journal number

Authorisation

Description of why double entry is necessary

Double entry

JOURNAL ENTRY		No: 06671		
Prepared by:	P Freer			
Authorised by:	P Simms			
Date:	3 October 20X2			
Narrative:				
To write off bad debt from L C Hamper				
Account		Code	Debit	Credit
Bad debts expense		GL28	102.00	
Debtors' control		GL06		102.00
TOTALS			102.00	102.00

Equal totals as journal must balance

Example

The total sales for the month was posted from the sales day book as £4,657.98 instead of £4,677.98. This must be corrected using a journal entry.

Solution

The journal entry to correct this error will be as follows:

JOURNAL ENTRY		No: 97		
Prepared by:	A Graimm			
Authorised by:	L R Ridinghood			
Date:	23.7.X3			
Narrative:				
To correct error in posting from SDB				
Account		Code	Debit	Credit
Sales ledger control		GL11	20	
Sales		GL56		20
TOTALS			20	20

The adjustment required is to increase debtors and sales by £20 therefore a debit to sales ledger control and a credit to sales is needed.

4.3 Adjustments in the subsidiary ledger

Adjustments in the subsidiary ledger do not need to be shown in a journal entry. Journal entries are only required for adjustments to the general ledger.

These adjustments should be recorded in memorandum form, with proper authorisation.

4.4 Procedure for a sales ledger control account reconciliation

(1) The balances on the sales ledger accounts for debtors are extracted, listed and totalled.

(2) The sales ledger control account is balanced.

(3) If the two figures differ, then the reasons for the difference must be investigated.

Reasons may include the following:

- An error in the casting of the day book. (The total is posted to the control account whereas the individual invoices are posted to the individual accounts and, therefore, if the total is incorrect, a difference will arise.)
- A transposition error (the figures are switched around, e.g. £87 posted as £78) which could be made in posting either:
  - (a) to the control account (the total figure); or
  - (b) to the individual accounts (the individual transactions).
- A casting error in the cash book column relating to the control account. (The total is posted.)
- A balance omitted from the list of individual accounts.
- A credit balance on an individual account in the sales ledger for debtors which has automatically and wrongly been assumed to be a debit balance.

(4) Differences which are errors in the control account should be corrected in the control account.

(5) Differences which are errors in the individual accounts should be corrected by adjusting the list of balances and, of course, the account concerned.

Activity 5

Would the following errors cause a difference to occur between the balance of the sales ledger control account and the total of the balances in the sales ledger?

(a) The total column of the sales day book was overcast by £100.

(b) In error H Lambert's account in the sales ledger was debited with £175 instead of M Lambert's account.

(c) An invoice for £76 was recorded in the sales day book as £67.

Example

The balance on the sales ledger control account for a business at 31 March 20X3 is £14,378.37. The total of the list of sales ledger balances for debtors is £13,935.37.

The difference has been investigated and the following errors have been identified:

- the sales day book was overcast by £1,000
- a credit note for £150 was entered into an individual debtor's account as an invoice
- discounts allowed of £143 were correctly accounted for in the sales ledger but were not entered into the general ledger accounts
- a credit balance on one debtor's account of £200 was mistakenly listed as a debit balance when totalling the individual debtor accounts in the sales ledger.

Prepare the reconciliation between the balance on the sales ledger control account and the total of the individual balances on the sales ledger accounts.

Solution

Step 1 Amend the sales ledger control account for any errors that have been made.

Sales ledger control account

	£		£
Balance b/d	14,378.37	SDB overcast	1,000.00
		Discounts allowed	143.00
		Balance c/d	13,235.37
	14,378.37		14,378.37
Balance b/d	13,235.37		

Step 2 Correct the total of the list of balances in the sales ledger.

		£
Original total		13,935.37
Less:	Credit note entered as invoice (2 × 150)	(300.00)
	Credit balance entered as debit balance (2 × 200)	(400.00)
		13,235.37

Activity 6

The balance on Diana's sales ledger control account at 31 December 20X6 was £15,450. The balances on the individual accounts in the sales ledger have been extracted and total £15,705. On investigation the following errors are discovered:

(a) a debit balance of £65 has been omitted from the list of balances;

(b) discounts totalling £70 have been recorded in the individual accounts but not in the control account

(c) the sales day book was 'overcast' by £200

(d) a contra entry for £40 has not been entered into the control account; and

(e) an invoice for £180 was recorded correctly in the sales day book but was posted to the debtors' individual account as £810.

Prepare the sales ledger control account reconciliation.

5 Accounting for creditors

5.1 Introduction

As we have previously seen, the total amount payable to creditors is recorded in the general ledger in the purchases ledger control account. The total of credit purchases from the purchases day book, returns to suppliers from the purchases returns day book, and the total payments to creditors, discounts received and any VAT adjustments taken from the cash payments book are all posted to this account.

The purchases ledger control account shows the total amount that is payable to creditors but it does not show the amount owed to individual suppliers. This information is provided by the purchases ledger which contains an account for each individual creditor.

Each individual invoice from the purchases day book and each individual credit note from the purchases returns day book is posted to the relevant creditor's account in the purchases ledger. Similarly each individual payment to creditors and discounts received are posted from the cash payments book to the individual creditors' accounts in the purchases ledger.

5.2 Relationship between the purchases ledger control account and the balances in the purchases ledger

The information that is being posted to the purchases ledger control account in total and to the individual accounts in the purchases ledger as individual entries are from the same sources and should in total be the same figures.

Therefore, just as with the sales ledger control account, if the double entry and entries to the purchases ledger have been correctly carried out then the balance on the purchases ledger control account should be equal to the total of the list of balances on the individual creditors' accounts in the purchases ledger.

5.3 Proforma purchases ledger control account

A purchases ledger control account normally appears like this.

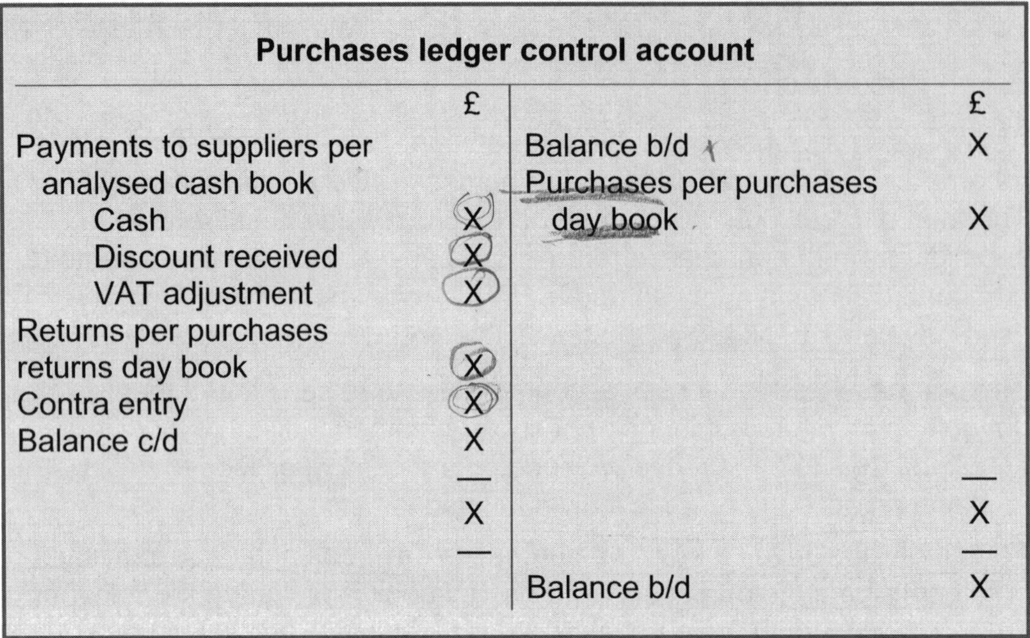

Purchases ledger control account

	£		£
Payments to suppliers per analysed cash book		Balance b/d	X
Cash	X	Purchases per purchases day book	X
Discount received	X		
VAT adjustment	X		
Returns per purchases returns day book	X		
Contra entry	X		
Balance c/d	X		
	X		X
		Balance b/d	X

If all of the accounting entries have been correctly made then the balance on this purchases ledger control account should equal the total of the balances on the individual supplier accounts in the purchases ledger.

6 Purchases ledger control account reconciliation

6.1 Introduction

At each month end the purchases ledger clerk must reconcile the purchases ledger control account and the purchases ledger, just as the sales ledger clerk performed the sales ledger control account reconciliation.

Remember that as well as investigating and discovering the differences, the control account and the individual accounts in the purchases ledger must also be amended for any errors.

6.2 Adjustments to the purchases ledger control account

Any corrections or adjustments made to the purchases ledger control account can be documented as a journal entry.

Example

The total purchases for the month were posted from the purchases day book as £2,547.98 instead of £2,457.98. Prepare a journal to correct this error.

Solution

The journal entry to correct this error will be as follows:

JOURNAL ENTRY		No: 253		
Prepared by:	P Charming			
Authorised by:	U Sister			
Date:	29.8.X5			
Narrative:				
To correct error in posting to creditors' control account				
Account		Code	Debit	Credit
Purchase ledger control		GL56	90	
Purchases		GL34		90
TOTALS			90	90

In this case both PLCA and purchases need to be reduced by £90. Therefore a debit to the purchases ledger control and a credit to purchases are required.

6.3 Adjustments in the purchases ledger

Adjustments in the purchases ledger do not need to be documented in a journal entry. Journal entries are only required for adjustments to the general ledger.

 **Example**

The balance on the purchases ledger control account for a business at 30 June was £12,309. The total of the balances on the individual creditors' accounts in the purchases ledger was £19,200. VAT is at 20%.

The following errors were also found:

- the cash payments book had been undercast by £20
- an invoice from Thomas Ltd, a credit supplier, for £2,400 was correctly entered in the purchases ledger but had been missed out of the addition of the total in the purchases day book
- an invoice from Fred Singleton for £2,000 plus VAT was included in his individual account in the purchases ledger at the net amount
- an invoice from Horace Shades for £6,000 was entered into the individual account in the purchases ledger twice
- the same invoice is for £6,000 plus VAT but the VAT had not been included in the purchases ledger
- returns to Horace Shades of £111 had been omitted from the purchases ledger.

You are required to reconcile the purchases ledger control account with the balances on the purchases ledger accounts at 30 June.

Solution

Step 1 Amend the purchases ledger control account to show the correct balance.

Purchases ledger control account

	£		£
Undercast of CPB	20	Balance b/d	12,309
Balance c/d	14,689	Invoice omitted from PDB	2,400
	14,709		14,709
		Amended balance b/d	14,689

Step 2 Correct the total of the list of purchases ledger balances.

	£
Original total	19,200
Add: Fred Singleton VAT	400
Less: Horace Shades invoice included twice	(6,000)
Add: Horace Shades VAT	1,200
Less: Horace Shades returns	(111)
Amended total of list of balances	14,689

Remember that invoices from suppliers should be included in the individual suppliers' accounts in the purchases ledger at the gross amount, including VAT.

Activity 7

How would each of the following be dealt with in the purchases ledger control account reconciliation?

(a) A purchase invoice for £36 from P Swift was credited to P Short's account in the subsidiary ledger.

(b) A purchase invoice for £96 not entered in the purchases day book.

(c) An undercast of £20 in the total column of the purchases day book.

(d) A purchase invoice from Short & Long for £42 entered as £24 in the purchases day book.

7 Cause of the difference

You may sometimes be asked to say what has caused the difference between the control account and the list of balances. If you are asked to do this, the difference will usually be caused by just one error.

An example will illustrate this.

Example

XYZ Ltd has made the following entries in the sales ledger control account.

	£
Opening balance 1 April 20X7	49,204
Credit sales posted from the sales day book	35,000
Discounts allowed	328
VAT adjustment	65
Bad debt written off	127
Cash received from debtors	52,359

The list of balances from the sales ledger totals £31,579.

(a) Calculate the closing balance on the SLCA at 31 April 20X7.

(b) State one reason for the difference between the SLCA balance and the total of the list of balances.

Solution

(a) The SLCA

Sales ledger control account

	£		£
Balance b/d	49,204	Discount allowed	328
SDB – sales	35,000	VAT adjustment	65
		Bad debt	127
		Cash received	52,359
		Balance c/d	31,325
	84,204		84,204

(b)	Total of sales ledger balances	31,579
	Balance of SLCA at 30 April 20X7	31,325
	Difference	254

Note: You have to look for the fairly obvious clues and also make some assumptions

(i) It's reasonable to assume that the control account is correct – it may not be, so be careful.

(ii) Calculate the difference and determine whether the list total is larger than the SLCA balance or vice versa.

(iii) See if one of the figures given in the question is the same as the difference or double the difference.

If a figure given is the same as the difference then it is likely that a number has been left out of an account.

If a figure given is double the difference then it is likely that a number has been entered on the wrong side of an account, or possibly entered twice.

- In the above question, the difference is £254.
- The total of the list of ledger balances is bigger than the SLCA balance.
- £254 is not a figure given in the question but the amount £127 is given and the difference is twice this figure.

One possible reason for this is that the bad debt write off (£127) was entered on the debit side of a ledger account in the sales ledger – that would have made the total of the list £254 larger. Of course there are a million possible reasons – perhaps there was an invoice for £254 and it was entered twice in a sales ledger account – that would have caused the difference, but the assessor is looking for something obvious in the figures given to you – not some speculative reason.

8 Batch control

8.1 Introduction

Throughout this chapter we have been dealing with control accounts in the general ledger and individual debtors and creditors accounts in the subsidiary ledgers. We have noted that there will sometimes be a discrepancy between the balance on the control account in the general ledger and the total of the balances in the subsidiary ledgers. Sometimes this difference is caused by correctly entered items that can be reconciled. However, sometimes the difference is caused by an error in the entering of the data. These latter errors can be eliminated or minimised by the use of batch control.

8.2 How a lack of batch control causes problems

Consider the situation where a small business has received 40 cheques from debtors and is going to post these into the accounts for the week. A typical system might be as follows.

(a) John writes the cheques into the total and SLCA columns of the analysed cash received book. John then totals the cash received book for the week and posts the total of the SLCA column to the sales ledger control account. He then writes out the bank paying-in slip and pays the cheques into the bank.

(b) George writes up the individual accounts in the sales ledger from the entries in the main cash book.

The above is a fairly typical system and of course all sorts of things can go wrong.

(a) A cheque could go missing and not be paid into the bank, causing a discrepancy between the entries in the cash book and the bank statement.

(b) John could write the values of one or more of the cheques incorrectly in the cash book, causing the cash book total and the sales ledger control account entry to be incorrect.

(c) George could also write the values of the cheques incorrectly in the sales ledger.

8.3 How batch control helps reduce errors

To improve the system the company employs a system of batch control.

(a) Before the cheques are entered in the cash book, a person unconnected with entering the cheques in the books (Jemima) will total the cheques using a computer spreadsheet such as Excel. She will not disclose the total of the cheques.

(b) John will now write the cheques into the cash book and total the cash book as before. He will then compare his total with Jemima's total. If the totals are different, Jemima and John will both check their work until they can agree on a total. This clearly minimises any errors that are likely to be made when entering the cheques in the books of account.

(c) George will write up the sales ledger as before. As a further check, the sales ledger could be passed to another person who would total the entries that George has just made and then compare that total with Jemima's total.

As you can see, by batching the cheques together and producing a total of their value before any entries are made in the books, the company has an excellent check on the accuracy of the entries that are made.

Of course nothing is foolproof. The accountants could enter incorrect amounts in the ledger which compensate for each other thereby still giving the correct total. Alternatively, a cheque might be lost thereby giving an incorrect banking total. But at least the possibility of human error is reduced.

9 The VAT control account

Within Level II we learned about the operation of VAT to enable us to calculate the amount we would charge on our sales, and the amounts we would reclaim on our purchases. We now need to consider how these transactions would look within the third control account within the general ledger, the VAT control account, and to appreciate that it is the difference between these two amounts that must be paid to or received from HMRC.

Example

The following VAT figures have been extracted from your day books. Complete the VAT control account, and find the balance.

Sales day book	22,436
Sales returns day book	674
Purchases day book	15,327

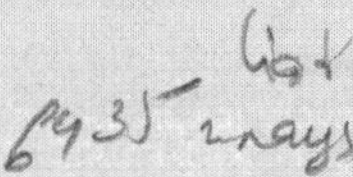

Solution

VAT account

Details	**Amount £**	**Details**	**Amount £**
Sales returns (SRDB)	674	Sales (SDB)	22,436
Purchases (PDB)	15,327		
Balance c/d	6,435		
	22,436		**22,436**

The VAT from the sales daybook is payable to HMRC, whereas the VAT from the sales returns and the purchases daybooks can be reclaimed. It is the net effect that is payable to HMRC.

Businesses are required to complete a VAT return, usually on a quarterly basis, to show the amount payable to or reclaimed from HMRC. We look at the completion of a VAT return later in this study text.

Activity 8

The following VAT figures have been extracted from the books of prime entry.

Sales day book	60,200
Sales returns day book	980
Purchases day book	34,300
Purchases returns day book	2,660
Cash receipts book	112

(a) What will be the entries in the VAT control account to record the VAT transactions in the quarter

(b) The VAT return has been completed and shows an amount owing from HMRC of £27,692. Is the VAT return correct?

VAT account

Details	**Amount £**	**Details**	**Amount £**
SRDB	980	SDB	60200
PDB	34300	PRDB	2660
		CRB	112
	35280		62972
Balance c/d	27692		
		Balance b/d	27692

10 Summary

We started this chapter with a revision of balancing accounts and extended this to entering opening balances in the ledger accounts. Then the chapter moved on to aspects of control and the use of control accounts and control account reconciliations in order to determine the accuracy of the figures in the ledger accounts. The reconciliations, sales ledger and purchases ledger are important and you should ensure that you are happy with the subject matter in this chapter.

Answers to chapter activities

Activity 1

Sales ledger control account

	£		£
SDB – invoices	5,426.23	CRB	3,226.56
		CRB - Discounts allowed	315.57
		CRB – VAT adjustment	63.11
		Balance c/d	1,820.99
	5,426.23		5,426.23
Balance b/d	1,820.00		

VAT account

	£		£
PDB	846.72	SDB	1,036.54
CRB – VAT adjustment	63.11		
Balance c/d	126.71		
	1,036.54		1,036.54
		Balance b/d	126.71

Sales account

	£		£
		SDB	2,667.45
Balance c/d	4,521.37	SDB	1,853.92
	4,521.37		4,521.37
		Balance b/d	4,521.37

Activity 2

(a) Credit balance

(b) Debit balance

(c) Credit balance

(d) Debit balance

Activity 3

Account name	Amount £	Debit / Credit
Bank overdraft	6,975	Credit
Cash	275	Debit
VAT payable	2,390	Credit
Motor vehicles	10,500	Debit
Plant and machinery	25,700	Debit
Loan from bank	12,000	Credit
Motor expenses	1,540	Debit
Rent and rates	2,645	Debit
Miscellaneous expenses	725	Debit

Activity 4

Purchases ledger

Bailey Limited

		£			£
01 Dec	Bank	799	01 Dec	Balance b/d	11,750
01 Dec	Discount received	20	01 Dec	Purchases	240
01 Dec	Balance c/d	11,171			
		11,990			11,990
			02 Dec	Balance b/d	11,171

Byng & Company

		£			£
			01 Dec	Balance b/d	1,269
01 Dec	Balance c/d	2,229	01 Dec	Purchases	960
		2,229			2,229
			02 Dec	Balance b/d	2,229

Office Supplies Limited

		£			£
01 Dec	Purchases returns	48	01 Dec	Balance b/d	4,230
01 Dec	Balance c/d	4,518	01 Dec	Purchases	336
		4,566			4,566
			02 Dec	Balance b/d	4,518

O'Connell Frames

		£			£
01 Dec	Purchases returns	2,160	01 Dec	Balance b/d	423
01 Dec	Balance c/d	3,303	01 Dec	Purchases	5,040
		5,463			5,463
			02 Dec	Balance b/d	3,303

General ledger

PLCA

		£			£
01 Dec	Purchases returns	2,208	01 Dec	Balance b/d	82,006
01 Dec	Bank	799	01 Dec	Purchases	6,576
01 Dec	Discounts received	20			
01 Dec	Balance c/d	85,555			
		88,582			88,582
			02 Dec	Balance b/d	85,555

SLCA

		£			£
01 Dec	Balance b/d	180,312	01 Dec	Bank	5,875
01 Dec	Sales	13,440	01 Dec	Balance c/d	187,877
		193,752			193,752
02 Dec	Balance b/d	187,877			

Purchases

		£			£
01 Dec	Balance b/d	90,563			
01 Dec	PLCA	5,200	01 Dec	Balance c/d	95,763
		95,763			95,763
02 Dec	Balance b/d	95,763			

Sales

		£			£
			01 Dec	Balance b/d	301,492
			01 Dec	SLCA	11,200
01 Dec	Balance c/d	313,132	01 Dec	Bank	440
		313,132			313,132
			02 Dec	Balance b/d	313,132

Purchases returns

		£			£
			01 Dec	Balance b/d	306
01 Dec	Balance c/d	2,106	01 Dec	PLCA	1,800
		2,106			2,106
			02 Dec	Balance b/d	2,106

Stationery

		£			£
01 Dec	Balance b/d	642	01 Dec	PLCA	40
01 Dec	PLCA	280	01 Dec	Balance c/d	882
		922			922
02 Dec	Balance b/d	882			

Discounts received

		£			£
			01 Dec	Balance b/d	50
01 Dec	Balance c/d	70	01 Dec	Creditors	20
		70			70
			02 Dec	Balance b/d	70

VAT

		£			£
01 Dec	PLCA	1,096	01 Dec	Balance b/d	17,800
			01 Dec	PLCA	368
			01 Dec	SLCA	2,240
01 Dec	Balance c/d	19,400	01 Dec	Bank	88
		20,496			20,496
			02 Dec	Balance b/d	19,400

Cash receipts book

Date	*Narrative*	*Total* £	*VAT* £	*SLCA* £	*Cash sales* £	*Discount* £
20X1						
01 Dec	Lili Chang	528	88		440	
01 Dec	Bentley Brothers	5,875		5,875		
		6,403	88	5,875	440	–

Cash payments book

Date	*Details*	*Cheque no*	*Code*	*Total* £	*VAT* £	*PLCA* £	*Cash purchases* £	*Other* £	*Discount received* £
20X1									
01 Dec	Bailey Ltd			799	–	799	–	–	20

	£
Opening balance	3,006
Add: Receipts	6,403
Less:	(799)
Closing balance	8,610

Activity 5

(a) Yes, because the correct detailed individual entries in the sales day book are posted to the sales ledger accounts and the incorrect total used in the control account.

(b) No, because the arithmetical balance is correct even though the wrong account is used. No imbalance would occur.

(c) No, because the total posted to the SLCA will include the £67 and the entry in the sales ledger will also be for £67. They are both wrong.

Activity 6

- We must first look for those errors which will mean that the sales ledger control account is incorrectly stated. The control account is then adjusted as follows:

Sales ledger control account

	£		£
Balance b/d	15,450	Discounts allowed	70
		Overcast of sales day book	200
		Contra with PLCA	40
		Adjusted balance c/d	15,140
	15,450		15,450
Balance b/d	15,140		

- We must then look for errors in the total of the individual balances per the sales ledger. The extracted list of balances must be adjusted as follows:

	£
Original total of list of balances	15,705
Debit balance omitted	65
Transposition error (810 – 180)	(630)
	15,140

- As can be seen, the adjusted total of the list of balances now agrees with the balance per the control account.

Activity 7

(a) This does not affect the reconciliation. A correction would simply be made in the subsidiary ledger.

(b) This must be adjusted for in the purchase ledger control account and in the purchases ledger.

(c) This is just an adjustment to the purchase ledger control account.

(d) This will require alteration in both the control account and the purchases ledger.

Activity 8

(a) **VAT account**

Details	**Amount £**	**Details**	**Amount £**
Sales Returns (SRDB)	980	Sales (SDB)	60,200
Purchases (PDB)	34,300	Purchases returns (PRDB)	2,660
Balance c/d	27,692	Cash sales (CRB)	112
	62,972		**62,972**

(b) **No.** The amount of £27,692 is payable to HMRC.

11 Test your knowledge

Workbook Activity 9

Indicate whether the opening balances listed below would be recorded in the general ledger as a debit or a credit balance.

Account name	Amount £	Dr ✓	Cr ✓
Cash	2,350		
Capital	20,360		
Motor Vehicles	6,500		
Electricity	800		
Office expenses	560		
Loan from bank	15,000		
Cash at bank	6,400		
Factory equipment	14,230		
Rent	2,500		
Insurance	1,000		
Miscellaneous expenses	1,020		

Workbook Activity 10

The following totals are taken from the books of a business:

	£
Credit balance on purchases ledger control account	5,926
Debit balance on sales ledger control account	10,268
Credit sales	71,504
Credit purchases	47,713
Cash received from credit customers	69,872
Cash paid to creditors	47,028
Sales ledger balances written off as bad debts	96
Sales returns	358
Purchases returns	202
Discounts allowed	1,435
Discounts received	867
Contra entry	75

Required:

(a) Prepare the purchases ledger control account and balance at the end of the month.

(b) Prepare the sales ledger control account and balance at the end of the month.

Workbook Activity 11

The balance on the sales ledger control account of Robin & Co on 30 September 20X0 amounted to £3,825 which did not agree with the net total of the list of sales ledger balances at that date of £3,362.

The errors discovered were as follows:

1 Debit balances in the sales ledger, amounting to £103, had been omitted from the list of balances.

2 A bad debt amounting to £400 had been written off in the sales ledger but had not been posted to the bad debts expense account or entered in the control accounts.

3 An item of goods sold to Sparrow, £250, had been entered once in the sales day book but posted to his account twice.

4 No entry had been made in the control account in respect of the transfer of a debit of £70 from Quail's account in the sales ledger to his account in the purchases ledger (a contra entry).

5 The discount allowed column in the cash account had been undercast by £140.

Required:

(a) Make the necessary adjustments in the sales ledger control account and bring down the balance.

(b) Show the adjustments to the net total of the original list of balances to reconcile with the amended balance on the sales ledger control account.

Workbook Activity 12

When carrying out the purchases ledger control account reconciliation the following errors were discovered:

(a) the purchases day book was overcast by £1,000 when it was posted to the purchase ledger control account;

(b) the total of the discount received column in the cash payments book was posted to the general ledger as £89 instead of £98;

(c) a contra entry of £300 had been entered in the subsidiary ledger but not in the general ledger.

Required:

Produce journal entries to correct each of these errors.

Workbook Activity 13

(a) Show whether each entry will be a debit or credit in the Sales ledger control account in the general ledger.

Details	Amount £	Dr ✓	Cr ✓
Balance of debtors at 1 July	60,580		
Goods sold on credit	18,950		
Payments received from credit customers	20,630		
Discounts allowed	850		
Bad debt written off	2,400		
Goods returned from credit customers	3,640		

(b) The following debit balances were in the sales ledger on 1 August:

	Amount £
Rock 'n Roll Ltd	10,700
Cavern Ltd	18,420
Tunnel Plc	2,400
Studio 51 Ltd	7,680
Hacienda Ltd	9,955
Warehouse Company	5,255

Required:

Calculate the balance brought down on the sales ledger control account on 1 August using the information from part (a). Then reconcile the balances shown above with the sales ledger control account balance.

	Amount £
Sales ledger control account balance as at 31 July	
Total of sales ledger accounts as at 31 July	
Difference	

(c) What may have caused the difference calculated above?

	✓
Goods returned may have been omitted from the sales ledger	
Bad debt written off may have been omitted from the sales ledger	
Goods returned may have been entered twice in the sales ledger	
Bad debt written off may have been entered twice in the sales ledger	

Workbook Activity 14

(a) Show whether each entry will be a debit or credit in the Purchases ledger control account in the general ledger.

Details	Amount £	Dr ✓	Cr ✓
Balance of creditors at 1 July	58,420		
Goods bought on credit	17,650		
Payments made to credit suppliers	19,520		
Discounts received	852		
Contra entry with sales ledger control	600		
Goods returned to credit suppliers	570		

(b) The following credit balances were in the purchases ledger on 1 August:

	Amount £
Price & Co	9,570
Andre Ltd	12,478
Hayes Plc	6,895
Lucas Ltd	7,950
Millers & Co	8,546
Griffiths Ltd	7,560

Required:

Calculate the balance brought down on the purchases ledger control account on 1 August using the information from part (a). Then reconcile the balances shown above with the purchases ledger control account balance.

	Amount £
Purchases ledger control account balance as at 31 July	54528
Total of purchase ledger accounts as at 31 July	52999
Difference	1529

(c) What may have caused the difference calculated above?

	✓
Payments made to suppliers may have been understated in the purchase ledger	
Goods returned to suppliers may have been overstated in the purchase ledger	
Goods bought on credit may have been overstated in the purchase ledger	
Contra entry may have been omitted from the purchase ledger	

Accounting for VAT

5

Introduction

ICB Level III requires an understanding of the accounting for VAT and the completion of a VAT return. We will consider the need to register for VAT, the requirements of a VAT invoice, common terms used, the use of a VAT control account, bad debt relief and the preparation of a VAT return. We will also look at the different types of VAT schemes a business can sign up to.

In this chapter we also learn how to complete a VAT return correctly. Businesses must complete a VAT return (a VAT 100 form) at the end of each quarter. The purpose of a VAT return is to summarise the transactions of a business for a period.

CONTENTS

1 Accounting for VAT

1.1 Introduction

This chapter will begin with just a brief reminder of how the VAT system operates.

1.2 What is VAT?

VAT is:

- an indirect tax
- charged on most goods and services supplied within the UK
- is borne by the final consumer, and
- collected by businesses on behalf of HM Revenue and Customs.

VAT is an indirect tax because it is paid indirectly when you buy most goods and services, rather than being collected directly from the taxpayer as a proportion of their income or gains.

VAT is charged by **taxable persons** when they make **taxable supplies** in the course of their business. VAT is not generally charged on non business transactions.

1.3 Taxable persons

Definition

Taxable persons are businesses which are (or should be) registered for VAT.

1.4 Registration and non-registration for VAT

When a business reaches a set annual turnover level (in 2014/15 this is £81,000) then it must register for VAT. If turnover is below this limit, the business can, if it wishes, register voluntarily. If a business is registered it must:

- charge VAT on its sales or services to its customers
- recover the VAT charged on its purchases and expenses rather than having to bear these costs as part of the business.

- In such cases, as the VAT charged and incurred is neither revenue nor expense, the revenues and costs of the business are entered in books at their value net of VAT, and the VAT is entered in the VAT account.

If the business is not registered for VAT then the cost of purchases and expenses must include the VAT as these amounts are said to be irrecoverable. Thus, the costs of the business are entered in the books at their gross, VAT inclusive, value and there is no VAT account.

1.5 Taxable supplies

Taxable supplies or outputs, are most sales made by a taxable person. Taxable supplies can also include gifts and goods taken from the business for personal use.

1.6 Output VAT

Definition

The VAT charged on sales or taxable supplies is called **output VAT.**

1.7 Input VAT

When a business buys goods or pays expenses (inputs), then it will also be paying VAT on those purchases or expenses.

Definition

VAT paid by a business on purchases or expenses is called **input VAT.**

Businesses are allowed to reclaim their input tax. They do this by deducting the input tax they have paid from the output tax which they owe, and paying over the net amount only. If the input tax exceeds the output tax, then the balance is recoverable from HMRC.

1.8 Rates of VAT

VAT is currently charged at the standard rate of 20%, the reduced rate of 5%, and the zero rate of 0%. The zero rate of VAT applies to items such as food, drink, books, newspapers, children's clothes and most transport.

1.9 Standard rated activities

Any taxable supply which is not charged at the zero or reduced rates is charged at the standard rate.

This is calculated by taking the VAT exclusive amount and multiplying by 20%.

If you are given the VAT inclusive figure then to calculate the VAT element, multiply this figure by the "VAT fraction", which is 1/6 or 20/120 for a rate of 20%. The following VAT structure can also be used to calculate VAT, VAT inclusive or VAT exclusive figures.

	£	%
VAT inclusive	120	120
VAT	20	20
VAT Exclusive	100	100

Example

Suppose that a business makes sales on credit of £1,000 and purchases on credit of £400 (both amounts exclusive of any VAT). How would these be accounted for in the ledger accounts. Assume a VAT rate of 20%.

Solution

The sales and purchases must be shown net and the VAT entered in the VAT account. As the sales and purchases were on credit the full double entry would be as follows:

DR	Debtors account	£1,200
CR	Sales account	£1,000
CR	VAT control account	£200

DR	Purchases account	£400
DR	VAT control account	£80
CR	Creditors account	£480

Sales account

	£		£
		Debtors	1,000

Debtors account

	£		£
Sales and VAT	1,200		

Purchases account

	£		£
Creditors	400		

Creditors account

	£		£
		Purchases	480

VAT control account

	£		£
Creditors	80	Debtors	200
Balance c/d	120		
	———		———
	200		200
	———		———
		Balance b/d	120

The amount due to HM Revenue and Customs is the balance on the VAT account, £120.

If a business is not registered for VAT then it will not charge VAT on its sales, and its expenses must be recorded at the gross amount (inclusive of VAT).

If a business is registered for VAT then it will charge VAT on its sales, although they will be recorded as sales at their net amount, and its expenses will also be recorded at the net amount.

The output and input VAT is recorded in the VAT account and the difference paid over to HM Revenue and Customs.

1.10 Zero-rated activities

If a business is registered for VAT and sells zero-rated products or services then it charges no VAT on the sales but can still reclaim the input VAT on its purchases and expenses. Such a business will normally be owed VAT by HM Revenue and Customs each quarter.

Example

Suppose that a business makes sales on credit of £1,000 plus VAT and purchases on credit of £400 plus VAT. How would these be accounted for if the rate of VAT on the sales was zero, whereas the purchases were standard rated? Standard rate is at 20%.

Solution

DR	Debtors (£1,000 at 0%)	£1,000
CR	Sales (£1,000 at 0%)	£1,000
DR	Purchases	£400
DR	VAT (£400 at 20%)	£80
CR	Creditors	£480

This would leave a debit balance on the VAT account which is the amount that can be claimed back from HM Revenue and Customs by the business.

1.11 Exempt activities

Certain supplies are exempt from VAT such as financial and postal services. If a business sells such services then not only is no VAT charged on the sales of the business but also no input VAT can be reclaimed on purchases and expenses.

Example

Suppose that a business makes sales on credit of £1,000 plus VAT and purchases on credit of £400 plus VAT. How would these be accounted for if the sales are exempt activities, whereas the purchases were standard-rated? (VAT rate is 20%)

Solution

DR	Debtors	£1,000
CR	Sales	£1,000
DR	Purchases	£480
CR	Creditors	£480

There is no VAT on sales due to HM Revenue and Customs and the business cannot claim the £80 from HM Revenue and Customs. However, the seller of the purchases should pay the £80 of VAT over to HM Revenue and Customs.

Activity 1

A business that is registered for VAT makes credit sales of £110,000 in the period and credit purchases of £75,000. Each of these figures is net of VAT at the standard rate of 20%.

Show how these transactions should be entered into the ledger accounts and state how much VAT is due to HM Revenue and Customs.

1.12 Differences between zero rated and exempt supplies

You must be careful to distinguish between traders making zero rated and exempt supplies.

	Exempt	**Zero rated**
Can register for VAT?	No	Yes
Charge output VAT to customers?	No	Yes at 0%
Can recover input tax?	No	Yes

Activity 2

Robbie's business bank account shows administrative expenses of £27,216 which is inclusive of VAT at the standard rate 20%.

1 Calculate the administrative expenses to be included in the trial balance.

2 Calculate the VAT figure on administrative expenses for inclusion in the VAT control account.

3 Update the VAT control account below and find the closing balance figure for VAT.

VAT control account

	£		£
VAT on purchases	35,000	Balance b/d	5,000
Paid to HMRC	5,000	VAT on sales	26,250

1.13 Partial exemption

A taxable person who makes both taxable supplies and exempt supplies is referred to as a **partially exempt** trader. For this purpose it does not matter if the taxable supplies are standard or zero rated.

The problem with partial exemption is that taxable supplies entitle the supplier to a credit for input tax in respect of related costs, whereas exempt supplies do not.

It is therefore necessary to apportion input tax between taxable and exempt supplies using a method set out by HMRC.

The most common method used is to divide input tax into three parts:

- Relating wholly to taxable supplies – all recoverable
- Relating wholly to exempt supplies – irrecoverable (but see below)
- Relating to overheads – proportion which relate to taxable supplies can be recovered, leaving the rest irrecoverable (but see below).

If the total irrecoverable input tax is no more than a certain amount, the **de minimus limit**, then it **can** be recovered.

Note that for assessment purposes, you need an awareness of the basics of this topic but calculations of the amount of exempt input tax will not be required.

1.14 Tax point (time of supply)

Definition

The **tax point** is the date on which the liability for output tax arises – it is the date on which a supply is recorded as taking place for the purposes of the tax return. It is also referred to as the time of supply.

Most taxable persons make a VAT return each quarter. The return must include all supplies whose tax points fall within that quarter.

1.15 The basic tax point

The **basic tax point** for goods is the date when goods are 'removed' which usually means the date of delivery of those goods or the date the customer takes the goods away.

A tax point also occurs if goods are not 'removed' but are made available to a customer – for example if a specialist installer is constructing a new machine for a customer on site in their factory, the tax point will occur when the machine is handed over and not when all the materials are delivered to the site.

For services, the tax point is the date the services are performed or completed.

Example

Queue Ltd received an order for goods from a customer on 14 March. The goods were despatched on 18 March and the customer paid on 15 April when they received their invoice dated 13 April.

State the basic tax point date.

Solution

The tax point is 18 March, i.e. the date of despatch.

1.16 Actual tax point

The basic tax point is amended in two situations.

Earlier tax point	Later tax point
• A tax invoice is issued or a payment is received before the basic tax point • In these circumstances the date of invoice or payment is the time when the supply is treated as taking place	• A tax invoice is issued within 14 days after the basic tax point (14 day rule) • In these circumstances the date of issue of the invoice is the time when the supply is treated as taking place

Provided that written approval is received from the local VAT office, the 14 day rule can be varied.

For example, it can be extended to accommodate a supplier who issues all of his invoices each month on the last day of the month and would like the month end invoice date to be the tax point date.

Note that the 14 day rule cannot apply to invoices which are only for zero rated goods as these are not tax invoices.

Most exports are zero rated so the tax point for these goods is always the earlier of the supply of goods and the receipt of payment.

1.17 Deposits received in advance

If a business receives a deposit or part payment in advance then this creates a tax point when the deposit is received. However, this is only for the deposit, not the whole supply. The business must account for the VAT included in the deposit.

No tax point is created for a returnable deposit, e.g. a deposit required to ensure the safe return of a hired item, where the deposit will be returned to the customer when they bring the item back safely.

Example

Ahmed receives a £60 deposit from a customer on 1 July. The total cost of the item is £210 including VAT at 20% and the customer pays the balance of £150 on 12 September when they collect the goods.

On 15 September Ahmed issues an invoice to his customer which he marks as paid in full.

How is VAT accounted for on this transaction?

Solution

The deposit of £60 creates a tax point on 1 July.

The amount of VAT is £10 (£60 × 20/120) and this must be entered in the VAT return which includes 1 July.

When the goods are collected and paid for on 12 September this creates a further tax point. The VAT is £25 (£150 × 20/120) and this must be included in the VAT return which includes 12 September.

2 Form and content of a VAT invoice

2.1 Introduction

All businesses that are registered for VAT must provide evidence to VAT registered customers of the VAT they have been charged.

In order to do this the supplier must give or send to the purchaser a VAT invoice **within 30 days** of the earlier of:

- supply of the goods or services or
- receipt of the payment.

VAT invoices are not required:

- if the purchaser is not VAT registered or
- if the supply is wholly zero rated.

In practice it is impossible to tell if a purchaser is VAT registered or not, so traders normally issue a VAT invoice anyway. If they are retailers selling to the public they have special rules (see below).

Similarly, traders will normally issue invoices for zero rated sales which show the same details as for other supplies, but technically this is not a VAT invoice.

The original VAT invoice is sent to the customer and forms their evidence for reclaiming input VAT. A copy must be kept by the supplier to support the calculation of output VAT.

2.2 Form of a VAT invoice

There is **no standard format for invoices**. The exact design is the choice of the business, but it must show the following details (unless the invoice is a **less detailed tax invoice** that you will see later):

- identifying number which must follow a sequence (if an invoice is spoilt or cancelled it must be kept as a VAT officer may wish to inspect it)
- date of supply (tax point) and the date of issue of the invoice
- supplier's name and address and registration number
- name and address of customer, i.e. the person to whom the goods or services are supplied
- type of supply
  - sale
  - hire purchase, credit sale, conditional sale or similar transaction
  - loan
  - exchange
  - hire, lease or rental
  - process (making goods using the customer's own materials)
  - sale on commission (e.g. an estate agent)
  - supply on sale or return
- description of the goods or services
- quantity of goods or extent of services
- rate of tax and amount payable (in sterling) excluding VAT for each separate description
- total amount payable (excluding VAT) in sterling

- rate of any cash discount offered (these are also called settlement discounts)
- separate rate and amount of VAT charged for each rate of VAT
- total amount of VAT chargeable.

2.3 VAT and discounts

The treatment of discounts and VAT was included in Level II. By way of revision, the basic principles are:

- if a **trade discount** is given then this is deducted before VAT is calculated
- if a **settlement discount** is offered, the supplier will not know whether the settlement discount will be taken up by the customer until they have either been paid in accordance with the terms of the settlement discount offer, or the time limit for the settlement discount has elapsed.

A two stage process for dealing with VAT is therefore required as follows where a settlement discount is offered:

- When issuing a sales invoice on which a settlement discount is offered, suppliers will enter the invoice into their accounts and record the VAT on the full invoice price in the normal way (i.e. ignoring the settlement discount).
- When the supplier receives payment within the settlement period, they can choose between two methods of adjusting their accounts to reflect a settlement discount which is taken up by a customer.
  (i) The supplier will issue a credit note as evidence of the reduction in the sales value.

     A copy of this credit note must be kept as evidence.

     This method will however be time-consuming for the business.

  (ii) Alternatively, the supplier can include the following information on the sales invoice (in addition to the usual invoicing requirements) and it will not then need to issue a credit note:

     – The terms of the settlement discount (this must include the time by which the discounted price must be paid).

     – A statement that the customer can only recover as input VAT, the VAT paid to the supplier (see below).

It is also helpful if the invoice shows:

- the discounted price
- the VAT on the discounted price, and
- the total amount due if the settlement discount is taken up.

The supplier must retain the VAT invoice together with proof of receipt of the discounted amount as evidence of the reduction both in the value of the sale and the output VAT.

HMRC recommends that businesses use the following wording on the sales invoice:

> "A discount of X% of the full price applies if payment is made within Y days of the invoice date.
>
> No credit note will be issued.
>
> Following payment you must ensure you have only recovered the VAT actually paid."

Example

Joachim is in business manufacturing angle brackets which he sells to retailers. He offers a 5% discount if goods are paid for within 10 days. He sells angle brackets with a pre-discount price of £1,000 to Kim Ltd.

How much VAT at 20% should he charge on the invoice ?

Solution

VAT should be calculated on the full invoice ignoring the settlement discount a customer could pay. It does not matter whether the customer takes the discount or not. The VAT will be £200 (£1,000 x 20%).

The invoice will also show the VAT on the discounted price. This will be £190 (£1,000 × 95% × 20%).

Activity 3

An invoice is issued for standard rated goods with a list price of £380.00 (excluding VAT).

A 10% trade discount is given and a 4% settlement or cash discount is offered.

How much VAT at the standard rate of 20% should be included on the invoice?

A £76.00

B £65.66

C £68.40

D £72.96

Sometimes a business will offer to pay a customer's VAT. This is really just another form of discount.

Example

XY Ltd sells beds with a normal retail price of £240 (including VAT at 20% of £40). They run a promotional offer to pay the customers' VAT for them and hence the customer pays £200.

XY Ltd must treat the £200 paid as a VAT inclusive price and account for VAT of £33.33 (£200 × 20/120).

2.4 Example of a VAT invoice

Example

MICRO TRAINING GROUP LTD
Unit 34, Castlewell Trading Estate
Manchester, M12 5RHF

To:

Slough Labels Ltd	Sales invoice number:	35
Station Unit	VAT registration number:	234 5566 87
Slough	Date of issue:	30 September 20X0
SL1 3EJ	Tax point:	12 September 20X0

Quantity	Description and price	Amount excl VAT £ p	VAT rate	VAT £ p
6	Programmable calculators FR34 at £24.76	148.56	20%	
12	Programmable calculators GT60 at £36.80	441.60	20%	
		590.16		118.03
	Delivery	23.45	20%	4.69
		613.61		122.72
VAT		122.72		
TOTAL		736.33		

A discount of 2% of the full price (excluding delivery charge) applies if payment is made within 10 days. No credit note will be issued. Following payment you must ensure you have only recovered the VAT actually paid

If you pay within 14 days, the discounted price is:

Net	601.80
VAT	120.36
TOTAL	722.16

Note that on this invoice, the VAT payable if the settlement discount is taken is calculated after applying the discount of 2% to the **goods** element of the invoice as the discount is not given on the delivery charge.

2.5 Rounding VAT

Usually, the amount of VAT calculated will not be a whole number of pounds and pence. You will therefore need a rounding adjustment.

The rules governing this adjustment are quite tricky, and permit more than one method.

However, for assessment purposes you only need to know the basic rounding rule – that is that the total amount of VAT payable on an invoice can be rounded down to the nearest penny.

Activity 4

Calculate the total VAT to be charged in respect of each of the three VAT invoices below.

Invoice	Description and price	Net of VAT £ p	VAT rate	VAT £ p
1	16 × 6 metre hosepipes @ £3.23 each	51.68	20%	
2	24 × bags of compost @ £5.78 each	138.72	20%	
3	Supply of kitchen units	1,084.57	20%	

2.6 Less detailed (simplified) VAT invoices

Retailers (selling to the public), do not have to issue a detailed VAT invoice every time they make a sale as this would make trading in a busy shop very difficult.

If the total amount of the supply **(including VAT)** by the retailer does not exceed £250, then **when a customer requests a tax invoice** a retailer may issue a **less detailed tax invoice**. However, if requested by a customer a full VAT invoice must be issued.

The details required on the less detailed invoice are:

- supplier's name and address
- supplier's VAT registration number
- date of supply

- description sufficient to identify the goods or services
- amount payable (including VAT) for each rate (standard and zero)
- the VAT rate applicable.

The main differences between the less detailed invoice and the full invoice are that the customer's name and address can be omitted and the total on the invoice includes the VAT without the VAT itself being shown separately.

Although this invoice shows less detail, it is still a valid tax invoice. This means that if the purchaser is a VAT registered business they can use the invoice to support a claim for input VAT.

 **Example**

Delta Office Supplies
46, Central Mall, Glastonbury, Somerset
G34 7QT
Telephone: 01392 43215
15 April 20X0

1 box of 50 blank DVD-R
Total including VAT @ 20% £25.85

VAT registration number: 653 7612 44

If the business accepts credit cards they can use the sales voucher given to the cardholder as a less detailed invoice.

However, it must still contain the details above.

Exempt supplies must not be included in a less detailed invoice.

Retailers **do not have to keep** copies of the less detailed VAT invoices that they issue, whereas non retailers must keep copies of all sales invoices issued.

This is because retailers generally calculate their VAT from their **daily gross takings** rather than from individual invoices.

2.7 Modified invoices

If a trader sells goods or a service for more than £250 including VAT, and the customer agrees, they may issue a modified VAT invoice.

This shows the VAT inclusive amount for each item sold and then at the bottom of the invoice the following amounts must be shown:

- the overall VAT inclusive total
- the total amount of VAT included in the total
- the total value of the supplies net of VAT
- the total value of any zero-rated and exempt supplies.

This only saves the trader from including the individual cost net of VAT and the VAT rate for each item. All other details must be the same as for a full VAT invoice.

3 VAT accounting schemes

3.1 Return periods

All registered traders have to complete a VAT return every return period. Information to complete the return is taken from sales and purchase information – usually from daybook totals. Any amounts of VAT due must be paid over to HMRC or a claim made for VAT to be reimbursed.

Return periods are normally 3 months.

3.2 Submission of returns

Returns must normally be submitted to **arrive with HMRC** one month after the end of the return period.

Traders who submit their returns online, rather than using a paper return, usually get an extra 7 days to submit.

All traders (with a few exceptions) must submit their returns online, and pay their VAT electronically.

3.3 Payment of VAT

The due date for payment of VAT depends on whether the trader is paying by sending a cheque through the post or paying electronically.

Postal payments can only be made with paper VAT returns and payment is due at the same time as the return, i.e. payments must have cleared HMRC bank account by **one month after the end of the return period.** Paper VAT returns are now very rare.

Electronic payments **must** be made if returns are submitted online and **may** be made when paper returns are submitted. The payment date is normally 7 days later than for a postal payment.

This extra 7 days does not apply:

- if the trader uses the annual accounting scheme
- if the trader has to make monthly payments (compulsory for large businesses).

Example

Jonas has a quarterly return period to 30 April.

If Jonas submits a paper VAT return it must be with HMRC by 31 May. If he submits electronically he will have until 7 June to submit.

If Jonas submits a paper return he can send a cheque with his return to clear HMRC's bank account by 31 May. Otherwise he must pay electronically by 7 June.

If you pay by direct debit the payment is taken from your account three working days after the 7 day period allowed for electronic payments.

Other electronic payment methods include:

- By debit or credit card over the internet
- Telephone banking payments
- BACS direct credit
- Bank Giro.

3.4 Refunds of VAT

If the business has more input tax than output tax in a particular VAT period then it will be due a refund.

Before making a repayment HMRC makes additional checks on the return to ensure the claim is valid.

Repayments are made directly into the trader's bank account. In most cases this will be within 10 working days of receiving the return.

Traders who regularly receive repayments can choose to submit monthly returns.

3.5 Other schemes

There are a number of special schemes for accounting for VAT. These are designed to help small businesses by reducing administration and may improve cash flow. The schemes which you must know about are:

- annual accounting
- cash accounting
- the flat rate scheme
- retail schemes.

Note that in your ICB assessment, questions will not be set testing data entry or completion of VAT returns for such schemes.

4 Annual accounting

4.1 Purpose of the scheme

Smaller businesses may find it costly or inconvenient to prepare the normal four quarterly VAT returns.

An 'annual' accounting scheme is available whereby a single VAT return is filed for a 12-month period (normally the accounting period of the business). This helps relieve the burden of administration.

4.2 How the scheme works

Only one VAT return is submitted each year, but VAT payments must still be made regularly. The scheme works as follows:

- The annual return must be filed within 2 months of the end of the annual return period.
- Normally, nine payments on account of the VAT liability for the year are made at the end of months 4 to 12 of the year. Each payment represents 10% of the VAT liability for the previous year.
- A new business will base its payments on an estimate of the VAT liability for the year.
- Businesses may apply to HMRC to agree quarterly payments on account instead of the normal nine monthly payments. In this case, the payments will be 25% of the VAT liability for the previous year and will be made by the ends of months 4, 7 and 10.
- A balancing payment or repayment is made when the return is filed.
- All payments must be made electronically with no 7 days extension.
- Additional payments can be made by the business when desired.

4.3 Conditions for the annual accounting scheme

The scheme is aimed at smaller businesses.

- Businesses can join the scheme provided their taxable turnover (excluding VAT and the sale of capital assets) expected in the next 12 months is no more than £1,350,000.
- The business must be up-to-date with its VAT returns. However a business does not need a history of VAT returns to join. It can join the scheme from the day it registers.
- Businesses must leave the scheme if their estimated taxable turnover (excluding VAT) for the next 12 months is more than £1,600,000.

4.4 Who might use the scheme?

The scheme is useful to businesses that want to:

- reduce administration because only one VAT return is needed instead of four and businesses get 2 months to prepare the return instead of the usual one.
- fix their VAT payments in advance, at least for their nine monthly or three quarterly payments. This is useful for budgeting cash flow.

It is not useful if:

- the business receives repayments as only one repayment per year will be received.
- the business turnover decreases, as then the interim payments might be higher than under the standard scheme and the business will have to wait until they submit the VAT return to get any repayment due.

Activity 5

Jump Ltd applies to use the annual accounting scheme from 1 January 20X1. The company's net VAT liability for the year ended 31 December 20X0 was £3,600.00.

The actual net VAT liability for the year ended 31 December 20X1 is £3,820.00.

1 When must Jump Ltd's VAT return be filed?

A 31 January 20X2

B 28 February 20X2

C 31 March 20X2

2 Which ONE of the following statements about Jump Ltd's payment of VAT during the year ended 31 December 20X1 is true?

Assume Jump Ltd has not chosen quarterly payments.

A Jump Ltd must make nine monthly payments of £360.00

B Jump Ltd must make nine monthly payments of £382.00

C Jump Ltd must make twelve monthly payments of £300.00

D Jump Ltd must make twelve monthly payments of £318.33

3 What is the balancing payment/repayment due from/to Jump Ltd when their VAT return for the year ended 31 December 20X1 is filed?

5 Cash accounting

5.1 How the scheme works

Normally VAT is accounted for on the basis of invoices issued and received in a return period. Accordingly:

- Output VAT is paid to HMRC by reference to the period in which the tax point occurs (usually the delivery or invoice date), regardless of whether payment has been received from the customer.
- Input VAT is reclaimed from HMRC by reference to the invoices received in the return period, even if payment has not been made to the supplier.

However, under the cash accounting scheme a business accounts for VAT on the basis of when payment is actually received from customers or made to suppliers. The tax point becomes the date of receipt or payment.

If registered under the scheme invoices will still be sent to customers and received from suppliers in the normal way, but the key record that must be kept is a cash book. This should summarise all the payments made and received and have a **separate column for VAT.**

5.2 Conditions

As with annual accounting, the scheme is aimed at smaller businesses. The conditions are:

- The trader's VAT returns must be up-to-date and they must have no convictions for VAT offences or penalties for dishonest conduct.
- Estimated taxable turnover, excluding VAT and sales of capital assets, must not exceed £1,350,000 for the next year.
- Once in the scheme, a trader must leave once their annual taxable turnover, excluding VAT, exceeds £1,600,000.
- When they leave the scheme they must account for all outstanding VAT (i.e. on debtors less creditors), as they will be moving to a system where VAT is accounted for on invoices not on a cash basis.

5.3 Advantages and disadvantages

Advantages	Disadvantages
• Businesses selling on credit do not have to pay output VAT to HMRC until they receive it from customers.	• Input tax cannot be claimed until the invoice is paid. This delays recovery of input VAT.
• This gives automatic bad debt relief because if the customer does not pay, then the VAT on their invoice is not paid over to HMRC. Cash flow is improved.	• Not suitable for businesses with a lot of cash sales or zero-rated supplies. Using cash accounting in these situations just causes a delay in the recovery of input VAT.
• Cash accounting can be used with annual accounting.	• If a business uses cash accounting as soon as it registers, it will be unable to reclaim VAT on stock and assets until the invoices for these items are paid.

Activity 6

Would each of the following businesses benefit from joining the cash accounting scheme? Select Yes or No for each business.

1 JB Ltd which operates a retail shop selling directly to the public. All sales are for cash and all purchases are made on credit. JB Ltd's supplies are all standard rated.

YES/NO

2 Amber and Co, which manufactures and sells computer printers to other businesses. This is a standard rated business and all sales and purchases are made on credit.

YES/NO

3 John Smith, a sole trader who manufactures children's shoes and sells them to retailers. This is a zero-rated activity and all sales and purchases are made on credit.

YES/NO

6 The flat rate scheme

6.1 Purpose of the scheme

The optional flat rate scheme is aimed at simplifying the way in which very small businesses calculate their VAT liability.

6.2 How the scheme works

Under the flat rate scheme, a business **calculates its VAT liability** by simply applying a flat rate percentage to total turnover. This removes the need to calculate and record output and input VAT. In some cases it can save the business money.

- The flat rate percentage is applied to the gross (VAT inclusive) **total turnover** figure. This includes standard rated, zero rated and exempt supplies. No input VAT is recovered.
- The percentage varies according to the type of trade in which the business is involved. In their first year in the scheme a business gets a 1% discount on their normal percentage. If you need to know a percentage in the assessment it will be given to you.
- A **VAT invoice must still be issued** to customers and VAT charged at the appropriate rate.

- A VAT account must still be maintained.
- The flat rate scheme is **only** used to calculate the VAT due to HMRC.
- The flat rate scheme can be used together with the annual accounting scheme.
- It is not possible to join both the flat rate scheme and the cash accounting scheme, however it is possible to request that the flat rate scheme calculations are performed on a cash paid/ receipts basis.

6.3 Conditions for the scheme

In order to join the scheme, the **taxable** turnover of the business, (excluding VAT), for the next 12 months, must not be expected to exceed £150,000.

Once in the scheme, a business can stay in until their **tax inclusive** turnover (**including taxable and exempt income**) for the previous 12 months exceeds £230,000.

 **Example**

Simon runs a business selling computer supplies. He has joined the flat rate scheme.

If the flat rate percentage for this type of business is 12%, how much VAT should Simon pay over for the quarter ended 30 June 20X0 when his turnover (including VAT) is £39,000?

Solution

£4,680.00 (£39,000 × 12%)

6.4 Advantages and disadvantages of the flat rate scheme

The advantages of the scheme include the following:

- A business does not have to record the VAT charged on each individual sale and purchase.
- Easier administration as the business does not have to decide which amounts of input VAT can be reclaimed and which cannot.
- The business gets a discount of 1% in the first year.
- The business may pay less VAT than using the standard method.
- The business has certainty as the percentage of turnover that has to be paid over as VAT is known in advance.
- There is less chance of making a mistake in calculating VAT.

The percentage used in flat rate accounting is fixed for particular trade sectors and takes into account the mix of standard rated, zero rated and exempt sales made by the average business in that sector.

The scheme may not be suitable for businesses which do not have the same mix as an average business.

In particular it would not be suitable for:

- businesses that regularly receive repayments under standard VAT accounting
- businesses that buy a higher proportion of standard rated items than others in their trade sector as they would not be able to reclaim the input VAT on these purchases
- businesses that make a higher proportion of zero rated or exempt sales than others in their trade.

Activity 7

In the year ended 31 December 20X0, Apple Ltd has annual sales to the general public of £100,000, all of which are standard rated.

The company incurs standard rated expenses of £4,500 per annum.

These figures include VAT at 20%.

1 What is Apple Ltd's VAT liability using the standard method?

A £19,100.00

B £15,916.66

C £20,000.00

D £16,666.66

2 What is Apple Ltd's VAT liability using the flat rate method assuming a percentage of 9%?

A £20,000.00

B £16,666.66

C £9,000.00

D £8,595.00

7 Retail schemes

7.1 Introduction

We have seen that using standard VAT accounting a registered trader must record the VAT on each sale in the accounting records. However with the retail schemes the value of the VAT can be based on the total taxable sales for a period.

For example if a retail trader's outputs were all standard rated and sales for a day were £2,100 VAT inclusive, then a fraction would be applied to calculate the VAT: £2,100 x 1/6 = £350. NB the 1/6 is the fraction that applies as the standard rate is currently 20%.

If a VAT registered customer requests a VAT invoice from a business using a retail scheme then one must be issued.

There are different types of retail schemes.

7.2 Standard Retail Schemes

This scheme enables VAT to be calculated using the point of sale, direct calculation or apportionment methods. These are explained below.

Standard schemes can only be used if the annual retail turnover excluding VAT is under £130m.

7.3 Point of sale scheme

Elements of the scheme include.

- Identify the appropriate VAT rate for each item sold at the time of sale. Tills will differentiate between goods sold at different rates e.g.: standard and zero.
- Determine gross takings including VAT.
- Determine the proportions of daily gross takings made at the various VAT rates – from till reading.
- Multiply the proportions by the relevant fraction to determine the VAT on the outputs for the period.

7.4 Direct calculation

This scheme works by calculating the Expected Selling Price of goods for retail sale at one or two rates of VAT in order to establish the proportion of the Daily Gross Takings on which VAT is due. The Expected Selling Prices of 'minority goods' must always be calculated. These are the goods at the rate of tax which forms the smallest proportion of the business's retail supplies.

For example, if a business makes:

- 60% standard-rated sales, and
- 40% zero-rated sales,

the minority goods are the zero-rated goods. The business will therefore calculate the Expected Selling Prices for the zero-rated goods received, made or grown for retail sale and then deduct this from their Daily Gross Takings. This gives the figure for standard-rated sales, to which the VAT fraction must be applied to arrive at the business's output tax liability.

On the other hand, if the business makes:

- 60% zero-rated sales, and
- 40% standard-rated sales,

the minority goods are the standard-rated goods. The business will calculate the ESPs for the standard-rated goods received, made or grown for retail sale. The business will then apply the VAT fraction to this figure to arrive at its output tax liability.

7.5 Apportionment scheme

There are two different apportionment schemes:

Retail turnover excluding VAT of not over £1m.

Elements of the scheme.

- Determine the proportion of goods bought for retail sale for each applicable rate of VAT. For example it may be 50:50, Standard and Zero.
- Apply these proportions to your retail sales. If for example 60% of your purchases are standard rated then 60% of your sales value is treated as standard rated.
- Calculate the VAT due on the outputs by applying the appropriate fraction to the relevant proportion of the gross sales for the period.

This scheme cannot be used for:

- The provision of services.
- Goods made or grown by the trader.
- Catering services.

Retail Turnover excluding VAT of not over £130m.

Elements of the scheme:

- Determine the expected selling prices of goods bought for resale either by mark up or by using recommended retail prices.
- Determine the proportions to be sold at different VAT rates. If this was for example 70:30, standard and zero then 70% of the retail sales are treated as standard rated sales and 30% zero rated sales.
- Calculate the VAT due by applying the appropriate VAT fraction to the gross sales figure in proportions as determined.

7.6 VAT margin scheme

Under a Margin Scheme VAT is paid on the Gross Margin (the difference between what you paid for an item and what you sold it for), rather than on the full selling price of the item.

Margin Schemes apply to various to various types of business and eligible goods include:

- Second hand goods.
- Works of art.
- Antiques and collectable items

There are also special rules under the margin scheme if you are selling

- Horses and ponies
- Second hand motor vehicles.

or if you are a

- Dealer
- Auctioneer
- Pawnbroker

Use of the Margin Scheme

When applying the scheme, the difference between the purchase and selling price - the margin - is treated as VAT inclusive. To calculate the VAT due on the sale of an item, determine the margin and apply the VAT fraction of 1/6 (or 20/120).

Example

A standard rated item was purchased for £1,600 and is sold for £2,200. The margin is therefore £600 and this is treated as VAT inclusive. T

The VAT due on the sale is £600 x 1/6 = £100 (or £600 x 20/120 = £100)

Purchase price

This is the amount paid for an item: it does not include any costs of making the item ready for sale, such as costs of repairs and refurbishment. However a claim for VAT on these costs can be made using standard VAT accounting.

Record keeping

The following records must be kept:

A stock book showing each item bought and sold under the scheme and the margin.

Purchase invoices showings the details of items bought under the scheme. If an item is bought from a private individual then the owner of the business must make out a purchase invoice.

8 The VAT return

8.1 What a VAT return looks like

An example of a paper VAT return is given below in section 8.2 although very few businesses will use these.

Most businesses have to file their returns online rather than on paper, however the boxes and numbers used for the electronic form are exactly the same.

8.2 Paper VAT return

Value Added Tax Return
For the period

For Official Use

Registration number *Period*

You could be liable to a financial penalty if your completed return and all the VAT payable are not received by the due date.

Due date:

For Official Use

Your VAT Office telephone number is 0123 4567

Before you fill in this form please read the notes on the back and the VAT Leaflet '*Filling in your VAT return*'. *Fill in all boxes clearly in ink and write 'none' where necessary. Don't put a dash or leave any box blank. If there are no pence write '00' in the pence column. Do not enter more than one amount in any box*

For official use				
	VAT due in this period on sales and other options	1		
	VAT due in this period on acquisitions from other EC Member states	2		
	Total VAT due (the sum of boxes 1 and 2)	3		
	VAT reclaimed in this period on purchases and other inputs (including acquisitions from the EC)	4		
	Net VAT to be paid to Customs or reclaimed by you (Difference between boxes 3 and 4)	5		
	Total value of sales and all other outputs excluding any VAT. Include your box 8 figure	6		00
	Total value of purchases and all other inputs excluding any VAT. Include your box 9 figures.	7		00
	Total value of all supplies of goods and related services excluding any VAT to other EC Member States	8		00
	Total value of all supplies of goods and related services excluding any VAT, from other EC Member States	9		00

Retail schemes. If you have used any of the schemes in the period covered by this return, enter the relevant letter(s) in this box.

If you are enclosing a payment please tick this box	DECLARATION You or someone on your behalf must sign below. I .... declare that the information given (Full name of signatory in BLOCK LETTERS) above is true and complete. Signature .... Date 20 A false declaration can result in prosecution.

8.3 VAT return – online template

		£
VAT due in this period on **sales** and other outputs	**Box 1**	
VAT due in this period on **acquisitions** from other **EC Member States**	**Box 2**	
Total VAT due (**the sum of boxes 1 and 2**)	**Box 3**	
VAT reclaimed in the period on **purchases** and other inputs, including acquisitions from the EC	**Box 4**	
Net VAT to be paid to HM Revenue & Customs or reclaimed by you (**Difference between boxes 3 and 4**)	**Box 5**	
Total value of **sales** and all other outputs excluding any VAT. **Include your box 8 figure**	**Box 6**	
Total value of purchases and all other inputs excluding any VAT. **Include your box 9 figure**	**Box 7**	
Total value of all **supplies** of goods and related costs, excluding any VAT, to other **EC Member States**	**Box 8**	
Total value of all **acquisitions** of goods and related costs, excluding any VAT, from other **EC Member States**	**Box 9**	

As you will see there are nine boxes to complete with the relevant figures.

Boxes 2, 8 and 9 are to do with supplies of goods and services to other European Community (EC) Member States and acquisitions from EC Member States.

8.4 Completing the VAT return

The main source of information for the VAT return is the VAT account which must be maintained to show the amount that is due to or from HMRC at the end of each quarter.

It is important to realise that the balance on the VAT account should agree to the balance of VAT payable/reclaimable on the VAT return.

8.5 How the VAT account should look

Given below is a pro-forma of a VAT account as suggested by the VAT Guide.

1 April 20X5 to 30 June 20X5

VAT deductible – input tax		**VAT payable – output tax**	
	£ p		£ p
VAT on purchases		VAT on sales	
April	X	April	X
May	X	May	X
June	X	June	X
VAT on imports	X		
VAT on acquisition from EC	X	VAT on acquisition from EC	X
Adjustments of previous errors			
(if within the error limit – Chapter 6)			
Net under claim	X	Net over claim	X
Bad debt relief (section 2.6)	X		
Less: Credit notes received	(X)	Less: Credit notes issued	(X)
	—		—
Total tax deductible	X	Total tax payable	X
	—	Less: Total tax deductible	(X)
			—
		Payable to HMRC	X
			—

You will note that the VAT shown is not strictly a double entry account as the VAT on credit notes received is deducted from input tax and the VAT on credit notes issued is deducted from output tax instead of being credited and debited respectively.

8.6 Information required for the VAT return

Boxes 1 to 4 of the VAT return can be fairly easily completed from the information in the VAT account. However, Boxes 6 and 7 require figures for total sales and purchases excluding VAT.

This information will need to be extracted from the totals of the accounting records such as sales day book and purchases day book totals. It is also possible that information relating to VAT could be shown in a journal.

Boxes 8 and 9 require figures, excluding VAT, for the value of supplies to other EC Member States and acquisitions from other EC Member States.

Therefore the accounting records should be designed in such a way that these figures can also be easily identified.

Activity 8

Panther

You are preparing the VAT return for Panther Alarms Ltd and you must first identify the sources of information for the VAT account.

Here is a list of possible sources of accounting information.

1 Sales day book
2 Sales returns day book
3 Bad and doubtful debts account
4 Purchase returns day book
5 Drawings account
6 Purchases day book
7 Cash book
8 Assets account
9 Petty cash book

Select from the list the best sources of information for the following figures by entering a number against each.

If you think the information will be in more than one place then give the number for both.

A sales
B cash sales
C credit notes issued
D purchases
E cash purchases
F credit notes received
G capital goods sold
H capital goods purchased
I bad debt relief

Example

Given below is a VAT account for Thompson Brothers for the second VAT quarter of 20X5.

Thompson Brothers Ltd **1 April 20X5 to 30 June 20X5**

VAT deductible – input tax		**VAT payable – output tax**	
VAT on purchases	£	*VAT on sales*	£
April	700.00	April	1,350.00
May	350.00	May	1,750.00
June	350.00	June	700.00
	1,400.00		3,800.00
Other adjustments			
Less: Credit notes received	(20.00)	Less: Credit notes issued	(120.00)
Total tax deductible	1,380.00	Total tax payable	3,680.00
		Less: Total tax deductible	(1,380.00)
		Payable to HMRC	2,300.00

You are also given the summarised totals from the day books for the three-month period:

Sales Day Book

	Net	*VAT*	*Total*
	£	£	£
Standard rated	19,000.00	3,800.00	22,800.00
Zero rated	800.00	–	800.00

Sales Returns Day Book

	Net	*VAT*	*Total*
	£	£	£
Standard rated	600.00	120.00	720.00
Zero rated	40.00	–	40.00

Purchases Day Book

	Net	*VAT*	*Total*
	£	£	£
Standard rated	7,000.00	1,400.00	8,400.00
Zero rated	2,000.00	–	2,000.00

Purchases Returns Day Book

	Net	*VAT*	*Total*
	£	£	£
Standard rated	100.00	20.00	120.00
Zero rated	–	–	–

We are now in a position to complete the VAT return.

Solution

Step 1

Fill in Box 1 with the VAT on sales less the VAT on credit notes issued.

This can be taken either from the VAT account or from the day book summaries:
(£3,800 – £120) = £3,680.00.

Note that the figures in Boxes 1 – 5 should include pence so put '00' if there are no pence in the total.

Step 2

Fill in Box 2 with the VAT payable on acquisitions from other EC Member states – none here.

Step 3

Complete Box 3 with the total of Boxes 1 and 2:
(£3,680.00 + £Nil) = £3,680.00.

Step 4

Fill in Box 4 with the total of VAT on all purchases less the total VAT on any credit notes received. These figures can either be taken from the VAT account or from the day book totals:
(£1,400.00 – £20.00) = £1,380.00.

Step 5

Complete Box 5 by deducting the figure in Box 4 from the total in Box 3:
(£3,680.00 – £1,380.00) = £2,300.00.

This is the amount due to HMRC and should equal the balance on the VAT account.

If the Box 4 figure is larger than the Box 3 total then there is more input tax reclaimable than output tax to pay – this means that this is the amount being reclaimed from HMRC.

For a paper return, a negative figure like a repayment should be put in brackets. For an online return a negative figure should have a negative sign in front and no brackets.

Step 6

Fill in Box 6 with the VAT exclusive figure of all sales less credit notes issued – this information will come from the day books:
(£19,000 + £800– £600 – £40) = £19,160

Note that this figure includes zero-rated supplies and any exempt supplies that are made.

Note that the figures in Boxes 6 – 9 should be whole pounds only (pence will already be completed as '00' on a paper return).

Step 7

Fill in Box 7 with the VAT exclusive total of all purchases less credit notes received – again this will be taken from the day books:
(£7,000 + £2,000– £100) = £8,900

Step 8

Boxes 8 and 9 are for transactions with EU member states.

Note that if there is no entry for any box then 'none' should be written in the box for a paper return and 0 for an online return.

Step 9

If VAT is due to HMRC then payment must be made in accordance with the usual time limits. For assessment purposes you may be asked to state the payment date, or draft an email advising when this amount will be paid.

		£
VAT due in this period on **sales** and other outputs	**Box 1**	3,680.00
VAT due in this period on **acquisitions** from other **EC Member States**	**Box 2**	0.00
Total VAT due (**the sum of boxes 1 and 2**)	**Box 3**	3,680.00
VAT reclaimed in the period on **purchases** and other inputs, including acquisitions from the EC	**Box 4**	1,380.00
Net VAT to be paid to HM Revenue & Customs or reclaimed by you (**Difference between boxes 3 and 4**)	**Box 5**	2,300.00
Total value of **sales** and all other outputs excluding any VAT. **Include your box 8 figure**	**Box 6**	19,160
Total value of purchases and all other inputs excluding any VAT. **Include your box 9 figure**	**Box 7**	8,900
Total value of all **supplies** of goods and related costs, excluding any VAT, to other **EC Member States**	**Box 8**	0
Total value of all **acquisitions** of goods and related costs, excluding any VAT, from other **EC Member States**	**Box 9**	0

If the business makes sales or purchases for cash then the relevant net and VAT figures from the cash receipts and payments books should also be included on the VAT return.

Activity 9

Given below is a summary of the day books of a business for the three months ended 31 March 20X1.

The business is called Long Supplies Ltd and trades from Vale House, Lilly Road, Trent, TR5 2KL.

The VAT registration number of the business is 285 3745 12.

Sales Day Book	Net	VAT	Total
	£	£	£
Standard-rate	15,485.60	3,097.12	18,582.72
Zero-rated	1,497.56	–	1,497.56

Sales Returns Day Book	Net	VAT	Total
	£	£	£
Standard-rate	1,625.77	325.15	1,950.92
Zero-rated	106.59	–	106.59

Purchase Day Book	Net	VAT	Total
	£	£	£
Standard-rate	8,127.45	1,625.49	9,752.94
Zero-rated	980.57	–	980.57

Purchases Returns Day Book	Net	VAT	Total
	£	£	£
Standard-rate	935.47	187.09	1,122.56
Zero-rated	80.40	–	80.40

Required:

(a) Write up the VAT account to reflect these figures.

(b) Complete the VAT return given.

Answer proformas

(a) Proforma VAT account for completion

	£ p		£ p
VAT on purchases		VAT on sales	
Less: Credit notes received		Less: Credit notes issued	
Total tax deductible		Total tax payable	
		Less: Total tax deductible	
		Payable to HMRC	

(b) Proforma VAT return for completion

		£
VAT due in this period on **sales** and other outputs	**Box 1**	
VAT due in this period on **acquisitions** from other **EC Member States**	**Box 2**	
Total VAT due (**the sum of boxes 1 and 2**)	**Box 3**	
VAT reclaimed in the period on **purchases** and other inputs, including acquisitions from the EC	**Box 4**	
Net VAT to be paid to HM Revenue & Customs or reclaimed by you (**Difference between boxes 3 and 4**)	**Box 5**	
Total value of **sales** and all other outputs excluding any VAT. **Include your box 8 figure**	**Box 6**	
Total value of purchases and all other inputs excluding any VAT. **Include your box 9 figure**	**Box 7**	
Total value of all **supplies** of goods and related costs, excluding any VAT, to other **EC Member States**	**Box 8**	
Total value of all **acquisitions** of goods and related costs, excluding any VAT, from other **EC Member States**	**Box 9**	

8.7 VAT: Adjustment of previous errors

You will notice in the pro-forma VAT account that there are entries for net under claims and net over claims.

Net errors made in previous VAT returns which are below the disclosure threshold can be adjusted for on the VAT return through the VAT account.

Errors can be corrected on the next VAT return if they are:

- No more than £10,000
- Between £10,000 and £50,000 but no more than 1% of turnover for the current return period (specifically the figure included in Box 6 of the return).

The one single figure for net errors will then be entered as additional input tax in Box 4 if there has been an earlier net under claim of VAT and as additional output tax in Box 1 if the net error was a net over claim in a previous return.

8.8 Errors above the threshold

The VAT office should be informed immediately either by a letter or on Form VAT 652. This is known as voluntary disclosure.

The information provided to the VAT office should be:

- how the error happened
- the amount of the error
- the VAT period in which it occurred
- whether the error was involving input or output tax
- how you worked out the error
- whether the error is in favour of the business or HMRC.

8.9 VAT: Bad debt relief

You will notice that there is an entry in the pro-forma VAT account for bad debt relief as additional input tax.

When a supplier invoices a customer for an amount including VAT, the supplier must pay the VAT to HMRC.

If the customer then fails to pay the debt, the supplier's position is that he has paid output VAT which he has never collected. This is obviously unfair, and the system allows him to recover such amounts.

Suppliers cannot issue credit notes to recover VAT on bad debts.

Instead, the business must make an **adjustment through the VAT return**. The business can reclaim VAT already paid over if:

- output tax was paid on the original supply
- six months have elapsed between the date payment was due (or the date of supply if later) and the date of the VAT return, and
- the debt has been written off as a bad debt in the accounting records
- the debt is less than 3 years and 6 months old
- the debt has not been sold to a factoring company
- you did not charge more than the selling price for the items.

If the business receives a **repayment of the debt later**, it must make an adjustment to the VAT relief claimed.

The bad debt relief is entered in Box 4 of the return along with the VAT on purchases.

Be very careful when computing the VAT on the bad debt.

The amount of the bad debt will be VAT inclusive, because the amount the debtor owes is the amount that includes VAT.

To calculate the VAT you have to multiply the bad debt by 20/120 (or 1/6) for the standard VAT rate of 20%.

Example

A business has made purchases of £237,000 (net of VAT) in the VAT quarter and has written off a bad debt of £750. They also have a net under claim of VAT of £1,250.00 from earlier periods.

Calculate the figure that will be entered on the VAT return for the quarter in Box 4.

Solution

	£	£ p
Purchases (net of VAT)	237,000	
VAT thereon (£237,000 × 0.20)		47,400.00
Bad debt	750	
VAT thereon (£750 × 20/120)		125.00
Net under claim of VAT		1,250.00
Total VAT for Box 4		48,775.00

9 Summary

For your assessment you will need to be able to account for VAT and deal with the amount of VAT that is due either to or from HM Revenue and Customs.

In particular you must understand what is meant by the balance on the VAT control account in the trial balance.

This chapter has covered two important areas for VAT – invoicing and tax points.

The tax point for a supply of goods is important as this determines the VAT period in which the VAT on those goods is included. The basic tax point is the date on which goods are delivered or collected by a customer but there are also situations in which the tax point can be earlier or later. These rules must be understood.

VAT invoices must include certain details and in normal circumstances must be given or sent to a VAT registered purchaser. In practice this means that all purchasers will be provided with a VAT invoice whether they are registered or not. However retailers are allowed to issue less detailed or modified invoices.

A business should keep a VAT account which summarises all of the VAT from the accounting records and this can be used to complete the first five boxes on the VAT return. The figure for VAT due to or from HM Revenue and Customs on the VAT return should equal the balance on the VAT account.

This chapter has also covered the various VAT schemes which you need an understanding of for Level III.

Answers to chapter activities

Activity 1

Sales account

	£		£
		Sales ledger control account	110,000

Sales ledger control account

	£		£
Sales + VAT 110,000 + 22,000	132,000		

Purchases account

	£		£
Purchases ledger control account	75,000		

VAT control account

	£		£
Purchases ledger control account 75,000 × 20/100	15,000	Sales ledger control account 110,000 × 20/100	22,000
Balance c/d	7,000		
	22,000		22,000
		Balance b/d	7,000

Purchases ledger control account

	£		£
		Purchases + VAT 75,000 + 15,000	90,000

The amount due to HM Revenue and Customs is the balance on the VAT control account, £7,000.

Activity 2

1 The amount that should be included in the trial balance is the NET amount. As £27,216 is the VAT inclusive amount, the NET is calculated as follows:

27,216 × 100/120 = 22,680

2 The VAT can be calculated using the gross figure £27,216 × 20/120 = £4,536

3 The VAT control would be completed as follows:

VAT control account

	£		£
VAT on purchases	35,000	Balance b/d	5,000
Paid to HMRC	5,000	VAT on sales	26,250
Vat on expenses	4,536	**Balance c/d**	**13,286**
	44,536		44,536
Balance b/d	**13,286**		

A debit balance represents a refund due from HMRC.

Activity 3

The correct answer is C

	£
List price of goods less trade discount (380 – (380 × 10%)	342.00
VAT (20% × £342.00)	68.40

Activity 4

1 VAT on 6 metre hosepipes = £10.33 (£51.68 × 20% = £10.336)

2 VAT on bags of compost = £27.74 (£138.72 × 20% = £27.744)

3 VAT on kitchen units = £216.91 (£1,084.57 × 20% = £216.914)

All rounded down to the nearest penny.

Activity 5

1 The correct answer is B.

28 February 20X2 = 2 months after the year end.

2 The correct answer is A.

Nine monthly payments must be made, each of which are 10% of the VAT liability for the previous year.

3 The balancing payment will be £580.00 (£3,820.00 – (£360.00 × 9))

Activity 6

1 NO. As sales are all in cash, the adoption of the cash accounting scheme would not affect the time when output tax would be accounted for but would delay the recovery of input tax until the business had paid its suppliers.

2 YES. The business would benefit because it would only account for output VAT when the customer paid. Even though the recovery of input VAT would be delayed until the suppliers were paid, the amount of input VAT is likely to be less than output VAT so the business does gain a net cash flow advantage.

3 NO. As the sales are zero rated no output tax is payable. The adoption of the cash accounting scheme would simply delay the recovery of input VAT until the suppliers were paid.

Activity 7

1 The correct answer is B.

£15,916.66 (20/120 × (£100,000 – £4,500))

2 The correct answer is C.

£9,000.00 (9% × £100,000)

Activity 8

Panther

A	Sales	1
B	Cash sales	7
C	Credit notes issued	2
D	Purchases	6
E	Cash purchases	7 and 9
F	Credit notes received	4
G	Capital goods sold	8 or 1 (if it is an analysed sales day book)
H	Capital goods purchased	8 or 6 (if analysed)
I	Bad debt relief	3

Activity 9

(a)

Long Supplies Ltd
VAT account 1 January to 31 March 20X1

	£		£
VAT on purchases	1,625.49	VAT on sales	3,097.12
Less: Credit notes received	(187.09)	Less: Credit notes issued	(325.15)
Total tax deductible	1,438.40	Total tax payable	2,771.97
		Less: Total tax deductible	(1,438.40)
		Payable to HMRC	1,333.57

(b)

		£
VAT due in this period on **sales** and other outputs	**Box 1**	2,771.97
VAT due in this period on **acquisitions** from other **EC Member States**	**Box 2**	0.00
Total VAT due (**the sum of boxes 1 and 2**)	**Box 3**	2,771.97
VAT reclaimed in the period on **purchases** and other inputs, including acquisitions from the EC	**Box 4**	1,438.40
Net VAT to be paid to HM Revenue & Customs or reclaimed by you (**Difference between boxes 3 and 4**)	**Box 5**	1,333.57
Total value of **sales** and all other outputs excluding any VAT. **Include your box 8 figure**	**Box 6**	15,251
Total value of purchases and all other inputs excluding any VAT. **Include your box 9 figure**	**Box 7**	8,092
Total value of all **supplies** of goods and related costs, excluding any VAT, to other **EC Member States**	**Box 8**	0
Total value of all **acquisitions** of goods and related costs, excluding any VAT, from other **EC Member States**	**Box 9**	0

Workings:

Box 1

	£
VAT on sales	3,097.12
Less: VAT on credit notes	(325.15)
	2,771.97

Box 4

	£
VAT on purchases	1,625.49
Less: VAT on credit notes	(187.09)
	1,438.40

Box 6

	£
Standard-rated sales	15,485.60
Zero-rated sales	1,497.56
	16,983.16
Less: Credit notes	
Standard-rated	(1,625.77)
Zero-rated	(106.59)
	15,250.80

Box 7

	£
Standard-rated purchases	8,127.45
Zero-rated purchases	980.57
	9,108.02
Less: Credit notes	
Standard-rated	(935.47)
Zero-rated	(80.40)
	8,092.15

10 Test your knowledge

Workbook Activity 10

A business that is registered for VAT has the following record relating to sales, purchases and expenses.

Sales for the quarter ending 31 March 20X4 of £236,100 (including VAT)

Purchases and expenses of £143,600 (excluding VAT).

At 1 January 20X4 there was an amount of £8,455 owing to HM Revenue and Customs and this was paid on 28 January 20X4.

Required:

Write up the VAT control account for the quarter ending 31 March 20X4 . (VAT rate is 20%)

VAT control account

	£		£
Purchases	28720	Balance b/d	8450
Payment	8450	Sales	39350
		to be paid	10630

Explain what the balance on the account represents.

Workbook Activity 11

Indicate whether the following statements are true or false.

Tick one box on each line.

		True	*False*
1	Traders do not have to supply a VAT invoice unless their customer is VAT registered.		
2	Retailers can issue less detailed VAT invoices if the total amount of the supply, excluding VAT, does not exceed £250.		
3	The VAT invoice is used by a customer as their evidence for reclaiming input VAT.		
4	A VAT invoice must be issued to a customer within 30 days of the tax point.		

Workbook Activity 12

Calculate the amount of output VAT at the standard rate of 20% that should be charged on the following invoices (to the nearest pence).

Goods pre discount price £	*Trade discount*	*Settlement discount*	*Output tax* £ p
1,000	10%	2%	
2,000	Nil	5%.	
750	8%	None	

Workbook Activity 13

Look at the following list of items.

Select by entering the appropriate number whether the items:

1 Should only be shown on a normal detailed VAT invoice; or

2 Should be shown on both a normal detailed VAT invoice and on a less detailed invoice; or

3 Should not be shown on either form of invoice.

	Item	*Number (1, 2, or 3)*
A	Identifying number	
B	Tax point date	
C	Delivery date	
D	Total amount of VAT payable	
E	Customer's registration number	

Workbook Activity 14

Which of the following statements about proforma invoices are FALSE?

Enter a tick in the final box for each false statement.

		False
A	A proforma invoice IS a valid tax invoice	
B	A proforma invoice IS NOT a valid tax invoice	
C	A customer receiving a proforma invoice can use it to reclaim the input tax shown	
D	A proforma invoice is really just a demand for payment	

Workbook Activity 15

In each of the following cases, state the tax point date.

		Tax point
1	Goods delivered to a customer on 15 August, invoice sent out on 20 August and payment received 30 August.	
2	Proforma invoice issued 3 June, payment received 10 June, goods delivered 30 June with a tax invoice dated on that day.	
3	Goods delivered to a customer on 4 March, invoice sent out on 25 March and payment received 15 April.	
4	Invoice sent to a customer on 10 December, goods delivered 18 December and payment received 27 December.	

Workbook Activity 16

A VAT registered business receives a £100 non-refundable deposit on 19 October from a customer for the supply of goods which are despatched on 25 October.

The goods are invoiced on 31 October and the balance of £350 is paid on 10 November.

Both amounts are VAT inclusive.

1 What is the tax point for the deposit?

A 19 October

B 25 October

C 31 October

D 10 November

2 What is the output VAT on the deposit?

A £20.00

B £16.66

3 What is the tax point for the balance?

A 19 October

B 25 October

C 31 October

D 10 November

4 What is the output VAT on the balance?

A £70.00

B £58.33

Workbook Activity 17

You are a self-employed bookkeeper and Duncan Bye, a motor engineer, is one of your clients. He is registered for VAT.

His records for the quarter ended 30 June 20X1 showed the following:

Sales day book

	Gross	*Net*	*VAT*
	£	£	£
April	8,100.00	6,750.00	1,350.00
May	7,812.00	6,510.00	1,302.00
June	9,888.00	8,240.00	1,648.00
	25,800.00	21,500.00	4,300.00

Purchases day book

	Gross	*Net*	*VAT*
	£	£	£
April	3,780.00	3,150.00	630.00
May	3,924.00	3,270.00	654.00
June	3,216.00	2,680.00	536.00
	10,920.00	9,100.00	1,820.00

He also gives you some details of petty cash expenditure in the quarter.

	£ p
Net purchases	75.60
VAT	15.12
	90.72

Duncan understated his output VAT by £24 on his last return.

Prepare the following VAT form 100 for the period.

		£
VAT due in this period on **sales** and other outputs	**Box 1**	4300 24
VAT due in this period on **acquisitions** from other **EC Member States**	**Box 2**	
Total VAT due (**the sum of boxes 1 and 2**)	**Box 3**	4324
VAT reclaimed in the period on **purchases** and other inputs, including acquisitions from the EC	**Box 4**	1820 15.12
Net VAT to be paid to HM Revenue & Customs or reclaimed by you (**Difference between boxes 3 and 4**)	**Box 5**	2488.88
Total value of **sales** and all other outputs excluding any VAT. **Include your box 8 figure**	**Box 6**	21500
Total value of purchases and all other inputs excluding any VAT. **Include your box 9 figure**	**Box 7**	9175.60
Total value of all **supplies** of goods and related costs, excluding any VAT, to other **EC Member States**	**Box 8**	
Total value of all **acquisitions** of goods and related costs, excluding any VAT, from other **EC Member States**	**Box 9**	

Activity 18

You are provided with the following summary of Mark Ambrose's books and other information provided by Mark for the quarter ended 30 September 20X1.

MARK AMBROSE

Summary of day books and petty cash expenditure
Quarter ended 30 September 20X1

Sales day book

	Work done	VAT	Total
	£	£	£
July	12,900.00	2,580.00	15,480.00
August	13,200.00	2,640.00	15,840.00
September	12,300.00	2,460.00	14,760.00
	38,400.00	7,680.00	46,080.00

Purchase day book

	Net	VAT	Total
	£	£	£
July	5,250.00	1,050.00	6,300.00
August	5,470.00	1,094.00	6,564.00
September	5,750.00	1,150.00	6,900.00
	16,470.00	3,294.00	19,764.00

Petty cash expenditure for quarter (VAT inclusive)

July	£108.00
August	£96.00
September	£120.00

Bad debts list – 30 September 20X1

Date	Customer	Total (including VAT)
30 November 20X0	High Melton Farms	£300.00
3 January 20X1	Concorde Motors	£180.00
4 April 20X1	Bawtry Engineering	£120.00

These have now been written off as bad debts.

Complete boxes 1 to 9 of the VAT return for the quarter ended 30 September 20X1.

		£
VAT due in this period on **sales** and other outputs	**Box 1**	
VAT due in this period on **acquisitions** from other **EC Member States**	**Box 2**	
Total VAT due (**the sum of boxes 1 and 2**)	**Box 3**	
VAT reclaimed in the period on **purchases** and other inputs, including acquisitions from the EC	**Box 4**	
Net VAT to be paid to HM Revenue & Customs or reclaimed by you (**Difference between boxes 3 and 4**)	**Box 5**	
Total value of **sales** and all other outputs excluding any VAT. **Include your box 8 figure**	**Box 6**	
Total value of purchases and all other inputs excluding any VAT. **Include your box 9 figure**	**Box 7**	
Total value of all **supplies** of goods and related costs, excluding any VAT, to other **EC Member States**	**Box 8**	
Total value of all **acquisitions** of goods and related costs, excluding any VAT, from other **EC Member States**	**Box 9**	

Workbook Activity 19

Indicate whether the following statements about the flat rate scheme are true or false.

Tick one box on each line.

		True	*False*
1	VAT invoices are not issued to customers.		
2	A VAT account need not be kept.		
3	Traders using the flat rate scheme can also join the annual accounting scheme.		
4	Traders can join the flat rate scheme if their taxable turnover for the last 12 months is below £230,000.		
5	The flat rate scheme percentage varies according to the trade sector of the business.		

Workbook Activity 20

A VAT registered business has a year end of 30 June 20X2 and uses the annual accounting scheme.

1 Which one of the following statements is true?

A The whole VAT liability for the year is payable on 30 June 20X2

B The whole VAT liability for the year is payable on 31 August 20X2

C The VAT liability is payable in nine monthly instalments starting on 31 October 20X1 with a balancing payment on 31 July 20X2

D The VAT liability is payable in nine monthly instalments starting on 31 October 20X1 with a balancing payment on 31 August 20X2

2 The annual VAT return is due to be submitted by which date?

A 31 July 20X2

B 31 August 20X2

Bank reconciliations

Introduction

Completion of this chapter will ensure we are able to correctly prepare the cash book, compare the entries in the cash book to details on the bank statement and then finally to prepare a bank reconciliation statement.

CONTENTS

1 Writing up the cash book

1.1 Introduction

Most businesses will have a separate cash receipts book and a cash payments book which form part of the double entry system. If this form of record is used, the cash balance must be calculated from the opening balance at the beginning of the period, plus the receipts shown in the cash receipts book for the period and minus the payments shown in the cash payments book for the period.

1.2 Balancing the cash book

The following brief calculation will enable us to find the balance on the cash book when separate receipts and payments books are maintained.

	£
Opening balance per the cash book	X
Add: Receipts in the period	X
Less: Payments in the period	(X)
Closing balance per the cash book	X

Example

Suppose that the opening balance on the cash book is £358.72 on 1 June. During June the Cash Payments Book shows that there were total payments made of £7,326.04 during the month of June and the Cash Receipts Book shows receipts for the month of £8,132.76.

What is the closing balance on the cash book at the end of June?

Solution

		£
Opening balance at 1 June		358.72
Add:	Receipts for June	8,132.76
Less:	Payments for June	(7,326.04)
Balance at 30 June		1,165.44

Take care if the opening balance on the cash book is an overdraft balance. Any receipts in the period will reduce the overdraft and any payments will increase the overdraft.

Suppose that the opening balance on the cash book is £631.25 overdrawn on 1 June. During June the Cash Payments Book shows that there were total payments made of £2,345.42 during the month of June and the Cash Receipts Book shows receipts for the month of £1,276.45

What is the closing balance on the cash book at the end of June?

Solution

		£
Opening balance at 1 June		(631.25)
Add:	Receipts for June	1,276.45
Less:	Payments for June	(2,345.42)
Balance at 30 June		(1,700.22)

Activity 1

The opening balance at 1 January in a business cash book was £673.42 overdrawn. During January payments totalled £6,419.37 and receipts totalled £6,488.20.

What is the closing balance on the cash book?

Example

The following transactions are to be written up in the cash book of Jupiter Limited and the balance at the end of the week calculated. The opening balance on the bank account on 28 June 20X1 was £560.61.

2 July Received a cheque for £45.90 from Hill and French Limited (no settlement discount allowed) – paying in slip 40012.

2 July Corrected a salary error by paying a cheque for £56.89 – cheque number 100107.

3 July Paid £96.65 by cheque to Preston Brothers after deducting a settlement discount of £1.65 (VAT adjustment £0.33) – cheque number 100108.

3 July Banked £30 of cash held – paying in slip 40013.

4 July Received a cheque from Green and Holland for £245.89. They were allowed a settlement discount of £3.68 (VAT adjustment £0.73) – paying in slip 40014.

5 July Reimbursed the petty cash account with £34.89 of cash drawn on cheque number 100109.

The cash receipts and payments books are to be written up and the closing balance calculated.

Solution

Step 1 Enter all of the transactions into the receipts and payments cash books.

Step 2 Total the cash book columns.

Cash receipts book

Date	*Narrative*	*Total* £	*VAT* £	*SLCA* £	*Other* £	*Discount* Allowed £	*VAT Adj* £
20X1							
2 July	Hill and French 40012	45.90		45.90			
3 July	Cash 40013	30.00			30.00		
4 July	Green and Holland 40014	245.89		245.89		3.68	0.73
		321.79	–	291.79	30.00	3.68	0.73

Cash payments book

Date	*Details*	*Cheque*	*Code no*	*Total* £	*VAT* £	*PLCA* £	*Other* £	*Discount received* £	*VAT Adj* £
20X1									
2 July	Salary error	100107		56.89			56.89		
3 July	Preston Bros	100108		96.65		96.65		1.65	0.33
5 July	Petty cash	100109		34.89			34.89		
				188.43	–	96.65	91.78	1.65	0.33

Step 3 Find the balance on the cash book at the end of the week.

		£
Opening balance at 1 July		560.61
Add:	Receipts total	321.79
Less:	Payments total	(188.43)
Balance at the end of the week		693.97

When totalling the cash book columns always check your additions carefully as it is easy to make mistakes when totalling columns of numbers on a calculator. Check that the totals of each analysis column (excluding the discounts and VAT adjustments columns) add back to the total of the total column.

2 Preparing the bank reconciliation statement

2.1 Introduction

At regular intervals (normally at least once a month) the cashier must check that the cash book is correct by comparing the cash book with the bank statement.

2.2 Differences between the cash book and bank statement

At any date the balance shown on the bank statement is unlikely to agree with the balance in the cash book for two main reasons.

(a) Items in the cash book not on the bank statement

Certain items will have been entered in the cash book but will not appear on the bank statement at the time of the reconciliation. Examples are:

- Cheques received by the business and paid into the bank which have not yet appeared on the bank statement, due to the time lag of the clearing system. These are known as **outstanding lodgements** (can also be referred to as "uncleared lodgements").
- Cheques written by the business but which have not yet appeared on the bank statement, because the recipients have not yet paid them in, or the cheques are in the clearing system. These are known as **unpresented cheques**.
- Errors in the cash book (e.g. transposition of numbers, addition errors).

(b) Items on the bank statement not in the cash book

At the time of the bank reconciliation certain items will appear on the bank statement that have not yet been entered into the cash book. These can occur due to the cashier not being aware of the existence of these items until receiving the bank statements. Examples are:

- Direct debit or standing order payments that are in the bank statement but have not yet been entered in the cash payments book.
- BACS or other receipts paid directly into the bank account by a customer.
- Bank charges or bank interest that are unknown until the bank statement has been received and therefore will not be in the cash book.
- Errors in the cash book that may only come to light when the cash book entries are compared to the bank statement.
- Returned cheques i.e. cheques paid in from a customer who does not have sufficient funds in his bank to pay the cheque (see later in this chapter).

2.3 The bank reconciliation

Definition

A bank reconciliation is simply a statement that explains the differences between the balance in the cash book and the balance on the bank statement at a particular date.

A bank reconciliation is produced by following a standard set of steps.

Step 1: Compare the cash book and the bank statement for the relevant period and identify any differences between them.

You should begin with agreeing the opening balances on the bank statement and cash book so that you are aware of any prior period reconciling items that exist.

This is usually done by ticking in the cash book and bank statement items that appear in both the cash book and the bank statement. Any items left unticked therefore only appear in one place, either the cash book or the bank statement. We saw in 2.2 above the reasons why this might occur.

Step 2: Update the cash book for any items that appear on the bank statement that have not yet been entered into the cash book.

Tick these items in both the cash book and the bank statement once they are entered in the cash book.

At this stage there will be no unticked items on the bank statement.

(You clearly cannot enter on the bank statement items in the cash book that do not appear on the bank statement – the bank prepares the bank statement, not you. These items will either be unpresented cheques or outstanding lodgements – see 2.2 above.)

Step 3: Bring down the new cash book balance following the adjustments in step 2 above.

Step 4: Prepare the bank reconciliation statement.

This will typically have the following proforma.

Bank reconciliation as at 31.0X.200X

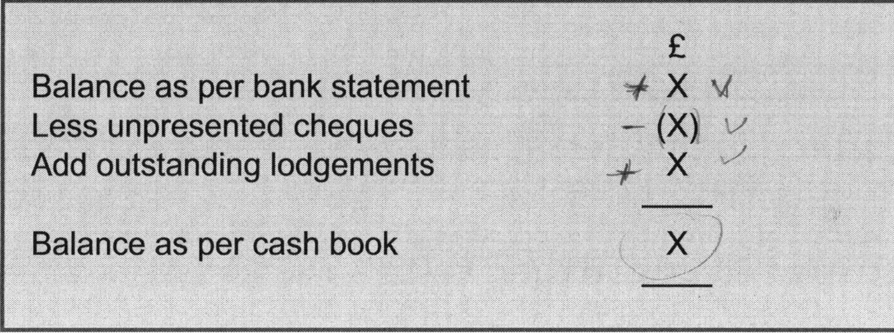

	£
Balance as per bank statement	X
Less unpresented cheques	(X)
Add outstanding lodgements	X
Balance as per cash book	X

Think for a moment to ensure you understand this proforma.

We deduct the unpresented cheques (cheques already entered in the cash book but not yet on the bank statement) from the bank balance, because when they are presented this bank balance will be reduced.

We add outstanding lodgements (cash received and already entered in the cash book) because when they appear on the bank statement they will increase the bank balance.

It is also useful to remember that the bank reconciliation can be performed the opposite way round as shown below:

Bank reconciliation as at 31.0X.200X

	£
Balance as per cash book	X
Add unpresented cheques	(X)
Less outstanding lodgements	X
Balance as per bank statement	X

If we start with the cash book balance, to reconcile this to the bank statement balance we add back the unpresented cheques as though they haven't been paid out of the cash book (as the bank statement has not recognised these being paid out).

We deduct outstanding lodgements as though we haven't recognised these in the cash book (as the bank statement has not recognised these receipts). The cash book balance should then agree to the bank statement balance i.e. we have reconciled these balances.

2.4 Debits and credits in bank statements

When comparing the cash book to the bank statement it is easy to get confused with debits and credits.

- When we pay money into the bank, we debit our cash book but the bank credits our account.
- This is because a debit in our cash book represents the increase in our asset 'cash'. For the bank, the situation is different: they will debit their cash book and credit our account because they now owe us more money; we are a payable.
- When our account is overdrawn, we owe the bank money and consequently our cash book will show a credit balance. For the bank an overdraft is a debit balance.

On the bank statement a credit is an amount of money paid into the account and a debit represents a payment. A bank statement conveys the transactions in the bank's point of view rather than the business' point of view.

Example

Given below are the completed cash books for Jupiter Limited from the previous example.

Cash receipts book

Date	*Narrative*	*Total* £	*VAT* £	*SLCA* £	*Other* £	*Discount* Allowed £	*VAT Adj* £
20X1							
2 July	Hill and French 40012	45.90		45.90			
3 July	Cash 40013	30.00			30.00		
4 July	Green and Holland 40014	245.89		245.89		3.68	0.73
		321.79	–	291.79	30.00	3.68	0.73

Cash payments book

Date	*Details*	*Cheque*	*Code no*	*Total* £	*VAT* £	*PLCA* £	*Other* £	*Discount received* £	*VAT Adj* £
20X1									
2 July	Salary error	100107		56.89			56.89		
3 July	Preston Bros	100108		96.65		96.65		1.65	0.33
5 July	Petty cash	100109		34.89			34.89		
				188.43	–	96.65	91.78	1.65	0.33

You have now received the bank statement for the week commencing 1 July 20X1 which is also shown below.

FIRST NATIONAL BANK
Cheque Account SHEET NUMBER 012
ACCOUNT NUMBER 38 41 57 33794363

			Paid in	*Paid out*	*Balance*
			£	£	£
28 June	Balance brought forward				560.61
1 July	CT	A/C 38562959	123.90		684.51
4 July	CHQ	100107		56.89 √	
4 July	CR	40013	30.00 √		657.62
5 July	CR	40012	45.90 √		
5 July	DR	Bank charges		5.23	
5 July	DD	English Telecom		94.00	
5 July	CHQ	100109		34.89 √	569.40

CHQ	Cheque	CT	Credit transfer	CR	Payment in
DR	Payment out	DD	Direct debit		

You are required to compare the cash book and the bank statement and determine any differences. Tick the items in the bank statement and in the cash book above, then prepare the bank reconciliation statement at 5 July 20X1.

The balance on the cash book at 28 June was £560.61.

Solution

Step 1 The cash book, duly ticked, appears below.

Cash receipts book

Date	*Narrative*	*Total*	*VAT*	*SLCA*	*Other*	*Discount* allowed	*VAT* Adj
		£	£	£	£	£	£
20X1							
2 July	Hill and French 40012	45.90	✓	45.90			
3 July	Cash 40013	30.00	✓		30.00		
4 July	Green and Holland 40014	245.89		245.89		3.68	0.73
		321.79	–	291.79	30.00	3.68	0.73

Cash payments book

Date	*Details*	*Cheque*	*Code no*	*Total* £	*VAT* £	*PLCA* £	*Other* £	*Discount received* £	*VAT Adj* £
20X1									
2 July	Salary error	100107		56.89 ✓			56.89		
3 July	Preston Bros	100108		96.65		96.65		1.65	0.33
5 July	Petty cash	100109		34.89 ✓			34.89		
				188.43	–	96.65	91.78	1.65	0.33

The bank statement should have been ticked as shown below.

FIRST NATIONAL BANK
Cheque Account
SHEET NUMBER 012
ACCOUNT NUMBER 38 41 57 33794363

			Paid in £	*Paid out* £	*Balance* £
28 June	Balance brought forward				560.61
1 July	CT	A/C 38562959	123.90		684.51
4 July	CHQ	100107		56.89 ✓	
4 July	CR	40013	30.00 ✓		657.62
5 July	CR	40012	45.90 ✓		
5 July	DR	Bank charges		5.23	
5 July	DD	English Telecom		94.00	
5 July	CHQ	100109		34.89 ✓	569.40

CHQ	Cheque	CT	Credit transfer	CR	Payment in
DR	Payment out	DD	Direct debit		

Step 2 A comparison of the items in the cash book with those in the bank statement reveals unticked items in both.

(a) We will first consider the items that are unticked on the bank statement;

- there is a credit transfer on 1 July of £123.90 – this must be checked to the related documentation and then entered into the cash receipts book;
- the bank charges of £5.23 must be entered into the cash payments book;
- the direct debit of £94.00 should be checked and then entered into the cash payments book.

(b) We will now consider the items that are unticked in the cash book. Remember that no adjustment is needed to these but we have to decide where they will appear in the bank reconciliation statement.

- the cheque paid in on 4 July has not yet appeared on the bank statement due to the time it takes for cheques to clear through the clearing system – an outstanding lodgement;
- cheque number 100108 has not yet cleared through the banking system – an unpresented cheque.

The cash receipts and cash payments book will now appear as follows after the adjustments in (a) above.

Cash receipts book

Date	*Narrative*	*Total* £	*VAT* £	*SLCA* £	*Other* £	*Discount* allowed £	*VAT* Adj £
20X1							
2 July	Hill and French	45.90	✓	45.90			
	40012						
3 July	Cash	30.00	✓		30.00		
	40013						
4 July	Green and Holland	245.89		245.89		3.68	0.73
	40014						
1 July	Credit transfer	123.90	✓	123.90			
		445.69	–	415.69	30.00	3.68	0.73

Cash payments book

Date	*Details*	*Cheque*	*Code no*	*Total* £	*VAT* £	*PLCA* £	*Other* £	*Discount received* £	*VAT Adj* £
20X1									
2 July	Salary error	100107		56.89	✓		56.89		
3 July	Preston Bros	100108		96.65		96.65		1.65	0.33
5 July	Petty cash	100109		34.89	✓		34.89		
5 July	Bank charges			5.23	✓		5.23		
5 July	English Telecom	DD		94.00	✓	94.00			
				287.66	–	190.65	97.01	1.65	0.33

Note that the items we have entered in the cash book from the bank statement are ticked in both. There are no unticked items on the bank statement (not shown) and two unticked items in the cash book.

Step 3 Find the amended cash book balance.

	£
Balance at 28 June	560.61
Cash receipts in first week of July	445.69
Cash payments in first week of July	(287.66)
Balance at 5 July	718.64

Step 4 Reconcile the amended cash book balance to the bank statement balance.

Bank reconciliation as at 5 July 20X1

	£
Balance per bank statement	569.40
Less: unpresented cheque	(96.65)
Add: outstanding lodgement	245.89
Balance per cash book	718.64

This is the completed bank reconciliation.

Activity 2

The following are summaries of the cash receipts book, cash payments book and bank statement for the first two weeks of trading of Gambank, a firm specialising in selling cricket bats.

Cash receipts book

Date	*Narrative*	*Total* £	*VAT* £	*SLCA* £	*Other* £
20X0					
01 Jan	Capital	2,000			2,000
05 Jan	A Hunter	1,000		1,000	
09 Jan	Cancel cheque no 0009	90			90
10 Jan	I M Dunn	4,800		4,800	

Cash payments book

Date	Details	Cheque no	Code	Total £	VAT £	PLCA £	Cash purchases £	Other £
20X0								
01 Jan	Wages	0001		50				50
01 Jan	Fine	0002		12				12
03 Jan	Dodgy Dealers	0003		1,500		1,500		
04 Jan	E L Pubo	0004		45		45		
05 Jan	Drawings	0005		200				200
07 Jan	E L Wino	0007		30		30		
08 Jan	Toby	0008		1,400		1,400		
09 Jan	El Pubo	0009		70		70		
10 Jan	Marion's Emp	0010		200		200		
11 Jan	Speeding Fine	0011		99				99

FINANCIAL BANK plc

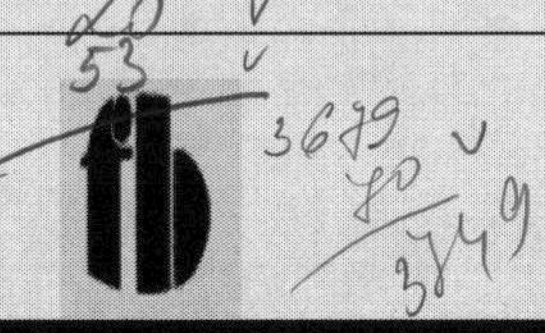

CONFIDENTIAL

YOU CAN BANK ON US

10 Yorkshire Street
Headingley
Leeds LS1 1QT
Telephone: 0113 633061

Account CURRENT GAMBANK

Sheet no. 1

Statement date 14 Jan 20X0 *Account Number* 40023986

Date	*Details*		*Withdrawals (£)*	*Deposits (£)*	*Balance (£)*
01 Jan	CR			2,000	2,000
02 Jan	0001		50		1,950
04 Jan	0003		1,500		450
05 Jan	0005		200		250
07 Jan	CR			1,000	
	0002		12		
	0004		45		
	0006		70		1,123
08 Jan	0007		30		1,093
10 Jan	0009		70		
	0009			70	
	0010		200		893
11 Jan	0012		20		
	Charges		53		820

SO	Standing order	DD	Direct debit	CR	Credit
AC	Automated cash	OD	Overdrawn	TR	Transfer

Prepare a bank reconciliation statement at 14 January 20X0.

2.5 Opening balances disagree

Usually the balances on the bank statement and in the cash book do not agree at the start of the period for the same reasons that they do not agree at the end, e.g. items in the cash book that were not on the bank statement. When producing the reconciliation statement it is important to take this opening difference into account.

Example

The bank statement and cash book of Jones for the month of December 20X8 start as follows.

Bank statement

		Debit	*Credit*	*Balance*
		£	£	£
1 Dec 20X8	Balance b/d (favourable)			8,570
2 Dec 20X8	0073	125		
2 Dec 20X8	0074	130		
3 Dec 20X8	Sundries		105	

Cash book

	£		£
1 Dec 20X8 b/d	8,420	Cheque 0075 Wages	200
Sales	320	Cheque 0076 Rent	500
	X		X
	X		X

Required:

Explain the difference between the opening balances.

Solution

The difference in the opening balance is as follows.

£8,570 – £8,420 = £150

This difference is due to the following.

	£
Cheque 0073	125
Cheque 0074	130
	255
Lodgement (sundries)	(105)
	150

These cheques and lodgements were in the cash book in November, but only appear on the bank statement in December. They will therefore be matched and ticked against the entries in the November cash book. The December reconciliation will then proceed as normal.

3 Returned cheques

A customer C may send a cheque in payment of an invoice without having sufficient funds in his account with Bank A.

The seller S who receives the cheque will pay it into his account with Bank B and it will go into the clearing system. Bank B will credit S's account with the funds in anticipation of the cheque being honoured.

Bank A however will not pay funds into the S's account with Bank B and Bank B will then remove the funds from S's account.

The net effect of this is that on S's bank statement, the cheque will appear as having been paid in (a credit on the bank statement),and then later will appear as having been paid out (a debit on the bank statement).

The original credit on the bank statement will be in S's cash book as a debit in the normal way. But the debit on the bank statement (the dishonour of the cheque) will not be in S's cash book. This will have to be credited in the cash book as money paid out.

These cheques are technically referred to as 'returned cheques', but they are also called 'dishonoured cheques' or 'bounced cheques'.

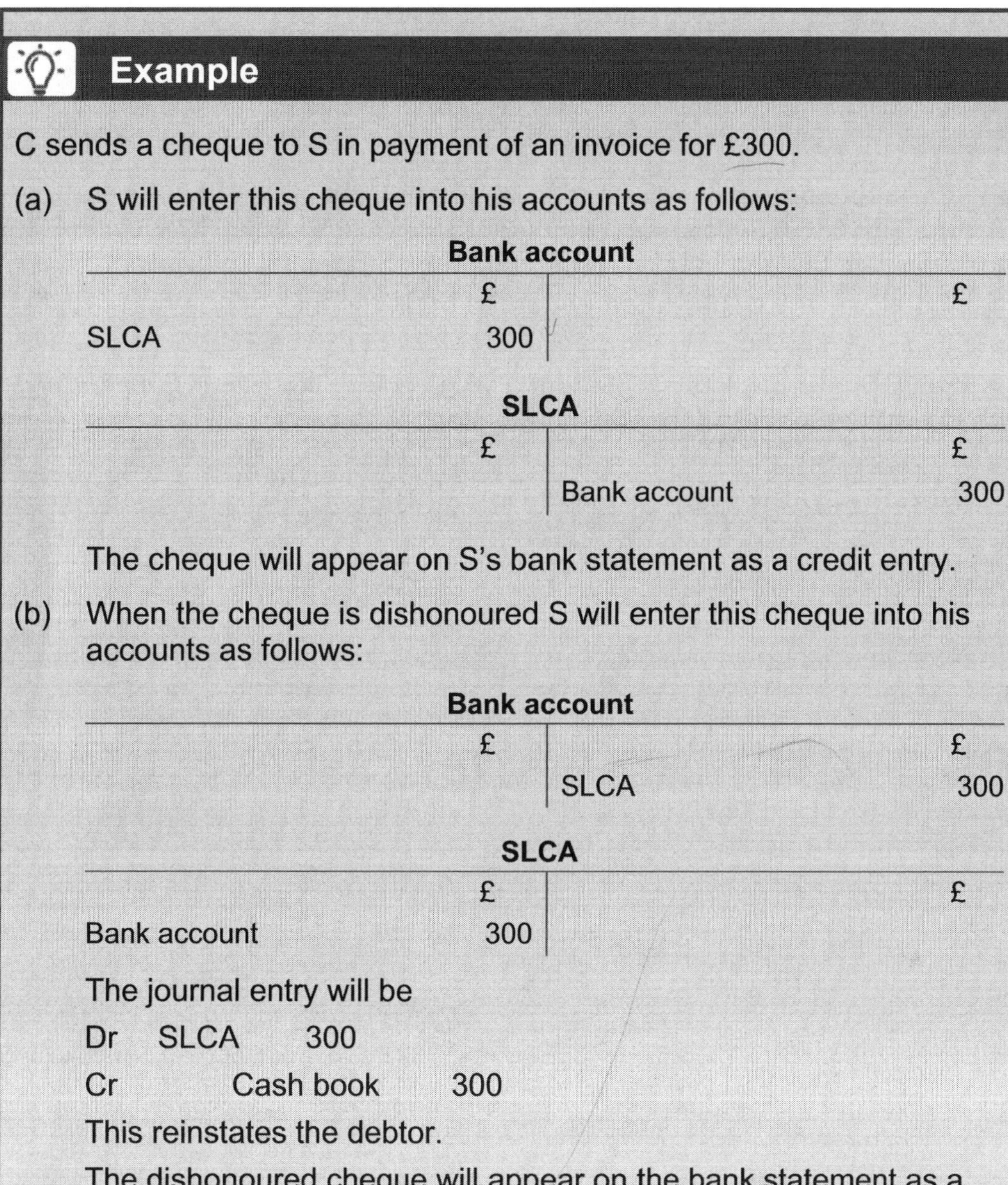

Example

C sends a cheque to S in payment of an invoice for £300.

(a) S will enter this cheque into his accounts as follows:

Bank account

	£		£
SLCA	300		

SLCA

	£		£
		Bank account	300

The cheque will appear on S's bank statement as a credit entry.

(b) When the cheque is dishonoured S will enter this cheque into his accounts as follows:

Bank account

	£		£
		SLCA	300

SLCA

	£		£
Bank account	300		

The journal entry will be

Dr SLCA 300

Cr Cash book 300

This reinstates the debtor.

The dishonoured cheque will appear on the bank statement as a debit entry.

4 Summary

In this chapter you have had to write up the cash receipts and cash payments books and then total and balance the cash book. However, most importantly for this unit a comparison has to be made between the cash book and the bank statement and a bank reconciliation prepared. Do note that when comparing the bank statement to the cash book, figures appearing on the bank statement may be from the cash book some time ago due to the nature of the clearing system.

Answers to chapter activities

Activity 1

	£
Opening balance	(673.42)
Payments	(6,419.37)
Receipts	6,488.20
Closing balance	(604.59)

The closing balance is £604.59 overdrawn.

Activity 2

Step 1 Tick the cash books and bank statement to indicate the matched items.

Cash receipts book

Date	*Narrative*	*Total* £	*VAT* £	*Sales ledger* £	*Other* £
20X0					
01 Jan	Capital	2,000 ✓			2,000
05 Jan	A Hunter	1,000 ✓		1,000	
09 Jan	Cancel cheque no 0009	90			90
10 Jan	I M Dunn	4,800		4,800	
		7,890	–	5,800	2,090

Cash payments book

Date	*Details*	*Cheque no*	*Code*	*Total* £	*VAT* £	*Purchases ledger* £	*Cash purchases* £	*Other* £
20X0								
01 Jan	Wages	0001		50	✓			50
01 Jan	Fine	0002		12	✓			12
03 Jan	Dodgy Dealers	0003		1,500	✓	1,500		
04 Jan	E L Pubo	0004		45	✓	45		
05 Jan	Drawings	0005		200	✓			200
07 Jan	E L Wino	0007		30	✓	30		
08 Jan	Toby	0008		1,400		1,400		
09 Jan	El Pubo	0009		70	✓	70		
10 Jan	Marion's Emp	0010		200	✓	200		
11 Jan	Speeding Fine	0011		99				99
				3,606	–	3,245	–	361

FINANCIAL BANK plc  CONFIDENTIAL

YOU CAN BANK ON US

10 Yorkshire Street
Headingley
Leeds LS1 1QT
Telephone: 0113 633061

Account CURRENT
GAMBANK

Sheet no. 1

Statement date 14 Jan 20X0 *Account Number* 40023986

Date	*Details*	*Withdrawals (£)*	*Deposits (£)*	*Balance (£)*
01 Jan	CR		2,000✓	2,000
02 Jan	0001	50✓		1,950
04 Jan	0003	1,500✓		450
05 Jan	0005	200✓		250
07 Jan	CR		1,000✓	
	0002	12✓		
	0004	45✓		
	0006	70		1,123
08 Jan	0007	30✓		1,093
10 Jan	0009	70✓		
	0009		70	
	0010	200✓		893
11 Jan	0012	20		
	Charges	53		820

SO	Standing order	DD	Direct debit	CR	Credit
AC	Automated cash	OD	Overdrawn	TR	Transfer

Step 2 Deal with each of the unticked items.

Cash receipts book – cheque number 0009 does appear to have been cancelled as it has appeared as a debit and a credit entry in the bank statement – however the bank statement shows that the cheque was for £70 and not the £90 entered into the cash receipts book – this must be amended in the cash book.

– the receipt from I M Dunn has not yet cleared through the banking system and is therefore not on the bank statement – it is an outstanding lodgement.

Cash payments book – cheque number 0008 to Toby and cheque number 0011 have not yet cleared through the clearing system – they are unpresented cheques.

Bank statement – cheque number 0006 has not been entered into the cash payments book but it has cleared the bank account – the cash book must be amended to show this payment.

– cheque number 0012 has not been entered into the cash payments book but it has cleared the bank account – the cash book must be amended to show this payment.

– the bank charges of £53 must be entered into the cash payments book.

Step 3 Amend the cash books and total them. Cash receipts book

Cash receipts book

Date	*Narrative*	*Total* £	*VAT* £	*Sales ledger* £	*Other* £	*Discount allowed* £
20X0						
01 Jan	Capital	2,000 ✓			2,000	
05 Jan	A Hunter	1,000 ✓		1,000		
09 Jan	Cancel cheque no 0009	90			90	
10 Jan	I M Dunn	4,800		4,800		
10 Jan	Cancelled cheque adjustment 0009	(20) ✓			(20)	
		7,870	–	5,800	2,070	–

Cash payments book

Date	*Details*	*Cheque no*	*Code*	*Total* £	*VAT* £	*PLCA* £	*Cash purchases* £	*Other* £	*Discount received* £
20X0									
01 Jan	Wages	0001		50	✓			50	
01 Jan	Fine	0002		12	✓			12	
03 Jan	Dodgy Dealers	0003		1,500	✓	1,500			
04 Jan	E L Pubo	0004		45	✓	45			
05 Jan	Drawings	0005		200	✓			200	
07 Jan	E L Wino	0007		30	✓	30			
08 Jan	Toby	0008		1,400		1,400			
09 Jan	El Pubo	0009		70	✓	70			
10 Jan	Marion's Emp	0010		200	✓	200			
11 Jan	Speeding Fine	0011		99				99	
6 Jan		0006		70	✓	70			
10 Jan		0012		20	✓	20			
11 Jan	Bank charges			53	✓			53	
				3,749	–	3,335	–	414	

Step 4 Determine the amended cash book balance

	£
Opening balance	–
Cash receipts	7,870
Cash payments	(3,749)
Amended cash book balance	4,121

Step 5 Reconcile the amended cash book balance to the bank statement balance

		£	£
Balance per bank statement			820
Add: outstanding lodgement			4,800
Less: unpresented cheques	0008	1,400	
	0011	99	
			(1,499)
Amended cash book balance			4,121

5 Test your knowledge

Workbook Activity 3

Given below are the cash receipts book, cash payments book and bank statement for a business for the week ending 11 March 20X1.

Required:

- Compare the bank statement to the cash book.
- Correct the cash receipts and payments books for any items which are unmatched on the bank statement.
- Total the cash receipts book and cash payments book and determine the final cash balance
- Using the reconciliation proforma reconcile the closing balance on the bank statement to the closing cash balance

Cash receipts book

Date	*Narrative*	*Bank*	*VAT*	*Debtors*	*Other*	*Discount allowed*	*VAT Adj*
20X1		£	£	£	£	£	£
7/3	Balance b/f	860.40					
7/3	Paying in slip 0062	1,117.85	84.05	583.52	450.28	23.60	4.72
8/3	Paying in slip 0063	1,056.40	68.84	643.34	344.22	30.01	6.00
9/3	Paying in slip 0064	1,297.81	81.37	809.59	406.85	34.20	6.84
10/3	Paying in slip 0065	994.92	57.02	652.76	285.14	18.03	3.60
11/3	Paying in slip 0066	1,135.34	59.24	779.88	296.22	23.12	4.62

Cash payments book

Date	*Details*	*Cheque no*	*Code*	*Bank* £	*VAT* £	*Creditors* £	*Cash purchases* £	*Discount received* £	*Other* £	*VAT Adj* £
20X1										
7/3	P Barn	012379	PL06	383.21		383.21				
	Purchases	012380	ML	274.04	45.67		228.37			
	R Trevor	012381	PL12	496.80		496.80		6.30		1.26
8/3	F Nunn	012382	PL07	218.32		218.32				
	F Taylor	012383	PL09	467.28		467.28		9.34		1.86
	C Cook	012384	PL10	301.40		301.40				
9/3	L White	012385	PL17	222.61		222.61				
	Purchases	012386	ML	275.13	45.85		229.28			
	T Finn	012387	PL02	148.60		148.60				
10/3	S Penn	012388	PL16	489.23		489.23		7.41		1.48
11/3	P Price	012389	PL20	299.99		299.99				
	Purchases	012390	ML	270.12	45.02		225.10			

Loan 200

4046.73

FINANCIAL BANK plc  CONFIDENTIAL

YOU CAN BANK ON US

10 Yorkshire Street
Headingley
Leeds LS1 1QT
Telephone: 0113 633061

Account CURRENT

Account name T R FABER LTD

Sheet no. 00614

Statement date 11 March 20X1 *Account Number* 27943316

Date	*Details*	*Withdrawals (£)*	*Deposits (£)*	*Balance (£)*
7/3	Balance from sheet 00613			860.40
	Bank giro credit L Fernley		406.90	1,267.30
9/3	Cheque 012380	274.04		
	Cheque 012381	496.80		
	Credit 0062		1,117.85	1,614.31
10/3	Cheque 012383	467.28		
	Cheque 012384	301.40		
	Credit 0063		1,056.40	
	SO – Loan Finance	200.00		1,702.03
11/3	Cheque 012379	383.21		
	Cheque 012386	275.13		
	Cheque 012387	148.60		
	Credit 0064		1,297.81	
	Bank interest		6.83	2,199.73

DD	Standing order	DD	Direct debit	CP	Card purchase
AC	Automated cash	OD	Overdrawn	TR	Transfer

BANK RECONCILIATION STATEMENT AS AT 11 MARCH 20X1

	£
Balance per bank statement	2199.73
Outstanding lodgements:	2130.26
Unpresented cheques:	(1500.27)
Balance per cash book	£2829.72

Workbook Activity 4

Given below is the cash book of a business and the bank statement for the week ending 20 April 20X1.

Required:

Compare the cash book to the bank statement and note any differences that you find.

Cash Book

		£			£
16/4	Donald & Co	225.47	16/4	Balance b/d	310.45
17/4	Harper Ltd	305.68	17/4	Cheque 03621	204.56
	Fisler Partners	104.67	18/4	Cheque 03622	150.46
18/4	Denver Ltd	279.57	19/4	Cheque 03623	100.80
19/4	Gerald Bros	310.45		Cheque 03624	158.67
20/4	Johnson & Co	97.68	20/4	Cheque 03625	224.67
			20/4	Balance c/d	173.91
		1,323.52			1,323.52

EXPRESS BANK CONFIDENTIAL

High Street
Fenbury
TL4 6JY
Telephone: 0169 422130

Account CURRENT Sheet no. 0213

Account name P L DERBY LTD

Statement date 20 April 20X1 *Account Number* 40429107

Date	*Details*	*Withdrawals (£)*	*Deposits (£)*	*Balance (£)*
16/4	Balance from sheet 0212			310.45 OD
17/4	DD – District Council	183.60		494.05 OD
18/4	Credit		225.47	
19/4	Credit		104.67	
	Cheque 03621	240.56		
	Bank interest	3.64		408.11 OD
20/4	Credit		305.68	
	Credit		279.57	
	Cheque 03622	150.46		
	Cheque 03624	158.67		131.99 OD

DD	Standing order	DD	Direct debit	CP	Card purchase
AC	Automated cash	OD	Overdrawn	TR	Transfer

Workbook Activity 5

Graham

The bank account of Graham showed a debit balance of £204 on 31 March 20X3. A comparison with the bank statements revealed the following:

			£
1	Cheques drawn but not presented		3,168
2	Amounts paid into the bank but not credited		723
3	Entries in the bank statements not recorded in the cash account		
	(i)	Standing orders	35
	(ii)	Interest on bank deposit account	18
	(iii)	Bank charges	14
4	Balance on the bank statement at 31 March		2,618

Required:

(a) Show the appropriate adjustments required in the bank account of Graham bringing down the correct balance at 31 March 20X3.

(b) Prepare a bank reconciliation statement at that date.

Workbook Activity 6

The following are the cash book and bank statements of KT Ltd.

Receipts June 20X1

CASH BOOK – JUNE 20X1

Date	*Details*	*Total*	*Sales ledger control*	*Other*
1 June	Balance b/d	7,100.45		
8 June	Cash and cheques	3,200.25✓	3,200.25	–
15 June	Cash and cheques	4,100.75 ✓	4,100.75	–
23 June	Cash and cheques	2,900.30 ✓	2,900.30	–
30 June	Cash and cheques	6,910.25	6,910.25	–
		£24,212.00	£17,111.55	

Payments June 20X1

Date	Payee	Cheque no	Total £	Purchase ledger control £	Operating overhead £	Admin overhead £	Other £
1 June	Hawsker Chemical	116	6,212.00	6,212.00			
7 June	Wales Supplies	117	3,100.00	3,100.00			
15 June	Wages and salaries	118	2,500.00		1,250.00	1,250.00	
16 June	Drawings	119	1,500.00				1,500.00
18 June	Blyth Chemical	120	5,150.00	5,150.00			
25 June	Whitby Cleaning Machines	121	538.00	538.00			
28 June	York Chemicals	122	212.00	212.00			
			19,212.00	15,212.00	1,250.00	1,250.00	1,500.00

Bank Statement

Crescent Bank plc
High Street
Sheffield

Statement no: 721
Page 1

Account: Alison Robb t/a KT Ltd
Account no: 57246661

Date	Details	Payments £	Receipts £	Balance £
20X1				
1 June	Balance b/fwd			8,456.45
1 June	113	115.00		8,341.45
1 June	114	591.00		7,750.45
1 June	115	650.00		7,100.45
4 June	116	6,212.00		888.45
8 June	CC		3,200.25	4,088.70
11 June	117	3,100.00		988.70
15 June	CC		4,100.75	5,089.45
15 June	118	2,500.00		2,589.45
16 June	119	1,500.00		1,089.45
23 June	120	5,150.00		4,060.55 O/D
23 June	CC		2,900.30	1,160.25 O/D

Key:

S/O	Standing Order	DD	Direct Debit
CC	Cash and cheques	CHGS	Charges
BACS	Bankers automated clearing	O/D	Overdrawn

Required:

Examine the business cash book and the business bank statement shown in the data provided above. Prepare a bank reconciliation statement as at 30 June 20X1. Set out your reconciliation in the proforma below.

Proforma

BANK RECONCILIATION STATEMENT AS AT 30 JUNE 20X1

	£
Balance per bank statement	
Outstanding lodgements:	
Unpresented cheques:	
Balance per cash book	£

Fixed Assets

7

Introduction

The ICB Level III syllabus covers all areas of accounting for fixed assets including acquisition, depreciation and disposal.

In this chapter we will start to look at the details of authorising and accounting for capital expenditure.

CONTENTS

1 Capital and revenue expenditure

1.1 Introduction

In the Balance Sheet, assets are split between fixed assets and current assets.

1.2 Fixed assets

Definition

The fixed assets of a business are the assets that were purchased with the intention of long term-use within the business.

Examples of fixed assets include buildings, machinery, motor vehicles, office fixtures and fittings and computer equipment.

1.3 Capital expenditure

Definition

Capital expenditure is expenditure on the purchase or improvement of fixed assets.

The purchase of fixed assets is known as capital expenditure. This means that the cost of the fixed asset is initially taken to the Balance Sheet rather than the Profit and Loss Account. We will see in a later chapter how this cost is then charged to the Profit and Loss Account over the life of the fixed asset by the process of depreciation.

1.4 Revenue expenditure

Definition

Revenue expenditure is all other expenditure incurred by the business other than capital expenditure.

When determining whether a purchase should be treated as capital or revenue expenditure it is important to consider how significant the cost is i.e. materiality. For example, an item of stationery such as a stapler may be used for a long time within a business but the cost is rather insignificant.

Revenue expenditure is charged as an expense to the Profit and Loss Account in the period that it is incurred.

Capital expenditure is shown as a fixed asset in the Balance Sheet.

1.5 Authorising capital expenditure

Many types of fixed asset are relatively expensive. Most fixed assets will be used to generate income for the business for several years into the future. Therefore they are important purchases. Timing may also be critical. It may be necessary to arrange a bank overdraft or a loan, or alternatively capital expenditure may have to be delayed in order to avoid a bank overdraft.

For these reasons, most organisations have procedures whereby capital expenditure must be authorised by a responsible person. In small organisations, most fixed asset purchases are likely to be authorised by the owner of the business. In large organisations, there is normally a system whereby several people have the authority to approve capital expenditure up to a certain limit which depends on the person's level of seniority.

The method of recording the authorisation is also likely to vary according to the nature and size of the organisation, and according to the type of fixed asset expenditure it normally undertakes. In a small business, there may be no formal record other than a signature on a cheque.

In a large company, the directors may record their approval of significant expenditure in the minutes of a board meeting. Other possibilities include the use of requisition forms and signing of the invoice.

In most organisations, disposals of fixed assets must also be authorised in writing.

Where standard forms are used, these will vary from organisation to organisation, but the details for acquisition of an asset are likely to include:

- date
- description of asset
- reason for purchase
- supplier
- cost/quotation

- details of quotation (if applicable)
- details of lease agreement (if applicable)
- authorisation (number of signatures required will vary according to the organisation's procedures)
- method of financing.

Activity 1

When authorising the purchase of a new machine, choose the most suitable policy.

New machinery purchases should be authorised by:

(a) The office assistant

(b) The accounting technician

(c) The machine operator

(d) A partner of the business

2 Recording the purchase of fixed assets

2.1 Introduction

We have seen that the cost of a fixed asset will appear in the Balance Sheet as capitalised expenditure. Therefore it is important that the correct figure for cost is included in the correct ledger account.

2.2 Cost

The cost figure that will be used to record the fixed asset is the full purchase price of the asset. Care should be taken when considering the cost of some assets, in particular motor cars, as the invoice may show that the total amount paid includes some revenue expenditure, for example petrol and road fund licences. These elements of revenue expenditure must be written off to the Profit and Loss Account and only the capital expenditure included as the cost of the fixed asset.

Definition

Cost should include the cost of the asset and the cost of getting the asset to its current location and into working condition. Therefore cost is:

Purchase price + additional costs

Additional costs may include delivery costs, legal and professional fees, installation costs (site preparation and construction) and test runs.

Activity 2

When a business purchases CDs for the new computer, the amount of the purchase is debited to computer equipment (cost) account.

(a) Is this treatment correct?

(b) If so, why; if not, why not?

2.3 Ledger accounts

If a fixed asset is paid for by cheque then the double entry is:

Dr Fixed asset account

Cr Bank account

If the fixed asset was bought on credit the double entry is:

Dr Fixed asset account

Cr PLCA/loan account

In practice most organisations will have different fixed asset accounts for the different types of fixed assets, for example:

- land and buildings account
- plant and machinery account
- motor vehicles account
- office fixtures and fittings account
- computer equipment account.

2.4 Purchase of fixed assets and VAT

When most fixed assets are purchased VAT will be added and this can normally be recovered from HMRC as input VAT. Therefore the cost of the fixed asset is the amount net of VAT.

Activity 3

A piece of machinery has been purchased on credit from a supplier for £4,200 plus VAT.

How will this purchase be recorded?

	Account name	*Amount* £
Dr	Machinery/Building/Fixtures	4,200/5,040
Dr	Machinery/VAT/PLCA	5,040/840
Cr	Bank /PLCA/VAT	4,200/5,040

Circle the correct account name and the amount.

2.5 Purchase of cars and VAT

When new cars are purchased the business is not allowed to reclaim the VAT. Therefore the cost to be capitalised for the car must include the VAT.

Example

Raymond has just purchased a new car for his business by cheque and an extract from the invoice shows the following:

	£
Cost of car	18,000
Road fund licence	155
	18,155
VAT on cost of car	3,600
Total cost	21,755

Record this cost in the ledger accounts of the business.

Motor cars account

	£		£
Bank (18,000 + 3,600)	21,600		

Motor expenses account

	£		£
Bank	155		

Bank account

	£		£
		Motor vehicle + expenses	21,755

Note that only the motor cars account balance would appear in the Balance Sheet, i.e. be capitalised, while the motor expenses account balance would appear in the Profit and Loss Account as an expense for the period.

2.6 Transfer journal

Fixed asset acquisitions do not normally take place frequently in organisations and many organisations will tend to record the acquisition in the transfer journal.

Definition

The transfer journal is a primary record which is used for transactions that do not appear in the other primary records of the business.

The transfer journal will tend to take the form of an instruction to the bookkeeper as to which accounts to debit and credit and what this transaction is for.

An example of a transfer journal for the purchase of a fixed asset is given below.

Journal entry			**No: 02714**
Date	**20 May 20X1**		
Prepared by	C Jones		
Authorised by	F Peters		
Account	**Code**	**Debit** £	**Credit** £
Computers: Cost	0120	5,000	
VAT	0138	1,000	
Bank	0163		6,000
Totals		6,000	6,000

A transfer journal is used for entries to the ledger accounts that do not come from any other primary records.

Activity 4

Below is an invoice for the purchase of a motor car purchased on the 1 June 20X1. The payment was made by cheque.

	£
Cost of car	20,000
Road fund licence	165
	20,165
VAT (20,000 × 20%)	4,000
	24,165

Note that in the assessment you may be given different forms to fill in for journal entries, and may be told to ignore any reference columns for the entry. Complete the journal entries to record the purchase of the asset.

Ref	**Account name**	**Dr (£)**	**Cr (£)**

2.7 Fixed assets produced internally

In some instances a business may make its own fixed assets. For example a construction business may construct a new head office for the organisation.

Where fixed assets are produced internally then the amount that should be capitalised as the cost is the production cost of the asset.

Definition

Production cost is the direct cost of production (materials, labour and expenses) plus an appropriate amount of the normal production overheads relating to production of this asset.

2.8 Capitalising subsequent expenditure

It is frequently the case that there will be further expenditure on a fixed asset during its life in the business. In most cases this will be classed as revenue expenditure and will therefore be charged to the Profit and Loss Account. However in some cases the expenditure may be so major that it should also be capitalised as an addition to the cost of the fixed asset.

Current accounting standards state that subsequent expenditure should only be capitalised in three circumstances:

- where it enhances the value of the asset
- where a major component of the asset is replaced or restored
- where it is a major inspection or overhaul of the asset.

2.9 Financing fixed asset acquisitions

Fixed assets generally cost a lot of money and are purchased with the intention that they be used over a period of years. For most businesses the full purchase cost cannot be funded from cash available in the business, and so other financing methods must be found, including the following:

Borrowing – a bank or other lender lends the business cash to pay for the asset, at a negotiated interest rate. Often the loan will be secured on the asset, so that it can be sold directly for the benefit of the bank or lender in the event of non-payment or liquidation.

Hire purchase – the business makes regular payments to the finance company (comprising capital amounts plus interest) but the asset remains the finance company's property until the last regular payment is made, when the business can elect to take over the asset's full ownership.

Leasing – the business makes regular payments to the finance company and makes full use of the asset. They may then make a final payment to the finance company so that they become the owner of the asset.

Part exchange – part of the purchase price of the asset is satisfied by transferring ownership of another asset to the seller. This is frequently seen in the case of motor vehicles, and represents a disposal of the old asset and a purchase of the new asset at the same time. (This will be covered in a later chapter.)

3 Types of fixed assets

3.1 Introduction

We have seen how the fixed assets of a business will be classified between the various types, e.g. buildings, plant and machinery, etc. However there is a further distinction in the classification of fixed assets that must be considered. This is the distinction between tangible fixed assets and intangible fixed assets.

3.2 Tangible fixed assets

Definition

Tangible fixed assets are assets which have a tangible, physical form.

Tangible fixed assets therefore are all of the types of assets that we have been considering so far such as machinery, cars, computers, etc.

3.3 Intangible fixed assets

Definition

Intangible fixed assets are assets for long-term use in the business that have no physical form e.g. patents, licences and goodwill.

3.4 Goodwill

Many businesses will have a particular intangible fixed asset known as goodwill. Goodwill is the asset arising from the fact that a going concern business is worth more in total than the value of its tangible net assets in total. The reasons for this additional asset are many and varied but include factors such as good reputation, good location, quality products and quality after sales service.

3.5 Accounting treatment of goodwill

Although it is recognised that goodwill exists in many businesses, it is generally not included as a fixed asset on the Balance Sheet. This is for a number of reasons including the difficulty in valuation of goodwill and also its innate volatility. Consider a restaurant with an excellent reputation which suddenly causes a bout of food poisoning. The asset, goodwill, could literally be wiped out overnight.

4 Fixed asset register

4.1 Introduction

The fixed assets of a business will tend to be expensive items that the organisation will wish to have good control over. In particular the organisation will wish to keep control over which assets are kept where and check on a regular basis that they are still there.

Therefore most organisations that own a significant number of fixed assets will tend to maintain a fixed asset register as well as the ledger accounts that record the purchase of the fixed assets. The fixed asset register forms a record from which control can be maintained through physical verifications and reconciliations with the ledger accounts.

4.2 Layout of a fixed asset register

The purpose of a fixed asset register is to record all relevant details of all of the fixed assets of the organisation. The format of the register will depend on the organisation, but the information to be recorded for each fixed asset of the business will probably include the following:

- asset description
- asset identification code/barcode
- asset location/member of staff the asset has been issued to
- date of purchase
- purchase price
- supplier name and address
- invoice number
- any additional enhancement expenditure
- depreciation method
- estimated useful life
- estimated residual value
- accumulated depreciation to date
- carrying value
- disposal details.

A typical format for a fixed asset register is shown below.

4.3 Example of a fixed asset register

Date of purchase	*Invoice number*	*Serial number*	*Item*	*Cost*	*Accum'd depreciation b/f at 1.1.X8*	*Date of disposal*	*Dep'n charge in 20X8*	*Accum'd depreciation c/f*	*Disposal proceeds*	*Loss/ gain on disposal*
				£	£		£	£	£	£
3.2.X5	345	3488	Chair	340						
6.4.X6	466	–	Bookcase	258						
10.7.X7	587	278	Chair	160						
				——						
				758						
				——						

There may also be a further column or detail which shows exactly where the particular asset is located within the business. This will facilitate checks that should be regularly carried out to ensure that all of the assets the business owns are still on the premises.

Activity 5

Record the cost of the motor car in the fixed asset register below for the previous Activity 4.

Date of purchase	*Invoice number*	*Serial number*	*Item*	*Cost*	*Accum'd depreciation b/f at 1.1.X8*	*Date of disposal*	*Depreciation charge in 20X8*	*Accum'd depreciation c/f*	*Disposal proceeds*	*Loss/gain on disposal*
				£	£		£	£	£	£
				——						
				——						

Activity 6

1 Purchase of a motor van is classified as **revenue / capital** expenditure?

2 Decorating the office is an example of **revenue / capital** expenditure

3 Other than its actual purchase price, what additional costs can be capitalised as part of the cost of the fixed asset?

4 What are the three occasions where subsequent expenditure on a fixed asset can be capitalised according to current accounting standards?

5 Goodwill is an example of **a tangible asset / a current asset / an intangible asset**?

5 Revaluation of fixed assets

5.1 Introduction

Businesses may decide to revalue certain fixed assets to reflect any increase in their market value. For the purposes of your studies, this will only apply to assets on which no depreciation is charged, such as land and buildings.

Any gain on revaluation is credited to the capital account

5.2 Accounting for a revaluation

When accounting for the revaluation of an asset, the following procedure should be adopted:

- Restate the asset to the revalued amount (rather than at cost)
- Credit the capital account with the amount of the revaluation.

Example

A building was purchased at a cost of £200,000 on 1 January 20X8. No depreciation is charged on this asset. At 31 December 20X8 the building was revalued at £247,000.

Show how this revaluation should be dealt with in the financial statements as at 31 December 20X8.

Solution

The revaluation gain is £47,000 (from a cost of £200,000 up to £247,000). This gain would not be reported in the Profit and Loss Account for the year, as it is not a realised gain. It would be taken to the capital account.

The revaluation is accounted for as follows:

	£	£
Dr Building	47,000	
Cr Capital account		47,000

Activity 7

At the end of its financial year, Tanner has the following fixed assets:

Land and buildings at cost	£10.4 million

The company has decided to revalue its land and buildings at the year end to £15 million.

What will be the amount of the adjustment on revaluation?

A £4.48m

B £4.6m

C £4.72m

D £15.12m

5.3 Reporting valuation gains and losses

Valuation gains are not recorded in the Profit and Loss account for the year but are credited to the capital account in the Balance Sheet. This is because the gain has not yet been realised as the asset has not yet been sold.

6 Summary

In this chapter we have considered the acquisition of fixed assets. The acquisition of a fixed asset must be properly authorised and the most appropriate method of funding used. The correct cost figure must be used when capitalising the fixed asset and care should be taken with VAT and the exclusion of any revenue expenditure in the total cost. The details of the acquisition of the asset should also be included in the fixed asset register. Finally, any revaluations of fixed assets must be dealt with in the appropriate way.

Answers to chapter activities

Activity 1

The answer is D

Activity 2

(a) No.

(b) Although, by definition, the CDs may be considered as fixed assets, their treatment would come within the remit of the concept of materiality and would probably be treated as office expenses – revenue expenditure.

Activity 3

	Account name	*Amount* £
Dr	Machinery	4,200
Dr	VAT	840
Cr	Purchase ledger control account	5,040

Activity 4

Ref	Account name	Dr (£)	Cr (£)
	Motor car	24,000	
	Motor expenses	165	
	Bank		24,165

Activity 5

Date of purchase	*Invoice number*	*Serial number*	*Item*	*Cost*	*Accum'd depreciation b/f at 1.1.X8*	*Date of disposal*	*Depreciation charge in 20X8*	*Accum'd depreciation c/f*	*Disposal proceeds*	*Loss/gain on disposal*
				£	£		£	£	£	£
1 Jun X1			Motor car	24,000						
				——						
				24,000						
				——						

Activity 6

1 Capital expenditure.

2 Revenue expenditure.

3 The full purchase price of the asset plus the cost of getting the asset to its location and into working condition.

4 Where the expenditure enhances the economic benefits of the asset.

Where the expenditure is on a major component which is being replaced or restored.

Where the expenditure is on a major inspection or overhaul of the asset.

5 Intangible asset.

Activity 7

Answer is B

	£m	
Fixed assets at cost	10.40	
Revaluation amount	15.00	
Gain to capital account	4.6	

The accounting entry is:

Dr Land	4.6	
Cr Capital account		4.6

7 Test your knowledge

Workbook Activity 8

Stapling machine

When a business purchases a new stapler so that accounts clerks can staple together relevant pieces of paper, the amount of the purchase is debited to the fittings and equipment (cost) account.

(a) Is this treatment correct?

(b) If so, why; if not; why not

Workbook Activity 9

Office equipment

A business bought a small item of computer software costing £32.50. This had been treated as office equipment. Do you agree with this treatment?

Give brief reasons.

Workbook Activity 10

Engine

If an airline replaces one of its plane's engines, which are depreciated at a different rate to the rest of the plane's components, at a cost of £1,800,000 would this represent capital or revenue expenditure? Give brief reasons.

Depreciation

Introduction

You need to be able to understand the purpose of depreciation on fixed assets, calculate the annual depreciation charge using one of two standard methods, account correctly for the annual depreciation charge and treat the depreciation accounts in the trial balance correctly in a set of final accounts.

All of this will be covered in this chapter.

CONTENTS

1 The purpose of depreciation

1.1 Introduction

Fixed assets are capitalised in the accounting records which means that they are treated as capital expenditure and their cost is initially recorded in the balance sheet and not charged to the profit and loss account. However this is not the end of the story and this cost figure must eventually go through the profit and loss account by means of the annual depreciation charge.

1.2 Accruals concept

The accruals concept states that the costs incurred in a period should be matched with the income produced in the same period. When a fixed asset is used it is contributing to the production of the income of the business. Therefore in accordance with the accruals concept some of the cost of the fixed asset should be charged to the profit and loss account each year that the asset is used.

1.3 What is depreciation?

Definition

Depreciation is the measure of the cost of the economic benefits of the tangible fixed assets that have been consumed during the period. Consumption includes the wearing out, using up or other reduction in the useful economic life of a tangible fixed asset whether arising from use, passage of time or obsolescence through either changes in technology or demand for the goods and services produced by the asset. (Taken from current UK Accounting Standards.)

This makes it quite clear that the purpose of depreciation is to charge the profit and loss account with the amount of the cost of the fixed asset that has been used up during the accounting period.

1.4 How does depreciation work?

The basic principle of depreciation is that a proportion of the cost of the fixed asset is charged to the profit and loss account each period and deducted from the cost of the fixed asset in the balance sheet. Therefore as the fixed asset gets older its value in the balance sheet reduces and each year the profit and loss account is charged with this proportion of the initial cost.

Definition

Net book value is the cost of the fixed asset less the accumulated depreciation to date.

	£
Cost	X
Less: Accumulated depreciation	(X)
Net book value (NBV)	X

The aim of depreciation of fixed assets is to show the cost of the asset that has been consumed during the year. It is not to show the true or market value of the asset. So this net book value will probably have little relation to the actual market value of the asset at each balance sheet date. The important aspect of depreciation is that it is a charge to the profit and loss account of the amount of the fixed asset consumed during the year.

2 Calculating depreciation

2.1 Introduction

The calculation of depreciation can be done by a variety of methods (see later in the chapter) but the principles behind each method remain the same.

2.2 Factors affecting depreciation

There are three factors that affect the depreciation of a fixed asset:

- the cost of the asset
- the length of the useful economic life of the asset
- the estimated residual value of the asset.

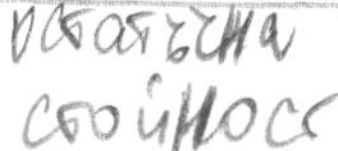

2.3 Useful economic life

Definition

The useful economic life of an asset is the estimated life of the asset for the current owner.

This is the estimated number of years that the business will be using this asset and therefore the number of years over which the cost of the asset must be spread via the depreciation charge.

One particular point to note here is that land is viewed as having an infinite life and therefore no depreciation charge is required for land. However, any buildings on the land should be depreciated.

2.4 Estimated residual value

Many assets will be sold for a form of scrap value at the end of their useful economic lives.

Definition

The estimated residual value of a fixed asset is the amount that it is estimated the asset will be sold for when it is no longer of use to the business.

The aim of depreciation is to write off the cost of the fixed asset less the estimated residual value over the useful economic life of the asset.

2.5 The straight line method of depreciation

Definition

The straight line method of depreciation is a method of charging depreciation so that the profit and loss account is charged with the same amount of depreciation each year.

The method of calculating depreciation under this method is:

$$\text{Annual depreciation charge} = \frac{\text{Cost} - \text{estimated residual value}}{\text{Useful economic life}}$$

Example

An asset has been purchased by an organisation for £400,000 and is expected to be used in the organisation for 6 years. At the end of the six -year period it is currently estimated that the asset will be sold for £40,000.

What is the annual depreciation charge on the straight line basis?

Solution

Annual depreciation charge $= \dfrac{400{,}000 - 40{,}000}{6}$

$= £60{,}000$

Activity 1

The following task is about recording fixed asset information in the general ledger.

A new asset has been acquired. VAT can be reclaimed on this asset.

- The cost of the asset excluding VAT is £85,000 and this was paid for by cheque.
- The residual value is expected to be £5,000 excluding VAT
- The asset is to be depreciated using the straight line basis and the assets useful economic life is 5 years.

Make entries to account for:

(a) The purchase of the new asset

(b) The depreciation on the new asset

Asset at cost account

	£		£

Accumulated depreciation

	£		£

Depreciation charge

	£		£

2.6 The reducing balance method

Definition

The reducing balance method of depreciation allows a higher amount of depreciation to be charged in the early years of an asset's life compared to the later years.

The depreciation is calculated using this method by multiplying the net book value of the asset at the start of the year by a fixed percentage.

Example

A fixed asset has a cost of £100,000.

It is to be depreciated using the reducing balance method at 30% over its useful economic life of four years, after which it will have an estimated residual value of approximately £24,000.

Show the amount of depreciation charged for each of the four years of the asset's life.

Solution

	£
Cost	100,000
Year 1 depreciation 30% × 100,000	(30,000)
Net book value at the end of year 1	70,000
Year 2 depreciation 30% × 70,000	(21,000)
Net book value at the end of year 2	49,000
Year 3 depreciation 30% × 49,000	(14,700)
Net book value at the end of year 3	34,300
Year 4 depreciation 30% × 34,300	(10,290)
Net book value at the end of year 4	24,010

Activity 2

A business buys a motor van for £20,000 and depreciates it at 10% per annum by the reducing balance method.

Calculate:

- The depreciation charge for the second year of the motor van's use.
- Calculate the net book value at the end of the second year.

Solution

	£
Cost	20000
Year 1 depreciation	(2000)
Net book value at the end of year 1	18000
Year 2 depreciation	(1800)
Net book value at the end of year 2	16200

2.7 Choice of method

Whether a business chooses the straight line method of depreciation or the reducing balance method (or indeed any of the other methods which are outside the scope of this syllabus) is the choice of management.

The straight line method is the simplest method to use. Often, however, the reducing balance method is chosen for assets which reduce in value more in the early years of their life than the later years. This is often the case with cars and computers and the reducing balance method is often used for these assets.

Once the method of depreciation has been chosen for a particular class of fixed assets then this same method should be used each year in order to satisfy the accounting objective of comparability. The management of a business can change the method of depreciation used for a class of fixed assets but this should only be done if the new method shows a truer picture of the consumption of the cost of the asset than the previous method.

Activity 3

Give one reason why a business might choose reducing balance as the method for depreciating its delivery vans?

(a) It is an easy method to apply.

(b) It is the method applied for fixed assets that lose more value in their early years.

(c) It is the method that is most consistent.

3 Accounting for depreciation

3.1 Introduction

Now we have seen how to calculate depreciation we must next learn how to account for it in the ledger accounts of the business.

3.2 Dual effect of depreciation

The two effects of the charge for depreciation each year are:

- there is an expense to the profit and loss account and therefore a debit entry to a depreciation expense account;

- therefore we create a provision for accumulated depreciation account and there is a credit entry to this account. Accumulated depreciation may also be referred to as 'provision for depreciation'.

Definition

The provision for accumulated depreciation account is used to reduce the value of the fixed asset in the balance sheet.

Example

An asset has been purchased by an organisation for £400,000 and is expected to be used in the organisation for six years.

At the end of the six year period it is currently estimated that the residual value will be £40,000.

The asset is to be depreciated on the straight line basis.

Show the entries in the ledger accounts for the first two years of the asset's life and how this asset would appear in the balance sheet at the end of each of the first two years.

Solution

Step 1

Record the purchase of the asset in the fixed asset account.

Fixed asset account

	£		£
Year 1 Bank	400,000		

Step 2

Record the depreciation expense for Year 1.

$$\text{Depreciation charge} = \frac{£400,000 - £40,000}{6}$$

$$= £60,000 \text{ per year}$$

DR Depreciation expense account

CR Accumulated depreciation account

Depreciation expense account

	£		£
Year 1	60,000		
Accumulated depreciation			

Accumulated depreciation account

	£		£
		Expense account	60,000

Note the balance sheet will show the cost of the asset and the accumulated depreciation is then deducted to arrive at the net book value of the asset.

Step 3

Show the entries for the year 2 depreciation charge

Depreciation expense account

	£		£
Year 2	60,000		
Accumulated depreciation			

Accumulated depreciation account

	£		£
		Balance b/d	60,000
		Expense account	60,000

Note that the expense account has no opening balance as this was cleared to the profit and loss account at the end of year 1.

However the accumulated depreciation account being a balance sheet account is a continuing account and does have an opening balance being the depreciation charged so far on this asset.

Step 4

Balance off the accumulated depreciation account and show how the fixed asset would appear in the balance sheet at the end of year 2.

Accumulated depreciation account

	£		£
		Balance b/d	60,000
Balance c/d	120,000	Expense account	60,000
	120,000		120,000
		Balance b/d	120,000

Balance Sheet extract

	Cost	Accumulated depreciation	Net book value
	£	£	£
Fixed asset	400,000	120,000	280,000

Activity 4

At 31 March 20X3, a business owned a motor vehicle which had a cost of £12,100 and accumulated depreciation of £9,075.

Complete the balance sheet extract below.

	Cost	Accumulated depreciation	NBV
Motor Vehicle	12100	9075	3025

3.3 Net book value

As you have seen from the balance sheet extract the fixed assets are shown at their net book value. The net book value is made up of the cost of the asset less the accumulated depreciation on that asset or class of assets.

The net book value is purely an accounting value for the fixed asset. It is not an attempt to place a market value or current value on the asset and it in fact often bears little relation to the actual value of the asset.

3.4 Ledger entries with reducing balance depreciation

No matter what method of depreciation is used the ledger entries are always the same. So here is another example to work through.

Example

On 1 April 20X2 a machine was purchased for £12,000 with an estimated useful life of 4 years and estimated scrap value of £4,920. The machine is to be depreciated at 20% reducing balance.

The ledger accounts for the years ended 31 March 20X3, 31 March 20X4 and 31 March 20X5 are to be written up.

Show how the fixed asset would appear in the balance sheet at each of these dates.

Solution

Step 1

Calculate the depreciation charge.

			£
Cost			12,000
Year-end March 20X3 – depreciation	12,000 × 20%	=	2,400
			9,600
Year-end March 20X4 – depreciation	9,600 × 20%	=	1,920
			7,680
Year-end March 20X5 – depreciation	7,680 × 20%	=	1,536
			6,144

Step 2

Enter each year's figures in the ledger accounts bringing down a balance on the machinery account and accumulated depreciation account but clearing out the entry in the expense account to the profit and loss account.

Machinery account

	£		£
April 20X2 Bank	12,000	Mar 20X3 Balance c/d	12,000
April 20X3 Balance b/d	12,000	Mar 20X4 Balance c/d	12,000
April 20X5 Balance b/d	12,000	Mar 20X5 Balance c/d	12,000
April 20X5 Balance b/d	12,000		

Depreciation expense account

	£		£
Mar 20X3 Accumulated dep'n a/c	2,400	Mar 20X3 P&L a/c	2,400
Mar 20X4 Accumulated dep'n a/c	1,920	Mar 20X4 P&L a/c	1,920
Mar 20X5 Accumulated dep'n a/c	1,536	Mar 20X5 P&L a/c	1,536

Machinery: Accumulated depreciation account

		£			£
Mar 20X3	Balance c/d	2,400	Mar 20X3	Depreciation expense	2,400
			Apr 20X3	Balance b/d	2,400
Mar 20X4	Balance c/d	4,320	Mar 20X4	Depreciation expense	1,920
		4,320			4,320
			Apr 20X4	Balance b/d	4,320
Mar 20X5	Balance c/d	5,856	Mar 20X5	Depreciation expense	1,536
		5,856			5,856
			Apr 20X5	Balance b/d	5,856

Balance Sheet extract

Fixed assets		Cost	Accumulated depreciation	Net book value
		£	£	£
At 31 Mar 20X3	Machinery	12,000	2,400	9,600
At 31 Mar 20X4	Machinery	12,000	4,320	7,680
At 31 Mar 20X5	Machinery	12,000	5,856	6,144

Make sure that you remember to carry down the accumulated depreciation at the end of each period as the opening balance at the start of the next period.

Activity 5

ABC Co owns the following assets as at 31 December 20X6:

	£
Plant and machinery	5,000
Office furniture	800

Depreciation is to be provided as follows:

(a) plant and machinery, 20% reducing-balance method;

(b) office furniture, 25% on cost per year, straight-line method.

The plant and machinery was purchased on 1 January 20X4 and the office furniture on 1 January 20X5.

Required:

Show the ledger accounts for the year ended 31 December 20X6 necessary to record the transactions.

4 Assets acquired during an accounting period

4.1 Introduction

So far in our calculations of the depreciation charge for the year we have ignored precisely when in the year the fixed asset was purchased. This can sometimes be relevant to the calculations depending upon the policy that you are given for calculating depreciation. There are two main methods of expressing the depreciation policy and both of these will now be considered.

4.2 Calculations on a monthly basis

The policy may state that depreciation is to be charged on a monthly basis. This means that the annual charge will be calculated using the depreciation method given and then pro-rated for the number of months in the year that the asset has been owned.

Example

A piece of machinery is purchased on 1 June 20X1 for £20,000. It has a useful life of 5 years and zero scrap value. The organisation's accounting year ends on 31 December.

What is the depreciation charge for 20X1? Depreciation is charged on a monthly basis using the straight line method.

Solution

Annual charge $= \frac{£20,000}{5} = £4,000$

Charge for 20X1: £4,000 × 7/12 (i.e. June to Dec) = £2,333

Activity 6

A business buys a machine for £40,000 on 1 January 20X3 and another one on 1 July 20X3 for £48,000.

Depreciation is charged at 10% per annum on cost, and calculated on a monthly basis.

What is the total depreciation charge for the two machines for the year ended 31 December 20X3?

4.3 Acquisition and disposal policy

The second method of dealing with depreciation in the year of acquisition is to have a depreciation policy as follows:

'A full year's depreciation is charged in the year of acquisition and none in the year of disposal.'

Ensure that you read the instructions in any question carefully as in the assessment you will always be given the depreciation policy of the business.

Activity 7

A business purchased a motor van on 7 August 20X3 at a cost of £12,640.

It is depreciated on a straight-line basis using an expected useful economic life of five years and estimated residual value of zero.

Depreciation is charged with a full year's depreciation in the year of purchase and none in the year of sale.

The business has a year end of 30 November.

What is the net book value of the motor van at 30 November 20X4?

What does this amount represent?

4.4 Working backwards to calculate the cost of an asset

It may be the case in the assessment that you are given the NBV of an asset after a number of years and the rate of depreciation from which you will need to calculate its original cost.

Example

Noble owns a commercial vehicle.

Its estimated residual value at the date of purchase was £5,000.

It is being depreciated over 5 years on a straight-line basis.

Its net book value after 3 years is £13,000.

What was the vehicle's original cost?

Solution

The NBV of £13,000 is made up as follows:

	£
(Cost less residual value) x 40%	8,000
Residual value	5,000

Depreciation of 20% per year for three years has been deducted from the cost to arrive at the NBV.

Therefore £8,000 x 100/40 = £20,000 is the amount that was subject to the depreciation charge.

The cost of the vehicle is therefore £20,000 add the residual value of £5,000 = £25,000

5 Summary

This chapter considered the manner in which the cost of fixed assets is charged to the profit and loss account over the life of the fixed assets, known as depreciation.

Whatever the method of depreciation, the ledger entries are the same. The profit and loss account is charged with the depreciation expense and the accumulated depreciation account shows the accumulated depreciation over the life of the asset to date.

The accumulated balance is netted off against the cost of the fixed asset in the balance sheet in order to show the fixed asset at its net book value.

Answers to chapter activities

Activity 1

Annual depreciation charge $= \dfrac{85,000 - 5,000}{5}$

$= £16,000$

Asset at cost account

	£		£
Bank	85,000	Balance c/d	85,000
	85,000		**85,000**

Accumulated depreciation

	£		£
Balance c/d	16,000	Depreciation charge	16,000
	16,000		**16,000**

Depreciation charge

	£		£
Accumulated depreciation	16,000	Profit and loss account	16,000
	16,000		**16,000**

Activity 2

	£
Cost	20,000
Year 1 depreciation	(2,000)
Net book value at the end of year 1	18,000
Year 2 depreciation	(1,800)
Net book value at the end of year 2	16,200

Activity 3

The answer is B.

The reducing balance method is used to equalise the combined costs of depreciation and maintenance over the vehicle's life (i.e. in early years, depreciation is high, maintenance low; in later years, depreciation is low, maintenance is high).

The reducing balance method is also used for fixed assets that are likely to lose more value in their early years than their later years such as cars or vans.

Activity 4

Balance sheet extract below.

	Cost	Accumulated depreciation	NBV
Motor Vehicle	12,100	9,075	3,025

Activity 5

Plant and machinery account

Date		£	Date		£
1.1.X6	Balance b/d	5,000	31.12.X6	Balance c/d	5,000
		——			——
1.1.X7	Balance b/d	5,000			

Office furniture account

Date		£	Date		£
1.1.X6	Balance b/d	800	31.12.X6	Balance c/d	800
		——			——
1.1.X7	Balance b/d	800			

Depreciation expense account

Date		£	Date		£
31.12.X6	Accumulated dep'n a/c – plant and machinery	640	31.12.X6	Trading and profit and loss account	840
31.12.X6	Accumulated dep'n a/c – office furniture	200			
		——			——
		840			840
		——			——

Accumulated depreciation account – Plant and machinery

Date		£	Date		£
31.12.X6	Balance c/d	2,440	1.1.X6	Balance b/d	1,800
			31.12.X6	Dep'n expense	640
		——			——
		2,440			2,440
		——			——
			1.1.X7	Balance b/d	2,440

Accumulated depreciation account – Office furniture

Date		£	*Date*		£
31.12.X6	Balance c/d	400	1.1.X6	Balance b/d	200
			31.12.X6	Dep'n expense	200
		400			400
			1.1.X7	Balance b/d	400

The opening balance on the accumulated depreciation account is calculated as follows:

		Plant and machinery	*Office furniture*
		£	£
20X4	20% × £5,000	1,000	–
20X5	20% × £(5,000 – 1,000)	800	
	25% × £800		200
Opening balance 1.1.X6		1,800	200

The depreciation charge for the year 20X6 is calculated as follows:

	Plant and machinery	*Office furniture*	*Total*
	£	£	£
20% × (5,000 – 1,800)	640		
25% × £800		200	840

Activity 6

		£
Machine 1	£40,000 × 10%	4,000
Machine 2	£48,000 × 10% × 6/12	2,400
		6,400

Activity 7

Annual depreciation $= \frac{£12{,}640}{5} = £2{,}528$

NBV = £12,640 – (2 × £2,528) = £7,584

This is the cost of the van less the accumulated depreciation to date. It is the amount remaining to be depreciated in the future. It is not a market value.

6 Test your knowledge

Workbook Activity 8

Mead is a sole trader with a 31 December year end. He purchased a car on 1 January 20X3 at a cost of £12,000. He estimates that its useful life is four years, after which he will trade it in for £2,400. The annual depreciation charge is to be calculated using the straight line method.

Required:

Write up the motor car cost and accumulated depreciation accounts and the depreciation expense account for the first three years, bringing down a balance on each account at the end of each year.

Workbook Activity 9

S Telford purchases a machine for £6,000. He estimates that the machine will last eight years and its scrap value then will be £1,000.

Required:

(1) Prepare the machine cost and accumulated depreciation accounts for the first three years of the machine's life, and show the balance sheet extract at the end of each of these years charging depreciation on the straight line method.

(2) What would be the net book value of the machine at the end of the third year if depreciation was charged at 20% on the reducing balance method?

Workbook Activity 10

Hillton

(a) Hillton started a veggie food manufacturing business on 1 January 20X6. During the first three years of trading he bought machinery as follows:

January	20X6	Chopper	Cost	£4,000
April	20X7	Mincer	Cost	£6,000
June	20X8	Stuffer	Cost	£8,000

Each machine was bought for cash.

Hillton's policy for machinery is to charge depreciation on the straight line basis at 25% per annum. A full year's depreciation is charged in the year of purchase, irrespective of the actual date of purchase.

Required:

For the three years from 1 January 20X6 to 31 December 20X8 prepare the following ledger accounts:

(i) Machinery account

(ii) Accumulated depreciation account (machinery)

(iii) Depreciation expense account (machinery)

Bring down the balance on each account at 31 December each year.

Tip: *Use a table to calculate the depreciation charge for each year.*

(b) Over the same three year period Hillton bought the following motor vehicles for his business:

January 20X6	Metro van	Cost £3,200
July 20X7	Transit van	Cost £6,000
October 20X8	Astra van	Cost £4,200

Each vehicle was bought for cash.

Hillton's policy for motor vehicles is to charge depreciation on the reducing balance basis at 40% per annum. A full year's depreciation is charged in the year of purchase, irrespective of the actual date of purchase.

Required:

For the three years from 1 January 20X6 to 31 December 20X8 prepare the following ledger accounts:

(i) Motor vehicles account

(ii) Accumulated depreciation account (motor vehicles)

(iii) Depreciation expense account (motor vehicles)

Bring down the balance on each account at 31 December each year.

Tip: Use another depreciation table.

Workbook Activity 11

On 1 December 20X2 Infortec Computers owned motor vehicles costing £28,400. During the year ended 30 November 20X3 the following changes to the motor vehicles took place:

		£
1 March 20X3	Sold vehicle – original cost	18,000
1 June 20X3	Purchased new vehicle – cost	10,000
1 September 20X3	Purchased new vehicle – cost	12,000

Depreciation on motor vehicles is calculated on a monthly basis at 20% per annum on cost.

Complete the table below to calculate the total depreciation charge to profits for the year ended 30 November 20X3.

	£
Depreciation for vehicle sold 1 March 20X3	
Depreciation for vehicle purchased 1 June 20X3	
Depreciation for vehicle purchased 1 September 20X3	
Depreciation for other vehicles owned during the year	
Total depreciation for the year ended 30 November 20X3	

Disposal of fixed assets

Introduction

When a fixed asset is disposed of there are a variety of accounting calculations and entries that need to be made.

Firstly, the asset being disposed of must be removed from the accounting records as it is no longer controlled. In most cases the asset will be disposed of for either more or less than its carrying value leading to a profit or a loss on disposal which must be accounted for.

Finally, the fact that the asset has been disposed of must be recorded in the fixed asset register.

For your assessment you will be required to know how to put through the accounting entries for the disposal of a capital asset (i.e. a fixed asset) and to record the disposal in the fixed asset register.

This is a favourite area in assessments and must be fully understood. In particular the method of acquiring a new fixed asset, with an old asset as a part-exchange, is a trickier topic, which will be covered in detail in this chapter.

Finally in this chapter we must consider the purpose of the fixed asset register and how it can be used to regularly check that all of the fixed assets owned by the business are in place.

CONTENTS

1 Accounting for the disposal of capital assets

1.1 Introduction

When a capital or fixed asset is sold then there are two main aspects to the accounting for this disposal:

Firstly the existing entries in the ledger accounts for the asset being disposed of must be removed as the asset is no longer controlled.

Secondly there is likely to be a profit or loss on disposal and this must be calculated and accounted for.

1.2 Removal of existing ledger account balances

When an asset is sold, the balances in the ledger accounts that relate to that asset must be removed. There are two such balances:

(a) the original cost of the asset in the fixed asset cost account

(b) the depreciation to date on the asset in the accumulated depreciation account.

In order to remove these two balances we must do the following:

Step 1

Open a disposal account.

Step 2

Transfer the two amounts to the disposal account.

Step 3

Enter any proceeds from the sale of the asset in the disposal account.

 **Definition**

The disposal account is the account which is used to make all of the entries relating to the sale of the asset and also determines the profit or loss on disposal.

1.3 Profit or loss on disposal

The value that the fixed asset is recorded at in the books of the organisation is the carrying value, i.e. cost less accumulated depreciation. However this is unlikely to be exactly equal to the amount for which the asset is actually sold. The difference between these two is the profit or loss on disposal.

	£
Cost of asset	X
Less: accumulated depreciation	(X)
Carrying value	X
Disposal proceeds	(X)
(Profit)/loss on disposal	X

If the disposal proceeds are greater than the carrying value a profit has been made, if the proceeds are less than the carrying value a loss has been made.

Example

A fixed asset cost £14,000

The accumulated depreciation on this asset is £9,600.

This asset has just been sold for £3,800.

(a) What is the profit or loss on disposal? 600 loss

(b) Write up the relevant ledger accounts to record this disposal.

Solution

(a)

	£
Cost	14,000
Accumulated depreciation	(9,600)
Carrying value	4,400
Proceeds	(3,800)
Loss on disposal	600

(b) Step 1

Determine the cost and accumulated depreciation ledger account balances for this asset.

Fixed asset cost

	£		£
Balance b/d	14,000		

Accumulated depreciation

	£		£
		Balance b/d	9,600

Step 2

Open the disposal account and transfer balances on the above two accounts.

Cost

Debit	Disposal account	£14,000
Credit	Fixed asset cost account	£14,000

Accumulated depreciation

Debit	Accumulated depreciation	£9,600
Credit	Disposal account	£9,600

Fixed asset cost

	£		£
Balance b/d	14,000	Disposal	14,000
	14,000		14,000

Accumulated depreciation

	£		£
Disposal	9,600	Balance b/d	9,600
	9,600		9,600

Disposal

	£		£
Cost	14,000	Accumulated dep'n	9,600

Step 3

Enter the proceeds in the disposal account and balance the disposal account with the profit/loss on disposal.

Disposal

	£		£
Cost	14,000	Accumulated dep'n	9,600
		Cash	3,800
		Loss – P &L A/C	600
	14,000		14,000

Note 1: The loss of £600 is credited to the disposal account to balance the account. The corresponding debit is in the Profit and Loss Account and represents the loss on the disposal.

Note 2: The profit or loss on disposal can actually be calculated as the balancing figure in the disposal account:

- if there is a debit entry to balance the account then this is a profit on disposal which is credited to the Profit and Loss Account as income
- if there is a credit entry to balance the account then this is a loss on disposal which is debited to the Profit and Loss Account as an additional expense.

Activity 1

A business buys a car for £20,000 and expects it to have a useful life of five years.

It depreciates the car at 50% reducing balance and sells it after three years for £10,000.

Record the ledger entries for the three years.

Clearly show the profit or loss on disposal.

Car account

	£		£

Accumulated depreciation

	£		£

Disposal account

	£		£

1.4 Journal entries

We have already seen that journal entries are an instruction to the bookkeeper to put through double entry in the ledger accounts where the transaction is not necessarily recorded in any of the books of prime entry.

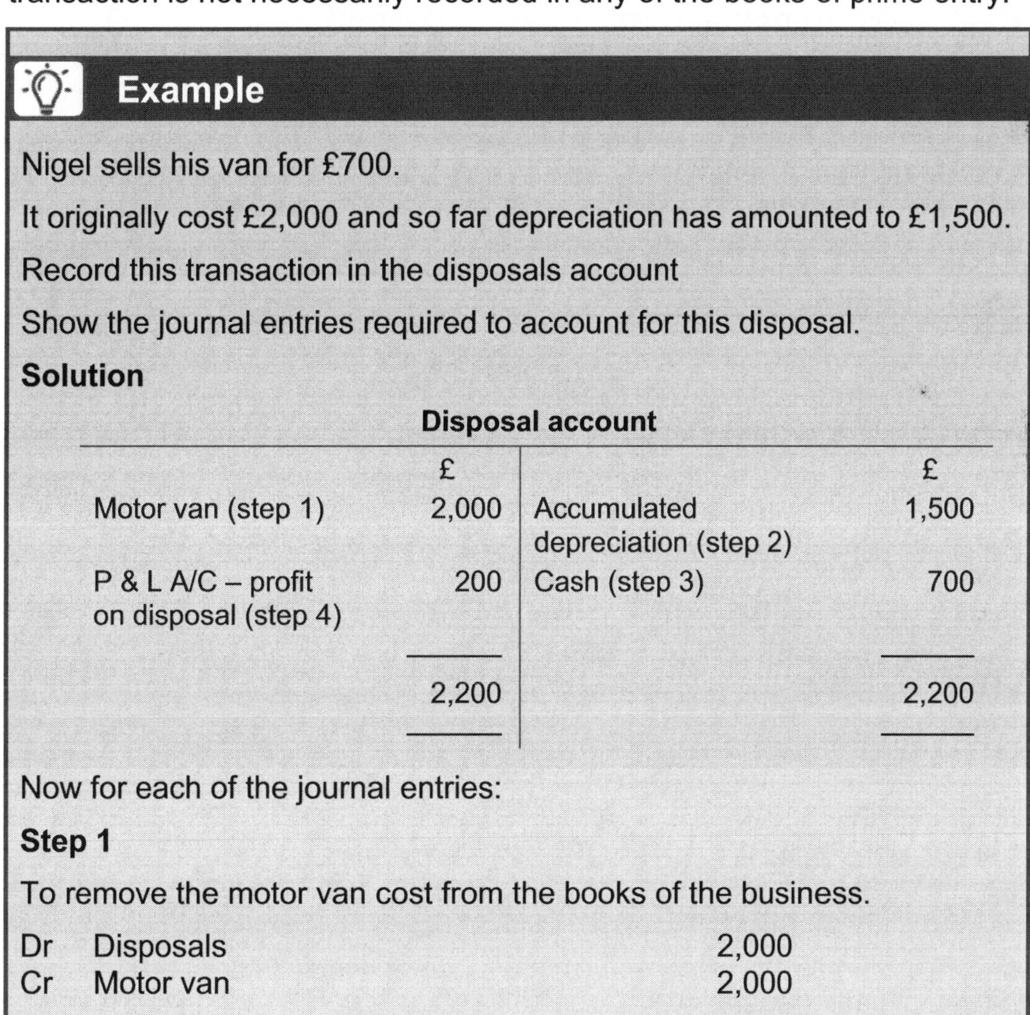

Example

Nigel sells his van for £700.

It originally cost £2,000 and so far depreciation has amounted to £1,500.

Record this transaction in the disposals account

Show the journal entries required to account for this disposal.

Solution

Disposal account

	£		£
Motor van (step 1)	2,000	Accumulated depreciation (step 2)	1,500
P & L A/C – profit on disposal (step 4)	200	Cash (step 3)	700
	2,200		2,200

Now for each of the journal entries:

Step 1

To remove the motor van cost from the books of the business.

Dr	Disposals	2,000	
Cr	Motor van		2,000

Step 2

To remove the associated depreciation from the books of the business.

Dr	Accumulated depreciation	1,500
Cr	Disposals	1,500

Note: These two entries together effectively remove the carrying value of the van to the disposals account.

Step 3

To record the cash proceeds.

Dr	Cash	700
Cr	Disposals	700

Step 4

Balance the disposal account

The resulting balance is the profit on sale which is transferred to the Profit and Loss Account.

Dr	Disposals	200
Cr	Profit and Loss Account	200

1.5 Journal

As with the acquisition of non-current assets, the journal or journal voucher is used as the book of prime entry. The journal voucher for this entire disposal is shown as follows:

Journal entry			**No: 234**
Date	**4 July 20X8**		
Prepared by	J Allen		
Authorised by	A Smith		
Account	**Code**	**Debit** £	**Credit** £
Disposals	0240	2,000	
Motor vehicles cost	0130		2,000
Motor vehicles acc. dep'n	0140	1,500	
Disposals	0240		1,500
Cash at bank (receipts)	0163	700	
Disposals	0240		700
Totals		4,200	4,200

Activity 2

Complete the journal voucher below for the following information:

A company buys a car for £20,000.

The depreciation charged to date is £7,500.

The car is sold for £10,000 at the end of three years.

Using the information above and the following account names and codes, complete the journal voucher below:

0130 Motor vehicles at cost

0140 Motor vehicles accumulated depreciation

0163 Cash at bank (receipts)

0240 Disposals

Journal entry No 235

Date	**13 June 20X8**		
Prepared by	A Tech		
Authorised by	B Jones		
Account	**Code**	**Debit** £	**Credit** £
Motor Vehicle	0130		20000
MV acc. depr.	0140	7 500	
Cash	0163	10 000	
Disposals	0240	20 000	
Disposals			7500
Disposals			10 000
		37500	37500

2500 loss

2 Part-exchange of assets

2.1 Introduction

There is an alternative to selling a fixed asset for cash, particularly if a new asset is to be purchased to replace the one being sold. This is often the case with cars or vans where the old asset may be taken by the seller of the new asset as part of the purchase price of the new asset. This is known as a part-exchange deal.

2.2 Part-exchange deal value

When a part exchange deal takes place the seller of the new asset will place a value on the old asset and this will be its part-exchange value.

Example

A new car is being purchased for a list price of £18,000. An old car of the business has been accepted in part-exchange and the cheque required for the new car is £14,700.

What is the part-exchange value of the old car?

Solution

	£
List price	18,000
Cheque required	14,700
Part-exchange value	3,300

2.3 Accounting for the part-exchange value

The part-exchange value has two effects on the accounting records:

(a) it is effectively the sale proceeds of the old asset

(b) it is part of the full cost of the new asset together with the cash/cheque paid.

The double entry for the part exchange value is:

- credit the disposal account as these are the effective proceeds of the old asset
- debit the new asset cost account as this value is part of the total cost of the new asset.

Example

Suppose Nigel had part exchanged his van for a new one.

The old van had cost £2,000 and depreciation amounted to £1,500.

The garage gave him an allowance of £700 against the price of the new van which was £5,000. He paid the balance by cheque.

Show all the accounting entries for the disposal of the old van and the acquisition of the new van.

Solution

Step 1

Transfer balances from van and accumulated depreciation accounts to the disposal account.

Old van

	£		£
Balance b/d	2,000	Disposal	2,000
	2,000		2,000

Accumulated depreciation

	£		£
Disposal	1,500	Balance b/d	1,500
	1,500		1,500

Disposal

	£		£
Old van	2,000	Depreciation	1,500

Note: We have closed off the van and depreciation account to make the entries clearer.

Step 2

Open a new van account and enter in it:

(a) the part exchange value (£700) from the disposal account; and

(b) the balance of the cost of the new van (£4,300).

The £700 part exchange value is also credited to the disposal account as the effective proceeds of the old van.

Disposal

	£		£
Old van	2,000	Depreciation	1,500
		New van	700

New van

	£		£
Disposal	700		
Bank	4,300		

Step 3

Balance the accounts

(a) Close the disposal account to the Profit and Loss Account with a profit of £200 being recorded.

(b) Bring down the total cost (£5,000) of the new van.

Disposal

	£		£
Old van	2,000	Depreciation	1,500
P & L Account– profit on disposal – old van	200	New van	700
	2,200		2,200

New van

	£		£
Disposal	700	Balance c/d	5,000
Bank	4,300		
	5,000		5,000
Balance b/d	5,000		

Note 1: You could put all the entries in the one van account. It would look like this.

Motor van

	£		£
Balance b/d	2,000	Disposal	2,000
Disposal	700	Balance c/d	5,000
Bank	4,300		
	7,000		7,000
Balance b/d	5,000		

Example

A business is purchasing a new van and the invoice for this van has just been received showing the following details:

	£
Registration number GU44 HFF – list price	18,000.00
VAT at 20%	3,600.00
Carrying value	21,600.00
Vehicle excise duty	140.00
Total due	21,740.00
Less: part-exchange value Y624 UFD	(4,000.00)
Balance to pay	17,740.00

The old van taken in part exchange originally cost £11,000 and at the time of disposal had accumulated depreciation charged to it of £8,340.

From the invoice you can find the total cost of the new van, £18,000, and the part-exchange value of the old van, £4,000.

Write up the van account, accumulated depreciation on vans account and the disposal account to reflect this transaction.

Solution

Van account

	£		£
Old van – cost	11,000	Disposal account	11,000
New van (18,000-4,000)	14,000		
Disposal account – exchange value	4,000	Balance c/d	18,000
	29,000		29,000
Balance b/d	18,000		

Remember that the vehicle excise duty is revenue expenditure and is therefore not part of the cost of the new van and that VAT on the purchase of vans (rather than cars) is recoverable. Therefore the VAT is debited to the VAT control account rather than the van account. The balance b/d on the van account after all of these transactions is simply the full cost of the van of £18,000.

Accumulated depreciation accounts – van

	£		£
Disposal account	8,340	Balance b/d	8,340

Disposal account

	£		£
Van at cost	11,000	Acc. Depreciation	8,340
Profit on disposal	1,340	Van account – part exchange value	4,000
	12,340		12,340

2.4 Original documentation

You should also understand how to find some of the information necessary from the sales invoice for the new asset.

Activity 3

On 31 December 20X3 a business part-exchanges a van which it bought on 1 January 20X0 for £6,000 and has depreciated each year at 25% pa by the straight-line method (assuming nil residual value). The business charges a full year's charge in the year of acquisition and none in the year of disposal.

It trades this van in for a new one costing £10,000 and pays the supplier £9,200 by cheque.

1 Record the entries in ledger accounts for the disposal of the OLD van.

2 Record the entries in ledger accounts for the addition of the NEW van.

3 Complete the disposal account and calculate the profit/loss on disposal.

3 Authorising disposals

3.1 Introduction

It is important that disposals of fixed assets are properly controlled. For most organisations, this means that there must be some form of written authorisation before a disposal can take place. In some ways, authorisation is even more important for disposals than for additions.

3.2 Importance of authorisation

Disposals can easily be made without the knowledge of management and are difficult to detect from the accounting records alone. Sales of assets are often for relatively small amounts of cash and they may not be supported by an invoice (for example, if they are to an employee of the business). Although the transaction itself may not be significant, failure to detect and record the disposal correctly in the accounting records may result in the overstatement of fixed assets in the accounts.

3.3 Requirements of valid authorisation

Possibilities for written authorisation include board minutes (for material disposals), memos or authorisation forms. The following information is needed:

- date of purchase
- date of disposal
- description of asset
- reason for disposal
- original cost
- accumulated depreciation
- sale proceeds
- authorisation (number of signatures required will depend upon the organisation's procedures).

4 Disposals and the fixed asset register

4.1 Introduction

When a fixed asset is disposed of then this must be recorded not only in the ledger accounts but also in the fixed asset register.

Example

Date of purchase	*Invoice number*	*Serial number*	*Item*	*Cost*	*Accum'd depreciation b/f at 1.1.X8*	*Date of disposal*	*Depreciation charge in 20X8*	*Accum'd depreciation c/f*	*Disposal proceeds*	*Loss/ gain on disposal*
				£	£		£	£	£	£
3.2.X5	345	3488	Chair	340	102		34	136		
6.4.X6	466	–	Bookcase	258	52		26	78		
10.7.X7	587	278	Chair	160	16	12.7.X8	–			
30.8.X8	634	1228	Table	86			9	9		
				——	——		——	——		
				844	170		69	223		
				——	——		——	——		

Using the fixed asset register reproduced above we will now complete the entries for the chair (serial number 278) being disposed of.

The disposal proceeds are £15.

The profit or loss must also be entered into the fixed asset register and the total of all of the profits or losses should equal the amount transferred to the Profit and Loss Account for the period.

Solution

(W1)	£
Cost	160
Cumulative dep'n	(16)
	——
CV	144
Proceeds	(15)
	——
Loss	129

Date of purchase	*Invoice number*	*Serial number*	*Item*	*Cost*	*Accum'd depreciation b/d at 1.1.X8*	*Date of disposal*	*Depreciation charge in 20X8*	*Accum'd depreciation c/d*	*Disposal proceeds*	*Loss/gain on disposal*
				£	£		£	£	£	£
3.2.X5	345	3488	Chair	340	102		34	136		
6.4.X6	466	–	Bookcase	258	52		26	78		
10.7.X7	587	√278	Chair	160	16	12.7.X8	–	—	15	(129)(W1)
30.8.X8	634	1228	Table	86			9	9		
				——	——					
				844	170					
12.7.X8		√278	Chair	(160)	(16)					
				——	——		——	——		——
				684	154		69	223		(129)
				——	——		——	——		——

5 Reconciliation of physical assets to the fixed asset register

5.1 Introduction

One of the purposes of the fixed asset register is to allow control over the fixed assets of a business. Obviously many of the fixed assets are extremely valuable and some are also easily moved, especially assets such as personal computers and cars. Therefore on a regular basis the organisation should carry out random checks to ensure that the fixed assets recorded in the fixed asset register are actually on the premises.

5.2 Details in the fixed asset register

The fixed asset register will show the purchase cost, depreciation and disposal details of the fixed assets that the business owns and have recently disposed of.

The fixed asset register should also normally show the location of the assets. This will either be by an additional column in the fixed asset register or by grouping assets in each department or area of the business together. This enables periodic checks to be carried out to ensure that the physical assets in each department agree to fixed asset register.

5.3 Discrepancies

A variety of possible discrepancies might appear between the physical assets and the book records.

- An asset recorded in the fixed asset register is not physically present – this might be due to the asset being disposed of but not recorded in the fixed asset register, the asset having been moved to another location or the asset having been stolen or removed without authorisation.
- An asset existing that is not recorded in the fixed asset register – this might be due to the fixed asset register not being up to date or the asset having been moved from another location.

Whatever type of discrepancy is discovered it must be either resolved or reported to the appropriate person in the organisation so that it can be resolved.

5.4 Agreement of accounting records to fixed asset register

The ledger accounts for the fixed assets should also be agreed on a regular basis to the fixed asset register.

The cost total with any disposals deducted should agree to the fixed asset at cost accounts totals.

The accumulated depreciation column total for each class of assets should also agree to the accumulated depreciation account balance for each class of asset.

Any total in the loss or gain on disposals column should also agree to the amount charged or credited to the Profit and Loss Account.

On a regular basis the fixed asset register details should be agreed to the physical assets held and to the ledger accounts.

6 Summary

The two main aspects to accounting for disposals of fixed assets are to remove all accounting entries for the asset disposed of and to account for any profit or loss on disposal. This can all be done by using a disposal account.

Some assets will not be sold outright but will be transferred as a part-exchange deal when purchasing a new asset. The part-exchange value is not only equivalent to the proceeds of sale but is also part of the cost of the new asset being purchased.

Control over the disposal of fixed assets is extremely important and as such authorisation of a disposal and whether it is as a sale or a part-exchange is key to this. Allied to this is the control feature of the fixed asset register.

All purchases and disposals of fixed assets should be recorded in the fixed asset register and the actual physical presence of the fixed assets should be checked on a regular basis to the fixed asset register details.

Answers to chapter activities

Activity 1

	£	*Depreciation*
Cost	20,000	
Year 1 depreciation **(20,000 × 50%)**	(10,000)	10,000
	10,000	
Year 2 dep'n (10,000 × 50%)	(5,000)	5,000
	5,000	
Year 3 depreciation (5,000 × 50%)	(2,500)	2,500
		17,500

Car account

	£		£
Yr 1 Bank	20,000	Yr 1 Balance c/d	20,000
	20,000		20,000
Yr 2 Balance b/d	20,000	Yr 2 Balance c/d	20,000
	20,000		20,000
Yr 3 Balance b/d	20,000	Yr 3 Disposal account	20,000
	20,000		20,000

Accumulated depreciation

	£		£
Yr 1 Balance c/d	10,000	Yr 1 Depreciation exps	10,000
	10,000		10,000
Yr 2 Balance c/d	15,000	Yr 2 Balance b/d	10,000
		Yr 2 Depreciation exps	5,000
	15,000		15,000
Yr 3 Disposal account	17,500	Yr 3 Balance b/d	15,000
		Yr 3 Depreciation exps	2,500
	17,500		17,500

Disposal account

	£		£
Yr 3 Car cost	20,000	Yr 3 Accumulated dep'n	17,500
Yr 3 Profit on disposal	7,500	Yr 3 Proceeds	10,000
	27,500		27,500

Activity 2

Journal entry No 235

Date	13 June 20X8		
Prepared by	A Tech		
Authorised by	B Jones		
Account	**Code**	**Debit** £	**Credit** £
Disposals	0240	20,000	
MV at cost	0130		20,000
MV acc dep'n	0140	7,500	
Disposals	0240		7,500
Cash at bank	0163	10,000	
Disposals	0240		10,000

Activity 3

Van account

	£		£
Cost b/d	6,000	Disposals account	6,000
Disposal account	800		
Bank	9,200	Balance c/d	10,000
	16,000		16,000
Balance b/d	10,000		

Accumulated depreciation

	£		£
Disposal account	4,500	Balance b/d (£6,000 × 25% × 3)	4,500
Balance c/d	2,500	Depreciation charge (£10,000 × 25%)	2,500
	7,000		7,000
		Balance b/d	2,500

Disposal account

	£		£
Van	6,000	Accumulated depreciation	4,500
		Part exchange allowance	800
		Loss on disposal	700
	6,000		6,000

7 Test your knowledge

Workbook Activity 4

Spanners Ltd has a car it wishes to dispose of. The car cost £12,000 and has accumulated depreciation of £5,000. The car is sold for £4,000.

Tasks

(a) Clearly state whether there is a profit or a loss on disposal.

(b) Show the entries in the motor car account, accumulated depreciation account and disposal account.

Workbook Activity 5

Baldrick's venture

On 1 April 20X6, Baldrick started a business growing turnips and selling them to wholesalers. On 1 September 20X6 he purchased a turnip-digging machine for £2,700. He sold the machine on 1 March 20X9 for £1,300.

Baldrick's policy for machinery is to charge depreciation on the reducing balance method at 25% per annum. A full year's charge is made in the year of purchase and none in the year of sale.

Required:

For the three years from 1 April 20X6 to 31 March 20X9 prepare the following ledger accounts:

(a) Machinery account

(b) Accumulated depreciation account (machinery)

(c) Depreciation expense account (machinery)

(d) Disposals account

Bring down the balance on each account at 31 March each year.

Workbook Activity 6

Keith

The following transactions relate to Keith Manufacturing Co Ltd's plant and machinery:

1 January 20X7	Lathe machine purchased for £10,000. It is to be depreciated on a straight line basis with no expected scrap value after four years.
1 April 20X7	Cutting machine purchased for £12,000. It is estimated that after a five-year working life it will have a scrap value of £1,000.
1 June 20X8	Laser machine purchased for £28,000. This is estimated to have a seven year life and a scrap value of £2,800.
1 March 20X9	The cutting machine purchased on 1 April 20X7 was given in part exchange for a new micro-cutter with a purchase price of £20,000. A part-exchange allowance of £3,000 was given and the balance paid by cheque. It is estimated that the new machine will last for five years with a scrap value of £3,000. It will cost £1,500 to install.

The accounting year-end is 31 December. The company depreciates its machines on a straight line basis, charging a full year in the year of purchase and none in the year of sale.

At 31 December 20X6 the plant register had shown the following:

Date of purchase	*Machine*	*Cost*	*Anticipated residual value*	*Rate of depreciation*
		£	£	
1 June 20X5	Piece machine	10,000	Nil	Straight line over 5 years
1 January 20X6	Acrylic machine	5,000	1,000	Straight line over 5 years
1 June 20X6	Heat seal machine	6,000	Nil	Straight line over 5 years

Required:

Write up the plant and machinery account, the accumulated depreciation account and the disposal accounts for 20X7, 20X8 and 20X9. Show the relevant extracts from the financial statements.

Workbook Activity 7

A motor vehicle which had originally been purchased on 31 October 20X1 for £12,000 was part exchanged for a new vehicle on 31 May 20X3. The new vehicle cost £15,000 and was paid for using the old vehicle and a cheque for £5,000.

Prepare a disposals account for the old vehicle showing clearly the transfer to the Profit and Loss Account. (Depreciation for motor vehicles is calculated on a monthly basis at 20% per annum straight line method assuming no residual value.)

Disposals account

Workbook Activity 8

A business is purchasing a new van for deliveries from Grammoth Garages. It has just received the following invoice from Grammoth Garages:

GRAMMOTH GARAGES
Park Road • Valedon • HE4 8NB
SALES INVOICE

Delivery of Ford Transit Van Registration GS55 OPP

	£
List price	21,000.00
VAT	4,200.00
	25,200.00
Less: part exchange value Ford Transit Van Reg X234 JDF	(5,500.00)
Amount due	19,700.00

The van that is being part-exchanged originally cost £16,400 and has been depreciated on a straight-line basis for four years at 15% per annum.

Required:

Write up the motor vans at cost account, accumulated depreciation and the disposal account to reflect the purchase of the new van and the part-exchange of the old van.

Accounting for stock

Introduction

In this chapter we will consider the accounting for opening and closing stock and the issues that surround valuing and recording closing stock.

As well as being able to enter a valuation for closing stock correctly in the trial balance and financial statements, you can also expect to be assessed on other aspects of stock valuation.

This will include:

- valuing stock at the lower of cost and net realisable value
- determining the cost of stock and its net realisable value
- various methods of costing stock units and
- a closing stock reconciliation.

CONTENTS

1 Closing stock in the financial statements

1.1 Introduction

Most businesses will have a variety of different types of stock. In a retail business this will be the goods that are in stock and held for resale. In a manufacturing business there are likely to be raw materials (that are used to make the business's products), partly finished products (known as work in progress) and completed goods ready for sale (known as finished goods).

These items of stock are assets of the business and therefore must be included in the financial statements as current assets.

1.2 Counting closing stock

At the end of the accounting period a stock count will normally take place where the quantity of each line of stock is counted and recorded. The organisation will then know the number of units of each type of stock that it has at the year end. The next stage is to value the stock. Both of these areas will be dealt with in detail later in the chapter.

1.3 Closing stock and the financial statements

Once the stock has been counted and valued it must then be included in the financial statements. The detailed accounting for this will be considered later in the chapter.

At this stage we will just look at an overview of how the closing stock will appear in the financial statements.

1.4 Balance Sheet

The closing stock is an asset of the business and as such will appear on the Balance Sheet. It is a current asset and will normally be shown as the first item in the list of current assets, as it is the least liquid of the current assets.

1.5 Trading and Profit and Loss Account

An extract from the Trading and Profit and Loss Account is shown below: this shows how stock appears as part of the cost of sales in the Trading and Profit and Loss Account. This extract below is referred to as the Trading Account.

	£	£
Sales		X
Less: cost of sales		
Opening stock	X	
Plus: purchases	X	
	X	
Less: closing stock	(X)	
		(X)
Gross profit		X

As you will see the 'cost of sales' figure is made up of the opening stock, plus the purchases of the business for the period, less the closing stock.

The opening stock is the figure included in the accounts as last year's closing stock.

The purchases figure is the balance on the purchases account.

From this the closing stock is deducted in order to determine the cost of the goods actually sold in the period, as this stock has clearly not yet been sold. This is part of the matching concept, and matches the cost of the goods sold with the revenue generated from the sales.

Closing stock therefore appears in both the Balance Sheet and the Profit and Loss Account.

2 Closing stock reconciliation

2.1 Introduction

Before the stock of a business can be valued, the physical amount of stock held must be counted and the amounts physically on hand checked to the stores records. Any discrepancies must be investigated. This is known as a closing stock reconciliation.

2.2 Stores records

For each line of stock the stores department should keep a bin card or stock card which shows the following:

- the quantity of stock received from suppliers (sourced from delivery notes or goods received notes). This should be netted off by any goods returned to the suppliers (sourced from credit notes or despatch notes)
- the quantity issued for sale or use in manufacture (sourced from store requisitions)
- any amounts returned to the stores department (sourced from goods returned notes), and
- the amount/balance that should be on hand at that time.

At any point in time the balance on the stores record should agree with the number of items of that line of stock physically held by the stores department.

2.3 Possible reasons for differences

If there is a difference between the quantity physically counted and the stores records this could be for a variety of reasons:

- Goods may have been delivered and therefore have been physically counted but the stores records have not yet been updated to reflect the delivery.
- Goods may have been returned to suppliers and therefore will not have been counted but again the stores records have not yet been updated.
- Goods may have been issued for sales or for use in manufacturing, therefore they are not in the stores department but the stores records do not yet reflect this issue.
- Some items may have been stolen so are no longer physically in stock.
- Errors may have been made, either in counting the number of items held, or in writing up the stores records.

Example

At 30 June 20X4 a sole trader carried out a stock count and compared the quantity of each line of stock to the stock records. In most cases the actual stock quantity counted agreed with the stores records but, for three lines of stock, the sole trader found differences.

	Stock code		
	FR153	*JE363*	*PT321*
Quantity counted	116	210	94
Stock record quantity	144	150	80

The stock records and documentation were thoroughly checked for these stock lines and the following was discovered:

- On 28 June, 28 units of FR153 had been returned to the supplier as they were damaged. A credit note has not yet been received and the despatch note had not been recorded in the stock records.
- On 29 June, a goods received note showed that 100 units of JE363 had arrived from a supplier but this had not yet been entered in the stock records.
- Also on 29 June, 14 units of PT321 had been recorded as an issue to sales, however they were not physically dispatched to the customer until after the stock was counted.
- On 28 June, the sole trader had taken 40 units of JE363 out of stock in order to process a rush order for a customer and had forgotten to update the stock record.

The closing stock reconciliation must now be performed and the actual quantities for each line of stock that are to be valued must be determined.

Solution

Closing stock reconciliation – 30 June 20X4

FR153	*Quantity*
Stock record	144
Less: Returned to supplier	(28)
Counted	116

When valuing the FR153 stock line, the actual quantity counted of 116 should be used. There should also be a journal entry to reflect the purchase return:

Debit Purchases ledger control account

Credit Purchases returns

JE363	*Quantity*
Stock record	150
Add: GRN not recorded	100
Less: Sales requisition	(40)
Counted	210

The quantity to be valued should be the quantity counted of 210 units. If the sale has not been recorded then an adjustment will be required for the value of the sales invoice:

Debit Sales ledger control account

Credit Sales account

In addition, if the purchase has not been recorded then an adjustment will be required for the value of the purchase invoice:

Debit Purchases

Credit Purchase ledger control account

PT321	*Quantity*
Stock record	80
Add: Subsequent sale	14
Counted	94

In this case the amount to be valued is the stock record amount of 80 units and if the sale has not been recorded then an adjustment must be made at the selling price of the 14 units, (note that this is done as the stock was sold on 30th June, pre period end, but after the stock count):

Debit Sales ledger control account

Credit Sales account

3 Valuation of closing stock

3.1 Introduction

Now that we know how many units of stock we have from the stock count, we will consider how the units of stock are valued.

3.2 Accounting standards

The basic rule from current accounting standards is that stock should be valued at: 'the lower of cost and net realisable value'.

Definition

Cost is defined in current accounting standards as 'that expenditure which has been incurred in the normal course of business in bringing the product or service to its present location and condition. This expenditure should include, in addition to cost of purchase, such costs of conversion as are appropriate to that location and condition'.

3.3 Cost

Purchase cost is defined as:

'including import duties, transport and handling costs and any other directly attributable costs, less trade discounts, rebates and subsidies'.

Costs of conversion includes:

- direct production costs
- production overheads, and
- other overheads attributable to bringing the product to its present location and condition.

This means the following:

- Only **production overheads** – not those for marketing, selling and distribution – should be included in cost.
- Exceptional spoilage, idle capacity and other abnormal costs are not part of the cost of inventories.
- General management and non-production related administration costs should not be included in stock cost.

So far, then, we can summarise that the **cost of stock** is:

- the amount it was bought for from the supplier, less any trade discounts
- any extra costs (delivery costs) to get it to its current location, and
- the production cost of any work performed on it since it was bought.

This means that different items of the same stock in different locations may have different costs.

Activity 1

A company had to pay a special delivery charge of £84 on a delivery of urgently required games software it had purchased for resale. This amount had been debited to office expenses account.

(a) This treatment is incorrect. Which account should have been debited? (Tick)

Purchases account	☑
Stock account	☐
Returns Inwards account	☐

(b) Give the journal entry to correct the error.

Office exp. account Cr. £84

Purchase account dt £84

3.4 Net realisable value

Definition

Current accounting standards define net realisable value (NRV) as 'the actual or estimated selling price (net of trade but before settlement discounts) less all further costs to completion and all costs to be incurred in marketing, selling and distributing'.

NRV can be summarised as the actual or estimated selling price less any future costs that will be incurred before the product can be sold.

Example

Jenny manufactures widgets. Details of the basic version are given below:

	Cost	*Selling price*	*Selling cost*
	£	£	£
Basic widgets	5	10	2

What value should be attributed to each widget in stock?

Solution

Stock valuation	£
Cost	5
Net realisable value (£10 – £2)	8

Therefore stock should be valued at £5 per widget, the lower of cost and NRV.

It is wrong to add the selling cost of £2 to the production cost of £5 and value the stock at £7 because it is not a production cost.

3.5 Justification of the current accounting standards

The valuation rule that stock must be valued at the lower of cost and net realisable value is an example of the accounting concept known as 'prudence.' It is also now seen as a simple application of the accruals concept and revenue recognition rules.

Normally stock items are likely to sell for a high enough prices that NRV is higher than cost (i.e. they are sold for a profit). If stock were valued at NRV then the accounts would include the profit before they were sold. This is not allowed and so the stock should be valued at cost.

In some circumstances it is possible that the selling price of the goods has fallen so that NRV is now lower than the original cost of the goods (i.e. they will be sold at a loss). In these circumstances the business should take a prudent approach and record the loss immediately. Therefore these goods should be valued at net realisable value.

3.6 Separate items or groups of stock

Current accounting standards also make it quite clear that when determining whether the stock should be valued at cost or net realisable value EACH item of stock or groups of similar items should be considered separately.

Example

A business has three lines of stock A, B and C. The details of cost and NRV for each line is given below:

	Cost	*NRV*
	£	£
A	1,200	2,000
B	1,000	800
C	1,500	2,500
	3,700	5,300

What is the value of the closing stock of the business?

Solution

It is incorrect to value the stock at £3,700, the total cost, although it is clearly lower than the total NRV. Each line of stock must be considered separately.

	Cost	*NRV*	*Stock value*
	£	£	£
A	1,200	2,000	1,200
B	1,000	800	800
C	1,500	2,500	1,500
	3,700	5,300	3,500

You will see that the NRV of B is lower than its cost and therefore the NRV is the value that must be included for B.

Make sure that you look at each stock line separately and do not just take the total cost of £3,700 as the stock value.

Activity 2

Karen sells three products: A, B and C. At the company's year-end, the inventories held are as follows:

	Cost	*Selling price*
	£	£
A	1,200	1,500
B	6,200	6,100
C	920	930

At sale a 5% commission is payable by the company to its agent.

What is the total value of these inventories in the company's accounts?

(Complete the following table)

	Cost	*Selling price*	*NRV*
	£	£	£
A			
B			
C			

Total stock valuation =

3.7 Adjustment to closing stock value

If closing stock has been valued at cost and it is subsequently determined that some items of have a net realisable value which is lower than cost, then the valuation of the closing stock must be reduced.

4 Methods of costing

4.1 Introduction

In order to determine the valuation of closing stock the cost must be compared to the net realisable value. We have seen how cost is defined and the major element of cost will be the purchase price of the goods.

In many cases organisations buy goods at different times and at different prices, as such it is difficult to determine the exact purchase price of the goods that are left in stock at the end of the accounting period. Therefore assumptions have to be made about the movement of stock in and out of the warehouse.

You need to be aware of two methods of determining the purchase price of the goods – first in first out and weighted average cost. The last-in-first-out method, which used to be common, is not permitted by current accounting standards.

4.2 First in, first out

The first in, first out (FIFO) method of costing stock makes the assumption that the goods going out of the warehouse are the earliest purchases. Therefore the stock items left are the most recent purchases.

4.3 Weighted average cost

The weighted average cost method values stock at the weighted average of the purchase prices each time stock is issued. This means that the total purchase price of the stock is divided by the number of units of stock, but this calculation must be carried out before every issue out of the warehouse.

4.4 Costing methods

In practice, as already stated, a business is unlikely to know exactly how much a particular item of stock originally cost. A standard policy for valuation is therefore adopted and the most common is FIFO. You should, however, make sure that you are clear about the other methods as well.

5 Accounting for closing stock

5.1 Introduction

You will need to be able to enter closing stock in the Trading Account and Balance Sheet; and to correctly enter the figure for closing stock in the trial balance. Therefore in this section the actual accounting for stock will be considered.

5.2 Opening stock

Opening stock is the balance on the stock account that appeared in last year's Balance Sheet as the closing stock figure. This stock account then has no further entries put through it until the year end which is why it still appears in the trial balance.

Remember that all purchases of goods are accounted for in the purchases account, they should never be entered into the stock account.

5.3 Year end procedure

At the year end there is a set of adjustments that must be made in order to correctly account for stock in the Trading Account and the Balance Sheet.

Step 1

The opening stock balance in the stock account (debit balance as this was a current asset at the end of last year) is transferred to the Trading Account as part of cost of sales.

The double entry for this is:

Dr Trading Account (opening stock in cost of sales)

Cr Stock account

This opening stock balance has now been removed.

Step 2

The closing stock, at its agreed valuation, is entered into the ledger accounts with the following double entry:

Dr Closing stock (asset on the Balance Sheet)

Cr Closing stock (in cost of sales)

We will study this double entry with an example.

Example

John prepares accounts to 31 December 20X4.

His opening stock on 1 January 20X4 is £20,000. During the year he purchases goods which cost £200,000. At 31 December 20X4 his closing stock is valued at £30,000.

You are required to enter these amounts into the ledger accounts and transfer the amounts as appropriate to the Trading and Trading Account.

(You should open a Trading Account in the ledger and treat it as part of the double entry as this will help you to understand the double entry).

Solution

Step 1

Open the required accounts and enter the opening stock and purchases into the accounts.

Opening stock

		£		£
1.1.X4	Balance b/d	20,000		

Purchases

		£		£
1.1.X4	PDB	200,000		

Trading Account

	£		£

Step 2

Write off the opening stock and purchases to the Trading Account

Opening stock

	£		£
1.1.X4 Balance b/d	20,000	31.12.X4 Trading A/C	20,000

Purchases

	£		£
PDB	200,000	31.12.X4 Trading A/C	200,000
	200,000		200,000

Trading Account

	£		£
31.12.X4 Opening stock	20,000		
31.12.X4 Purchases	200,000		

Note

(a) The opening stock of £20,000 was brought down as an asset at the end of December 20X3, and has remained in the ledger account for the whole year without being touched.

At 31 December 20X4 it is finally written off to the debit of the Trading Account as part of the cost of sales.

(b) Purchases of goods made during the year are accumulated in the purchases account. At the end of the year (31 December 20X4) the entire year's purchases are written off to the debit of the Trading Account as the next element of cost of sales. The purchases account now balances and we have closed it off. Next year will start with a nil balance on the purchases account.

Step 3

Enter the closing stock £30,000 into the stock account.

Closing stock Trading Account

	£		£
		31.12.X4 Closing stock	30,000

Closing stock Balance Sheet

	£		
31.12.X4 Closing stock	30,000		

Note

The double entry for closing stock is therefore:

Debit Closing stock Balance Sheet

Credit Closing stock Trading Account

(a) On the closing stock Balance Sheet account, we are just left with a debit entry of £30,000. This is the closing stock at 31 December 20X4 and is the opening stock at 1 January 20X5. This £30,000 will be entered on the Balance Sheet and it will remain untouched in the stock account until 31 December 20X5.

(b) The Trading Account has a balance of £190,000. This is the cost of sales for the year. If we write this out in its normal form, you will see what we have done.

Step 4

Transfer the credit entry for closing stock to the Trading Account and bring down the balances on the stock and the Trading Account

Closing stock Trading Account

	£		£
31.12.X4 Trading A/C	30,000	31.12.X4 Closing stock	30,000
	30,000		30,000

Trading Account

	£		£
31.12.X4 Op. stock	20,000	31.12.X4 Closing stock	30,000
31.12.X4 Purchases	200,000	31.12.X4 Balance c/d	190,000
	220,000		220,000
31.12.X4 Balance b/d (Cost of sales)	190,000		

Trading Account at 31.12.X4

	£	£
Sales (not known)		X
Cost of sales		
Opening stock (1.1.X4)	20,000	
Add: purchases	200,000	
	220,000	
Less: closing stock (31.12.X4)	(30,000)	
		190,000

For the purposes of the assessment you need to remember the following:

Opening stock is recorded as part of **cost of sales** (as above) in the **Trading Account.**

Closing stock is recorded as part of **cost of sales** (as above) and as **current assets** in the **Balance Sheet**.

Example

A business has a figure for opening stock in its trial balance of £10,000. The closing stock has been counted and valued at £12,000.

Show the entries in the ledger accounts to record this.

Solution

Opening stock Trading Account

	£		£
Balance b/d – opening stock	10,000	Trading A/C	10,000
	10,000		10,000

Closing stock Trading Account

Trading A/C	12,000	Closing stock (BS)	12,000
	12,000		12,000

Closing stock Balance Sheet

Closing stock (Trading A/C)	12,000	Balance c/d	12,000
	12,000		12,000
Balance b/d	12,000		

Trading Account

	£		£
Opening stock	10,000	Closing stock	12,000

Activity 3

1 Where will the closing stock appear in the Balance Sheet? (Tick)

Fixed assets ☐

Current assets ☑

2 Where will the closing stock appear in the Trading Account? (Tick)

Expenses ☐

Cost of sales ☑

3 A line of stock has been counted and the stock count shows that there are 50 units more in the stock room than is recorded on the stock card. What possible reasons might there be for this difference?

____

____

____

____

4 Complete the following sentence.

Stock should be valued at the __________ of __________ and __________

5 The closing stock of a sole trader has been valued at cost of £5,800 and recorded in the trial balance. However, one item of stock which cost £680 has a net realisable value of £580. What is the journal entry required for this adjustment? (Tick)

Debit	**Credit**	
Closing stock (BS)	Closing stock (Trading A/C)	☐
Closing stock (Trading A/C)	Closing stock (BS)	☐

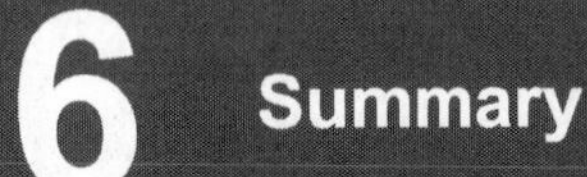

6 Summary

In this chapter you have learnt how stock should be valued at the lower of its cost and net realisable value. You have also learnt the various costing methods that can be used to determine the value of items held in stock. Finally, you have looked at how to deal with opening and closing stock in both the Trading Account and the Balance Sheet: make sure you are confident on this as it is an area which many students struggle with in the assessment.

Answers to chapter activities

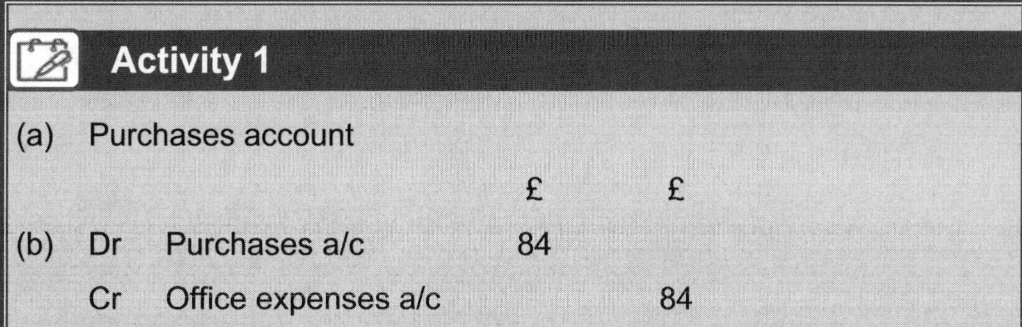

Activity 1

(a) Purchases account

			£	£
(b)	Dr	Purchases a/c	84	
	Cr	Office expenses a/c		84

Activity 2

Stock is valued at the lower of cost and net realisable value (costs to be incurred 5% in selling stock are deducted from selling price in computing NRV).

	Cost	*Selling price*	*NRV*
	£	£	£
A	1,200	1,500	1,425
B	6,200	6,100	5,795
C	920	930	884

Total stock values (1,200 + 5,795 + 884) = **£7,879**

Activity 3

1 As a current asset.

2 As a reduction to cost of sales.

3
- A delivery has not yet been recorded on the stock card.
- A return of goods from a customer has not yet been recorded on the stock card.
- An issue to sales has been recorded on the stock card but not yet despatched.
- A return to a supplier has been recorded on the stock card but not yet despatched.

4 Stock should be valued at the lower of cost and NRV (net realisable value).

5

Debit	Closing stock– Trading A/C	£100
Credit	Closing stock – Balance Sheet	£100

7 Test your knowledge

Workbook Activity 4

Infortec has ten Mica40z PCs in stock at the year end, each of which cost £500 and is priced to sell to customers at £580. Unfortunately they all have faulty hard drives which will need to be replaced before they can be sold. The cost of a replacement hard drive is £100 for each machine.

Required:

What is the value of the closing stock to include in the year end financial statements?

Workbook Activity 5

Smith has closing stock value at £5,000 at the year end.

Required:

Complete the journal below to enter the closing stock in Smith's accounts.

Ledger Account	DR £	CR £
Trading account		5000
Closing stock Balance	5000	

Accruals and prepayments

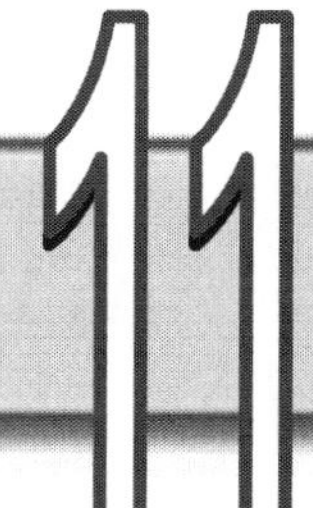

Introduction

In this chapter we start to deal with adjustments that are required to the trial balance figures in order to go from an initial trial balance to a final set of accounts.

In almost all cases these adjustments will include accruals and prepayments of expenses and possibly income.

CONTENTS

1 Recording income and expenditure

1.1 Introduction

One of the fundamental accounting concepts is the accruals concept. This states that the income and expenses recognised in the accounting period should be that which has been earned or incurred during the period rather than the amounts received or paid in cash in the period.

1.2 Recording sales and purchases on credit

Sales on credit are recorded in the ledger accounts from the sales day book. The double entry is to credit sales and debit the sales ledger control account (debtors account).

Therefore all sales made in the period are accounted for in the period whether the money has yet been received by the seller or not.

Purchases on credit are recorded in ledger accounts from the purchases day book and debited to purchases and credited to the purchases ledger control account (creditors account).

Again this means that the purchases are already recorded whether or not the creditor has yet been paid.

1.3 Recording expenses of the business

Most of the expenses of the business such as rent, rates, telephone, power costs etc. will tend to be entered into the ledger accounts from the cash payments book. This means that the amount recorded in the ledger accounts is only the cash payment.

In order to accord with the accruals concept the amount of the expense to be recognised in the profit and loss account may be different to this cash payment made in the period.

Expenses should be charged to the profit and loss account as the amount that has been incurred in the accounting period rather than the amount of cash that has been paid during the period.

2 Accruals

2.1 Introduction

If an expense is to be adjusted to represent the amount incurred in a period rather than what has been paid, then the adjustment may be an accrual or a prepayment.

Definition

An accrual is an expense that has been incurred during the period but has not been paid for by the period end and has therefore not been entered in the ledger accounts.

Example

A business has a year end of 31 December. During the year 20X1 the following electricity bills were paid:

		£
15 May	4 months to 30 April	400
18 July	2 months to 30 June	180
14 Sept	2 months to 31 August	150
15 Nov	2 months to 31 October	210

It is estimated that the average monthly electricity bill is £100.

What is the total charge for the year 20X1 for electricity?

Solution

	£
Jan to April	400
May to June	180
July to August	150
Sept to Oct	210
Accrual for Nov/Dec (2 × 100)	200
Total charge	1,140

Activity 1

Olwen commenced business on 1 May 20X0 and is charged rent at the rate of £6,000 per annum. During the period to 31 December 20X0, he actually paid £3,400.

What should his charge in the profit and loss account for the period to 31 December 20X0 be in respect of rent?

2.2 Accounting for accruals

The method of accounting for an accrual is to:

(a) **debit the expense account**

to increase the expense to reflect the fact that an expense has been incurred; and

(b) **credit an accruals account** (or the same expense account)

to reflect the fact that there is a creditor for the expense.

Note that the credit entry can be made in one of two ways:

(1) credit a separate accruals account; or

(2) carry down a credit balance on the expense account.

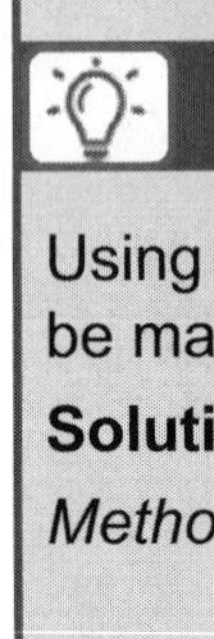

Example

Using the electricity example from above, the accounting entries will now be made in the ledger accounts.

Solution

Method 1 – Separate accruals account Electricity Account

Electricity account

	£		£
15 May CPB	400		
18 July CPB	180		
14 Sept CPB	150		
15 Nov CPB	210		
31 Dec Accrual	200	P&L Account	1,140
	1,140		1,140

Accruals account

	£		£
		Electricity account	200

Using this method the profit and loss account is charged with the full amount of electricity used in the period and there is an accrual or creditor to be shown in the balance sheet of £200 in the accruals account. Any other accruals such as telephone, rent, etc. would also appear in the accruals account as a credit balance. The total of the accruals would appear in the balance sheet as a creditor.

Method 2 – Using the expense account Electricity Account

Electricity account

	£		£
15 May CPB	400		
18 July CPB	180		
14 Sept CPB	150		
15 Nov CPB	210		
31 Dec Accrual	200	P&L Account	1,140
	1,140		1,140
		Balance b/d	200

Again with this method the profit and loss account charge is the amount of electricity used in the period and the credit balance on the expense account is shown as an accrual or creditor in the balance sheet.

Activity 2

Olwen commenced business on 1 May 20X0 and is charged rent at the rate of £6,000 per annum. During the period to 31 December 20X0, he actually paid £3,400.

Write up the ledger account for rent for the period to 31 December 20X0.Clearly state whether the year-end adjustment is an accrual or prepayment.

Rent account

	£		£
Paid rent	3400	Profit and loss	4000
Accruals	600		
	4000		

2.3 Opening and closing balances

When the accrual is accounted for in the expense account then care has to be taken to ensure that the accrual brought down is included as the opening balance on the expense account at the start of the following year.

Example

Continuing with our earlier electricity expense example the closing accrual at the end of 20X0 was £200. During 20X1 £950 of electricity bills were paid and a further accrual of £220 was estimated at the end of 20X1.

Write up the ledger account for electricity for 20X1 clearly showing the charge to the profit and loss account and any accrual balance.

Solution

Electricity account

	£		£
Cash paid during the year	950	Balance b/d – opening accrual	200
Balance c/d – closing accrual	220	P&L account	970
	1,170		1,170
		Balance b/d	220

The opening accrual of £200 acts as a reduction against the increase to the expense account on the debit side of the cash paid of £950. The £200 opening accrual is part of this £950 payment but the accrued amount was recognised within the expense in the prior year- when the expense was incurred and hence we should not double count the expense.

Activity 3

The insurance account of a business has an opening accrual of £340 at 1 July X0. During the year insurance payments of £3,700 were made and it has been calculated that there is a closing accrual of £400.

Prepare the insurance expense account for the year ended 30th June X1 and close it off by showing the transfer to the profit and loss account

Insurance expenses

	£		£

3 Prepayments

3.1 Introduction

The other type of adjustment that might need to be made to an expense account is to adjust for a prepayment.

Definition

A prepayment is a payment made during the period (and therefore debited to the expense account) for an expense that relates to a period after the year end.

Example

The rent of a business is £3,000 per quarter payable in advance. During 20X0 the rent ledger account shows that £15,000 of rent has been paid during the year.

What is the correct charge to the profit and loss account for the year and what is the amount of any prepayment at 31 December 20X0?

Solution

The profit and loss account charge should be £12,000 for the year, four quarterly charges of £3,000 each. The prepayment is £3,000 (£15,000 – £12,000), rent paid in advance for next year.

Activity 4

Julie paid £1,300 insurance during the year to 31 March 20X6.The charge in the profit and loss account for the year to 31 March 20X6 is £1,200.

What is the amount of the prepayment at 31 March 20X6?

3.2 Accounting for prepayments

The accounting for prepayments is the mirror image of accounting for accruals.

(a) **credit the expense account**

to reduce the expense by the amount of the prepayment; and

(b) **debit a prepayment account**

to show that the business has an asset (the prepayment) at the period end.

The debit entry can appear in one of two places:

(1) debit a separate prepayments account; or

(2) carry down a debit balance on the expense account.

 **Example**

The rent of a business is £3,000 per quarter payable in advance. During 20X0 the rent ledger account shows that £15,000 of rent has been paid during the year.

Show how these entries would be made in the ledger accounts.

Solution

Method one – Separate prepayments account and rent account

Rent account

	£		£
Cash payments	15,000	Prepayments account	3,000
		P&L account	12,000
	15,000		15,000

Prepayments account

	£		£
Rent account	3,000		

The charge to the profit and loss account is now the correct figure of £12,000 and there is a debit balance on the prepayments account.

This balance on the prepayments account will appear as a debtor or prepayment in the balance sheet.

Method two – Balance shown on the expense account.

Rent account

	£		£
Cash payments	15,000	P&L account	12,000
		Balance c/d – prepayment	3,000
	15,000		15,000
Balance b/d – prepayment	3,000		

The expense to the profit and loss account is again £12,000 and the debit balance on the account would appear as the prepayment on the balance sheet.

3.3 Opening and closing balances

Again as with accounting for accruals, care must be taken with opening prepayment balances on the expense account. If there is a closing prepayment balance on an expense account then this must be included as an opening balance at the start of the following year. As we must recognise the expense of the prepayment in the year it relates to, despite is being paid in the prior year.

Example

Continuing with the previous rent example the prepayment at the end of 20X0 was £3,000. The payments for rent during the following year were £15,000 and the charge for the year was £14,000.

Write up the ledger account for rent clearly showing the charge to the profit and loss account and the closing prepayment at 31 December 20X1.

Solution

Rent account

	£		£
Balance b/d – opening prepayment	3,000	P&L account charge	14,000
Cash payments	15,000	Balance c/d – prepayment (bal fig)	4,000
	18,000		18,000
Balance b/d – prepayment	4,000		

Note that you were given the charge for the year in the question and therefore the prepayment figure is the balancing amount. The opening prepayment increases the current year expense as it is now being recognised due to it being the year the expense relates to. The closing prepayment reduces the expense as despite the £15,000 payment being partly related to this closing prepayment we shouldn't be recognising the expense of it until the next year.

Activity 5

The following information relates to a company's rent and rates account:

Balances as at:	**1 April 20X0** £	**31 March 20X1** £
Prepayment for rates expenses	20	30
Accrual for rent expense	100	120

The bank summary for the year shows payments for rent and rates of £840.

Prepare the rent and rates account for the year ended 31st March 20X1 and close it off by showing the transfer to the profit and loss account.

Rent and rates expense account

	£		£
Prepayment Balance	20	Accrual rent b/d	100
Payment	840	Profit and loss	850
Balance c/d	120	Balance c/d	30
	980		980
Balance	30	Balance	120

3.4 Approach to accruals and prepayments

There are two approaches to writing up expenses accounts with accruals or prepayments. This will depend upon whether the charge to the profit and loss account is the balancing figure or whether the accrual or prepayment is the balancing figure.

Approach 1 – enter any opening accrual /prepayment

– enter the cash paid during the period

– enter the closing accrual/prepayment that has been given or calculated

– enter the charge to the profit and loss account as a balancing figure.

Approach 2 – enter any opening accrual/prepayment
- enter the cash paid during the period
- enter the profit and loss account charge for the period
- enter the closing accrual/prepayment as the balancing figure.

4 Income accounts

4.1 Introduction

As well as having expenses some businesses will also have sundry forms of income. The cash received from this income may not always be the same as the income earned in the period and therefore similar adjustments to those for accruals and prepayments in the expense accounts will be required.

4.2 Accruals of income

If the amount of income received in cash is less than the income earned for the period then this additional income must be accrued for. This is done by:

(1) a credit entry in the income account;

(2) a debit entry/debtor in the balance sheet for the amount of cash due.

4.3 Income prepaid

If the amount of cash received is greater than the income earned in the period then this income has been prepaid by the payer. The accounting entries required here are:

(1) a debit entry to the income account;

(2) a credit entry/creditor shown in the balance sheet for the amount of income that has been prepaid.

Example

Minnie's business has two properties, A and B, that are rented out to other parties. The rental on property A for the year is £12,000 but only £10,000 has been received. The rental on property B is £15,000 and the client has paid £16,000 this year.

Write up separate rent accounts for properties A and B showing the income credited to the profit and loss account and any closing balances on the income accounts.

Explain what each balance means.

Solution

Rental income – A

	£		£
P&L account	12,000	Cash received	10,000
		Balance c/d – income accrued	2,000
	12,000		12,000
Balance b/d income accrued	2,000		

Accrued income would be a debtor balance in the balance sheet showing that £2,000 is owed for rental income on this property.

Rental income – B

	£		£
P&L account	15,000	Cash received	16,000
Balance c/d – income prepaid	1,000		
	16,000		16,000
		Balance b/d – income prepaid	1,000

Prepaid income would be a creditor balance in the balance sheet indicating that too much cash (cash in advance) has been received for this rental.

Activity 6

Hyde, an acquaintance wishes to use your shop to display and sell framed photographs. He will pay £40 per month for this service in cash.

(a) How would you account for this transaction each month?

(b) If, at the end of the year, the acquaintance owed one month's rental, how would this be treated in the accounts?

(c) Which accounting concept is being applied?

5 Journal entries

5.1 Introduction

The accruals and prepayments are adjustments to the accounts which do not appear in the accounting records from the primary records. Therefore the adjustments for accruals and prepayments must be entered into the accounting records by means of a journal entry.

Example

An accrual for electricity is to be made at the year-end of £200. Show the journal entry required for this adjustment.

Solution

Journal entry			**No:**
Date			
Prepared by			
Authorised by			
Account	**Code**	**Debit £**	**Credit £**
Electricity account	0442	200	
Accruals	1155		200
Totals		200	200

Activity 7

A prepayment adjustment is to be made at the year end of £1,250 for insurance expense.

Record the journal entry required for this adjustment.

The following account codes and account names should be used.

0445 Insurance

1000 Prepayment

Journal entry			**No:**
Date			
Prepared by			
Authorised by			
Account	**Code**	**Debit £**	**Credit £**
Insurane	0445		1250
Prepayment	1000	1250	
Totals			

6 Summary

In order for the final accounts of an organisation to accord with the accruals concept, the cash receipts and payments for income and expenses must be adjusted to ensure that they include all of the income earned during the year and expenses incurred during the year.

The sales and purchases are automatically dealt with through the sales ledger and purchases ledger control account.

However the expenses and sundry income of the business are recorded in the ledger accounts on a cash paid and received basis and therefore adjustments for accruals and prepayments must be made by journal entries.

Answers to chapter activities

Activity 1

$(\frac{8}{12} \times £6,000) = £4,000$

Activity 2

Rent account

	£		£
Cash payments	3,400	Profit and loss account (6,000 × $\frac{8}{12}$)	4,000
Balance c/d – accrual	600		
	4,000		4,000
		Balance b/d – accrual	600

Activity 3

Insurance expenses

	£		£
Cash payments	3,700	Balance b/d – opening accrual	340
Balance c/d – closing accrual	400	P & L account charge (bal fig)	3,760
	4,100		4,100
		Balance b/d – accrual	400

Activity 4

The prepayment is £1,300 – 1,200 = £100

Activity 5

Rent and rates expense account

	£		£
Balance b/d	20	Balance b/d	100
Cash	840	Profit and loss account	850
Balance c/d	120	(bal fig)	
		Balance c/d	30
	980		980
Balance b/d	30	Balance b/d	120

Activity 6

(a) DR Cash account £40

CR Sundry Income a/c £40

(b) Accrued income – a sundry debtor

(1) revenue in the Profit and Loss a/c

(2) current asset in the Balance Sheet

(c) Accruals concept

Activity 7

Journal entry			**No:**
Date			
Prepared by			
Authorised by			
Account	**Code**	**Debit £**	**Credit £**
Prepayment	1000	1,250	
Insurance	0445		1,250
Totals		1,250	1,250

7 Test your knowledge

Workbook Activity 8

Siobhan

Siobhan, the proprietor of a sweet shop, provides you with the following information in respect of sundry expenditure and income of her business for the year ended 31 December 20X4:

1 **Rent payable**

£15,000 was paid during 20X4 to cover the 15 months ending 31 March 20X5.

2 **Gas**

£840 was paid during 20X4 to cover gas charges from 1 January 20X4 to 31 July 20X4. Gas charges can be assumed to accrue evenly over the year. There was no outstanding balance at 1 January 20X4.

3 **Advertising**

Included in the payments totalling £3,850 made during 20X4 is an amount of £500 payable in respect of a planned campaign for 20X5.

4 **Bank interest**

The bank statements of the business show that the following interest has been charged to the account.

For period up to 31 May 20X4	Nil (no overdraft)
For 1 June – 31 August 20X4	£28
1 September – 30 November 20X4	£45

The bank statements for 20X5 show that £69 was charged to the account on 28 February 20X5.

5 **Rates**

Towards the end of 20X3 £4,800 was paid to cover the six months ended 31 March 20X4.

In May 20X4 £5,600 was paid to cover the six months ended 30 September 20X4.

In early 20X5 £6,600 was paid for the six months ending 31 March 20X5.

6 **Rent receivable**

During 20X4, Siobhan received £250 rent from Joe Soap for the use of a lock-up garage attached to the shop, in respect of the six months ended 31 March 20X4.

She increased the rent to £600 pa from 1 April 20X4, and during 20X4 Joe Soap paid her rent for the full year ending 31 March 20X5.

Required:

Write up ledger accounts for each of the above items, showing:

(a) the opening balance at 1 January 20X4, if any;

(b) any cash paid or received;

(c) the closing balance at 31 December 20X4;

(d) the charge or credit for the year to the profit and loss account.

Workbook Activity 9

A Crew

The following is an extract from the trial balance of A Crew at 31 December 20X1:

	DR
	£
Stationery	560
Rent	900
Rates	380
Lighting and heating	590
Insurance	260
Wages and salaries	2,970

Stationery which had cost £15 was still in hand at 31 December 20X1.

Rent of £300 for the last three months of 20X1 had not been paid and no entry has been made in the books for it.

£280 of the rates was for the year ended 31 March 20X2. The remaining £100 was for the three months ended 31 March 20X1.

Fuel had been delivered on 18 December 20X1 at a cost of £15 and had been consumed before the end of 20X1. No invoice had been received for the £15 fuel in 20X1 and no entry has been made in the records of the business.

£70 of the insurance paid was in respect of insurance cover for the year 20X2. Nothing was owing to employees for wages and salaries at the close of 20X1.

Required:

Record the above information in the relevant accounts, showing the transfers to the profit and loss account for the year ended 31 December 20X1.

Workbook Activity 10

A Metro

A Metro owns a number of antique shops and, in connection with this business, he runs a small fleet of motor vans. He prepares his accounts to 31 December in each year.

On 1 January 20X0 the amount prepaid for motor tax and insurance was £570.

On 1 April 20X0 he paid £420 which represented motor tax on six of the vans for the year ended 31 March 20X1.

On 1 May 20X0 he paid £1,770 insurance for all ten vans for the year ended 30 April 20X1.

On 1 July 20X0 he paid £280 which represented motor tax for the other four vans for the year ended 30 June 20X1.

Required:

Write up the account for 'motor tax and insurance' for the year ended 31 December 20X0.

Accounting for bad and doubtful debts

Introduction

When producing a trial balance or extended trial balance, and eventually a set of final accounts, a number of adjustments are often required to the initial trial balance figures.

One of these adjustments may be to the sales ledger balance in order to either write off any bad debts or to provide for any provision for doubtful debts.

CONTENTS

1 Problems with sales ledger accounts

1.1 Introduction

When sales are made to credit customers the double entry is to debit the sales ledger control account and credit the sales account. Therefore the sale is recorded in the accounts as soon as the invoice is sent out to the customer on the basis that the customer will pay for these goods.

1.2 Conditions of uncertainty

The accounting concept of prudence was mentioned in an earlier chapter. Part of that accounting concept means that in conditions of uncertainty more evidence is needed of the existence of an asset than is needed for the existence of a liability.

Therefore if there is any evidence of significant uncertainty about the receipt of cash from a debtor then it may be that this asset, the debt, should not be recognised.

1.3 Aged debtors analysis

Definition

An aged debtors analysis shows when the elements of the total debt owed by each customer were incurred.

An aged debtors analysis should be produced on a regular basis and studied with care. If a customer has old outstanding debts or if the customer has stopped paying the debts owed regularly then there may be a problem with this debt.

1.4 Other information about trade debtors

It is not uncommon for businesses to go into liquidation or receivership in which case it is often likely that any outstanding credit supplier will not receive payment. This will often be reported in the local or national newspapers or the information could be discovered informally from conversation with other parties in the same line of business.

If information is gathered about a debtor with potential problems which may mean that your organisation will not receive full payment of the amounts due then this must be investigated.

However care should be taken as customers are very important to a business and any discussion or correspondence with the customer must be carried out with tact and courtesy.

2 Bad debts

2.1 Information

If information is reliably gathered that a debtor is having problems paying the amounts due then a decision has to be made about how to account for the amount due from that customer. This will normally take the form of deciding whether the debt is a bad debt or a doubtful debt.

2.2 What is a bad debt?

Definition

A bad debt is a debt that is not going to be received from the debtor.

Therefore a bad debt is one that the organisation is reasonably certain will not be received at all from the debtor. This may be decided after discussions with the customer, after legal advice if the customer has gone into liquidation or simply because the customer has disappeared.

2.3 Accounting treatment of a bad debt

A bad debt is one where it has been determined that it will never be recovered and therefore it is to be written out of the books totally.

The double entry reflects the fact that:

(a) the business no longer has the debt, so this asset must be removed from the books

(b) the business accounts for an expense equal to the debt in its Profit and Loss Account because it has 'lost' this money. It does this by putting the expense initially through a bad debt expense account.

The double entry for the bad debt is therefore:

Dr Bad debt expense account

Cr Sales ledger control account (SLCA)

There is also a credit entry in the individual customer's account in the subsidiary sales ledger to match the entry in the SLCA.

Example

Lewis reviews his sales ledger balances (which total £10,000) and notices an amount due from John of £500. He knows that this will never be recovered so he wants to write it off.

Solution

Sales ledger control account

	£		£
Balance b/d	10,000	Bad debt expense	500
		Balance c/d	9,500
	10,000		10,000
Balance b/d	9,500		

Bad debt expense

	£		£
SLCA	500	P & L	500

In the subsidiary sales ledger there will also be an entry in John's account:

John's account

	£		£
Balance b/d	500	Bad debt written off	500

Activity 1

A business has total trade debtors of £117,489. One of these debts from J Casy totalling £2,448 is now considered to be bad and must be accounted for.

Record the accounting entries in the general ledger for the bad debt.

Sales ledger control account

	£		£
Balance b/d	117489	Bad debt	2448
		Balance c/d	115041
Balance b/d	115041		

Bad debt expense

	£		£
SLCA	2448		

The accounting treatment of bad debts means that the debt is completely removed from the accounting records and the Profit and Loss Account is charged with an expense.

3 Doubtful debts

3.1 Introduction

In the previous section we considered debts that we were reasonably certain would not be recovered. However the position with some debts is not so clear cut. The organisation may have doubts about whether the debt may be received but may not be certain that it will not.

3.2 Doubtful debts

Definition

Doubtful debts are debts about which there is some question as to whether or not the debt will be received.

The situation here is not as clear cut as when a debt is determined to be bad and the accounting treatment is therefore different. If there is doubt about the recoverability of this debt then according to the prudence concept this must be recognised in the accounting records but not to the extreme of writing the debt out of the accounts totally.

3.3 Accounting treatment of doubtful debts

As the debt is only doubtful rather than bad we do not need to write it out of the accounting records totally but the doubt has to be reflected. This is done by setting up a provision for doubtful debts.

Definition

A provision for doubtful debts is an amount that is netted off against the trade debtors balance in the Balance Sheet to show that there is some doubt about the recoverability of these amounts.

A provision for doubtful debts account is credited in order to net this off against the sales ledger balance and the debit entry is made to the bad debt expense account recognised in the Profit and Loss Account.

The double entry therefore is:

Dr Bad debt expense account (Profit and Loss Account)

Cr Provision for doubtful debts (Balance Sheet)

Example

At the end of his first year of trading Roger has trade debtors of £120,000 and has decided that of these there is some doubt as to the recoverability of £5,000 of debts.

Set up the provision for doubtful debts in the ledger accounts and show how the trade debtors would appear in Balance Sheet at the end of the year.

Solution

Provision for doubtful debts

	£		£
		Bad debt expense	5,000

Bad debt expense

	£		£
Provision for doubtful debts	5,000		

Balance Sheet extract

	£
Trade debtors	120,000
Less: Provision for doubtful debts	(5,000)
	115,000

The accounting treatment of doubtful debts ensures that the Balance Sheet clearly shows that there is some doubt about the collectability of some of the debts and the Profit and Loss Account is charged with the possible loss from not collecting these debts.

3.4 Changes in the provision

As the provision for doubtful debts account is a Balance Sheet balance, the balance on that account will remain in the ledger accounts until it is changed. When the provision is altered, **only the increase or the decrease** is charged or credited to the bad debt expense account.

Increase in provision:

Dr Bad debt expense account (Profit and Loss Account)

Cr Provision for doubtful debts account (Balance Sheet)

Decrease in provision:

Dr Provision for doubtful debts account (Balance Sheet)

Cr Bad debt expense account (Profit and Loss Account)

Example

At the end of the second year of trading Roger feels that the provision for doubtful debts should be increased to £7,000. At the end of the third year of trading Roger wishes to decrease the provision to £4,000.

Show the entries in the ledger accounts required at the end of year 2 and year 3 of trading.

Solution

Provision for doubtful debts account

	£		£
		Balance b/d	5,000
End of year 2 balance c/d	7,000	Year 2 – Bad debt expense account	2,000
	7,000		7,000
Year 3 – Bad debt expense account	3,000	Balance b/d	7,000
End of year 3 balance c/d	4,000		
	7,000		7,000
		Balance b/d	4,000

Bad debt expense account

	£		£
Year 2 Provision for doubtful debts account	2,000	Profit and Loss Account year 2	2,000
	2,000		2,000
Profit and Loss Account year 3	3,000	Year 3 Provision for doubtful debts account	3,000
	3,000		3,000

Take care that the Profit and Loss Account is only charged or credited with the increase or decrease in the provision each year.

4 Types of provisions for doubtful debts

4.1 Introduction

There are two main types of provisions for doubtful debts:

- specific provisions
- general provisions.

This does not affect the accounting for provision for doubtful debts but it does affect the calculation of the provision.

4.2 Specific provisions

Definition

A specific provision is a provision against identified specific debts.

This will normally be determined by close scrutiny of the aged debtors analysis in order to determine whether there are specific debts that the organisation feels may not be paid.

4.3 General provision

Definition

A general provision is a provision against trade debtors as a whole, normally expressed as a percentage of the trade debtors balance.

Most businesses will find that not all of their customers pay their debts. Experience may indicate that generally a percentage of debts, say 3%, will not be paid.

The organisation may not know which debts these are going to be but they will maintain a provision for 3% of the sales ledger balance at the year end.

Care should be taken with the calculation of this provision as the percentage should be of the trade debtors balance after deducting any specific provisions as well as any bad debts written off.

Order of dealing with a general provision:

1 Write off bad debts

2 Create specific provisions

3 Calculate the net trade debtors figures after both bad debts and specific provisions

4 Calculate the general provision using the net trade debtors figure from point 3.

Example

A business has trade debtors of £356,000 of which £16,000 are to be written off as bad debts.

Of the remainder a specific provision is to be made against a debt of £2,000 and a general provision of 4% is required against the remaining trade debtors.

The opening balance on the provision for doubtful debts account is £12,000.

Show the entries in the provision for doubtful debts account and the bad debt expense account.

Solution

Calculation of provision required:	£
Trade debtors	356,000
1 Less: bad debt to be written off	(16,000)
2 Less: specific provisions	(2,000)
3 Remaining trade debtors	338,000
4 General provision 4% × £338,000	13,520
Specific provision	2,000
Provision at year end	15,520

Provision for doubtful debts (note 1)

	£		£
		Balance b/d	12,000
Balance c/d	15,520	Bad debt expense - increase in provision	3,520
	15,520		15,520
		Balance b/d	15,520

Sales ledger control account (note 2)

	£		£
Balance b/d	356,000	Bad debt expense – written off	16,000
		Balance c/d	340,000
	356,000		356,000
Balance b/d	340,000		

Bad debt expense account

	£		£
Trade debtors (Note 2)	16,000	Profit and Loss A/c	19,520
Provision for doubtful debts (Note 1)	3,520		
	19,520		19,520

Note 1

The balance on the provision account is simply 'topped-up' (or down) at each year end. In this case the required provision has been calculated to be £15,520. The existing provision is £12,000 so the increase is calculated as:

	£
Provision at start of year b/f	12,000
Provision required at year end	15,520
Increase in provision	3,520

This is credited to the provision account and debited to the bad debt expense account.

Note 2

The £16,000 bad debt is written out of the books. The double entry for this is to credit the SLCA and debit the bad debt expense.

Note that the provision does not affect the SLCA.

Any specific provision must be deducted from the trade debtors balance before the general provision percentage is applied.

Activity 2

DD makes a provision for doubtful debts of 5% of trade debtors.

On 1 January 20X5 the balance on the provision for doubtful debts account was £1,680.

During the year the business incurred bad debts amounting to £1,950. On 31 December 20X5 trade debtors amounted to £32,000 after writing off the bad debts of £1,950.

Required:

Write up the relevant accounts for the year ended 31 December 20X5.

Activity 3

Peter had the following balances in his trial balance at 31 March 20X4:

	£
Total trade debtors	61,000
Provision for doubtful debts at 1 April 20X3	1,490

After the trial balance had been prepared it was decided to carry forward at 31 March 20X4 a specific provision of £800 and a general provision equal to 1% of remaining trade debtors. It was also decided to write off debts amounting to £1,000.

What is the total charge for bad and doubtful debts which should appear in the company's Profit and Loss Account for the year ended 31 March 20X4?

5 Writing off a debt already provided for

5.1 Introduction

It may happen that a doubtful debt provision is made at a year end, and then it is decided in a later year to write the debt off completely as a bad debt as it will not be received.

Example

At 31 December 20X2, John has a balance on the SLCA of £20,000 and a provision for doubtful debts of £1,000 which was created in 20X1.

This £1,000 relates to A whose debt was thought to be doubtful. There is no general provision.

At 31 December 20X2, A has still not paid and John has decided to write the debt off as bad.

Make the related entries in the books.

Solution

Step 1

Open the SLCA and the provision account.

SLCA

	£		£
Balance b/d	20,000		

Provision for doubtful debts

	£		£
		Balance b/d	1,000

Step 2

Remove A's debt from the accounts.

A's £1,000 is included in the £20,000 balance on the SLCA, and this has to be removed. Similarly, the £1,000 in the provision account related to A.

The double entry is simply to:

Debit Provision account with £1,000

Credit SLCA with £1,000

SLCA

	£		£
Balance b/d	20,000	Provision	1,000

Provision for doubtful debts

	£		£
SLCA	1,000	Balance b/d	1,000

Note that there is no impact on the Profit and Loss Account. The profits were charged with £1,000 when a provision was made for A's debt, and there is no need to charge profits with another £1,000.

6 Money received from bad and doubtful debts

6.1 Receipt of a debt previously written off as bad

Occasionally money may be received from a customer whose balance has already been written off as a bad debt.

The full double entry for this receipt has two elements:

Dr Sales ledger control account

Cr Bad debt expense account

In order to reinstate the debt that has been previously written off.

Dr Bank account

Cr Sales ledger control account

To account for the cash received from this debtor.

However this double entry can be simplified to:

Dr Bank account

Cr Bad debts expense account (or a separate bad debts recovered account)

Note that the debtor is not reinstated as there is both a debit and credit to the sales ledger control account which cancel each other out.

6.2 Receipt of a debt previously provided against

On occasion money may be received from a customer for whose balance a specific provision was previously made.

The double entry for this receipt is:

Dr Bank account

Cr Sales ledger control account

This is accounted for as a normal receipt from a debtor (that has not been written out of the books) and at the year end, the requirement for a provision against this debt will no longer be necessary.

Example

At the end of 20X6 Bjorn had made a provision of £500 against doubtful trade debtors. This was made up as follows:

		£
Specific provision	A	300
Specific provision	50% × B	200
		500

At the end of 20X7 Bjorn's trade debtors total £18,450. After reviewing each debt he discovers the following, none of which have been entered in the books:

(1) A has paid £50 of the debt outstanding at the beginning of the year.
(2) B has paid his debt in full.

Show the ledger entries required to record the above.

Step 1

Calculate the new provision required at the year end.

	£
A	250
B	Nil
	250

Step 2

Enter the cash on the SLCA.

Sales ledger control account

	£		£
Balance b/d	18,450	Cash – A	50
		Cash – B	400
		Balance c/d	18,000
	18,450		18,450
Balance b/d	18,000		

Step 3

Bring down the new provision required in the provision account.

Bad Debt expense account

	£		£
		Provision for doubtful debts	250

Provision for doubtful debts account

	£		£
Bad debt expense account	250	Balance b/d	500
Balance c/d	250		
	500		500
		Balance b/d	250

Note: Because the provision has been reduced from £500 to £250, there is a credit entry in the bad debt expense account which will be taken to the Profit and Loss Account.

6.3 Journal entries

As with the depreciation charge for the year and any accrual or prepayment adjustments at the year end, any bad debts or doubtful debt provisions are transactions that will not appear in any of the books of prime entry.

Therefore, the source document for any bad debt write offs or increases or decreases in doubtful debt provisions must be the transfer journal. The necessary journals must be written up and then posted to the relevant ledger accounts at the year end.

Activity 4

Record the following journal entries needed in the general ledger to deal with the items below.

(a) Entries need to be made for a bad debt of £240.

Journal	*Dr* £	*Cr* £
Bad debt	240	
SLCA		240

(b) Entries need to be made for a doubtful debt provision. The trade debtor's balance at the year end is £18,000 and a provision is to be made against 2% of these.

Journal	*Dr* £	*Cr* £
Doubtful debt prov.		360
Bad debt	360	

(c) A sole trader has an opening balance on his provision for doubtful debts account of £2,500. At his year end he wishes to make a provision for 2% of his year end trade debtors of £100,000.

Journal	*Dr* £	*Cr* £
Provis. doubt debts	500	
Bad debts		500

(d) Entries need to be made for an amount of £200 that has been recovered, it was previously written off in the last accounting period.

Journal	*Dr* £	*Cr* £
Bank	200	
Bad debt		200

7 Summary

When sales are made on credit they are recognised as income when the invoice is sent out on the assumption that the money due will eventually be received from the customer.

However according to the prudence concept if there is any doubt about the recoverability of any of the debts this must be recognised in the accounting records.

The accounting treatment will depend upon whether the debt is considered to be a bad debt or a doubtful debt.

Bad debts are written out of the sales ledger control account.

However, for doubtful debts, a provision is set up which is netted off against the trade debtors figure in the Balance Sheet. The charge or credit to the Profit and Loss Account each year for doubtful debts is either the increase or decrease in the provision for doubtful debts required at the end of the each year.

Answers to chapter activities

Activity 1

Sales ledger control account

	£		£
Balance b/d	117,489	Bad debts expense	2,448
		Balance c/d	115,041
	117,489		117,489
Balance b/d	115,041		

Bad debt expense account

	£		£
Sales ledger control account	2,448	P & L Account	2,448

Activity 2

Provision for doubtful debts account

	£		£
Bad debts expense	80	Balance b/d	1,680
Balance c/d	1,600		
	1,680		1,680

Note: The provision required at 31 December 20X5 is calculated by taking 5% of the total trade debtors at 31 December 20X5 (i.e. 5% × £32,000 = £1,600). As there is already a provision of £1,680, there will be a release of the provision (decrease) of £80.

Bad debt expense account

	£		£
Trade debtors	1,950	Provision for doubtful debts	80
		Profit and loss a/c	1,870
	1,950		1,950

Note: Only one account is being used to record the reduction in the provision and also the bad debt.

Activity 3

Provision for doubtful debts account

	£		£
Bad debt expense	98	Balance b/d	1,490
Balance c/d	1,392		
	1,490		1,490
		Balance b/d (800 + 592)	1,392

Required provision of £1,392 is made up of the specific provision of £800 and a general provision calculated as £592 ((£61,000 – £1,000 – £800) × 1%)

Bad debts expense

	£		£
Bad debts written off	1,000	Provision for doubtful debts	98
		Profit and Loss Account	902
	1,000		1,000

Activity 4

(a) Entries need to be made for a bad debt of £240; main ledger accounts therefore will be as below.

Journal	*Dr* £	*Cr* £
Bad debts expense account	240	
Sales ledger control account		240

(b) Provision is calculated as £18,000 × 2%.

Journal	*Dr* £	*Cr* £
Bad debt expense account	360	
Provision for doubtful debts account		360

(c) Provision for doubtful debts are ((100,000 × 2%) – 2,500)

Journal	*Dr* £	*Cr* £
Provision for doubtful debts	500	
Bad debt expense account		500

(d) Entries need to be made for an amount of £200 in the bank and bad debt expense account.

Journal	*Dr* £	*Cr* £
Bank account	200	
Bad debt expense account		200

8 Test your knowledge

Workbook Activity 5

John Stamp has opening balances at 1 January 20X6 on his trade debtors account and provision for doubtful debts account of £68,000 and £3,400 respectively.

During the year to 31 December 20X6 John Stamp makes credit sales of £354,000 and receives cash from his trade debtors of £340,000.

At 31 December 20X6 John Stamp reviews his trade debtors listing and acknowledges that he is unlikely ever to receive debts totalling £2,000. These are to be written off as bad.

John also wishes to provide a provision against 5% of his remaining trade debtors after writing off the bad debts.

You are required to write up the:

- Sales ledger control account
- Provision for doubtful debts account and the bad debts expense account for the year to 31 December 20X6
- Show the trade debtors and provision for doubtful debts extract from the Balance Sheet at that date.

Workbook Activity 6

Angola

Angola started a business on 1 January 20X7 and during the first year of business it was necessary to write off the following debts as bad:

		£
10 April	Cuba	46
4 October	Kenya	29
6 November	Peru	106

On 31 December 20X7, after examination of the sales ledger, it was decided to provide a provision against two specific debts of £110 and £240 from Chad and Chile respectively and to make a general provision of 4% against the remaining debts.

On 31 December 20X7, the total of the trade debtors balances stood at £5,031; Angola had not yet adjusted this total for the bad debts written off.

Required:

Show the accounts for bad debts expense and provision for doubtful debts.

Workbook Activity 7

Zambia

On 1 January 20X8 Angola sold his business, including the trade debtors, to Zambia. During the year ended 31 December 20X8 Zambia found it necessary to write off the following debts as bad:

		£
26 February	Fiji	125
8 August	Mexico	362

He also received on 7 July an amount of £54 as a final dividend against the debt of Peru which had been written off during 20X7.

No specific provisions were required at 31 December 20X8 but it was decided to make a general provision of 5% against outstanding trade debtors.

On 31 December 20X8 the total of the trade debtors balances stood at £12,500 (before making any adjustments for bad debts written off during the year) and the balance b/d on the provision for doubtful debts account stood at £530.

Required:

Show the accounts for bad debt expense and provision for doubtful debts, bringing forward any adjustments for Angola.

Workbook Activity 8

Julie Owens is a credit customer of Explosives and currently owes approximately £5,000.

She has recently become very slow in paying for purchases and has been sent numerous reminders for most of the larger invoices issued to her.

A cheque for £2,500 sent to Explosives has now been returned by Julie Owens' bankers marked 'refer to drawer'.

Which accounting concept would suggest that a provision for doubtful debts should be created to cover the debt of Julie Owens?

Preparation of final accounts for a sole trader

13

Introduction

You need to be able to prepare the final accounts; a profit and loss account and a balance sheet for a sole trader.

These final accounts may be prepared directly from a trial balance plus various adjustments or from an extended trial balance. The preparation of an extended trial balance is not part of the Level III syllabus and therefore we will just be considering the step by step approach to the final accounts preparation from an initial trial balance.

CONTENTS

1 The profit and loss account for a sole trader

1.1 Introduction

Definition

The profit and loss account summarises transactions over a period and determines whether a profit or a loss has been made during that period.

Technically the profit and loss account is split into two elements:

- the trading account
- the profit and loss account.

However, in general the whole statement is referred to as the profit and loss account.

1.2 Trading account

The trading account calculates the gross profit/loss that has been made from the trading activities of the sole trader; the buying and selling of goods.

 **Definition**

The gross profit/loss is the profit/loss from the trading activities of the sole trader.

The trading account looks like this:

		£	£
	Sales		X
Less:	Sales returns		(X)
			X
Less:	Cost of sales		
	Opening stock	X	
	Purchases	X	
Less:	Purchases returns	(X)	
		X	
	Less: Closing stock	(X)	
			(X)
	Gross profit (loss)		X

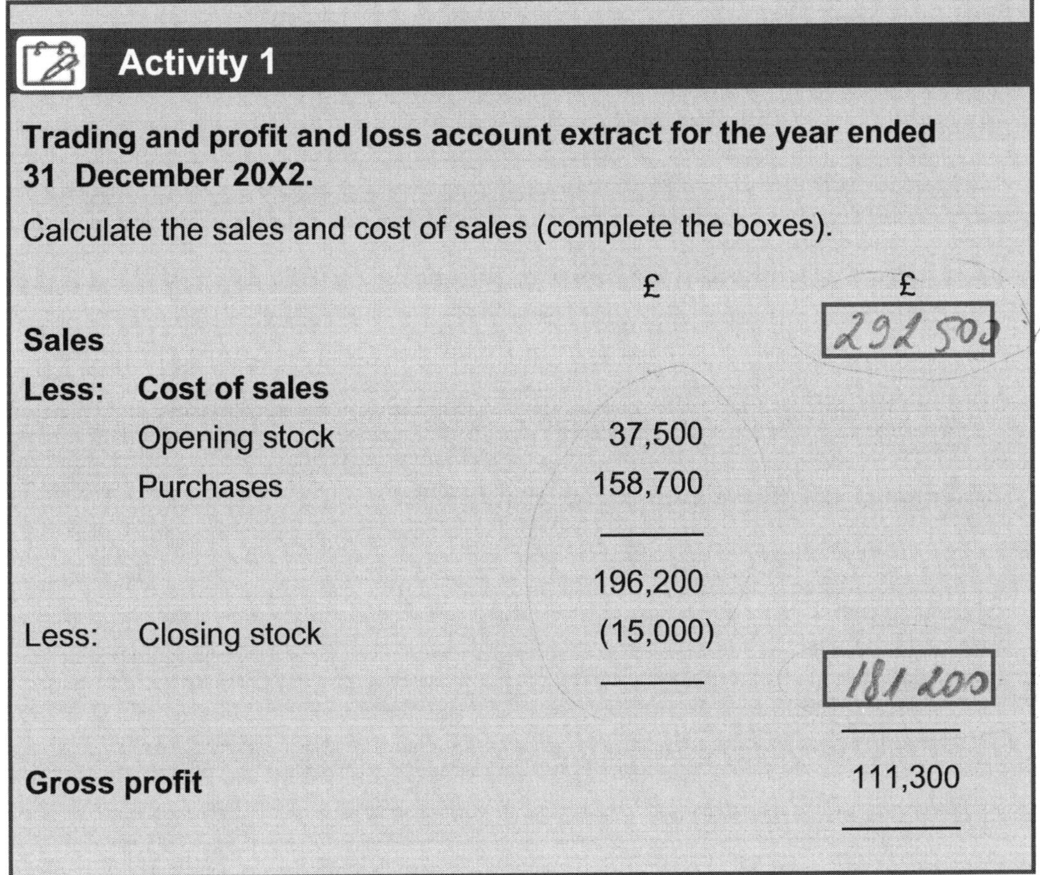

Activity 1

Trading and profit and loss account extract for the year ended 31 December 20X2.

Calculate the sales and cost of sales (complete the boxes).

		£	£
Sales			292 500
Less:	**Cost of sales**		
	Opening stock	37,500	
	Purchases	158,700	
		196,200	
Less:	Closing stock	(15,000)	
			181 200
Gross profit			111,300

1.3 Profit and loss account

The remaining content of the profit and loss account is a list of the expenses of the business. These are deducted from the gross profit to give the net profit or loss.

Definition

The net profit or loss is the profit or loss after deduction of all of the expenses of the business.

A proforma profit and loss account is shown on the following page.

Profit and loss account for the year ended 31 December 20X2

	£	£
Sales		X
Less: Sales returns		(X)
		X
Less: Cost of sales		
Stock on 1 January (opening stock)	X	
Add: Purchases of goods for resale	X	
Less: Purchases returns	(X)	
	X	
Less: Stock on 31 December (closing stock)	(X)	
		(X)
Gross profit		X
Sundry income:		
Discounts received	X	
Commission received	X	
Rent received	X	
		X
		X
Less: Expenses:		
Rent	X	
Rates	X	
Lighting and heating	X	
Telephone	X	
Postage	X	
Insurance	X	
Stationery	X	
Payroll expenses	X	
Depreciation	X	
Accountancy and audit fees	X	
Bank charges and interest	X	
Bad debts	X	
Delivery costs	X	
Van running expenses	X	
Selling expenses	X	
Discounts allowed	X	
		(X)
Net profit/(Loss)		X/(X)

1.4 Preparation of the profit and loss account

The profit and loss account is prepared by listing all of the entries from the trial balance that are profit and loss account balances.

It is important to consider any adjustments that are required to the trial balance amounts prior to inserting the amounts into the profit and loss account.

Example

Given below is the trial balance for Lyttleton along with additional columns for some adjustments that are required.

Account name	*Trial balance*		*Adjustments*	
	DR	CR	DR	CR
	£	£	£	£
Capital		7,830		
Cash	2,010			
Fixed assets	9,420			
Accumulated depreciation		3,470		942
SLCA	1,830			
Opening stock	1,680			
PLCA		390		
Sales		14,420		
Purchases	8,180			1,500
Rent	1,100		100	
Electricity	940		400	
Rates	950			200
Depreciation expense			942	
Bad debts expense			55	
Drawings			1,500	
Accruals				555
Prepayments			200	
Closing stock BS			1,140	
Closing stock P&L				1,140
	26,110	**26,110**	**4,337**	**4,337**

We will now show how the final profit and loss account for Lyttleton would look.

Solution

Trading and profit and loss account of Lyttleton for the year ended 31 December 20X5

		£	£
Sales			14,420
Less:	Cost of sales		
	Opening stock	1,680	
	Purchases	6,680	
		8,360	
Less:	Closing stock	(1,140)	
			(7,220)
Gross profit			7,200
Less: Expenses			
	Rent	1,200	
	Electricity	1,340	
	Rates	750	
	Depreciation	942	
	Bad debts expense	55	
Total expenses			(4,287)
Net profit			2,913

2 The balance sheet for a sole trader

2.1 Introduction

Definition

A balance sheet is a list of the assets and liabilities of the sole trader at the end of the accounting period.

The assets are split into fixed assets and current assets.

Definition

Fixed assets are assets for long-term use within the business e.g. buildings.

Definition

Current assets are assets that are either currently cash or are expected to soon be converted into cash e.g. stock.

The liabilities are split into current liabilities and long term liabilities.

Definition

Current liabilities are the short term creditors of the business. This generally means creditors who are due to be paid within twelve months of the balance sheet date e.g. trade creditors.

Definition

Long-term liabilities are creditors who are expected to be paid after more than 12 months e.g. long term loans. These are deducted to give the net assets.

A proforma for a typical sole trader's balance sheet is given below:

Balance sheet at 31 December 20X2

	Cost	Depreciation	
	£	£	£
Fixed assets			
Freehold factory	X	X	X
Machinery	X	X	X
Motor vehicles	X	X	X
	X	X	X
Current assets			
Stocks		X	
Trade debtors		X	
Prepayments		X	
Cash at bank		X	
Cash in hand		X	
		X	
Current liabilities			
Trade creditors	X		
Accruals	X		
		(X)	
Net current assets			X
Total assets less current liabilities			X
Long-term liabilities			
Bank loan			(X)
Net assets			X
Capital at 1 January			X
Net profit for the year			X
			X
Less: Drawings			(X)
Proprietor's funds			X

2.2 Assets and liabilities

The assets and liabilities in a formal balance sheet are listed in a particular order:

- firstly the fixed assets less the accumulated depreciation (remember that this net total is known as the net book value)
- next the current assets in the following order – stock, debtors, prepayments then bank and cash balances
- next the current liabilities – creditors and accruals that are payable within 12 months
- finally the long-term creditors such as loan accounts.

The assets are all added together and the liabilities are then deducted. This gives the balance sheet total.

2.3 Capital balances

The total of the assets less liabilities of the sole trader should be equal to the capital of the sole trader.

The capital is shown in the balance sheet as follows:

	£
Opening capital at the start of the year	X
Add: Net profit/(loss) for the year	X
	X
Less: Drawings	(X)
Closing capital	X

This closing capital should be equal to the total of all of the assets less liabilities of the sole trader shown in the top part of the balance sheet.

Example

Below is the trial balance along with adjustments for Lyttleton again. This time the balance sheet will be prepared.

Account name	*Trial balance*		*Adjustments*	
	DR	CR	DR	CR
	£	£	£	£
Capital		7,830		
Cash	2,010			
Fixed assets	9,420			
Accumulated depreciation		3,470		942
SLCA	1,830			
Opening Stock	1,680			
PLCA		390		
Sales		14,420		
Purchases	8,180			1,500
Rent	1,100		100	
Electricity	940		400	
Rates	950			200
Depreciation expense			942	
Bad debt expense			55	
Drawings			1,500	
Accruals				555
Prepayments			200	
Closing stock – Profit and loss				1,140
Closing stock – Balance sheet			1,140	
	26,110	**26,110**	**4,337**	**4,337**

We now need to consider which ledger accounts will form part of the balance sheet.

Solution

Balance sheet of Lyttleton at 31 December 20X5

	Cost	*Accumulated Dep'n*	
	£	£	£
Fixed assets	9,420	4,412	5,008
Current assets			
Stocks		1,140	
Trade debtors		1,830	
Prepayments		200	
Cash		2,010	
		5,180	
Less:			
Current liabilities			
Creditors	390		
Accruals	555		
		(945)	
Net current assets			4,235
Net assets			9,243
Capital 1 January			7,830
Net profit for the year			2,913
			10,743
Less: Drawings			(1,500)
Proprietor's funds			9,243

Notes:

- the fixed assets are shown at their net book value
- the current assets are sub-totalled as are the current liabilities – the current liabilities are then deducted from the current assets to give net current assets
- the net current assets are added to the fixed asset net book value to reach the balance sheet total, net assets.

The balance sheet total of net assets should be equal to the closing capital; the balance sheet is then said to balance. If your balance sheet does not balance then make some quick obvious checks such as the adding up and that all figures have been included at the correct amount but do not spend too much time searching for your error as the time can be better used on the rest of the assessment. If you have time left over at the end then you can check further for the difference.

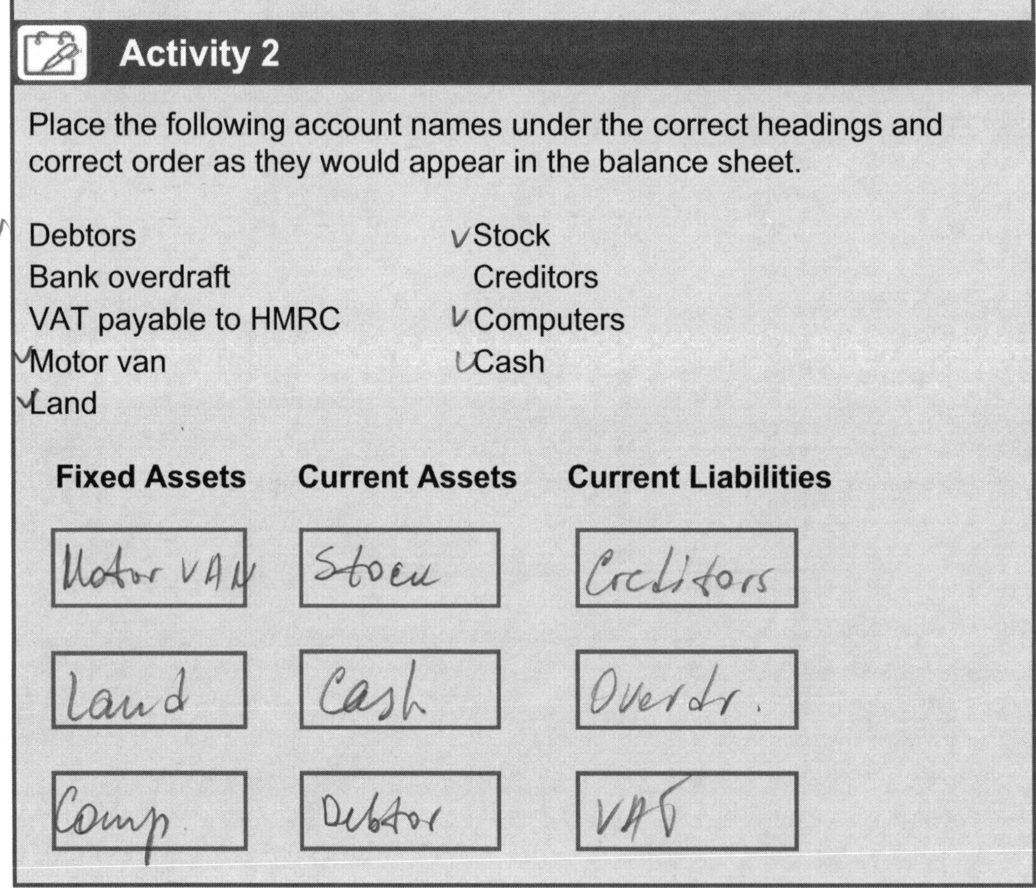

Activity 2

Place the following account names under the correct headings and correct order as they would appear in the balance sheet.

Debtors	Stock
Bank overdraft	Creditors
VAT payable to HMRC	Computers
Motor van	Cash
Land	

Fixed Assets	**Current Assets**	**Current Liabilities**

Activity 3

Given below is a trial balance along with some adjustments that are required.

Trial balance at 31 December 20X6

Account name	*Trial balance*		*Adjustments*	
	DR	CR	DR	CR
	£	£	£	£
Fittings	7,300			
Accumulated depreciation 1.1.X6		2,500		400
Leasehold	30,000			
Accumulated depreciation 1.1.X6		6,000		1,000
Stock 1 January 20X6	15,000			
Sales ledger control account	10,000			500
Cash in hand	50			
Cash at bank	1,250			
Purchases ledger control account		18,000		
Capital		19,850		
Drawings	4,750		1,200	
Purchases	80,000			1,200
Sales		120,000		
Wages	12,000			200
Advertising	4,000		200	
Rates	1,800			360
Bank charges	200			
Depreciation – Fittings			400	
Depreciation – Lease			1,000	
Bad debts			500	
Prepayments			360	
Closing stock BS			21,000	
Closing stock P&L				21,000
	166,350	166,350	24,660	24,660

Prepare the profit and loss account for the business.

For items in italics, select the appropriate account heading.

Profit and loss account for the year ended 31 December 20X6

		£	£
Sales			120000
Less: Cost of sales			
	Opening stock/Closing stock/Purchases	15000	
	Purchases/Opening stock/Closing stock	78800	
		93800	
Less:	Opening stock/Closing stock/Purchases	21000	
		72800	72800
Gross profit			47200
Less: Expenses			
	Trade debtors/Wages	11800	
	Advertising/Prepayments	4200	
	Drawings/Rates	1440	
	Bank charges/Capital	200	
	Depreciation/Accumulated depreciation – F&F	400	
	– lease	1000	
	Bad debts	500	
Total expenses		19540	(19540)
Net profit			27660

Prepare the balance sheet for the business.

For items in italics, select the appropriate account heading.

Balance sheet as at 31 December 20X6

	£	£	£
Fixed assets:			
Fittings/Closing stock	7300	2900	4400
Trade debtors/Leasehold	30000	7000	23000
	37300	9900	27400
Current assets:			
Closing stock/Opening stock		21000	
Trade creditors/Trade debtors		19500	
Accruals/Prepayments		360	
Cash at bank/Drawings		50	
Capital/Cash in hand		1250	
		32160	

Current liabilities:
Trade debtors/Trade creditors

Owner's capital
Capital at 1.1.X6
Drawings/Net profit for the year
Less: Capital/Drawings

3 Preparing final accounts from the trial balance

3.1 Introduction

Now that we have reviewed the preparation of the profit and loss account and the balance sheet from the trial balance, we will now work through a comprehensive example which will include the extraction of the initial trial balance, correction of errors and clearing a suspense account, accounting for year-end adjustments and finally the preparation of the final accounts.

Example

Given below are the balances taken from a sole trader's ledger accounts on 31 March 20X4

	£
Sales ledger control account	30,700
Telephone	1,440
Purchases ledger control account	25,680
Heat and light	2,480
Motor vehicles at cost	53,900
Computer equipment at cost	4,500
Carriage inwards	1,840
Carriage outwards	3,280
Wages	67,440
Loan interest	300
Capital	48,450
Drawings	26,000
Bank overdraft	2,880
Purchases	126,800
Petty cash	50
Sales	256,400
Insurance	3,360
Accumulated depreciation – motor vehicles	15,000
Accumulated depreciation – computer equipment	2,640
Stock at 1 April 20X3	13,200
Loan	8,000
Rent	23,760

The following information is also available:

(i) The value of stock at 31 March 20X4 was £14,400.

(ii) Motor vehicles are to be depreciated at 30% on reducing balance basis and computer equipment at 20% on cost.

(iii) A telephone bill for £180 for the three months to 31 March 20X4 did not arrive until after the trial balance had been drawn up.

(iv) Of the insurance payments, £640 is for the year ending 31 March 20X5.

(v) A bad debt of £700 is to be written off.

Solution

Step 1

The first stage is to draw up the initial trial balance. Remember that assets and expenses are debit balances and liabilities and income are credit balances.

	£	£
Sales ledger control account	30,700	
Telephone	1,440	
Purchases ledger control account		25,680
Heat and light	2,480	
Motor vehicles at cost	53,900	
Computer equipment at cost	4,500	
Carriage inwards	1,840	
Carriage outwards	3,280	
Wages	67,440	
Loan interest	300	
Capital		48,450
Drawings	26,000	
Bank overdraft		2,880
Purchases	126,800	
Petty cash	50	
Sales		256,400
Insurance	3,360	
Accumulated depreciation – motor vehicles		15,000
Accumulated depreciation– computer equipment		2,640
Stock at 1 April 20X3	13,200	
Loan		8,000
Rent	23,760	
	359,050	359,050

Step 2

Now to deal with the year-end adjustments:

(i) The value of stock at 31 March 20X4 was £14,400.

Closing stock – profit and loss

	£		£
		Closing stock balance sheet	14,400

Closing stock – balance sheet

	£		£
Closing stock profit and loss	14,400		

We now have the closing stock for the profit and loss account and in the balance sheet.

(ii) The motor vehicles and computer equipment have yet to be depreciated for the year. Motor vehicles are depreciated at 30% on reducing balance basis and computer equipment at 20% on cost.

Motor vehicles depreciation (53,900 – 15,000) × 30% = £11,670

Computer equipment depreciation 4,500 × 20% = £900

Depreciation expense account – motor vehicles

	£		£
Accumulated depreciation	11,670		

Accumulated depreciation account – motor vehicles

	£		£
		Balance b/d	15,000
Balance c/d	26,670	Depreciation expense	11,670
	26,670		26,670
		Balance b/d	26,670

Depreciation expense account – computer equipment

	£		£
Accumulated depreciation	900		

Accumulated depreciation account – computer equipment

	£		£
		Balance b/d	2,640
Balance c/d	3,540	Depreciation expense	900
	3,540		3,540
		Balance b/d	3,540

(iii) A telephone bill for £180 for the three months to 31 March 20X4 did not arrive until after the trial balance had been drawn up.

This needs to be accrued for:

Debit	Telephone	£180
Credit	Accruals	£180

Telephone account

	£		£
Balance b/d	1,440		
Accrual	180	Balance c/d	1,620
	1,620		1,620
Balance b/d	1,620		

Accruals

	£		£
		Telephone	180

(iv) Of the insurance payments £640 is for the year ending 31 March 20X5.

This must be adjusted for as a prepayment:

Debit	Prepayment	£640
Credit	Insurance account	£640

Prepayments

	£		£
Insurance	640		

Insurance account

	£		£
Balance b/d	3,360	Prepayment	640
		Balance c/d	2,720
	3,360		3,360
Balance b/d	2,720		

(v) A bad debt of £700 is to be written off.

Debit	Bad debts expense	£700
Credit	Sales ledger control account	£700

Bad debts expense account

	£		£
Sales ledger control account	700		

Sales ledger control account

	£		£
Balance b/d	30,700	Bad debts expense	700
		Balance c/d	30,000
	30,700		30,700
Balance b/d	30,000		

Step 3

Now that all of the adjustments have been put through the ledger accounts, an amended trial balance can be drawn up as a check and as a starting point for preparing the final accounts. The amended and additional ledger accounts are all shown below.

Closing stock – profit and loss

	£		£
Balance c/d	14,400	Closing stock balance sheet	14,400
	14,400		14,400
		Balance b/d	14,400

Closing stock – balance sheet

Closing stock profit and loss	14,400	Balance c/d	14,400
	14,400		14,400
Balance b/d	14,400		

Depreciation expense account – motor vehicles

	£		£
Accumulated depreciation	11,670		

Accumulated depreciation account – motor vehicles

	£		£
		Balance b/d	15,000
Balance c/d	26,670	Depreciation expense	11,670
	26,670		26,670
		Balance b/d	26,670

Depreciation expense account – computer equipment

	£		£
Accumulated depreciation	900		

Accumulated depreciation account – computer equipment

	£		£
		Balance b/d	2,640
Balance c/d	3,540	Depreciation expense	900
	3,540		3,540
		Balance b/d	3,540

Telephone account

	£		£
Balance b/d	1,440		
Accrual	180	Balance c/d	1,620
	1,620		1,620
Balance b/d	1,620		

Accruals

	£		£
		Telephone	180

Prepayments

	£		£
Insurance	640		

Insurance account

	£		£
Balance b/d	3,360	Prepayment	640
		Balance c/d	2,720
	3,360		3,360
Balance b/d	2,720		

Bad debts expense account

	£		£
Sales ledger control	700		
		Balance c/d	700
	700		700

Sales ledger control account

	£		£
Balance b/d	30,700	Irrecoverable debts expense	700
		Balance c/d	30,000
	30,700		30,700
Balance b/d	30,000		

Trial balance at 31 March 20X4

	£	£
Sales ledger control account	30,000	
Telephone	1,620	
Purchases ledger control account		25,680
Heat and light	2,480	
Motor vehicles at cost	53,900	
Computer equipment at cost	4,500	
Carriage inwards	1,840	
Carriage outwards	3,280	
Wages	67,440	
Loan interest	300	
Capital		48,450
Drawings	26,000	
Bank overdraft		2,880
Purchases	126,800	
Petty cash	50	
Sales		256,400
Insurance	2,720	
Accumulated depreciation – motor vehicles		26,670
Accumulated depreciation – computer equipment		3,540
Stock at 1 April 20X3	13,200	
Loan		8,000
Rent	23,760	
Stock at 31 March 20X4	14,400	14,400
Depreciation expense – motor vehicles	11,670	
Depreciation expense – computer equipment	900	
Accruals		180
Prepayments	640	
Bad debts expense	700	
	386,200	386,200

Step 4

We are now in a position to prepare the final accounts for the sole trader. Take care with the carriage inwards and carriage outwards. They are both expenses of the business but carriage inwards is treated as part of cost of sales, whereas carriage outwards is one of the list of expenses.

Profit and loss account for the year ended 31 March 20X4

	£	£
Sales		256,400
Less: Cost of sales		
Opening stock	13,200	
Carriage inwards	1,840	
Purchases	126,800	
	141,840	
Less: Closing stock	(14,400)	
		127,440
Gross profit		128,960
Less: Expenses		
Telephone	1,620	
Heat and light	2,480	
Carriage outwards	3,280	
Wages	67,440	
Loan interest	300	
Insurance	2,720	
Rent	23,760	
Depreciation expense – motor vehicles	11,670	
Depreciation expense – computer equipment	900	
Bad debts	700	
Total expenses		114,870
Net profit		14,090

Balance sheet as at 31 March 20X4

	Cost	*Accumulated depreciation*	*Net book value*
	£	£	£
Fixed assets			
Motor vehicles	53,900	26,670	27,230
Computer equipment	4,500	3,540	960
	58,400	30,210	28,190
Current assets			
Stock		14,400	
Trade debtors		30,000	
Prepayment		640	
Petty cash		50	
		45,090	
Current liabilities			
Bank overdraft	2,880		
Trade Creditors	25,680		
Accruals	180		
		28,740	
Net current assets			16,350
Total assets less current liabilities			44,540
Long term liability:			
Loan			(8,000)
Net assets			36,540
Capital			
Opening capital			48,450
Net profit for the year			14,090
			62,540
Less: Drawings			26,000
Proprietor's funds			36,540

Activity 4

Given below is the list of ledger balances for a sole trader at 30 June 20X4 after all of the year-end adjustments have been put through.

	£
Sales	165,400
Sales ledger control account	41,350
Wages	10,950
Bank	1,200
Rent	8,200
Capital	35,830
Purchases ledger control account	15,100
Purchases	88,900
Electricity	1,940
Telephone	980
Drawings	40,000
Stock at 1 July 20X3	9,800
Motor vehicles at cost	14,800
Accumulated depreciation – motor vehicles	7,800
Fittings at cost	3,200
Accumulated depreciation – fittings	1,800
Accruals	100
Prepayments	210
Stock at 30 June 20X4 – balance sheet	8,300
Stock at 30 June 20X4 – profit and loss	8,300
Depreciation expense – motor vehicles	3,700
Depreciation expense – fittings	800

(i) Trial balance as at 30 June 20X4

	£	£
Sales		
Sales ledger control account		
Wages		
Bank		
Rent		
Capital		
Purchases ledger control account		
Purchases		
Electricity		
Telephone		
Drawings		
Stock at 1 July 20X3		
Motor vehicles at cost		
Accumulated depreciation – motor vehicles		
Fittings at cost		
Accumulated depreciation – fittings		
Accruals		
Prepayments		
Stock at 30 June 20X4 – profit and loss		
Stock at 30 June 20X4 – balance sheet		
Depreciation expense – motor vehicles		
Depreciation expense – fittings		
	234,330	234,330

(ii) Profit and loss account for the year ended 30 June 20X4

	£	£
Sales		
Less: Cost of sales		
Less:		
Gross profit		

Less: Expenses	Wages	10950	
	~~Bank~~	~~1200~~	
	Rent	8200	
	EL.	1940	
	Tel.	980	
	Depr. mv	3700	
	Depr. F&F	800	
Total expenses		23420	26570
Net profit			48430

Balance sheet as at 30 June 20X4

	Cost	*Depreciation*	*NBV*
	£	£	£
Fixed assets	14800	7800	7000
	3200	1800	1400
	18000	9600	8400
Current assets			
SLCA	41350		
Stock	8300		
Bank	1200		
Prepayment	210		
		51060	
Current liabilities			
PLCA	15100		
Accruals	100		
		(15200)	
Net current assets			35860
Net assets			44,260
Capital			35830
Net profit for the year			48430
Drawings			40000
Proprietor's funds			44,260

Activity 5

Tick as appropriate.

1 Opening stock is recorded in the profit and loss account as

- An expense ☐
- Cost of sales ☒

2 Indicate where the drawings should be shown in the final accounts

- Profit and loss expenses ☐
- Balance sheet as a deduction to capital ☒

3 Payroll expenses are recorded as

- A liability in the balance sheet ☒ ?
- An expense in the profit and loss account ☒

4 Does the bad adjustment appear in the profit and loss account or balance sheet?

- Profit and loss account ☒ ?
- Balance sheet ☐

5 Sales returns are deducted from purchases

- True ☐
- False ☒

Activity 6

Trial balance at 31 December 20X2

	Dr £	Cr £
Capital on 1 January 20X2		106,149
Freehold factory at cost	360,000	
Motor vehicles at cost	126,000	
Stocks at 1 January 20X2	37,500	
Debtors	15,600	
Cash in hand	225	
Bank overdraft		82,386
Creditors		78,900
Sales		307,500
Purchases	158,700	
Wages and salaries	39,060	
Rent and rates	35,400	
Postage	400	
Discounts allowed	6,600	
Insurance	2,850	
Motor expenses	5,500	
Loan from bank		240,000
Sundry expenses	1,000	
Drawings	26,100	
	814,935	814,935

Prepare a profit and loss account and balance sheet.

4 Simpler taxation for the simplest small business (the cash basis scheme)

This chapter has covered the preparation of the final accounts of a Sole Trader which are based on the accruals or matching concept.

HMRC has recently introduced a scheme whereby small businesses can report their activities based on cash received and cash paid for expenses in the form of a simple Statement of Income rather than a Trading and Profit and Loss Account based on the accruals concept.

HMRC stated that a move to the cash basis will help small businesses simplify their accounting processes and save them time and money.

Sole Traders and Partnerships with an annual income of less than £82,000 (currently) can supply details of cash received and cash paid on allowable expenses in a tax year rather than prepare accounts on an accruals basis.

Limited Companies and Limited Liability Partnerships cannot adopt the cash based system for reporting to HMRC.

The scheme is designed to suit the needs of those small businesses mainly providing services as tradesmen. This may include taxi drivers, painters and decorators, gardeners, hairdressers, window cleaners, plumbers, electricians and photographers.

If a business enters the cash based scheme it can continue with the scheme until its income reaches double the VAT threshold, so currently until its income reaches £164,000.

The scheme allows the use of 'simplified expenses'. This will involve the use of flat rate allowances for actual business expenses for items as vehicle expenses, business mileage and use of part of the home for business purposes.

The Federation of Small Businesses estimates that the scheme could apply to some 3 million small businesses. The Institute of Chartered Accountants in England and Wales (ICAEW) has however said that a lack of formal accounts (Profit and Loss Account and a Balance Sheet) may make it difficult for some small businesses to access borrowing.

5 Summary

The profit and loss account for the period summarises the transactions in the period and leads to a net profit or loss for the period.

The balance sheet lists the assets and liabilities of the business on the last day of the accounting period in a particular order.

When preparing the final accounts from a trial balance, you will have to recognise whether the balances should appear in the profit and loss account or in the balance sheet and also consider adjustments required.

Answers to chapter activities

Activity 1

Trading and Profit and loss account extract for the year ended 31 December 20X2

Calculate the sales and cost of sales.

	£	£
Sales		292,500
Less: Cost of sales		
Opening stock	37,500	
Purchases	158,700	
	196,200	
Less: Closing stock	(15,000)	
		(181,200)
Gross profit		111,300

Activity 2

Fixed Assets	**Current Assets**	**Current Liabilities**
Land	Stock	Bank overdraft
Motor Van	Debtors	VAT payable to HMRC
Computers	Cash	Creditors

Activity 3

Profit and loss account for the year ended 31 December 20X6

		£	£
Sales			120,000
Less:	Cost of sales		
	Opening stock	15,000	
	Purchases	78,800	
		93,800	
Less:	Closing stock	(21,000)	
			(72,800)
Gross profit			47,200
Less:	**Expenses**		
	Wages	11,800	
	Advertising	4,200	
	Rates	1,440	
	Bank charges	200	
	Depreciation – F&F	400	
	– lease	1,000	
	Bad debts	500	
Total expenses			(19,540)
Net profit			27,660

Balance sheet as at 31 December 20X6

	£	£	£
Fixed assets			
Fittings	7,300	2,900	4,400
Leasehold	30,000	7,000	23,000
	37,300	9,900	27,400
Current assets			
Stock		21,000	
Trade debtors		9,500	
Prepayments		360	
Cash at bank		1,250	
Cash in hand		50	
		32,160	
Current liabilities			
Trade creditors		(18,000)	

Net current assets	14,160
Net assets	41,560
Owner's capital	
Capital at 1.1.X6	19,850
Net profit for the year	27,660
Less: Drawings	(5,950)
Proprietor's funds	41,560

Activity 4

(i) **Trial balance as at 30 June 20X4**

	£	£
Sales		165,400
Sales ledger control account	41,350	
Wages	10,950	
Bank	1,200	
Rent	8,200	
Capital		35,830
Purchases ledger control account		15,100
Purchases	88,900	
Electricity	1,940	
Telephone	980	
Drawings	40,000	
Stock at 1 July 20X3	9,800	
Motor vehicles at cost	14,800	
Accumulated depreciation – motor vehicles		7,800
Fittings at cost	3,200	
Accumulated depreciation – fittings		1,800
Accruals		100
Prepayments	210	
Stock at 30 June 20X4 – profit and loss		8,300
Stock at 30 June 20X4 – balance sheet	8,300	
Depreciation expense – motor vehicles	3,700	
Depreciation expense – fittings	800	
	234,330	234,330

(ii) **Profit and loss account for the year ended 30 June 20X4**

	£	£
Sales		165,400
Less: Cost of sales		
Opening stock	9,800	
Purchases	88,900	
	98,700	
Less: Closing stock	(8,300)	
		(90,400)
Gross profit		75,000
Less: Expenses		
Wages	10,950	
Rent	8,200	
Electricity	1,940	
Telephone	980	
Depreciation – motor vehicles	3,700	
Depreciation – fittings	800	
Total expenses		26,570
Net profit		48,430

Balance sheet as at 30 June 20X4

	Cost	*Depreciation*	*NBV*
	£	£	£
Fixed assets			
Motor vehicles	14,800	7,800	7,000
Fittings	3,200	1,800	1,400
	18,000	9,600	8,400
Current assets			
Stock		8,300	
Trade debtors		41,350	
Prepayments		210	
Bank		1,200	
		51,060	

Current liabilities			
Trade creditors	15,100		
Accruals	100	(15,200)	
Net current assets			35,860
Net assets			44,260
Capital			35,830
Net profit for the year			48,430
			84,260
Drawings			(40,000)
Proprietor's funds			44,260

Activity 5

1 Opening stock is recorded in the profit and loss account as

Cost of sales

2 Indicate where the drawings should be shown in the final accounts

Balance sheet

3 Payroll expenses are recorded as

An expense in the profit and loss account

4 Does the bad adjustment appear in the profit and loss account or balance sheet?

Profit and loss

5 Sales returns are deducted from purchases

False

Activity 6

Profit and loss account for the year ended 31 December 20X2

	£	£
Sales		307,500
Less: Cost of sales		
Opening stock	37,500	
Purchases	158,700	
	196,200	
Less: Closing stock	0	
		(196,200)
Gross profit		111,300
Less: Expenses		
Rent and rates	35,400	
Insurance	2,850	
Motor expenses	5,500	
Wages and salaries	39,060	
Postage	400	
Sundry expenses	1,000	
Discounts allowed	6,600	
		(90,810)
Net profit		20,490

Balance sheet as at 31 December 20X2

	£	£	£
Fixed assets:			
Freehold factory	360,000	0	360,000
Motor vehicles	126,000	0	126,000
	486,000	0	486,000
Current assets:			
Stock		0	
Debtors		15,600	
Cash in hand		225	
		15,825	

Current liabilities:		
Creditors	78,900	
Bank overdraft	82,386	
	161,286	
Net current assets/(liabilities)		(145,461)
Total assets less current liabilities		340,539
Loan from bank		(240,000)
Net assets		**100,539**
Owner's capital		
Capital at 1.1.X2		106,149
Net profit for the year		20,490
Less: drawings		(26,100)
Proprietors funds		**100,539**

5 Test your knowledge

Workbook Activity 7

David Pedley

The following information is available for David Pedley's business for the year ended 31 December 20X8. He started his business on 1 January 20X8.

	£
Creditors	6,400
Debtors	5,060
Purchases	16,100
Sales	28,400
Motor van	1,700
Drawings	5,100
Insurance	174
General expenses	1,596
Rent and rates	2,130
Salaries	4,162
Stock at 31 December 20X8	2,050
Sales returns	200
Cash at bank	2,628
Cash in hand	50
Capital introduced	4,100

Required:

Prepare a profit and loss account for the year ended 31 December 20X8 and a balance sheet at that date.

Workbook Activity 8

Karen Finch

On 1 April 20X7 Karen Finch started a business with capital of £10,000 which she paid into a business bank account.

The following is a summary of the cash transactions for the first year.

	£
Amounts received from customers	17,314
Salary of assistant	2,000
Cash paid to suppliers for purchases	10,350
Purchase of motor van on 31 March 20X8	4,000
Drawings during the year	2,400
Amounts paid for electricity	560
Rent and rates for one year	1,100
Postage and stationery	350

At the end of the year, Karen was owed £4,256 by her customers and owed £5,672 to her suppliers. She has promised her assistant a bonus for the year of £400. At 31 March 20X8 this had not been paid.

At 31 March 20X8 there were stocks of £4,257 and the business owed £170 for electricity for the last quarter of the year. A year's depreciation is to be charged on the motor van at 25% on cost.

Required:

Prepare a profit and loss account for the year ended 31 March 20X8 and a balance sheet at that date.

Workbook Activity 9

The trial balance of Elmdale at 31 December 20X8 is as follows

	DR	*CR*
	£	£
Capital		8,602
Stock	2,700	
Sales		21,417
Purchases	9,856	
Rates	1,490	
Drawings	4,206	
Electricity	379	
Freehold shop	7,605	
Debtors	2,742	
Creditors		3,617
Cash at bank		1,212
Cash in hand	66	
Sundry expenses	2,100	
Wages and salaries	3,704	
	34,848	34,848

In addition, Elmdale provides the following information:

(a) Closing stock has been valued for accounts purposes at £3,060.

(b) An electricity bill amounting to £132 in respect of the quarter to 28 February 20X9 was paid on 7 March 20X9. +44

(c) Rates include a payment of £1,260 made on 10 April 20X8 in respect of the year to 31 March 20X9. –315

Required:

(a) Show the adjustments to the ledger accounts for the end-of-period adjustments (a) to (c).

(b) Prepare a trading and profit and loss account for the year ended 31 December 20X8.

Suspense accounts and errors

Introduction

We have already seen the use of suspense accounts and the correction of errors in Level II but we will revise it again for Level III. When preparing a trial balance it may be necessary to open a suspense account to deal with any errors or omissions. The suspense account cannot be allowed to remain permanently in the trial balance, and must be cleared by correcting each of the errors that have caused the trial balance not to balance.

CONTENTS

1 The trial balance

1.1 Introduction

We saw in Bookkeeping Level II that one of the purposes of the trial balance is to provide a check on the accuracy of the double entry bookkeeping. If the trial balance does not balance then an error or a number of errors have occurred and this must be investigated and the errors corrected.

1.2 Errors detected by the trial balance

The following types of error will cause a difference in the trial balance and therefore will be detected by the trial balance and can be investigated and corrected:

A single entry – if only one side of a double entry has been made then this means that the trial balance will not balance e.g. if only the debit entry for receipts from debtors has been made then the debit total on the trial balance will exceed the credit balance.

A casting error – if a ledger account has not been balanced correctly due to a casting error then this will mean that the trial balance will not balance.

A transposition error – if an amount in a ledger account or a balance on a ledger account has been transposed and incorrectly recorded then the trial balance will not balance e.g. a debit entry was recorded correctly as £5,276 but the related credit entry was entered as £5,726.

An extraction error – if a ledger account balance is incorrectly recorded on the trial balance either by recording the wrong figure or putting the balance on the wrong side of the trial balance then the trial balance will not balance.

An omission error – if a ledger account balance is inadvertently omitted from the trial balance then the trial balance will not balance.

Two entries on one side – instead of a debit and credit entry if a transaction is entered as a debit in two accounts or as a credit in two accounts then the trial balance will not balance.

1.3 Errors not detected by the trial balance

A number of types of errors however will not cause the trial balance not to balance and therefore cannot be detected by preparing a trial balance:

An error of original entry – this is where the wrong figure is entered as both the debit and credit entry e.g. a payment of the electricity expense was correctly recorded as a debit in the electricity account and a credit to the bank account but it was recorded as £300 instead of £330.

A compensating error – this is where two separate errors are made, one on the debit side of the accounts and the other on the credit side, and by coincidence the two errors are of the same amount and therefore cancel each other out.

An error of omission – this is where an entire double entry is omitted from the ledger accounts. As both the debit and credit have been omitted the trial balance will still balance.

An error of commission – with this type of error a debit entry and an equal credit entry have been made but one of the entries has been to the wrong account e.g. if the electricity expense was debited to the rent account but the credit entry was correctly made in the bank account – here both the electricity account and rent account will be incorrect but the trial balance will still balance.

An error of principle – this is similar to an error of commission but the entry has been made in the wrong type of account e.g. if the electricity expense was debited to a fixed asset account – again both the electricity account and the fixed asset account would be incorrect but the trial balance would still balance.

It is important that a trial balance is prepared on a regular basis in order to check on the accuracy of the double entry. However not all errors in the accounting system can be found by preparing a trial balance.

1.4 Correction of errors

Errors will normally be corrected by putting through a journal entry for the correction.

The procedure for correcting errors is as follows:

Step 1

Determine the precise nature of the incorrect double entry that has been made.

Step 2

Determine the correct entries that should have been made.

Step 3

Produce a journal entry that cancels the incorrect part and puts through the correct entries.

Example

The rent expense of £1,000 has been correctly credited to the bank account but has been debited to the entertainment expense account.

Step 1

The incorrect entry has been to debit the entertainment expense with £1,000

Step 2

The correct entry is to debit the rent account with £1,000

Step 3

The journal entry required is:

DR Rent account £1,000

CR Entertainment expense account £1,000

Note that this removes the incorrect debit from the entertainment expense account and puts the correct debit into the rent account.

Activity 1

Jacob returned some goods to a supplier because they were faulty. The original purchase price of these goods was £900.

The ledger clerk has correctly treated the double entry but used the figure £9,000.

What is the correcting entry which needs to be made?

2 Opening a suspense account

2.1 Introduction

A suspense account is used as a temporary account to deal with errors and omissions. It means that it is possible to continue with the production of financial accounts whilst the reasons for any errors are investigated and then corrected.

2.2 Reasons for opening a suspense account

A suspense account will be opened in two main circumstances:

(a) the bookkeeper does not know how to deal with one side of a transaction;

or

(b) the trial balance does not balance.

2.3 Unknown entry

In some circumstances the bookkeeper may come across a transaction for which he is not certain of the correct double entry and therefore rather than making an error, one side of the entry will be put into a suspense account until the correct entry can be determined.

Example

A new bookkeeper is dealing with a cheque received from the writing of an article for a popular magazine for £250. He correctly debits the bank account with the amount of the cheque but does not know what to do with the credit entry.

Solution

He will enter it in the suspense account:

Suspense account

	£		£
		Bank account – receipt of article fee	250

2.4 Trial balance does not balance

If the total of the debits on the trial balance does not equal the total of the credits then an error or a number of errors have been made. These must be investigated, identified and eventually corrected. In the meantime the difference between the debit total and the credit total is inserted as a suspense account balance in order to make the two totals agree.

Example

The totals of the trial balance are as follows:

	Debits	*Credits*
	£	£
Totals as initially extracted	234,987	209,876
Suspense account, to make the TB balance		25,111
	234,987	234,987

Suspense

	£		£
		Opening balance	25,111

Activity 2

The credit balances on a trial balance exceed the debit balances by £3,333. Open up a suspense account to record this difference.

3 Clearing the suspense account

3.1 Introduction

Whatever the reason for the suspense account being opened it is only ever a temporary account. The reasons for the difference must be identified and then correcting entries should be put through the ledger accounts, via the journal, in order to correct the accounts and clear the suspense account balance to zero.

3.2 Procedure for clearing the suspense account

Step 1

Determine the incorrect entry that has been made or the omission from the ledger accounts.

Step 2

Determine the journal entry required to correct the error or omission – this will not always mean that an entry is required in the suspense account e.g. when the rent expense was debited to the entertainment expense account the journal entry did not require any entry to be made in the suspense account.

Step 3

If there is an entry to be made in the suspense account put this into the suspense account – when all the corrections have been made the suspense account should normally have no remaining balance on it.

Example

A trial balance has been extracted and did not balance. The debit column totalled £191,000 and the credit column totalled £190,000.

You discover the cash sales of £1,000 have been correctly entered into the cash account but no entry has been made in the sales account.

Draft a journal entry to correct this error, and complete the suspense ledger account.

Solution

As the debit entries and credit entries do not match, we will be required to open up a suspense account to hold this difference until we can correct it.

Suspense

Detail	Amount £	Detail	Amount £
Journal 1 (below)	1,000	TB	1,000
	1,000		**1,000**

A credit entry is required in the sales account and the debit is to the suspense account.

		£	£
Dr	Suspense account	1,000	
Cr	Sales account		1,000

Being correction of double entry for cash sales.

Remember that normally a journal entry needs a narrative to explain what it is for – however in some assessments you are told not to provide the narratives so always read the requirements carefully.

Activity 3

On extracting a trial balance, the accountant of ERJ discovered a suspense account with a debit balance of £1,075 included therein; she also found that the debits exceeded the credits by £957. She posted this difference to the suspense account and then investigated the situation. She discovered:

(1) A debit balance of £75 on the postage account had been incorrectly extracted on the list of balances as £750 debit.

(2) A payment of £500 to a credit supplier, X, had been correctly entered in the cash book but no entry had been made in the supplier's account.

(3) When a motor vehicle had been purchased during the year the bookkeeper did not know what to do with the debit entry so he made the entry Dr Suspense, Cr Bank £1,575.

(4) A credit balance of £81 in the sundry income account had been incorrectly extracted on the list of balances as a debit balance.

(5) A receipt of £5 from a credit customer, Y, had been correctly posted to his account but had been entered in the cash book as £625.

(6) The bookkeeper was not able to deal with the receipt of £500 from the owner's own bank account, and he made the entry Dr Bank and Cr Suspense.

(7) No entry has been made for a cheque of £120 received from a credit customer M.

(8) A receipt of £50 from a credit customer, N, had been entered into his account as £5 and into the cash book as £5.

Required:

(a) Show the journal entries necessary to correct the above errors.

(b) Show the entries in the suspense account to eliminate the differences entered in the suspense account.

4 Redrafting the trial balance

Once the suspense account has been cleared, it is important to redraft the trial balance to ensure that the debit column and credit column agree.

Example

On 30 June an initial trial balance was extracted which did not balance, and a suspense account was opened. On 1 July journal entries were prepared to correct the errors that had been found, and clear the suspense account. The list of balances and the journal entries are shown below.

Redraft the trial balance by placing the figures in the debit or credit column, after taking into account the journal entries which will clear suspense.

	Balances as at 30 June	*Balances as at 1 July*	
		Debit £	Credit £
Motor vehicles	19,000		
Stock	3,456		
Bank overdraft	190		
Petty cash	90		
Sales ledger control	5,678		
Purchases ledger control	3,421		
VAT owing to HMRC	1,321		
Capital	12,500		
Sales	52,678		
Purchases	23,982		
Purchase returns	1,251		
Wages	9,999		
Motor expenses	123		
Drawings	710		
Suspense (debit balance)	8,323		

Journals

Account	**Debit £**	**Credit £**
Sales ledger control	5,323	
Suspense		5,323
Being to correct allocation of credit sale as a debtor balance		

Account	**Debit £**	**Credit £**
Purchases	3,000	
Suspense		3,000
Being to correct allocation of purchase balance.		

Solution

	Balances as at 30 June	*Balances as at 1 July*	
		Debit £	Credit £
Motor vehicles	19,000	19,000	
Stock	3,456	3,456	
Bank overdraft	190		190
Petty cash	90	90	
Sales ledger control	5,678	**11,001**	
Purchases ledger control	3,421		3,421
VAT owing to HMRC	1,321		1,321
Capital	12,500		12,500
Sales	52,678		52,678
Purchases	23,982	**26,982**	
Purchase returns	1,251		1,251
Wages	9,999	9,999	
Motor expenses	123	123	
Drawings	710	710	
Suspense (debit balance)			
		71,361	**71,361**

The sales ledger control and the purchases figures have been amended for the journals and the trial balance columns agree without the need for a suspense account.

5 Summary

Preparation of the trial balance is an important element of control over the double entry system but it will not detect all errors. The trial balance will still balance if a number of types of error are made. If the trial balance does not balance then a suspense account will be opened temporarily to make the debits equal the credits in the trial balance. The errors or omissions that have caused the difference on the trial balance must be discovered and then corrected using journal entries. Not all errors will require an entry to the suspense account. However, any that do should be put through the suspense account in order to try to eliminate the balance on the account.

Answers to chapter activities

Activity 1

Step 1

The purchases ledger control account has been debited and the purchases returns account credited but with £9,000 rather than £900.

Step 2

Both of the entries need to be reduced by the difference between the amount used and the correct amount (9,000 – 900) = £8,100

Step 3

Journal entry:		£	£
Dr	Purchases returns account	8,100	
Cr	Purchases ledger control account		8,100

Being correction of misposting of purchases returns.

Activity 2

As the credit balances exceed the debit balances the balance needed is a debit balance to make the two totals equal.

Suspense account

	£		£
Opening balance	3,333		

Activity 3

		Dr £	Cr £
1	Debit Suspense account	675	
	Credit Postage		675
	being correction of extraction error of postage account		
2	Debit Creditors	500	
	Credit Suspense account		500
	being correction of omitted entry in creditors account		
3	Debit Motor Vehicles Cost	1,575	
	Credit Suspense account		1,575
	being correct recording of Motor Vehicle acquisition		
4	Debit Suspense account	162	
	Credit Sundry income		162
	Being correction of incorrect treatment of sundry income		
5	Debit Suspense account	620	
	Credit Cash		620
	Being correction of incorrect posting		
6	Debit Suspense account	500	
	Credit Capital		500
	Being correction treatment of capital		
7	Debit Bank	120	
	Credit Debtors		120
	Being correct treatment of debtor receipt		
8	Debit Cash	45	
	Credit Debtors		45
	Being incorrect amount posted for a debtor receipt		

Suspense account

	£		£
Balance b/f	1,075	Trial balance difference	957
Postage (1)	675	Creditor X (2)	500
Sundry income (4)	162	Motor Vehicle Cost (3)	1,575
Cash (5)	620		
Capital (6)	500		
	3,032		3,032

6 Test your knowledge

Workbook Activity 4

Which of the errors below are, or are not, disclosed by the trial balance? (Ignore VAT in all cases)

(a) Recording a discount allowed correctly in the general ledger but not recording it in the subsidiary ledger.

(b) Recording a cash sale as a debit to the receivables account and a credit to the sales account..

(c) Omitting a credit sale to a debtor completely from both the general and subsidiary ledgers.

(d) Recording purchase invoices on the debit side of the purchase ledger control account and the credit side of the purchases account for the correct amount.

(e) Recording a receipt from a receivable in the sales ledger control account only.

(f) Recording a payment of £300 to a credit supplier as: Dr PLCA £300, Cr Bank £30.

Workbook Activity 5

Mr Plum's trial balance was extracted and did not balance. The debit column of the trial balance totalled £109,798 and the credit column totalled £219,666.

What entry would be made in the suspense account to balance the trial balance?

Workbook Activity 6

On 30 June Rick's Racers extracted an initial trial balance which did not balance, and a suspense account was opened. On 1 July journal entries were prepared to correct the errors that had been found, and clear the suspense account. The list of balances in the initial trial balance, and the journal entries to correct the errors, are shown below.

Redraft the trial balance by placing the figures in the debit or credit column. You should take into account the journal entries which will clear the suspense account.

	Balances extracted on 30 June £	*Balances at 1 July*	
		Debit £	*Credit* £
Motor vehicles	24,200	24200	
Plant and Equipment	22,350	22350	
Stock	9,000	9000	
Cash at Bank	11,217	11217	
Cash	150	150	
Sales ledger control	131,275	131275	
Purchases ledger control	75,336		75336
VAT owing to HMRC	15,127		15127
Capital	14,417		26247
Bank Loan	12,500		12500
Sales	276,132		276132
Purchases	152,476	152476	
Wages	35,465	35465	
Motor expenses	3,617	3617	
Repairs and Renewals ?	2,103	2103	
Rent and rates	3,283	3283	
Light and Heat	4,012	4012	
Insurance	4,874	4874	
Sundry Expenses	1,230	1320	
Suspense account (credit balance)	11,740		
	Totals	405342	405342

Journal entries

Account name	Debit £	Credit £
Capital		9,500
Suspense	9,500	
Capital		2,330
Suspense	2,330	

Account name	Debit £	Credit £
Suspense	1,230	
Sundry Expenses		1,230
Sundry Expenses	1,320	
Suspense		1,320

Professional Ethics

Introduction

In this chapter we look at the fundamental principles of integrity, objectivity, professional and technical competence, due care, confidentiality and professional behaviour.

CONTENTS

1 Introduction to business ethics

1.1 What do we mean by 'ethics'?

Definition of ethics

Ethics can be defined as the 'moral principles that govern a person's behaviour or the conducting of an activity'.

The Oxford English Dictionary

Ethics is thus concerned with how one should act in a certain situation, about 'doing the right thing' and is ultimately about morality – the difference between right and wrong.

Example 1 – Ethical choices

Consider the following ethical dilemmas:

- You buy something in a shop and later discover that they have under-charged you for an item. Do you go back and tell them?
- You want a new designer label tee-shirt but think it is too expensive. Would you buy a cheap fake copy if you saw one for sale while on holiday?
- Have you ever told your employer that you were sick when the truth was you simply wanted a day off?
- Would you stop buying a particular product if you found out that the working conditions in the factories where they are made were far below UK standards (e.g. concerning hours worked, pay rates, sickness policy, discrimination, use of child labour, etc.)?
- Have you ever 'exaggerated' an expense claim?

Does the fact that you are a (student) member of a professional body affect your answers?

1.2 Business ethics

Business ethics is the application of ethical principles to the problems typically encountered in a business setting.

There is no separate 'business ethic' that puts it beyond the range of normal moral judgements.

Example 2 – Typical issues in business ethics

Some typical issues addressed in business ethics include:

- 'creative accounting' to misrepresent financial performance
- misleading advertising
- aggressive personal selling (e.g. insurance or double glazing)
- unfair terms in contracts (e.g. cancelling a gym membership)
- data protection and privacy
- the difference between corporate hospitality and bribery
- the difference between business intelligence and industrial espionage
- political contributions to gain influence
- corporate governance
- corporate crime, including insider trading and price fixing
- employee issues, such as discrimination or unfair dismissal
- whistle blowing
- environmental issues and related social concerns
- marketing, sales and negotiation techniques
- product issues such as patent and copyright infringement, planned obsolescence, product liability and product defects
- using legal loopholes to avoid paying tax.

When ethical values get distorted or compromised, the impact can be enormous. Ethics and ethical standards have thus become the focus of greater attention by organisations, especially in the area of reputation management. Greater emphasis is now placed on accountability, ethics, codes of conduct and monitoring and reporting of violations.

1.3 Ethical influences

Each of us has our own set of values and beliefs that we have evolved over the course of our lives through our education, experiences and upbringing. We all have our own ideas of what is right and what is wrong and these ideas can vary between individuals and cultures.

There are a number of factors that affect ethical obligations.

(i) The law

For example, deceptive advertising is illegal and violators of this law are liable to large fines, court action and/or loss of goodwill.

Legislation hopefully makes it very clear what is acceptable as a minimum standard. However, ethics is more than just obeying the law.

For example, using legal loopholes to minimise a global firm's tax bill may not be illegal but is increasingly viewed as unethical.

(ii) Government regulations

For example, regulations set standards on issues such as unfair competition, unsafe products, etc. Failure to comply with these regulations could lead to criminal charges, or fines etc.

Unfortunately, some firms will still find ways to get round such regulations.

Example 3 – Artificial sweeteners

In 1970 cyclamates (a type of artificial sweetener) were banned in the USA following evidence that they were carcinogenic.

Following the ban a major US food manufacturer still sold 300,000 cases of cyclamate sweetened food overseas instead.

(iii) Ethical codes

Many organisations have codes that clearly state the ethical standards and principles an employee or member should follow.

For example, as an ICB member you are expected to follow ICB Professional Conduct Regulations.

Generally, written codes clarify the ethical issues and principles but leave the resolution to the individual's conscience.

Ethical codes are usually followed if written down and enforced – say by disciplinary procedures. However, many companies have 'unwritten' codes of practice and/or have no method of enforcement.

(iv) Social pressure

Many people draw their values from what they see other people doing, whether on the news or people they know. However, social pressure can change, just as society changes.

For example, many politicians comment on a decline in family values in the UK.

Many protest groups and activists hope to change public values with the long term hope that new values become reflected in law. A good example of this is the change in discrimination legislation over the last hundred years.

(v) Corporate culture

Definition of corporate culture

Corporate culture is defined as "the sum total of all the beliefs, attitudes, norms and customs that prevail within an organization" or "the way we do things around here".

Ideally we want a culture that supports and encourages ethical behaviour.

For example, if everyone else is exaggerating expense claims or covering up mistakes, then this can quickly become a norm of behaviour that new employees soon adopt.

Of particular importance is the example set by senior management – sometimes referred to as the 'tone at the top'.

It is important to note that there can often be tension between personal standards and the goals of the organisation

Suppose you work for a company selling banned substances overseas. It is not illegal, but it may be against your personal values to sell these products to unsuspecting overseas clients. What would you do if this action were a direct order from a superior? Does this take away your responsibility?

1.4 The costs and benefits of business ethics

It can be argued that the primary purpose of a business is to try and earn a profit. In a company, for instance, the directors have been employed in order to earn the owners of the business a return on their investment.

Some have concluded from this that going beyond the **legal** minimum standard of behaviour is contrary to the directors' duty to make money and that behaving ethically increases costs and reduces profits.

For example:

- Increased cost of sourcing materials from ethical sources (e.g. Fairtrade products or free range eggs).
- Having to turn away business from customers considered to be unethical (e.g. an 'ethical' bank may choose not to invest in a company that manufactures weapons).
- The management time that can be taken up by planning and implementation of ethical practices.

However, as well as the moral argument to act ethically, there can be commercial benefits to firms from acting ethically:

- Having good ethics can attract customers.

  This can be because good ethics tend to enhance a company's reputation and therefore its brand. Given the choice, many customers will prefer to trade with a company they feel is ethical.

- Good ethics can result in a more effective workforce

  A reputation for good business ethics is likely to involve good working conditions for employees, allowing the business to attract a higher calibre of staff.

  Avoiding discrimination against workers is likely to give the company access to a wider human resource base.

  Ethics programmes can cultivate strong teamwork and improve productivity.

- Ethics can give cost savings.

  Avoiding pollution will tend to save companies in the long run – many governments are now fining or increasing taxes of more polluting businesses.

- Ethics can reduce risk

  Many firms have failed due to unethical practices within them.

Example 4 – Enron

Enron, a major US energy company, filed for bankruptcy in 2001. Among the many reasons for its failure were dubious accounting practices (for example, in how they recognised revenue), poor corporate governance and failure by their external auditors, Arthur Andersen.

There were even attempts to hide the problems, with workers being told to destroy all audit material, except for the most basic work papers.

1.5 The Institute of Business Ethics – Simple test

According to the Institute of Business Ethics, a simple ethical test for a business decision could be reached in answering the following three questions:

Question	**Explanation**
Transparency	Do I mind others knowing what I have decided?
Effect	Does my decision affect or hurt anyone?
Fairness	Would my decision be considered fair by those affected?

2 Fundamental principles

2.1 The Code of Ethics for Professional Accountants

The Code of Ethics for Professional Accountants, published by The International Federation of Accountants (IFAC), forms the basis for the ethical codes of many accountancy bodies. The code adopts a principles-based approach. It does not attempt to cover every situation where a member may encounter professional ethical issues, prescribing the way in which he or she should respond. Instead, it adopts a value system, focusing on fundamental professional and ethical principles which are at the heart of proper professional behaviour.

The five key principles are as follows:

(a) **Integrity**

(b) **Objectivity**

(c) **Professional competence and due care**

(d) **Confidentiality**

(e) **Professional behaviour**

These are discussed in more detail below.

2.2 A conceptual framework

Professional bookkeepers may face a range of specific threats to compliance with the fundamental principles.

Such threats vary according to the nature of engagements and work assignments and therefore it is not possible to set out every instance that may lead to such a threat. Furthermore, different safeguards will be necessary to counteract these different threats.

A conceptual framework means that, when identifying and addressing threats, members do not simply comply with a set of fixed rules which may not be relevant to the particular threat, but that they will comply with fundamental principles. These fundamental principles form a frame of reference which can then be used to make a decision specific to an identified threat.

A conceptual framework also requires that members shall use safeguards in such a way that threats which are not clearly insignificant are either eliminated or reduced to an acceptable level. This means that fundamental principles will not be compromised.

2.3 Compliance with ethical codes

A professional bookkeeper's responsibility is not just to satisfy the needs of an individual client or employer. It should also be to act in the public interest.

In acting in the public interest a professional bookkeeper should observe and comply with the fundamental ethical requirements shown in the IFAC Code.

ICB members should note that disciplinary action may be taken for non-compliance with the ICB Professional Conduct Regulations where the member's conduct is considered to prejudice their status as a member or to reflect adversely on the reputation of ICB. For the purposes of this paper, you do not need to be concerned with the differences between the IFAC code and the ICB code.

Where professional bookkeepers are members of more than one professional body, there may be differences in some areas between the professional and ethical conduct requirements of the different bodies. Where there are differences, members should follow the more stringent provision.

Unethical and dishonest behaviour (and its legal consequences) creates powerful negative public relations within the profession, the wider community and the organisation itself.

2.4 Integrity

Definition – Integrity

Integrity means that a member should act with strong moral principles, sincerity and honesty in all their professional and business relationships. They should also be straight-forward and truthful.

Bookkeepers are expected to present financial information fully, honestly and professionally and so that it will be understood in its context.

Example 5 – Integrity

A professional bookkeeper should not be associated with reports where the information:

- contains a materially false or misleading statement
- contains statements or information furnished recklessly
- has omissions that make it misleading.

Bookkeepers should abide by relevant law and regulations and remember that, as well as legal documents, letters and verbal agreements may constitute a binding arrangement.

Bookkeepers should strive to be fair and socially responsible and respect cultural differences when dealing with overseas colleagues or contacts. Promises may not be legally binding but repeatedly going back on them can destroy trust, break relationships and lose co-operation.

To maintain integrity, members have the following responsibilities:

2.5 Objectivity

Definition – Objectivity

Objectivity means that a member must be impartial and fair-minded. They should not allow business or professional judgements to be clouded by other interests and influences, prejudice or bias.

Example 6 – Objectivity

If you receive excessive hospitality and discounts from a client then this could be seen as an attempt to influence (bribe?) you and compromise your objectivity.

Objectivity can also be defined as 'the state of mind which has regard to all considerations relevant to the task in hand but no other.' It is closely linked to the concept of independence:

- **Independence of mind** is the state of mind that permits the provision of an opinion without being affected by influences that compromise professional judgement, allowing an individual to act with integrity and exercise objectivity and professional scepticism.
- **Independence of appearance** is the avoidance of facts and circumstances that are so significant that a reasonable and informed third party, having knowledge of all relevant information, would reasonably conclude that a firm's or a member's integrity, objectivity or professional scepticism had been compromised.

Whatever capacity members serve in, they should demonstrate their objectivity in varying circumstances.

Objectivity is a distinguishing feature of the profession. Members have a responsibility to:

- Communicate information fairly and objectively.
- Disclose fully all relevant information that could reasonably be expected to influence an intended user's understanding of the reports, comments, and recommendations presented.

2.6 Professional competence and due care

Definition – Professional competence

Professional competence means that a member has an ongoing responsibility to maintain their professional knowledge and skills at an acceptable level. This will enable them to carry out a competent professional service for both employers and clients based on up to date legislation, practice and techniques.

Definition – Due care

Due care means a member must be conscientious and follow relevant technical and professional standards when acting in the capacity of their profession.

In agreeing to provide professional services, a professional bookkeeper implies that there is a level of competence necessary to perform those services and that his or her knowledge, skill and experience will be applied with reasonable care and diligence.

Example 7 – Professional competence

Suppose you are a bookkeeper in practice. A new client asks you to perform their tax computations but this is something you know that you know that you are not qualified to do. You should refrain from performing this work.

Professional bookkeepers must therefore refrain from performing any services that they are not competent to carry out unless appropriate advice and assistance is obtained to ensure that the services are performed satisfactorily.

Professional competence may be divided into two separate phases:

1 Gaining professional competence – for example, by training to gain the ICB qualification.

2 Maintaining professional competence – bookkeepers need to keep up to date with developments in the profession including relevant national and international pronouncements on accounting and other relevant regulations and statutory requirements.

Members have a responsibility to:

- Maintain an appropriate level of professional competence by ongoing development of their knowledge and skills.
- Maintain technical and ethical standards in areas relevant to their work through continuing professional development.
- Perform their professional duties in accordance with relevant laws, regulations, and technical standards.
- Prepare complete and clear reports and recommendations after appropriate analysis of relevant and reliable information.

Members should adopt review procedures that will ensure the quality of their professional work is consistent with national and international pronouncements that are issued from time to time.

Due professional care applies to the exercise of professional judgement in the conduct of work performed and implies that the professional approaches matters requiring professional judgement with proper diligence.

2.7 Confidentiality

Definition – Confidentiality

Any information obtained as a result of business and professional relationships must be kept confidential by members, in accordance with the law. Information may only be disclosed to third parties without proper and specific permission when the member has a legal or professional obligation or right to disclose this.

Furthermore, any confidential information obtained as a result of business and professional relationships must not be used for the member's personal advantage or that of any third parties.

Note that confidentiality is not only a matter of disclosure of information – it also concerns using information for personal advantage or for the advantage of a third party.

Example 8 – Confidentiality

Suppose you are a bookkeeper in practice and you discover that a client has just won a major contract. This has yet to be publicised but when a press release is made, then the share price will go up significantly.

If you then buy the (undervalued) shares, then you have breached the principle of confidentiality – not because you told someone but because you used confidential information with the expectation of making a personal gain.

Members should:

- be prudent in the use and protection of information acquired in the course of their duties. (Please note that the duty of confidentiality continues even after the end of the relationship between the member and the employer or client.)
- not use information for any personal gain or in any manner that would be contrary to the law or detrimental to the legitimate and ethical objectives of the organisation.
- inform subordinates as appropriate regarding the confidentiality of information acquired in the course of their work and monitor their activities to assure the maintenance of that confidentiality.

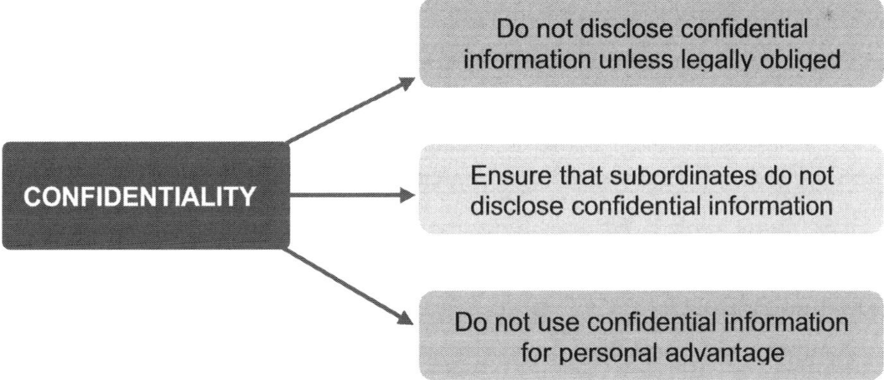

A member must take care to maintain confidentiality even in a social environment. The member should be alert to the possibility of inadvertent disclosure, particularly in circumstances involving close or personal relations, associates and long established business relationships.

Activity 1

You visit a client who is a dealer in sports cars. He sells one of his cars to a customer for £16,000; however he later tells you that the car has a faulty braking system.

What should you do?

- Nothing.
- Tell the customer.
- Tell the client you believe he acted unethically, but that you are bound by confidentiality therefore cannot tell anyone.
- Report your client to the authorities.

The problem with confidentiality is that there are times when disclosure may be permitted or even mandatory.

The following are circumstances where members are or may be required to disclose confidential information or when such disclosure may be appropriate:

(a) where disclosure is permitted by law and is authorised by the client or the employer

(b) where disclosure is required by law, for example:

  (i) producing documents or providing other evidence in the course of legal proceedings or

  (ii) disclosing any infringements of law that are discovered to the relevant public authority (such as HMRC) or

  (iii) disclosing any actual or suspected money laundering or terrorist financing to the member's firm's MLRO (Money Laundering Reporting Officer) or to the NCA (National Crime Agency) if the member is a sole practitioner, or

(c) where there is a professional duty or right to disclose, which is in the public interest, and is not forbidden by law. Examples may include:

  (i) complying with the quality review of any relevant professional body

  (ii) responding to an inquiry or investigation by the ICB or a relevant regulatory or professional body

  (iii) where it is necessary to protect the member's professional interests in legal proceedings or

  (iv) complying with technical standards and ethics requirements.

In deciding whether to disclose confidential information, members should consider the following points:

- Could the interests of all parties, including those of third parties, be harmed? This still applies where the client or employer to whom a duty of confidentiality is owed consents to the member disclosing information?
- Is all relevant information known and verified to be true as far as practicable? Where there is any incomplete or unverified information then professional judgement must be used as to what, if any, disclosure should be made.
- What type of disclosure should be made: how will this be communicated and to whom? The disclosure should only be communicated to appropriate parties.

2.8 Professional behaviour

Definition – Professional behaviour

A professional bookkeeper should act in accordance with relevant laws and regulations. They should also avoid acting in such a way that brings disrepute to the profession.

A profession is distinguished by certain characteristics including:

- mastery of a particular intellectual skill, acquired by training and education;
- adherence by its members to a common code of values and conduct established by its administrating body, including maintaining an outlook which is essentially objective; and
- acceptance of a duty to society as a whole (usually in return for restrictions in use of a title or in the granting of a qualification).

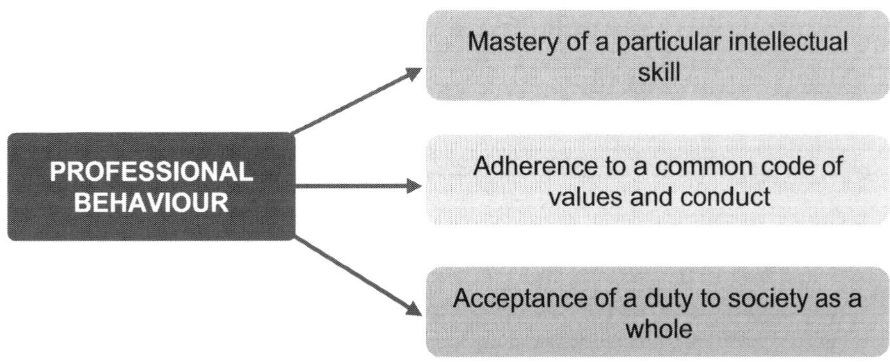

The objectives of the bookkeeping profession are to work to the highest standards of professionalism, to attain the highest levels of performance and generally to meet the public interest requirement. These objectives require four basic needs to be met:

(i) **Credibility** – there is a need for credibility in information and information systems.

(ii) **Professionalism** – there is a need to be clearly identified by employers, clients and other interested parties as a professional person in the accountancy field.

(iii) **Quality of services** – assurance is needed that all services obtained from a professional bookkeeper are carried out to the highest standards of performance.

(iv) **Confidence** – users of the services of professional bookkeepers should be able to feel confident that there is a framework of professional ethics to govern the provision of services.

The most important privilege conferred on professionals is the right to a 'professional opinion'. Professionals can be distinguished from others in society by their right to form an opinion and to base their services and/or products on this opinion. Misuse of this privilege can result in serious harm, thus it is only granted to those who are able to show by education and experience the ability to properly exercise this right.

What is understood by the term 'professionalism' will depend on the context and culture of the organisation.

It should include:

- **Professional/client relationship:**
  - the client presumes his or her needs will be met without having to direct the process
  - the professional decides which services are actually needed and provides them
  - the professional is trusted not to exploit his or her authority for unreasonable profit or gain.
- **Professional courtesy** – this is a bare minimum requirement of all business communication.
- **Expertise** – professionalism implies a level of competence that justifies financial remuneration. Incompetence is bad PR.
- **Marketing and promoting services** – bookkeepers should not make exaggerated or defamatory claims in their marketing.

Activity 2

When it comes to ethical principles, discussions often reveal that many employees think it is:

- acceptable to borrow money from the petty cash system if they have access (or their friends have access) and they are short of cash
- fine to browse the Internet or use the work telephone for unlimited numbers of personal calls
- quite appropriate to take a 'sickie' if they need a day off
- fun to invent a good story for being late or going early, and
- use work materials and tools for personal use.

Which of the fundamental principles is being flouted in these examples?

Activity 3

From time to time, you may receive or give gifts that are meant to show friendship, appreciation or thanks from or to people who do business with your company. You know you should never accept or offer gifts or entertainment when doing so may improperly influence or appear to influence your or the recipient's business decisions. If you are involved in any stage of a decision to do business with another company or person, you also know that you must refrain from accepting or giving any gift or entertainment that may influence or appear to influence the decision to do business.

Jot down some work based safeguards that colleagues would find helpful in deciding whether to accept or reject a gift.

3 Dealing with ethical conflicts

Given the above principles, threats and safeguards, a process of resolving ethical conflicts can be given as follows:

Step 1: Gather information

Rumour and hearsay are insufficient evidence upon which to base a decision. The bookkeeper should seek to gather further information to clarify the situation.

Step 2: Analysis

In analysing the scenario, the bookkeeper should first consider the legal perspective – have any laws been broken?

Next they can look at each of the fundamental principles to see which apply and whether there is an ethical issue to resolve.

Step 3: Action

If it is clear that there is a problem to resolve, the bookkeeper should weigh up the different courses of action:

- Is behaviour dictated by law?
- Who are the affected parties?
- Internal escalation – is there someone within the organisation who could/should be approached to discuss the matter further – for example, a manager?
- If the matter is still unresolved, then they should seek professional advice without breaching confidentiality.
- External escalation – should you report the matter externally?
- Ultimately the bookkeeper should consider resigning from the assignment.

Activity 4

You are a trainee bookkeeper within a small practice. A more senior trainee has been on sick leave, and you are due to go on study leave.

You have been told by your manager that, before you go on leave, you must complete a complicated task that the senior trainee was supposed to have done. The deadline suggested appears unrealistic, given the complexity of the work.

You feel that you are not sufficiently experienced to complete the work alone but your manager appears unable to offer the necessary support. You feel slightly intimidated by your manager, and also feel under pressure to be a 'team player' and help out.

However, if you try to complete the work to the required quality but fail, you could face repercussions on your return from study leave.

Required:

Analyse the scenario with particular reference to the following:

(a) Which fundamental principles are involved?

(b) Recommended action.

4 Summary

This chapter has introduced the concept of ethics in the business environment and has outlined the fundamental ethical principles that should be adhered to.

It is critical that you know and can apply the different principles.

5 Answers to chapter activities

Activity 1

Report your client to the authorities

When the law specifically requires disclosure, it could lead to a member producing documents or giving evidence in the course of legal proceedings and disclosing to the appropriate public authorities infringements of the law.

Activity 2

In all of these examples, the employees are not being honest or straightforward – they are therefore operating against the principle of **Integrity.**

Activity 3

Possible safeguards when considering whether to accept a gift:

Set up clear policies and guidance for staff stating the following:

– Cash gifts should never be accepted.

– Do not accept a gift if it could cause you to feel an obligation.

– Do not accept a gift from a vendor if it may give the vendor, other suppliers or subcontractors the impression that they have to provide similar gifts or favours in order to obtain company business.

– Do not justify accepting a gift by arguing, 'Everybody else does it,' 'I deserve a break today,' or 'No one will ever find out.'

Establish a code of ethics in the workplace that bans gifts.

Ensure senior management are not seen accepting gifts.

Activity 4

Key fundamental principles affected

(a) **Integrity**: Can you be open and honest about the situation?

(b) **Professional competence and due care**: Would it be right to attempt to complete work that is technically beyond your abilities, without proper supervision? Is it possible to complete the work within the time available and still act diligently to achieve the required quality of output?

(c) **Professional behaviour**: Can you refuse to perform the work without damaging your reputation within the practice? Alternatively, could the reputation of the practice suffer if you attempt the work?

(d) **Objectivity**: Pressure from your manager, combined with the fear of repercussions, gives rise to an intimidation threat to objectivity.

Possible course of action

You should explain to your manager that you do not have sufficient time and experience to complete the work to a satisfactory standard.

However, you should demonstrate a constructive attitude, and suggest how the problem may be resolved. (Your professional body is available to advise you in this respect.) For example, you might suggest the use of a subcontract bookkeeper.

Explore the possibility of assigning another member of staff to supervise your work.

If you feel that your manager is unsympathetic or fails to understand the issue, you should consider how best to raise the matter with the person within the practice responsible for training. It would be diplomatic to suggest to your manager that you raise the matter together, and present your respective views.

It would be unethical to attempt to complete the work if you doubt your competence.

However, simply refusing to, or resigning from your employment, would cause significant problems for both you and the practice. You could consult your professional body. If you seek advice from outside the practice (for example legal advice), then you should be mindful of the need for confidentiality as appropriate.

You should document, in detail, the steps that you take in resolving your dilemma, in case your ethical judgement is challenged in the future.

6 Test your knowledge

Workbook Activity 5

James, a member in practice, has been asked to assist a client with interviewing potential new recruits for the finance department. James has since discovered that a close personal friend of his has applied for the role.

Which fundamental principle needs to be safeguarded?

Workbook Activity 6

Explain why each of the following actions appears to be in conflict with fundamental ethical principles.

(1) An advertisement for a firm of bookkeepers states that their services are cheaper and more comprehensive than a rival firm.

(2) You believe your client has asked you to include what you believe to be misleading information in the accounts

(3) Your company is allowed, legally, to dump its waste into a river. This will kill all aquatic life along a 50 mile stretch.

Workbook Activity 7

Michael, a member in practice, performs bookkeeping services for a client called Ying Ltd. A company called Yang Ltd approaches Michael's firm and requests to become a new client. The two businesses are direct competitors and both have trade secrets which they wish to keep a secret.

Which fundamental principles are threatened?

Legal considerations

Introduction

As well as being influenced by ethical principles and professional considerations, the professional bookkeeper must ensure compliance with relevant legislation.

This chapter focuses primarily on the issues of money laundering and whistleblowing.

CONTENTS

1 Money laundering and terrorist financing

1.1 Money laundering

Definitions

Money laundering is the process by which criminally obtained money or other assets (criminal property) are exchanged for 'clean' money or other assets with no obvious link to their criminal origins. It also covers money, however come by, which is used to fund terrorism.

Criminal property is property which was obtained as a result of criminal conduct and the person knows or suspects that it was obtained from such conduct. It may take any form, including money or money's worth, securities, tangible property and intangible property.

In simple terms:

- Criminals make money through illegal actions.
- This money can be traced by the police so criminals try and stop it being tracked by buying and selling valuable items.
- The proceeds are constantly being re-invested in something else and it becomes very difficult to trace the money.
- 'Dirty cash' becomes a nice clean cheque.

There are three acknowledged phases to money laundering:

- **Placement**

  Cash generated from crime is placed in the financial system, for example paid into a bank account. This is the point when proceeds of crime are most apparent and at risk of detection.

- **Layering**

  Once proceeds of crime are in the financial system, layering obscures their origins by passing the money through complex transactions. These often involve different entities like companies and trusts and can take place in multiple jurisdictions.

- **Integration**

  Once the origin of the funds has been obscured, the criminal is able to make the funds reappear as legitimate funds or assets. They will invest funds in legitimate businesses or other forms of investment such as property.

Activities related to money laundering include:

- Acquiring, using or possessing criminal property.
- Handling the proceeds of crimes such as theft, fraud and tax evasion.
- Being knowingly involved in any way with criminal or terrorist property.
- Entering into arrangements to facilitate laundering criminal or terrorist property.
- Investing the proceeds of crimes in other financial products.
- Investing the proceeds of crimes through the acquisition of property/assets.
- Transferring criminal property.

1.2 Terrorist financing

Definitions

Terrorism is the use or threat of action designed to influence government, or to intimidate any section of the public, or to advance a political, religious or ideological cause where the action would involve violence, threats to health and safety, damage to property or disruption of electronic systems.

Terrorist financing is fund raising, possessing or dealing with property or facilitating someone else to do so, when intending, knowing or suspecting or having reasonable cause to suspect that it is intended for the purposes of terrorism.

Terrorist property is money or property likely to be used for terrorist purposes or the proceeds of commissioning or carrying out terrorist acts.

The definition of 'terrorist property' means that all dealings with funds or property which are likely to be used for the purposes of terrorism, even if the funds are 'clean' in origin, is a terrorist financing offence.

Money laundering involves the proceeds of crime whereas terrorist financing may involve both legitimate property and the proceeds of crime.

1.3 What are the money laundering and terrorist financing offences?

Anyone can commit a money laundering offence.

However, the Proceeds Of Crime Act (POCA) and the Terrorism Act (TA) include additional offences which can be committed by **individuals working in the regulated sector,** that is by people providing specified professional services such as accountancy and bookkeeping.

This means that a bookkeeper (i.e. an ICB member in practice) will be personally liable for breaching POCA and/or TA if he or she acts as a bookkeeping service provider while turning a 'blind eye' to a client's suspect dealings.

The Money Laundering Regulation (MLR) imposes duties on 'relevant persons' (sole traders and firms (not employees) operating within the regulated sector) to establish and maintain practice, policies and procedures to detect and deter activities relating to money laundering and terrorist financing. It is the sole trader or firm which will be liable therefore for any breach of the MLR.

The practice, policies and procedures required by the MLR of accountancy service providers include:

- Customer Due Diligence on clients
- reporting money laundering/terrorist financing
- record keeping.

Materiality or ***de minimis*** exceptions are not available in relation to either money laundering or terrorist financing offences – meaning no amount is too small not to bother about.

Definition

'de minimis' means **'considered trivial'**.

In this context it means that all potential offences must be reported as no amount is too small to be of consequence.

Under the POCA, the three money laundering offences are

- s327 – Concealing, disguising, converting, transferring or removing criminal property.
- s328 – Taking part in an arrangement to facilitate the acquisition, use or control of criminal property.
- s329 – Acquiring, using or possessing criminal property.

Conviction of any of these offences is punishable by up to 14 years imprisonment and/or an unlimited fine.

1.4 Money laundering regulation

UK anti-money laundering regime requirements are set out in the:

- Proceeds of Crime Act 2002 (POCA)
- The Money Laundering Regulations 2007 (2007 Regulations)
- The Terrorism Act 2000 (TA 2000) and the Terrorism Act 2006 (TA 2006).

The UK legislation on money laundering and terrorist financing applies to the proceeds of conduct that is a criminal offence in the UK and most conduct occurring elsewhere that would have been an offence if it had taken place in the UK.

2 Procedure for reporting money laundering

2.1 Summary of key points

- **Suspicious activity reports (SARs)** submitted by the regulated sector are an important source of information used by **NCA** in meeting its harm reduction agenda, and by law enforcement more generally.
- Businesses are required to have procedures which provide for the nomination of a person, this person is called a **Money Laundering Reporting Officer (MRLO**) to receive disclosures (internal reports) and requires that everyone in the business complies with the Proceeds of Crime Act (POCA) in terms of reporting knowledge, suspicion or reasonable grounds for knowledge or suspicion of money laundering.
- Without the presence within an organisation of an MLRO an individual MUST report directly to the National Crime Agency (NCA). **Note:** The NCA was previously known as the Serious Organised Crime Agency (SOCA).
- An individual other than the MLRO fulfils his reporting obligations by making an internal report to his MLRO.
- The MLRO is responsible for assessing internal reports, making further inquiries if need be (either within the business or using public domain information), and, if appropriate, filing SARs with NCA.
- When reports are properly made they are 'protected' under POCA in that nothing in them shall be taken to breach confidentiality.

- A person who considers he may have engaged or is about to engage in money laundering, should make an 'authorised' disclosure. Such a disclosure, provided it is made before the act is carried out, or is made as soon as possible on the initiative of that person after the act is done and with good reason being shown for the delay, may provide a defence against charges of money laundering. When properly made such reports shall not be taken to breach confidentiality.

2.2 An accountant's duty to report

POCA and TA impose an obligation on accountants (individuals within the regulated sector, including those involved in providing accountancy services to clients i.e. ICB members in practice), to submit in defined circumstances:

- An internal report to a Money Laundering Reporting Officer (MLRO), by those employed in a group practice.
- A Suspicious Activity Report (SAR) to the National Crime Agency (NCA), by sole practitioners and MLROs.

There are two circumstances when a required disclosure in an internal report or a SAR, collectively referred to below as a report, must be made by an accountant:

1 When the accountant wishes to provide services in relation to property which it is actually known or suspected relates to money laundering or terrorist financing. In such circumstances, the reporter must indicate in the report that consent is required to provide such services, and must refrain from doing so until consent is received.

2 When the accountant actually knows or suspects, or there are reasonable (objective) grounds for knowing or suspecting, that another person is engaged in money laundering or terrorist financing, whether or not he or she wishes to act for such person. The person in question could be a client, a colleague or a third party.

2.3 Required disclosure

The required disclosure which must be included in a suspicious activity report (SAR) is as follows:

- The identity of the suspect (if known).
- The information or other matter on which the knowledge or suspicion of money laundering (or reasonable grounds for such) is based.

- The whereabouts of the laundered property (if known) is passed as soon as is practicable to the MLRO.
- Additional information held by the individual that identifies other parties involved in or connected to the matter should also be given to the MLRO.

2.4 Failure to disclose

An offence is committed if an individual fails to make a report comprising the required disclosure as soon as is practicable either in the form of an:

- Internal report to his MLRO or
- A SAR to a person authorised by the National Crime Agency (NCA) to receive disclosures.
- The obligation to make the required disclosure arises when: a person knows or suspects, or has reasonable grounds for knowing or suspecting that another person is engaged in money laundering.

An MLRO is obliged to report to the NCA if he is satisfied that the information received in an internal report is serious in nature.

An MLRO may commit an offence if he fails to pass on reportable information in internal reports that he has received, as soon as is practicable, to NCA.

The maximum penalty for failure to disclose is 5 year imprisonment and/or an unlimited fine.

2.5 Exceptions to the duty to report

The obligation of an accountant to report does NOT apply if:

1. The information which forms the basis of knowledge or suspicion or the reasonable grounds to know or suspect was obtained other than in the course of the accountant's business, for example, on a social occasion;
2. The information came about in privileged circumstances, that is in order for the accountant to provide legal advice, such as explaining a client's tax liability (except when it is judged that the advice has been sought to enable the client to commit a criminal offence or avoid detection) or expert opinion or services in relation to actual or contemplated legal proceedings;
3. There is a reasonable excuse for not reporting, in which case the report must be made as soon as reasonable in the circumstances.

2.6 Protected and Authorised disclosures

Reports made under POCA are either protected disclosures or authorised disclosures.

Protected disclosure

Any report providing the required disclosure which is made by **any** person, not just an accountant, forming a money laundering suspicion, at work or when carrying out professional activities (whether or not providing accountancy services to clients), is a protected disclosure. This means the person is protected against allegations of breach of confidentiality; however the restriction on disclosure of information was imposed.

Authorised disclosure

Any person who realises they may have engaged in or be about to engage in money laundering should make what is known as an authorised disclosure to the appropriate authority. This may provide a defence against charges of money laundering provided it is made before the act is carried out (and NCA's consent to the act is obtained), or it is made as soon as possible on the initiative of that person after the act is done and with good reason being shown for the delay.

If NCA's consent is refused within seven working days, law enforcement has a further 31 calendar days (the 'moratorium period') to further the investigation into the reported matter and take further action e.g. restrain or seize funds.

If consent, or a refusal, is not received by the member within 7 working days, starting on the first working day after the consent request was made, consent is deemed.

If a refusal is received within that 7 working days, then the member may continue with the client relationship or transaction after a further 31 days has elapsed, starting with the day on which the member received notice of the refusal, unless a restraining order is obtained to prohibit this.

There is no deemed consent in relation to suspicions of terrorist financing.

Activity 1

Is the MLRO an internal or external person?

Is NCA is an internal or external body?

Activity 2

Tony is a bookkeeper working for McIntosh Ltd.

Recently Megavac Ltd, a customer of McIntosh Ltd, sent in a cheque for £50,000 in payment of an invoice for £10,000. When Tony queried this, the client said it was a mistake and asked for a cheque for the difference of £40,000 to be written to Omnivac Ltd, a sister company of Megavac Ltd.

Advise Tony.

Activity 3

Emma is a bookkeeper in practice working on the bookkeeping of a new client, Ghest Ltd.

Emma has discovered that some customers of Ghest Ltd have overpaid their invoices and some have paid twice. On further investigation Emma discovers that the Ghest Ltd has a policy of retaining all overpayments by customers and crediting them to the profit and loss account if they are not claimed within a year.

Advise Emma.

3 Tipping off

3.1 The offence of tipping off

 **Definition**

Tipping off is the legal term meaning

- to tell the potential offender of money laundering that the necessary authorities have been informed, or
- to disclose anything that might prejudice an investigation.

The criminal offence of tipping off arises where a person in the regulated sector (e.g. accountants) discloses either:

- that a disclosure has been made by a person of information to an MLRO or to NCA or to the police or HMRC and the disclosure is likely to prejudice any investigation that might be conducted following the disclosure referred to; **or**
- that an investigation into allegations that a money laundering offence has been committed, is being contemplated or is being carried out and the disclosure is likely to prejudice that investigation and the information disclosed came to the person in the course of a business in the regulated sector.

The penalty for this offence is a maximum of 5 years imprisonment, or an unlimited fine, or both.

The person making the disclosure does not have to intend to prejudice an investigation for this offence to apply

Tipping off is a serious criminal offence. You commit the offence if you make any disclosure likely to prejudice an investigation. An example might be if you tell the client that a SAR is or is about to be filed in respect of them. You don't have to speak to commit the offence. You can even tip off by failing to respond where an answer is expected.

There are exceptions that apply in certain circumstances, including those where a person does not know or suspect that the disclosure would prejudice a money laundering investigation, and where the disclosure is made in a valid attempt to persuade a client not to commit a money laundering offence.

Considerable care is required in carrying out any communications with clients or third parties following a report. Before any disclosure is made relating to matters referred to in an internal report or SAR, it is important to consider carefully whether or not it is likely to constitute offences of tipping off or prejudicing an investigation.

It is suggested that businesses keep records of these deliberations and the conclusions reached.

However, individuals and businesses in the regulated sector will frequently need to continue to deliver their professional services and a way needs to be found to achieve this without falling foul of the tipping off offence.

3.2 Prejudicing an investigation

'Prejudicing an investigation' is a potential offence for all persons. An offence may be committed where **any** person (not just an accountant):

- knows or suspects that a money laundering investigation is being conducted or is about to be conducted; and
- makes a disclosure which is likely to prejudice the investigation; or falsifies, conceals or destroys documents relevant to the investigation, or causes that to happen.

The person making the disclosure does not have to intend to prejudice an investigation for this offence to apply.

However, there is a defence available if the person making the disclosure did not know or suspect the disclosure would be prejudicial, did not know or suspect the documents were relevant, or did not intend to conceal any facts from the person carrying out the investigation.

3.3 Record keeping

Under the MLR, records should be maintained to assist any future law enforcement investigation relating to clients, and to demonstrate that the accountant has complied with statutory obligations. Such records should include:

- copies of or reference to the Customer Due Diligence identification evidence (see below). These records must be kept for 5 years starting with the date on which the accountant's relationship with the client ends
- copies or originals of documents relating to transactions that have been subject to Customer Due Diligence measures or ongoing monitoring. These must be kept for 5 years starting with the date on which the accountant completed the client's instructions.

Activity 4

What is the maximum prison term for tipping off?

4 Customer Due Diligence

4.1 ICB Professional Conduct Regulations

When considering any new client engagement, the ICB member in practice should assess the likelihood of money laundering.

The Money Laundering Regulations 2007 apply when: a member enters a professional relationship with a client, which the member estimates will have an element of duration; the member acts in relation to a transaction or series of related transactions amounting to €15,000 or more; or there is a suspicion of money laundering

4.2 When to apply Customer Due Diligence? (CDD)

CDD must be applied by accountants in practice to all clients **before** services are provided to them.

The one exception to this is where to do so would interrupt the normal conduct of business and there is little risk of money laundering or terrorist financing, in which case the accountant must always

- find out who the client claims to be before commencing the client's instructions and
- complete CDD as soon as reasonably possible afterwards.

Money laundering regulations state that CDD must be applied in the following situations:

- When establishing a business relationship.
- When carrying out an occasional transaction (i.e. involving €15,000 or the equivalent in sterling or more).
- Where there is a suspicion of money laundering or terrorist financing.
- Where there are doubts about previously obtained customer identification information.
- At appropriate times to existing clients on a risk-sensitive basis.

4.3 Elements of Customer Due Diligence for new clients

There are three elements to CDD for new clients:

1 Find out who the client claims to be – name, address, date of birth – and obtain evidence to check that the client is as claimed.

2 Obtain evidence so the accountant is satisfied that he or she knows who any beneficial owners are. This means beneficial owners must be considered on an individual basis. Generally, a beneficial owner is an individual who ultimately owns 25% or more of the client or the transaction property.

3 Obtain information on the purpose and intended nature of the transaction.

The evidence obtained can be documentary, data or information from a reliable and independent source, or a mix of all of these.

If CDD cannot be completed, **the bookkeeper must not act for the client** – and should consider whether to submit an Internal Report or Suspicious Activity Report, as appropriate

4.4 On-going monitoring of existing clients

On-going monitoring must be applied to existing clients. This means that an accountant must:

- Carry out appropriate and risk-sensitive CDD measures to any transaction which appears to be inconsistent with knowledge of the client or the client's business or risk profile.
- For example, if a client suddenly has an injection of significant funds, check the source of funds. If a beneficial owner is revealed, obtain evidence of the beneficial owner's identity and the nature and purpose of the injection of the funds.
- Keep CDD documents, data and information up to date.
- For example, if a client company has a change to its directorship, update records accordingly.

Activity 5

A prospective new client comes to see you and asks you to invest £20,000 in cash into a business opportunity. However, he does not want to tell you his name or address.

Do you continue with the transaction?

5 Whistleblowing

5.1 The ethics of whistleblowing

Thousands of workers witness wrongdoing at work. Most remain silent. They decide that it is not their concern; that nothing they can do would improve things, or they cannot afford problems at work.

Other workers choose to speak out. They 'blow the whistle' on unethical and illegal conduct in the workplace.

Definition

Whistleblowing means disclosing information that a worker believes is evidence of illegality, gross waste, gross mismanagement, abuse of power, or substantial and specific danger to the public health and safety.

Whistleblower actions may save lives, money, or the environment. However, instead of praise for the public service of 'committing the truth' whistleblowers are often targeted for retaliation, harassment, intimidation, demotion, dismissal and blacklisting.

Example - Whistleblowing

Tim, a civil engineer, believes that a certain building practice is unsafe and reports this to his employer. The employer does not act on the report so Tim takes it to his professional body. This body also does not act to Tim's satisfaction, so he then decides to take the report to the media. The employer dismisses Tim for gross misconduct in breaching confidentiality.

The ethics of whistleblowing highlights the matters that you should consider before you blow the whistle. It takes a realistic look at the effectiveness of the protection provided by the Public Interest Disclosure Act 1998.

5.2 Public Interest Disclosure Act (PIDA) 1998

Generally, as an employee, you owe a duty of loyalty to your employer as well as to the bookkeeping profession. However, there may be times where there is a conflict between the two.

For example, your manager may ask you to 'cook the books' to reduce the company's VAT liability. Although this is clearly wrong and you should not be involved in doing this, how do you resolve such a problem?

In this particular scenario, you would need to speak to your manager and advise him or her that you have concerns about doing this and cannot be involved in such an activity. If there is still a disagreement about a significant ethical issue with your manager, you should then raise the matter with higher levels of management or non-executive directors. Finally, if there is a material issue and you have exhausted all other avenues, you may wish to consider resigning – however, it is strongly recommended that you obtain legal advice before doing so.

In addition, you may decide to take the bolder step of external whistle blowing.

Where you have blown the whistle but decided not to resign, in certain circumstances you may be protected from dismissal by the Public Interest Disclosure Act 1998 (PIDA) where you disclose otherwise confidential information. The Act (which has also been referred to as 'the Whistleblowers' Charter') gives protection where you have made a 'qualifying disclosure' (i.e. disclosure of information which you reasonably believe shows that a criminal offence, breach of a legal obligation, miscarriage of justice, breach of health and safety legislation or environmental damage has occurred, is occurring or is likely to occur).

You need to show that you made the disclosure in good faith, reasonably believed that the information disclosed was true and that you would otherwise be victimised or the evidence concealed or destroyed; or that the concern has already been raised with the employer/external prescribed regulator (i.e. a body prescribed under PIDA such as Customs and Excise).

Activity 6

Vincent discovered that the company he worked for as a bookkeeper was involved in illegal pollution and decided to leak this information anonymously to the press.

A month later Vincent's department was closed down and Vincent made redundant. Vincent is now claiming that he has been victimised because he was a whistleblower and is seeking protection under PIDA.

Comment on Vincent's case.

6 Summary

This chapter has introduced you to some very important legislation.

It is vital you are able to both recite and apply the money laundering regulation: make sure you know what the definitions are!

7 Answers to chapter activities

Activity 1

The MLRO is an **internal** person.

The NCA is an **external** body.

Activity 2

The overpayment and request to pay a third party are grounds for suspicion of money laundering (see note below).

Any overpayment by a customer should be thoroughly investigated by a senior member of finance function staff and only repaid to the customer once it has been established that it is right/legal to do so.

Similarly the request to pay a third party should be scrutinised before any payment is agreed to. Without further information the transaction does not make commercial sense.

Unless investigations satisfy any concerns raised, then

- Tom should report the matter to the firm's MRLO.
- McIntosh Ltd should refuse the payment.
- The MRLO should fill in a Suspicious Activity Report (SAR) to be sent to NCA.

Tutorial note: It seems highly unlikely a customer would overpay by £40,000 by accident! Also, why doesn't the client, Megavac Ltd, simply want McIntosh Ltd to repay them, and then it is up to them whether they want to pay anything to Omnivac Ltd? Is it to make funds difficult to trace, so 'dirty' cash becomes a nice 'clean' cheque from a reputable accounting firm?

Activity 3

Emma should consider whether the retention of the overpayments might amount to theft by Ghest Ltd from its customers. If so, the client will be in possession of the proceeds of its crime, a money laundering offence.

In the case of minor irregularities where there is nothing to suggest dishonest behaviour, (for example where Ghest Ltd attempted to return the overpayments to its customers, or if the overpayments were mistakenly overlooked), Emma may be satisfied that no criminal property is involved and therefore a report is not required.

If there are no such indications that Ghest Ltd has acted honestly, Emma should conclude that Ghest Ltd may have acted dishonestly.

Emma must thus make a report to her firm's MLRO.

Activity 4

The maximum penalty for tipping off is a maximum of 5 years imprisonment, or an unlimited fine, or both.

Activity 5

You would be unable to complete a due diligence report on this potential customer, there you should not continue with the transaction.

Also the way in which you have been approached could be grounds for suspicious activity. It would be appropriate to report the dealings on the MLRO if possible, if not to NCA.

Activity 6

To gain protection from PIDA, Vincent would have to demonstrate that he was made redundant because he was a whistleblower.

In this case that would be very difficult as he made his disclosure anonymously.

8 Test your knowledge

Workbook Activity 7

(a) If you suspect money laundering is occurring, you should

A Talk it through with the people involved, to confirm that you have understood the situation fully.

B Report the problem to your line manager.

C Disclose the issue to your MLRO.

(b) If you are involved in money laundering, you face

A Life imprisonment.

B A £500 fine.

C 14 years imprisonment, and/or an unlimited fine.

Workbook Activity 8

David, a member in practice has been approached by a potential new client.

Answer the following question by selecting the TWO appropriate options.

As part of his customer due diligence process, which of the following actions must David undertake?

- Verify the client's identity on the basis of documents, data or other reliable information.
- Verify the value of the client's assets and liabilities.
- Obtain information on the purpose and intended nature of the client relationship.
- Notify the ICB.

Workbook Activity 9

(a) Customer due diligence refers to:

A Making sure that your client is hard working

B Verifying your client's identity

C Checking that your client will pay his bills

(b) Customer Due Diligence is performed to comply with:

A Companies Act 2006

B Money laundering legislation

C ICB ethical guidance

Partnership Accounts

Introduction

With partnerships, there is some new terminology to learn but more importantly there are a number of special accounting entries that have to be dealt with.

CONTENTS

1 Key features of partnerships

1.1 Identification of partnership

A partnership exists whenever two or more people trade together with the intention of making a profit. No legal formalities are needed to create a partnership, although most partnerships will have a partnership agreement. If no agreement exists then the partnership agreement set out in the Partnership Act of 1890 comes into effect. This states that all profits and losses should be shared equally between the partners.

1.2 The partnership agreement

Definition

A partnership agreement, which need not necessarily be in written form, will govern the relationships between the partners.

Important matters to be covered in the agreement include:

(a) name of firm, the type of business, and duration

(b) capital to be introduced by partners

(c) distribution of profits between partners

(d) drawings by partners

(e) arrangements for dissolution, or on the death or retirement of partners

(f) settling of disputes

(g) preparation and audit of accounts.

1.3 Advantages and disadvantages of operating as a partnership

Comparing a partnership to sole trading, the **advantages** of operating as a partnership are as follows:

(a) Business risks are spread among more than one person.

(b) Individual partners can develop special skills upon which the other partners can rely rather than being a jack of all trades.

(c) Certain partners may be able to draw upon larger capital resources to set up the partnership or expand the partnership.

The **disadvantages** are:

(a) There may be disputes between partners on such matters as the direction the business is taking or how much money individual partners are taking out of the business. Some partners may feel they are contributing more time and effort to the partnership than others and not being sufficiently financially rewarded as a result.

(b) A partner is 'jointly and severally liable' for his partners. This means that if one partner is being sued in relation to the business of the partnership, the other partners share in the responsibility.

A partnership has some advantages over a company as the arrangement is less formal than setting up a company requiring the issue of shares and the appointment of directors. If the partners wish to dissolve the business that is an easier matter to achieve by a partnership rather than a company.

The advantage of a company is that the owners of the business – the shareholders – may be protected from the creditors of the company as regards the payment of outstanding debts.

1.4 Summary

Relative to sole trading, a partnership can give access to the wider skills and capital resources of several partners, although disputes amongst partners and the problems which can arise from joint and several liability are disadvantages

Partnerships have fewer formalities than companies but do not have the protection of limited liability. Note that Limited Liability Partnerships do have the benefit of limited liability: these are covered in detail in your Level IV studies.

2 Division of profits and the partners' capital and current accounts

2.1 Division of profits

The partnership agreement will detail how the profits of the firm are to be divided amongst the partners. However, if the partners do not have a partnership agreement, verbal or written, the rules laid down in the Partnership Act 1890 will apply. The rules are:

- residual profits are shared equally
- there are no salaries paid to partners

- there is no interest paid on partners' capital invested in the business
- interest at 5% per annum is payable on partners' loans to the business.

The division of profit stated in the partnership agreement may be quite complex in order to reflect the expected differing efforts and contributions of the partners. For example, some or all of the partners may be entitled to a salary to reflect the differing management involvement in the business. Interest on capital may be provided to reflect the differing amounts of capital contributed. The profit shares may differ to reflect seniority or greater skills.

It is important to appreciate however that all of the above examples are means of dividing the profits of the partnership and are not expenses of the business. A partnership salary is merely a device for calculating the division of profit; it is not a salary in the normal meaning of the term.

2.2 Accounting distinctions between partnerships and sole traders

The accounting techniques developed for sole traders are generally applicable to partnerships, but there are certain important differences:

Item	*Sole trader's books*	*Partnership's books*
Capital introduced	Capital account	Partners' fixed capital accounts
Drawings and share of the profit	Capital account	Partners' current accounts
Division of profits	Inapplicable – one proprietor only	Appropriation account

2.3 Capital accounts

At the commencement of the partnership an agreement will have to be reached as to the amount of capital to be introduced. This could be in the form of cash or other assets. Whatever the form of assets introduced and debited to asset accounts, it is normal to make the credit entry to fixed capital accounts. These are so called because they are not then used to record drawings or shares of profits but only major changes in the relations between partners. In particular, fixed capital accounts are used to deal with:

(a) capital introduced or withdrawn by new or retiring partners

(b) revaluation adjustments

The balances on fixed capital accounts do not necessarily bear any relation to the division of profits. However, to compensate partners who provide a larger share of the capital, it is common for notional interest on capital accounts to be paid to partners. This is dealt with through the appropriation account (see section 3).

2.4 Current accounts

These are used to deal with the regular transactions between the partners and the firm i.e. matters other than those sufficiently fundamental to be dealt with through the capital accounts. Most commonly these are:

(a) share of profits, interest on capital and partners' salaries usually computed annually

(b) monthly drawings against the annual share of profit.

2.5 Revaluation adjustments

When there is a change in a partnership, such as the admission of a new partner, the sale of the business, or a change in the profit sharing ratio, it is usual for the partnership to revalue its fixed assets immediately before the change takes place.

This will reflect any profit or loss that has accrued on assets from the date of acquisition to the date of the partnership change. Each partner is entitled to their share of the assets in accordance with ratios set out in the partnership profit-sharing agreement. Therefore, any profit or loss arising on the revaluation of assets will be allocated to each partner in the profit-sharing ratio in existence at the date of the change.

A temporary revaluation account is used to calculate the overall gain or loss on revaluation: this will then be shared between the existing partners, at the date of change, in their capital accounts in accordance with the existing profit-sharing ratios.

Example

Dan and Matt are in partnership and share profits on a ratio of 2:1. On 1.1.X6, Tom will be joining the partnership. The book value of the assets on 31.12.X5 is £50,000 and they are revalued at £65,000 on that date.

The balances on the capital accounts at 31.12.X5 are:

Dan £4,000 CR
Matt: £3,000 CR

Prepare the revaluation account and the partners' capital accounts to reflect the revaluation of the assets at 31.12.X5.

Solution

The assets have been revalued by £15,000: this increase in value is initially credited to the revaluation account.

The balance on the revaluation account then needs to be shared between Dan and Matt using the profit-sharing ratio 2:1.

Therefore Dan will be allocated £10,000 of the profit and Matt will be allocated £5,000. These revaluation profits will be credited to their capital accounts.

Revaluation account

		£			£
20X5			20X5		
31/12	Dan capital account	10,000	31/12	Fixed Assets	15,000
	Matt capital account	5,000			
		15,000			15,000

Partners' capital accounts

		Dan	*Matt*			*Dan*	*Matt*
		£	£			£	£
				20X5			
				31/12	Balance b/d	4,000	3,000
20X5				31/12	Revaluation	10,000	5,000
31/12	Balance c/d	14,000	8,000				
		14,000	8,000			14,000	8,000
				20X6			
				1/1	Balance b/d	14,000	8,000

2.6 Recording the partners' shares of profits/losses and their drawings in the ledger accounts and balance sheet presentation

Example

Nab and Crag commenced business in partnership on 1 January 20X6, contributing as fixed capital £5,000 and £10,000 cash respectively. All profits and losses are shared equally. The profit for the year ended 31 December 20X6 amounted to £10,000. Drawings for Nab and Crag amounted to £3,000 and £4,000 respectively.

You are required to prepare the capital and current accounts and balance sheet extracts.

Solution

Partners' capital accounts

		Nab	*Crag*			*Nab*	*Crag*
		£	£			£	£
				20X6			
				1/1	Cash	5,000	10,000

Partners' current accounts

		Nab	*Crag*			*Nab*	*Crag*
		£	£			£	£
20X6				20X6			
31/12	Drawings	3,000	4,000	31/12	Share of profits	5,000	5,000
	Balance c/d	2,000	1,000				
		5,000	5,000			5,000	5,000
				20X7			
				1/1	Balance b/d	2,000	1,000

The above accounts are presented in a columnar format. This is quite common in a partnership set of books as each partner will have similar transactions during the year. A columnar format allows two (or more) separate accounts to be shown using the same narrative. It is important to remember though that each partner's account is separate from the other partner(s).

Balance sheet at 31 December 20X6 (extract)

	Capital accounts	*Current accounts*	
	£	£	£
Partners' accounts:			
Nab	5,000	2,000	7,000
Crag	10,000	1,000	11,000
	15,000	3,000	18,000

Note that the current account balances of £2,000 and £1,000 will be credited in the following year with profit shares and debited with drawings.

One of the main differences between the capital section of the balance sheet of a sole trader and a partnership, is that the partnership balance sheet will often only give the closing balances whereas the sole trader's movements in capital are shown. The main reason for the difference is simply one of space. Movements in the capital and current accounts for a few partners cannot be easily accommodated on the face of the balance sheet.

Example

The information is the same as in previous example, except that Nab's drawings are £5,300. The current accounts now become:

Partners' current accounts

		Nab	*Crag*			*Nab*	*Crag*
		£	£			£	£
20X6				20X6			
	Drawings	5,300	4,000		Share of profits	5,000	5,000
31/12	Balance c/d		1,000	31/12	Balance c/d	300	
		5,300	5,000			5,300	5,000
20X7				20X7			
1/1	Balance b/d	300		1/1	Balance b/d		1,000

Note that Nab's current account is overdrawn.

How do we present this in the balance sheet?

Balance sheet at 31 December 20X6 (extract)

	Capital accounts	*Current accounts*	
	£	£	£
Partners' accounts:			
Nab	5,000	(300)	4,700
Crag	10,000	1,000	11,000
	15,000	700	15,700

2.7 Recap

Partners' drawings and share of the annual profit is recorded in their current accounts. Their capital accounts are used to record fixed capital introduced or withdrawn and revaluation adjustments.

Activity 1

Tor and Hill have been in partnership for two years, sharing profits in the ratio 2:1. Figures for profit and drawings are as follows:

	Year ending 31 December	
	20X4	*20X5*
	£	£
Drawings: Tor	2,000	2,500
Drawings: Hill	1,500	1,500
Residual profit	9,000	12,000

You are required to prepare the partners' current accounts for 20X4 and 20X5, bringing down balances at the end of each year.

3 The appropriation account

3.1 Introduction

Definition

The **appropriation account** is a ledger account dealing with the allocation of net profit between the partners. In practice it is often included as the final part of the trading and profit and loss account. It can also be presented as a statement in columnar form.

An important point is that all allocations of profit to partners in their capacity as partners, and during the time they actually are partners, are made through the appropriation account. This applies even though such allocations may be described as partners' salaries, interest on capital or a share of profits.

3.2 Using the appropriation account

 **Example**

Pike and Scar are in partnership and have the following profit-sharing arrangements:

(a) interest on capital is to be provided at a rate of 8% pa

(b) Pike and Scar are to receive salaries of £6,000 and £8,000 pa respectively

(c) the balance of profit or loss is to be divided between Pike and Scar in the ratio 3:2.

Net profit for the year amounts to £20,000 and capital account balances are Pike £12,000 and Scar £9,000.

You are required to prepare:

(a) a statement showing the allocation of profit between the partners; and

(b) relevant entries in the trading and profit and loss and appropriation account.

Solution

(a) Allocation of net profit of £20,000

	Pike	*Scar*	*Total*
	£	£	£
Interest on capital	960	720	1,680
Salaries	6,000	8,000	14,000
Balance of profits (£20,000 – £15,680) in ratio 3:2	2,592	1,728	4,320
Totals	9,552	10,448	20,000

Note that this is only a calculation of the allocation of profit and not part of the double entry bookkeeping system, merely providing the figures for the appropriation account.

(b) Extract from trading and profit and loss and appropriation account for the year ended 20X1

	£	£
Sales		x
Cost of sales		x
Gross profit		x
Expenses		x
Net profit		20,000
Allocated to:		
Pike	9,552	
Scar	10,448	
		20,000

The profit and loss appropriation account is closed by transferring the profit shares to the credit of the partners' current accounts. The double entry is:

Debit	*Credit*	*With*
Profit and loss appropriation account	Pike's current account	£9,552
Profit and loss appropriation account	Scar's current account	£10,448

For the purposes of assessments (and in practice) parts (a) and (b) above can be amalgamated as follows

Extract from trading and profit and loss and appropriation account for the year ended 20X1

	£
Sales	x
Cost of sales	x
Gross profit	x
Expenses	x
Net profit for year	20,000

Appropriation statement

	Pike		*Scar*		*Total*
	£		£		£
Interest on capital	960		720		1,680
Salaries	6,000		8,000		14,000
Balance of profits (£20,000 – £15,680) in ratio 3:2	2,592	(3/5)	1,728	(2/5)	4,320
Totals	9,552		10,448		20,000

The debits actually being made are as before (£9,552 and £10,448).

Activity 2

Flame and Smoke are in partnership and have the following profit-sharing arrangements:

(a) Interest on capital is provided at a rate of 8% pa.

(b) Flame and Smoke are to receive salaries of £6,000 and £8,000 p.a.

(c) The balance of profit or loss is to be divided between Flame and Smoke in the ratio 3:2.

The balances on the capital accounts of the partners stand at Flame: £6,000 and Smoke: £4,000. The net profit for the year is £3,680.

You are required to show the allocation of profit between the partners

3.3 Partners' salaries

One point which regularly causes difficulties is the partners' salaries. The key is to remember at the outset that a partner's salary is an appropriation of profit, whereas a salary paid to an employee is an expense.

Accordingly a salary to which a partner is entitled, is included as part of the appropriation statement. Questions sometimes state that a partner has withdrawn his salary. In this case:

(a) include the salary in the appropriation statement as usual; and

(b) as a separate transaction, treat the withdrawal of the salary as drawings.

Debit	*Credit*	*With*
Partner's current account	Bank	Amount withdrawn

3.4 Guaranteed minimum profit share

In certain partnership agreements a partner may be guaranteed a minimum share of profits. The appropriation of profit would proceed in the normal way. If the result is that the partner has less than this minimum, the deficit will be made good by the other partners (normally in profit-sharing ratio). Sometimes the guarantee is given by one partner only, who will then bear the whole of the deficit.

Example

Tessa, Laura and Jane are in partnership and have the following profit-sharing arrangements:

(a) Tessa and Laura are to receive salaries of £20,000 and £30,000 respectively

(b) balance of profit or loss is to be divided in the ratio: Tessa 1, Laura 2, Jane 3

(c) Tessa is guaranteed a minimum profit share of £25,000.

The net profit for the year is £68,000.

You are required to show the appropriation account for the year.

Solution

Appropriation account

	Tessa	*Laura*	*Jane*	*Total*
	£	£	£	£
Net profit				68,000
Salaries	20,000	30,000		(50,000)
				18,000
Balance of profits in ratio 1 : 2 : 3	3,000	6,000	9,000	(18,000)
	23,000	36,000	9,000	
Adjustment	2,000			
Laura 2/5 × 2,000		(800)		
Jane 3/5 × 2,000			(1,200)	
Totals	25,000	35,200	7,800	68,000

3.5 Interest on drawings

Occasionally there is a provision in a partnership agreement for a notional interest charge on the drawings by each partner. The interest charges are merely a negative profit share – they are a means by which total profits are allocated between the partners.

The reason for an interest on drawings provision is that those partners who draw out more cash than their colleagues in the early part of an accounting period should suffer a cost.

Example

Dick and Dastardly are in partnership. The capital and current accounts as at 1 January 20X7 show:

	Capital	*Current*
	£	£
Dick	50,000	2,500
Dastardly	20,000	3,000

The partnership agreement provides for the following:

(a) profits and losses are shared between Dick and Dastardly in percentages 60 and 40

(b) interest on capital at 10% per annum is allowed

(c) interest on drawings is charged at 12% per annum.

Drawings for the year to 31 December 20X7 are:

	Dick	*Dastardly*
	£	£
1 February 20X7	5,000	2,000
30 September 20X7	2,000	5,000

The profit for the year is £20,000.

You are required to prepare the appropriation account and the current accounts for the year ended 31 December 20X7.

Solution

Appropriation account for the year ended 31 December 20X7

	Dick	*Dastardly*	
	£	£	£
Profit for the year			20,000
Add: Interest on drawings (see working)	610	370	980
			20,980
Less: Interest on capital:			
50,000 × 10%	(5,000)		
20,000 × 10%		(2,000)	(7,000)
			13,980

Balance in profit-sharing ratio:			
13,980 × 60%	(8,388)		
13,980 × 40%		(5,592)	(13,980)
			0
Total allocation	**12,778**	**7,222**	**20,000**

Current accounts

		Dick	Dast'ly			Dick	Dast'ly
		£	£			£	£
20X7:				20X7:			
1 Feb	Drawings	5,000	2,000		Balance b/d	2,500	3,000
30 Sep	Drawings	2,000	5,000	31 Dec	Share of profits	12,778	7,222
	Balance c/d	8,278	3,222				
		15,278	10,222			15,278	10,222

Workings

		Dick	Dast'ly
		£	£
Interest on drawings:			
1 February 20X7	5,000 × 12% × 11/12	550	
	2,000 × 12% × 11/12		220
30 September 20X7	2,000 × 12% × 3/12	60	
	5,000 × 12% × 3/12		150
		610	370

3.6 Conclusion

The appropriation account shows how the net profit for the year has been divided amongst the partners. Appropriations may take the form of:

- interest on capital
- 'salaries'
- a share of the remaining profit (in the agreed ratio)
- interest on drawings (occasionally).

4 Drafting financial statements

4.1 Preparing partnership accounts

You should now be ready to prepare a full set of partnership accounts.

Example

You are provided with the following information regarding the partnership of Dacre, Hutton and Tod.

(a) The trial balance at 31 December 20X6 is as follows:

	Dr	*Cr*
	£	£
Sales		50,000
Stock at 1 January 20X6	6,000	
Purchases	29,250	
Carriage inwards	250	
Carriage outwards	400	
Creditors		4,000
Cash at bank	3,900	
Current accounts:		
Dacre		900
Hutton		750
Tod		1,350
Capital accounts:		
Dacre		4,000
Hutton		5,000
Tod		6,000
Drawings:		
Dacre	2,000	
Hutton	3,000	
Tod	5,000	
Sundry expenses	2,800	
Debtors	13,000	
Shop fittings:		
Cost	8,000	
Accumulated depreciation		1,600
	73,600	73,600

(b) Closing stock is valued for accounts purposes at £5,500.

(c) Depreciation of £800 is to be provided on the shop fittings.

(d) The profit-sharing arrangements are as follows:

 (i) interest on capital is to be provided at a rate of 10% per annum

 (ii) Dacre and Tod are to receive salaries of £3,000 and £4,000 per annum respectively

 (iii) the balance of profit or loss is to be divided between Dacre, Hutton and Tod in the ratio of 3:8:4.

You are required to prepare final accounts together with current accounts of the partners.

Solution

Dacre, Hutton and Tod

Trading and profit and loss account for the year ended 31 December 20X6

	£	£
Sales		50,000
Opening stock	6,000	
Purchases	29,250	
Carriage inwards	250	
	35,500	
Less: Closing stock	5,500	
		30,000
Gross profit		20,000
Sundry expenses	2,800	
Carriage outwards	400	
Depreciation	800	
		4,000
Net profit		16,000
Allocated to:		
Dacre	4,900	
Hutton	4,500	
Tod	6,600	
		16,000

Balance sheet as at 31 December 20X6

	Cost	*Acc dep'n*	
	£	£	£
Fixed assets			
Shop fittings	8,000	2,400	5,600
Current assets			
Stock		5,500	
Debtors		13,000	
Cash at bank		3,900	
		22,400	
Current liabilities			
Creditors		4,000	
Net current assets			18,400
			24,000

Partners' accounts

	Capital accounts	**Current accounts**	
	£	£	£
Dacre	4,000	3,800	7,800
Hutton	5,000	2,250	7,250
Tod	6,000	2,950	8,950
	15,000	9,000	24,000

Partners' current accounts

		Dacre	*Hutton*	*Tod*			*Dacre*	*Hutton*	*Tod*
		£	£	£			£	£	£
20X6:					*20X6:*				
	Drawings	2,000	3,000	5,000	1 Jan	Bal b/d	900	750	1,350
31 Dec	Bal c/d	3,800	2,250	2,950		P&L app	4,900	4,500	6,600
		5,800	5,250	7,950			5,800	5,250	7,950
					20X7:				
					1 Jan	Balance b/d	3,800	2,250	2,950

Workings and commentary

The adjustments for stock and depreciation should be familiar by now.

The new development is that, having calculated the profit for the period, it has to be appropriated between Dacre, Hutton and Tod. To calculate their respective shares an appropriation statement is used:

	Dacre	*Hutton*	*Tod*	*Total*
	£	£	£	£
Interest on capital	400	500	600	1,500
Salaries	3,000	–	4,000	7,000
Balance of profit (£16,000 – £8,500) in ratio 3 : 8 : 4	1,500	4,000	2,000	7,500
	4,900	4,500	6,600	16,000

This gives us the figures for the double entry:

Dr Profit and loss appropriation
Cr Partners' current accounts

The majority of scenarios for your studies specify separate capital and current accounts. Occasionally you may be faced with a question specifying only one account for each partner. Such an account acts as a capital and current account combined.

4.2 Summary

Adopt a step by step approach to the preparation of partnership accounts, as follows:

1. Draw up a proforma balance sheet and profit and loss account and enter figures as soon as you calculate them.
2. Work through any adjustments required.
3. Complete the profit and loss account and appropriate the profit as per the partnership agreement.
4. Open up partners' current accounts; enter the opening balances, appropriations of profit and drawings.
5. Find the new balances on the partners' current accounts.
6. Complete the balance sheet.

5 Key terms

Partnership – exists whenever two or more people trade together with the intention of making a profit.

Partnership agreement – which need not necessarily be in written form, will govern the relationships between the partners.

Joint and several liability – each partner has unlimited liability for all of the losses incurred by the business. Usually losses will be shared in the profit sharing ratio, but if one or more partners become insolvent, then the loss must be borne by the other partners.

Partners' capital accounts – records the long-term investment by the partners in the business.

Partners' current accounts – used to deal with the regular transactions between the partners and the firm, such as profits and drawings.

Partners' appropriation account – a ledger account dealing with the allocation of net profit between the partners.

Partners' salaries – an appropriation of profit. They are not an expense of the business.

Profit-sharing ratio – the agreed ratio in which the residual profits of the partnership are shared between the partners.

Residual profits – the net profit of the partnership adjusted for interest on capital and drawings and salaries.

6 Answers to chapter activities

Activity 1

Current accounts

		Tor	*Hill*			*Tor*	*Hill*
		£	£			£	£
20X4				*20X4*			
	Drawings	2,000	1,500		Share of profit	6,000	3,000
31 Dec	Balance c/d	4,000	1,500				
		6,000	3,000			6,000	3,000
20X5				*20X5*			
31 Dec	Drawings	2,500	1,500	1 Jan	Balance b/d	4,000	1,500
	Balance c/d	9,500	4,000		Share of profit	8,000	4,000
		12,000	5,500			12,000	5,500
20X6				*20X6*			
				1 Jan	Balance b/d	9,500	4,000

Activity 2

Allocation of net profit of £3,680

	Flame	*Smoke*	*Total*
	£	£	£
Interest on capital	480	320	800
Salaries	6,000	8,000	14,000
Balance of loss £3,680 – £14,800 = (£11,120) to be shared in ratio 3:2	(6,672)	(4,448)	(11,120)
Totals	(192)	3,872	3,680

The double entry in this case would be:

Debit	*Credit*	*With*
Profit and loss appropriation account	Smoke's current account	£3,872
Flame's current account	Profit and loss appropriation account	£192

The relevant part of the profit and loss account would show:

	£	£
Net profit		3,680
Allocated to:		
Smoke	3,872	
Flame	(192)	
		3,680

7 Test your knowledge

Workbook Activity 3

Owen and Griffiths are in partnership, sharing profits equally after Owen has been allowed a salary of £5,000 per year. No interest is charged on drawings but interest of 10% pa is allowed on the opening capital account balances for each year.

The trial balance for the partnership as at 31 December is shown below.

	Debit	Credit
Capital account:		
Owen		9,000
Griffiths		10,000
10% loan account:		
Griffiths		5,000
Williams		6,000
Current account balance on 1 January:		
Owen		1,000
Griffiths		2,000
Drawings:		
Owen	6,500	
Griffiths	5,500	
Sales		123,100
Wages	17,000	
Purchases	70,000	
Sales ledger control account	40,000	
Purchase ledger control account		25,000
Operating expenses	26,100	
Fixed assets at cost	37,000	
Provision for depreciation		18,000
Bank overdraft		3,000
	202,100	**202,100**

The net profit for the year based on this trial balance was £10,000.

Requirement

Complete the current accounts below to show the allocation of the profit between the two partners.

Current accounts

	Owen	*Griffiths*		*Owen*	*Griffiths*
	£	£		£	£
Drawings			Balance b/d		
			Interest on capital		
			Salary		
Balance c/d			Profit		

Not-for-profit organisations

18

Introduction

You need to be able to prepare the final accounts, namely the income and expenditure account and a balance sheet, for a not-for-profit organisation. For the purposes of your studies, the not-for-profit organisation is most likely to be a club or society.

CONTENTS

1 Club and society accounts

1.1 Introduction

Club and society treasurers usually keep a simple cash book to record the income and expenditure over the accounting period.

An analysis of the cash book would result in a receipts and payments account being prepared.

However, as such non-profit making organisations need to prepare accounts using the accruals or matching concept, then the receipts and payments account together with adjustments for accruals and prepayments and the treatment of depreciation of tangible assets would form the basis of a club's income and expenditure account for its financial year.

In addition to this important financial statement, a balance sheet would also be prepared. The Balance Sheet of a club or society would include terminology that is unique to such organisations, that of the accumulated fund.

The accumulated fund is derived from the basic accounting equation:-

Assets less Liabilities = Accumulated Fund

This fund represents the members' interest in the club or society. Many of the concepts that apply there are those that you have covered in your previous studies in this text.

Worked example

Harthill Hockey Club had the following assets and liabilities at 1 January 20X7:

Net book value of fixed assets:

Pavilion	
(no depreciation charged to date)	£75,000
Machinery	£22,000
Equipment	£6,800
Bank	£4,250
Creditor for machine maintenance	£750
Accruals:	
Heat and light	£450
Ground rent	£490
Prepayments:	
Insurance	£510

Subscriptions in arrears and advance were £100 and £120 respectively.

The receipts and payments for the year ended 31 December 20X7 showed:-

(This is simply a summary of the Club's Cash Book)

	£
Bank Balance 1/1/X7	4,250
Income:	
Christmas Draw	1,800
Raffles	750
Jumble Sale	1,400
Subscriptions	1,001
Refreshments	869
Sponsorship	2,520
	12,590

Expenditure:	
Refreshments	1,250
Heat and light	900
Ground rent	1,400
Insurance	1,100
New equipment fence/nets	4,200
Ground maintenance	690
Maintenance machinery	960
	10,500
Bank Balance 31/12/X7	£2,090

Additional Information

At 31 December 20X7:

Insurance was prepaid by £610

Heat and light of £210 was accrued and £450 was outstanding for ground rent

Subscriptions of £100 were outstanding as overdue and £80 had been paid in advance

There was a creditor for machinery maintenance of £175

Depreciation Policy:

Machinery 10% on net book value

Equipment 20% on net book value

It was now agreed to depreciate the pavilion 2% on cost.

Task

Prepare the Income and Expenditure Account for year ended 31 December 20X7, together with a Balance Sheet for presentation to the members of Harthill Hockey Club.

Step 1

Calculate the opening accumulated fund.

Assets Less Liabilities = Accumulated Fund

	£
Assets:	
Pavilion	75,000
Machinery	22,000
Equipment	6,800
Bank	4,250
Prepayments	510
Subscriptions in arrears (due from members)	100
	£108,660
Less: Liabilities	
Creditors	750
Subscriptions in advance	120
Accruals:	
Heat and light	450
Ground rent	490
	1,810
Accumulated Fund	**£106,850**

This figure will be needed as the opening fund to be shown on the Balance Sheet.

Step 2

There are various figures shown in the receipts and payments account that require adjustment when preparing the income and expenditure account, to apply to accruals concept.

(1) Subscriptions (member's contribution)

It is often the case that member's subscriptions at the end of the year may be in advance or arrears. Here we have opening and closing values for subscriptions in arrears and advance.

The best approach to determine the figure required for the income and expenditure account is to construct a 'T' account.

Subscriptions a/c

		£			£
1/1/X7	Balance B/d	100	1/1/X7	Balance B/d	120
31/12/X7	Balance C/d		31/12/X7	Bank	1,001
	(in advance)	80	31/12/X7	Balance C/d	100
31/12/X7	I&E a/c	1,041		(outstanding)	
		1,221			1,221
1/1/X8	Balance B/d	100	1/1/X8	Balance B/d	80

The account now shows that the club has a current asset (DR balance) of £100 re subscriptions overdue from members and a current liability (CR balance) of £80 re subscriptions received in advance from members.

These values will appear on the club balance sheet, and the amount transferred to the income and expenditure account for the year will also account for these adjustments.

(2) The accruals and prepayments are also best dealt with by the use of a series of 'T' accounts.

Heat and Light

		£			£
31/12/X7	Bank	900	1/1/X7	Balance B/d	450
31/12/X7	Balance C/d		31/12/X7	I&E a/c	660
	(accruals)	210			
		1,110			1,110
			1/1/X8	Balance B/d	210

The account now shows the closing liability, the accrual and the amount to be transferred to the income and expenditure account.

Ground Rent

		£			£
31/12/X7	Bank	1,400	1/1/X7	Balance B/d	490
31/12/X7	Balance C/d		31/12/X7	I&E a/c	1,360
	(accruals)	450			
		1,850			1,850
			1/1/08	Balance B/d	450

Again, here we can see the closing liability in the form of the accrual, and the amount transferred to the income and expenditure account.

Machine Maintenance

		£			£
31/12/X7	Bank	960	1/1/X7	Balance B/d	750
31/12/X7	Balance C/d (closing creditor)	175	31/12/X7	I&E a/c	385
		1,135			1,135
			1/1/X8	Balance B/d	175

The closing liability is again clearly shown here, together with the transfer to the income and expenditure account.

There is also a prepayment to adjust for on insurance.

Insurance

		£			£
1/1/X7	Balance b/d	510	31/12/X7	Balance c/d (prepayment)	610
31/12/X7	Bank	1,100	31/12/X7	I&E a/c	1,000
		1,610			1,610
1/1/X8	Balance b/d	610			

Here we can see the closing prepayment is a (DR) balance brought down of £610. This will appear as a Current Asset on the balance sheet.

The transfer to I&E account is also shown in the account.

(3) **Depreciation**

We need to determine the charge for the year.

Pavilion £75,000		
2% on Cost =		£1,500
Machinery £22,000		
10% on NBV =		£2,200
Equipment		
at 1/1/07	£6,800	
Additions		
in year	£4,200	
	11,000	
20% on NBV		£2,200
		£5,900

The Income and Expenditure account and the Balance Sheet can now be prepared:

Harthill Hockey Club

Income and Expenditure Account

for the year ended 31 December 20X7

Income	**£**	**£**
Subscriptions		1,041
Christmas Draw		1,800
Raffles		750
Jumble Sale		1,400
Sponsorship		2,520
		7,511

Expenditure

Refreshments: (see note below)		
Income	869	
Expenditure	1,250	
		381
Heat and Light		660
Ground Rent		1,360
Insurance		1,000
Ground maintenance		690
Machinery maintenance		385
Depreciation:		
Machinery		2,200
Equipment		2,200
Pavilion		1,500
		£10,376

Excess of Expenditure over Income = **£2,865**

You will note that there is also new terminology on the Income and Expenditure account that of 'excess of expenditure over income for the year' (i.e. deficit). However, when a surplus is made, this would read excess of income over expenditure for the year.

Note that it is good practice to net off the income and expenditure from selling refreshments.

Balance Sheet as at 31 December 20X7

Fixed Assets		**NBV**
Pavilion		73,500
Machinery		19,800
Equipment		8,800
		102,100
Current Assets		
Bank	2,090	
Prepayment	610	
Subs in arrears	100	
	2,800	

Less Current Liabilities		
Creditors & Accruals	835	
Subs in advance	80	
	915	
Net Current Assets		1,885
Net Assets		£103,985
Financed By:		
Accumulated Fund 1/X7		106,850
Less excess expenditure over income for year		(2,865)
		£103,985

1.1 Summary of the accounts of Harthill Hockey Club for its membership

Firstly we should note that comparative figures for the previous year would be shown.

The following points would be made by the treasurer on the current year's accounts.

The Accumulated Fund or the Net Assets (the club's worth) at the start of the year was £106,850.

The club's income for the year was £7,511 and a detailed breakdown of this can be seen on the Income and Expenditure Account.

The total costs shown including the charge for depreciation were £10,376, the result being a deficit, or excess of expenditure over income for the year. It should be noted however that depreciation is a non-cash item.

The income set against the core expenses showed a surplus in excess of £2,000, and coupled with previous cash flow generated the club was able to invest a further £4,200 in new equipment.

The club's Balance Sheet shows that the Accumulated Fund has fallen marginally due to this year's deficit.

Activity 1

You are the bookkeeper for Redtown Snooker Club.

Membership fees of £4,500 have been received for the year ended 31 March 20X8 according to the cash book.

At 1 April 20X7, there was a total of £650 membership fees in arrears and at 31 March, there was a total of £350 membership fees in arrears.

Use the membership fees account to calculate the total income to be shown in the Income and Expenditure account for the year ended 31 March 20X8.

2 Summary

It is essential for your Level III studies that you know how to prepare a set of accounts for a not-for-profit organisation – most commonly a club or society for the purposes of your assessment. The most common adjustment you will need to make will be to adjust for membership fees/subscriptions paid in advance or in arrears.

Answers to chapter activities

Activity 1

Using a membership fee account, we can see that fees of £4,200 will be shown in the Income and Expenditure Account.

Membership fees

	£		£
1.4.X7 Balance b/d	650	31.3.X8 Cash	4,500
31.3.X8 I & E account	4,200	31.3.X8 Balance b/d	350
	4,850		**4,850**

3 Test your knowledge

Workbook Activity 2

Toptown Table Tennis Club has received membership fees of £3,600 during the year ended 31.12.X5. At 1.1.X5, membership fees of £30 had been paid in advance, and at 31.12.X5, fees of £20 had been paid in advance.

(a) Calculate the total membership fees to be shown as income in the Income & Expenditure Account for the year ended 31.12.X5.

(b) State how the membership fees paid in advance will be shown in the Balance Sheet at 31.12.X5.

WORKBOOK ACTIVITY ANSWERS

Workbook Activities Answers

Double entry bookkeeping

Workbook Activity 5

Assets	Fixed assets (5,000 + 6,000)	11,000
	Cash (15,000 – 6,000)	9,000
	Stock (4,000 – 1,500)	2,500
	Debtors	2,000
		24,500

Assets – Liabilities = Capital
£24,500 – £4,000 = £20,500

Capital (ownership interest) has increased by the profit made on the sale of stock.

Workbook Activity 6

The balance on the capital account represents the investment made in the business by the owner. It is a special liability of the business, showing the amount payable to the owner at the balance sheet date.

Workbook Activity 7

Tony

Bank Account

	£		£
Capital (a)	20,000	Purchases (b)	1,000
Sales (g)	1,500	Purchases (c)	3,000
Sales (i)	4,000	Insurance (d)	200
		Storage units (e)	700
		Advertising (f)	150
		Telephone (h)	120
		Stationery (j)	80
		Drawings (k)	500
		Balance c/d	19,750
	25,500		25,500
Balance b/d	19,750		

Capital

	£		£
Balance c/d	20,000	Bank (a)	20,000
	20,000		20,000
		Balance b/d	20,000

Purchases

	£		£
Bank ((b)	1,000	Balance c/d	4,000
Bank (c)	3,000		
	4,000		4,000
Balance b/d	4,000		

Insurance

	£		£
Bank (d)	200	Balance c/d	200
	200		200
Balance b/d	200		

Storage units – cost

	£		£
Bank (e)	700	Balance c/d	700
	700		700
Balance b/d	700		

Advertising

	£		£
Bank (f)	150	Balance c/d	150
	150		150
Balance b/d	150		

Telephone

	£		£
Bank (h)	120	Balance c/d	120
	120		120
Balance b/d	120		

Sales

	£		£
Balance c/d	5,500	Bank (g)	1,500
		Bank (i)	4,000
	5,500		5,500
		Balance b/d	5,500

Stationery

	£		£
Bank (j)	80	Balance c/d	80
	80		80
Balance b/d	80		

Drawings

	£		£
Bank (k)	500	Balance c/d	500
	500		500
Balance b/d	500		

Workbook Activity 8

Dave

Cash

	£		£
Capital	500	Rent	20
Sales	210	Electricity	50
		Car	100
		Drawings	30
		Balance c/d	510
	710		710
Balance b/d	510		

Capital

	£		£
Balance c/d	500	Cash	500
	500		500
		Balance b/d	500

Purchases

	£		£
Creditors (A Ltd)	200	Balance c/d	200
	200		200
Balance b/d	200		

Creditors (A Ltd)

	£		£
Balance c/d	200	Purchases	200
	200		200
		Balance b/d	200

Sales

	£		£
Balance c/d	385	Debtors (X Ltd)	175
		Cash	210
	385		385
		Balance b/d	385

Debtors (X Ltd)

	£		£
Sales	175	Balance c/d	175
	175		175
Balance b/d	175		

Electricity

	£		£
Cash	50	Balance c/d	50
	50		50
Balance b/d	50		

Rent

	£		£
Cash	20	Balance c/d	20
	20		20
Balance b/d	20		

Motor car

	£		£
Cash	100	Balance c/d	100
	100		100
Balance b/d	100		

Drawings

	£		£
Cash	30	Balance c/d	30
	30		30
Balance b/d	30		

Workbook Activity 9

Audrey Line

Bank

	£		£
Capital	6,000	Rent	500
Sales	3,700	Shop fittings	600
		Creditors	1,200
		Wages	600
		Electricity	250
		Telephone	110
		Drawings	1,600
		Balance c/d	4,840
	9,700		9,700
Balance b/d	4,840		

Capital

	£		£
		Bank	6,000

Sales

	£		£
		Bank	3,700

Shop fittings

	£		£
Bank	600		

Rent

	£		£
Bank	500		

Telephone

	£		£
Bank	110		

Drawings

	£		£
Bank	1,600		

Purchases

	£		£
Creditors	2,000		

Creditors

	£		£
Bank	1,200	Purchases	2,000
Balance c/d	800		
	2,000		2,000
		Balance b/d	800

Wages

	£		£
Bank	600		

Electricity

	£		£
Bank	250		

2 Accounting for sales – summary

Workbook Activity 8

(a) Cash receipts book

Cash receipts book								
Narrative	*SL Code*	*Discount* £	*VAT Adjust-ment* £	*Cash* £	*Bank* £	*VAT* £	*Cash sales* £	*SLCA* £
G Heilbron	SL04				108.45			108.45
L Tessa	SL15	3.31	0.66		110.57			110.57
J Dent	SL17	6.32	1.26		210.98			210.98
F Trainer	SL21				97.60			97.60
A Winter	SL09	3.16	0.63		105.60			105.60
Cash sales				240.00		40.00	200.00	
		12.79	2.55	240.00	633.20	40.00	200.00	633.20

(b) General ledger accounts

VAT account

	£		£
CRB – VAT adj	2.55	28/4 CRB	40.00

Sales ledger control account

	£		£
		28/4 CRB	633.20
		CRB – discount	12.79
		CRB – VAT adj	2.55

Sales account

	£		£
		28/4 CRB	200.00

Discount allowed account

	£		£
28/4 CRB	12.79		

(Note that the total of the 'Discount' and VAT adjustment columns are not included in the cross-cast total of £873.20. The discounts allowed and corresponding VAT adjustment are entered into the cash receipts book on a memorandum basis; the total discounts at the end of each period is posted to the sales ledger control account and to an expense account, and the total VAT adjustment at the end of each period is posted to the sales ledger control account and the VAT account.)

(c) Subsidiary ledger

G Heilbron **SL04**

	£		£
		28/4 CRB	108.45

L Tessa **SL15**

	£		£
		28/4 CRB	110.57
		CRB – discount	3.31
		CRB – VAT adj	0.66

		J Dent		**SL17**
	£			£
		28/4	CRB	210.98
			CRB – discount	6.32
			CRB – VAT adj	1.26

		F Trainer		**SL21**
	£			£
		28/4	CRB	97.60

		A Winter		**SL09**
	£			£
		28/4	CRB	105.60
			CRB – discount	3.16
			CRB – VAT adj	0.63

Workbook Activity 9

Cash receipts book

Narrative	*Discount* £	*VAT adjustment* £	*Cash* £	*Bank* £	*VAT* £	*Cash Sales* £	*SLCA* £
Irlam Transport			468.00		78.00	390.00	
Paulson Haulage			216.00		36.00	180.00	
Mault Motors			348.00		58.00	290.00	
James John Ltd	24.39	4.78		579.08			579.08
Exilm & Co	19.80	3.96		456.74			456.74
	44.19	8.74	1,032.00	1,035.82	172.00	860.00	1,035.82

Workbook Activity 10

	True/False
Documents can be disposed of as soon as the year end accounts are prepared. *Explanation – Businesses must keep copies of business and financial documents as they can be inspected by HMRC and used as evidence in legal action.*	FALSE
Documents cannot be inspected by anyone outside the business. *Explanation – Documents can be inspected by HMRC in a tax or VAT inspection.*	FALSE
Documents can be used as legal evidence in any legal actions.	TRUE
Businesses must keep an aged debtor analysis as part of their financial documents. *Explanation – Many businesses do keep an aged debtor analysis but it is not necessary to do so.*	FALSE
Businesses do not need to keep copies of invoices *Explanation – Businesses do need to keep copies of invoices as they can be inspected by HMRC.*	FALSE
Businesses need to keep copies of their bank statements available for inspection.	TRUE

3 Accounting for purchases – summary

Workbook Activity 6

CASH PAYMENTS BOOK										
Date	*Details*	*Code*	*Discount*	*VAT Adj*	*Cash*	*Bank*	*VAT*	*PLCA*	*Cash purchases*	*Other*
			£	£	£	£	£	£	£	£
12/3/X1	Homer Ltd	PL12	5.06	1.01		167.69		167.69		
	Forker & Co	PL07	5.38	1.07		178.38		178.38		
	Purchases				342.00		57.00		285.00	
	Print Ass.	PL08				190.45		190.45		
	ABG Ltd	PL02	6.62	1.32		219.35		219.35		
	Purchases				200.40		33.40		167.00	
	G Greg	PL19				67.89		67.89		
			17.06	3.40	542.40	823.76	90.40	823.76	452.00	–

General ledger

Purchases ledger control account

		£			£
12/3	CPB	823.76	5/3	Balance b/d	4,136.24
12/3	CPB discount	17.06			
12/3	CPB - VAT adj	3.40			

VAT account

		£			£
12/3	CPB	90.40	5/3	Balance b/d	1,372.56
			12/3	CPB - VAT adj	3.40

Purchases account

		£			£
5/3	Balance b/d	20465.88			
12/3	CPB	452.00			

Discounts received account

		£			£
			5/3	Balance b/d	784.56
			12/3	CPB	17.06

Purchases ledger

ABG Ltd PL02

		£			£
12/3	CPB 03652	219.35	5/3	Balance b/d	486.90
12/3	CPB discount	6.62			
12/3	CPB VAT adj	1.32			

Forker & Co PL07

		£			£
12/3	CPB 03649	178.38	5/3	Balance b/d	503.78
12/3	CPB discount	5.38			
12/3	CPB VAT adj	1.07			

Print Associates PL08

		£			£
12/3	CPB 03651	190.45	5/3	Balance b/d	229.56

Homer Ltd PL12

		£			£
12/3	CPB 03648	167.69	5/3	Balance b/d	734.90
12/3	CPB discount	5.06			
12/3	CPB VAT adj	1.01			

G Greg PL19

		£			£
12/3	CPB 03654	67.89	5/3	Balance b/d	67.89

Workbook Activity 7

Cash payments book

Narrative	*Discount* £	*VAT Adj* £	*Cash* £	*Bank* £	*VAT* £	*Cash Purchases* £	*PLCA* £	*Expenses* £
JD & Co			96.00		16.00	80.00		
LJ Ltd			240.00		40.00	200.00		
MK Plc			60.00		10.00	50.00		
TB Ltd	2.52	0.50		68.89			68.89	
CF Ltd	3.16	0.63		156.72			156.72	
Electricity				90.00				90.00
Stationery				84.00	14.00			70.00
	5.68	1.13	396.00	399.61	80.00	330.00	225.61	160.00

Workbook Activity 8

REMITTANCE ADVICE

To:

Building Contract Supplies
Unit 15 Royal Estate
Manchester
M13 2EF

Nethan Builders
Brecon House
Stamford House
Manchester
M16 4PL

Tel: 0161 521 6411
Fax: 0161 530 6412
VAT reg: 471 3860 42
Date: 18 May 20X1

Date	Invoice no	Amount £	Discount taken and VAT adj £	Paid £
18 May 20X1	07742	204.18	3.06	201.12

Total paid £201.12

Cheque no 200550

REMITTANCE ADVICE

To:

Jenson Ltd
30 Longfield Park
Kingsway
M45 2TP

Nethan Builders
Brecon House
Stamford House
Manchester
M16 4PL

Tel: 0161 521 6411
Fax: 0161 530 6412
VAT reg: 471 3860 42
Date: 18 May 20X1

Date	Invoice no	Amount £	Discount taken and VAT adj £	Paid £
18 May 20X1	47811	185.13	5.55	179.58

Total paid £179.58

Cheque no 200551

REMITTANCE ADVICE

To:

Magnum Supplies
140/150 Park Estate
Manchester
M20 6EG

Nethan Builders
Brecon House
Stamford House
Manchester
M16 4PL

Tel: 0161 521 6411
Fax: 0161 530 6412
VAT reg: 471 3860 42
Date: 18 May 20X1

Date	Invoice no	Amount £	Discount taken and VAT adj £	Paid £
18 May 20X1	077422	758.88	15.18	743.70

Total paid £743.70

Cheque no 200552

REMITTANCE ADVICE

To:

Haddow Bros
The White House
Standing Way
Manchester M13 6FH

Nethan Builders
Brecon House
Stamford House
Manchester
M16 4PL

Tel: 0161 521 6411
Fax: 0161 530 6412
VAT reg: 471 3860 42
Date: 18 May 20X1

Date	Invoice no	Amount £	Discount taken £	Paid £
18 May 20X1	G33940	512.64	10.25	502.39

Total paid: £502.39

Cheque no: 200553

4 Ledger balances and control accounts

Workbook Activity 9

Account name	Amount £	Dr ✓	Cr ✓
Cash	2,350	✓	
Capital	20,360		✓
Motor Vehicles	6,500	✓	
Electricity	800	✓	
Office expenses	560	✓	
Loan from bank	15,000		✓
Cash at bank	6,400	✓	
Factory equipment	14,230	✓	
Rent	2,500	✓	
Insurance	1,000	✓	
Miscellaneous expenses	1,020	✓	

Workbook Activity 10

(a)

Purchases ledger control account

	£		£
Cash paid	47,028	Balance b/d	5,926
Purchases returns	202	Purchases (total from PDB)	47,713
Discounts received	867		
Sales ledger control account (contra)	75		
Balance c/d (bal fig)	5,467		
	53,639		53,639

(b)

Sales ledger control account

	£		£
Balance b/d	10,268	Bank account	69,872
Sales (total from SDB)	71,504	Bad debts account	96
		Sales returns account (total from SRDB)	358
		Discounts allowed (total from discount column in CB)	1,435
		Purchases ledger control account (contra)	75
		Balance c/d (bal fig)	9,936
	81,772		81,772

Workbook Activity 11

(a) **Sales ledger control account**

		£			£
30 Sep	Balance b/f	3,825	30 Sep	Bad debts account (2)	400
				Purchases ledger control account (4)	70
				Discount allowed (5)	140
				Balance c/d	3,215
		3,825			3,825
1 Oct	Balance b/d	3,215			

(b) **List of sales ledger balances**

	£
Original total	3,362
Add: Debit balances previously omitted (1)	103
	3,465
Less: Item posted twice to Sparrow's account (3)	(250)
Amended total agreeing with balance on sales ledger control account	3,215

Workbook Activity 12

(a)

Account name	Amount £	Dr ✓	Cr ✓
Purchase ledger control account	1,000.00	✓	
Purchases	1,000.00		✓

(b)

Account name	Amount £	Dr ✓	Cr ✓
Purchase ledger control account	9.00	✓	
Discounts received	9.00		✓

(c)

Account name	Amount £	Dr ✓	Cr ✓
Purchase ledger control account	300.00	✓	
Sales ledger control account	300.00		✓

Workbook Activity 13

(a)

Details	Amount £	Dr ✓	Cr ✓
Balance of debtors at 1 July	60,580	✓	
Goods sold on credit	18,950	✓	
Payments received from credit customers	20,630		✓
Discounts allowed	850		✓
Bad debt written off	2,400		✓
Goods returned from credit customers	3,640		✓

(b)

	Amount £
Sales ledger control account balance as at 31 July	52,010
Total of sales ledger accounts as at 31 July	54,410
Difference	2,400

(c)

	✓
Goods returned may have been omitted from the sales ledger	
Bad debt written off may have been omitted from the sales ledger	✓
Goods returned may have been entered twice in the sales ledger	
Bad debt written off may have been entered twice in the sales ledger	

Workbook Activity 14

(a)

Details	**Amount £**	**Dr ✓**	**Cr ✓**
Balance of creditors at 1 July	58,420		✓
Goods bought on credit	17,650		✓
Payments made to credit suppliers	19,520	✓	
Discounts received	852	✓	
Contra entry with sales ledger control	600	✓	
Goods returned to credit suppliers	570	✓	

(b)

	Amount £
Purchases ledger control account balance as at 31 July	54,528
Total of purchase ledger accounts as at 31 July	52,999
Difference	1,529

(c)

	✓
Payments made to suppliers may have been understated in the purchase ledger	
Goods returned to suppliers may have been overstated in the purchase ledger	✓
Goods bought on credit may have been overstated in the purchase ledger	
Contra entry may have been omitted from the purchase ledger	

5 Accounting for VAT

Workbook Activity 10

VAT control account

	£		£
Bank	8,455	Opening balance	8,455
Input VAT 143,600 × 20%	28,720	Output VAT :	39,350
Balance carried down	10,630	236,100 × 20/120	
	47,805		47,805
		Balance brought down	10,630

The closing balance on the account represents the amount of VAT owing to HM Revenue and Customs.

Workbook Activity 11

1 True – it is only compulsory to issue VAT invoices to registered traders.

2 False – the £250 is VAT inclusive.

3 True – VAT invoices form the evidence for the reclaim of input tax.

4 True

Workbook Activity 12

VAT must be charged on the price payable after any trade discount and before any settlement discount.

£180.00 ((£1,000 – 10% of £1,000 = £900) × 20%)

£400.00 (£2,000 × 20%)

£138.00 (£750 – 8% of £750) × 20%

Workbook Activity 13

A 1

B 2

C 3

D 1

E 3

Workbook Activity 14

A and C are false. A proforma invoice is NOT a valid tax invoice, nor is it evidence that allows the customer to reclaim input tax.

Workbook Activity 15

1 20 August. The invoice is raised within 14 days of the delivery date (the basic tax point) and hence a later tax point is created.

2 10 June. The issue of the proforma invoice is ignored so the receipt of payment is the tax point.

3 4 March. The invoice is raised more than 14 days after the delivery date so the tax point stays on the delivery date.

4 10 December. The goods are invoiced before delivery so this creates an earlier tax point.

Workbook Activity 16

1 The correct answer is A.

Receipt of cash on 19 October creates a tax point

2 The correct answer is B.

£100 is VAT inclusive so the VAT element is £16.66 (£100 × 1/6)

3 The correct answer is C.

The goods are invoiced within 14 days of delivery so a later tax point is created.

4 The correct answer is B.

£350 is VAT inclusive so the VAT element is £58.33 (£350 × 1/6)

Workbook Activity 17

		£
VAT due in this period on **sales** and other outputs	**Box 1**	4,324.00
VAT due in this period on **acquisitions** from other **EC Member States**	**Box 2**	0.00
Total VAT due (**the sum of boxes 1 and 2**)	**Box 3**	4,324.00
VAT reclaimed in the period on **purchases** and other inputs, including acquisitions from the EC	**Box 4**	1,835.12
Net VAT to be paid to HM Revenue & Customs or reclaimed by you (**Difference between boxes 3 and 4**)	**Box 5**	2,488.88
Total value of **sales** and all other outputs excluding any VAT. **Include your box 8 figure**	**Box 6**	21,500
Total value of purchases and all other inputs excluding any VAT. **Include your box 9 figure**	**Box 7**	9,176
Total value of all **supplies** of goods and related costs, excluding any VAT, to other **EC Member States**	**Box 8**	0
Total value of all **acquisitions** of goods and related costs, excluding any VAT, from other **EC Member States**	**Box 9**	0

Workings for VAT return

		£
Box 1:	From SDB	4,300.00
	Error on previous return	24.00
		4,324.00

		£
Box 4:	From PDB	1,820.00
	Petty cash	15.12
		1,835.12

		£
Box 7:	From PDB	9,100
	Petty cash (£75.60 rounded up)	76
		9,176

Workbook Activity 18

		£
VAT due in this period on **sales** and other outputs	**Box 1**	7,680.00
VAT due in this period on **acquisitions** from other **EC Member States**	**Box 2**	0.00
Total VAT due (**the sum of boxes 1 and 2**)	**Box 3**	7,680.00
VAT reclaimed in the period on **purchases** and other inputs, including acquisitions from the EC	**Box 4**	3,428.00
Net VAT to be paid to HM Revenue & Customs or reclaimed by you (**Difference between boxes 3 and 4**)	**Box 5**	4,252.00
Total value of **sales** and all other outputs excluding any VAT. **Include your box 8 figure**	**Box 6**	38,400
Total value of purchases and all other inputs excluding any VAT. **Include your box 9 figure**	**Box 7**	16,740
Total value of all **supplies** of goods and related costs, excluding any VAT, to other **EC Member States**	**Box 8**	0
Total value of all **acquisitions** of goods and related costs, excluding any VAT, from other **EC Member States**	**Box 9**	0

***Workings* for VAT return**

		£
Box 4:	From PDB	3,294.00
	Petty cash (W1)	54.00
	Bad debts (W2)	80.00
		3,428.00

		£
Box 7:	From PDB	16,470
	Petty cash (£324 – £54) (W1)	270
		16,740

(W1) Total petty cash expenditure = (£108 + £96 + £120) = £324

VAT on £324 = (20/120 × £324) = £54.00

(W2) Bad debts more than six months old = (£300 + £180) = £480

VAT on £480 = (20/120 × £480) = £80

Workbook Activity 19

1 False – VAT invoices must still be supplied to customers.

2 False – A VAT account must still be kept.

3 True – It is possible to be in the flat rate and the annual accounting scheme.

4 False – the limit to join the scheme is £150,000.

5 True – The flat rate percentage is determined by your trade sector

Workbook Activity 20

1 The correct answer is D.

This is how the annual accounting scheme payments are made.

2 The correct answer is B.

31 August 20X2 – two months after the year end.

6 Bank reconciliations

Workbook Activity 3

Cash receipts book

Date	*Narrative*	*Bank*	*VAT*	*Debtors*	*Other*	*Discount allowed*	*VAT Adj*
20X1		£	£	£	£	£	£
7/3	Balance b/f	860.40✓					
7/3	Paying in slip 0062	1,117.85✓	84.05	583.52	450.28	23.60	4.72
8/3	Paying in slip 0063	1,056.40✓	68.84	643.34	344.22	30.01	6.00
9/3	Paying in slip 0064	1,297.81✓	81.37	809.59	406.85	34.20	6.84
10/3	Paying in slip 0065	994.92	57.02	652.76	285.14	18.03	3.60
11/3	Paying in slip 0066	1,135.34	59.24	779.88	296.22	23.12	4.62
	BGC – L Fernley	406.90✓		406.90			
	Bank interest	6.83✓			6.83		
		6,876.45	350.52	3,875.99	1,789.54	128.96	25.78

Cash payments book

Date	*Details*	*Cheque no*	*Code*	*Bank*	*VAT*	*Creditors*	*Cash purchases*	*Other*	*Discounts received*	*VAT Adj*
20X1				£	£	£	£	£	£	£
7/3	P Barn	012379	PL06	383.21✓		383.21				
	Purchases	012380	GL	274.04✓	45.67		228.37			
	R Trevor	012381	PL12	496.80✓		496.80			6.30	1.26
8/3	F Nunn	012382	PL07	218.32		218.32				
	F Taylor	012383	PL09	467.28✓		467.28			9.34	1.86
	C Cook	012384	PL10	301.40✓		301.40				
9/3	L White	012385	PL17	222.61		222.61				
	Purchases	012386	GL	275.13✓	45.85		229.28			
	T Finn	012387	PL02	148.60✓		148.60				
10/3	S Penn	012388	PL16	489.23		489.23			7.41	1.48
11/3	P Price	012389	PL20	299.99		299.99				
	Purchases	012390	GL	270.12	45.02		225.10			
	Loan finance	SO	GL	200.00✓				200.00		
				4,046.73	136.54	3,027.44	682.75	200.00	23.05	4.60

FINANCIAL BANK plc  CONFIDENTIAL

YOU CAN BANK ON US

10 Yorkshire Street
Headingley
Leeds LS1 1QT
Telephone: 0113 633061

Account CURRENT

Account name T R FABER LTD

Sheet no. 00614

Statement date 11 March 20X1 *Account Number* 27943316

Date	*Details*	*Withdrawals (£)*	*Deposits (£)*	*Balance (£)*
7/3	Balance from sheet 00613			860.40✓
	Bank giro credit L Fernley		406.90✓	1,267.30
9/3	Cheque 012380	274.04✓		
	Cheque 012381	496.80✓		
	Credit 0062		1,117.85✓	1,614.31
10/3	Cheque 012383	467.28✓		
	Cheque 012384	301.40✓		
	Credit 0063		1,056.40✓	
	SO – Loan Finance	200.00✓		1,702.03
11/3	Cheque 012379	383.21✓		
	Cheque 012386	275.13✓		
	Cheque 012387	148.60✓		
	Credit 0064		1,297.81✓	
	Bank interest		6.83✓	2,199.73

DD	Standing order	DD	Direct debit	CP	Card purchase
AC	Automated cash	OD	Overdrawn	TR	Transfer

BANK RECONCILIATION STATEMENT AS AT 11 MARCH 20X1

	£
Balance per bank statement	2,199.73
Add: Outstanding lodgements:	
Paying in slip 0065	994.92
Paying in slip 0066	1,135.34
Less: Unpresented cheques:	
Cheque 012382	(218.32)
Cheque 012385	(222.61)
Cheque 012388	(489.23)
Cheque 012389	(299.99)
Cheque 012390	(270.12)
Balance per cash book (Total of bank receipts – total of bank payments)	£2,829.72

Workbook Activity 4

Cash book

		£			£
16/4	Donald & Co	225.47✓	16/4	Balance b/d	310.45✓
17/4	Harper Ltd	305.68✓	17/4	Cheque 03621	204.56
	Fisler Partners	104.67✓	18/4	Cheque 03622	150.46✓
18/4	Denver Ltd	279.57✓	19/4	Cheque 03623	100.80
19/4	Gerald Bros	310.45		Cheque 03624	158.67✓
20/4	Johnson & Co	97.68	20/4	Cheque 03625	224.67
			20/4	Balance c/d	173.91
		1,323.52			1,323.52

There are three unticked items on the bank statement:

- direct debit £183.60 to the District Council;
- cheque number 03621 £240.56 – this has been entered into the cash book as £204.56;
- bank interest £3.64.

Cheques 03623 and 03625 are unticked items in the cash book but these are payments that have not yet cleared through the banking system.

EXPRESS BANK CONFIDENTIAL

High Street
Fenbury
TL4 6JY
Telephone: 0169 422130

Account CURRENT Sheet no. 0213

Account name P L DERBY LTD

Statement date 20 April 20X1 *Account Number* 40429107

Date	*Details*	*Withdrawals (£)*	*Deposits (£)*	*Balance (£)*
16/4	Balance from sheet 0212			310.45 OD
17/4	DD – District Council	183.60		494.05 OD
18/4	Credit		225.47✓	
19/4	Credit		104.67✓	
	Cheque 03621	240.56		
	Bank interest	3.64		408.11 OD
20/4	Credit		305.68✓	
	Credit		279.57✓	
	Cheque 03622	150.46✓		
	Cheque 03624	158.67✓		131.99 OD

DD	Standing order	DD	Direct debit	CP	Card purchase
AC	Automated cash	OD	Overdrawn	TR	Transfer

Workbook Activity 5

Graham

(a)

Bank account

	£		£
Balance b/f	204	Sundry accounts	
Interest on deposit account	18	Standing orders	35
		Bank charges	14
		Balance c/d	173
	222		222
Balance b/d	173		

(b)

BANK RECONCILIATION STATEMENT AT 31 MARCH 20X3

	£
Balance per bank statement	2,618
Add Uncleared lodgements	723
	3,341
Less Unpresented cheques	(3,168)
Balance per cash account	173

Workbook Activity 6

BANK RECONCILIATION STATEMENT AS AT 30 JUNE 20X1

	£	£
Balance per bank statement		(1,160.25) O/D
Outstanding lodgements:		6,910.25
30 June		
		5,750.00
Unpresented cheques:	538.00	
121		
122	212.00	
		(750.00)
Balance per cash book (7,100.45+ 17,111.55 – 19,212.00)		£5,000.00

7 Fixed Assets

Workbook Activity 8

Stapling machine

(a) No.

(b) Although, by definition, since the stapler will last a few years, it might seem to be a fixed asset, its treatment would come within the remit of the concept of materiality and would probably be treated as office expenses.

Workbook Activity 9

Office equipment

The item will have value in future years and could therefore be regarded as a fixed asset. However, the stronger argument is that this is not justified by the relatively small amount involved and the concept of materiality would suggest treatment as an expense of the year.

Workbook Activity 10

Engine

This would typically represent capital expenditure. As the engine is being depreciated separately from the rest of the plane it is effectively an asset in its own right. Therefore the replacement of the separate component is like the purchase of a new asset.

If, on the other hand, the engine was depreciated as part of the plane as a whole it is likely that the replacement cost would simply be treated as a repair/refurbishment cost and would be accounted for as an expense.

8 Depreciation

Workbook Activity 8

Motor car cost

	£		£
20X3		20X3	
1 Jan Purchase ledger control	12,000	31 Dec Balance c/d	12,000
20X4		20X4	
1 Jan Balance b/d	12,000	31 Dec Balance c/d	12,000
20X5		20X5	
1 Jan Balance b/d	12,000	31 Dec Balance c/d	12,000
20X6			
1 Jan Balance b/d	12,000		

$$\text{Annual depreciation charge} = \frac{12{,}000 - 2{,}400}{4}$$

$$= £2{,}400$$

Motor car – accumulated depreciation account

	£		£
20X3		20X3	
31 Dec Balance c/d	2,400	31 Dec Depreciation expense	2,400
20X4		20X4	
31 Dec Balance c/d	4,800	1 Jan Balance b/d	2,400
		31 Jan Depreciation expense	2,400
	4,800		4,800
20X5		20X5	
31 Dec Balance c/d	7,200	1 Jan Balance b/d	4,800
		31 Dec Depreciation expense	2,400
	7,200		7,200
		20X6	
		1 Jan Balance b/d	7,200

Depreciation expense account

		£		£
20X3			20X3	
31 Dec	Motor car accumulated depreciation	2,400	31 Dec P&L a/c	2,400
20X4			20X4	
31 Dec	Motor car accumulated depreciation	2,400	31 Dec P&L a/c	2,400
20X5			20X5	
31 Dec	Motor car accumulated depreciation	2,400	31 Dec P&L a/c	2,400

Workbook Activity 9

(1) Straight line method

$$\text{Annual depreciation} = \frac{\text{Cost} - \text{Scrap value}}{\text{Estimated life}}$$

$$= \frac{£6,000 - £1,000}{8 \text{ years}}$$

$$= £625 \text{ p.a.}$$

Machine account

	£		£
Year 1:			
Cost	6,000		

Accumulated depreciation

	£		£
Year 1:		Year 1:	
Balance c/d	625	Depreciation expense	625
Year 2:		Year 2:	
Balance c/d	1,250	Balance b/d	625
		Depreciation expense	625
	1,250		1,250

Year 3:		Year 3:	
Balance c/d	1,875	Balance b/d	1,250
		Depreciation expense	625
	1,875		1,875
		Year 4:	
		Balance b/d	1,875

Balance sheet extract:

		Cost	*Accumulated depreciation*	*Net book value*
		£	£	£
Fixed asset:				
Year 1	Machine	6,000	625	5,375
Year 2	Machine	6,000	1,250	4,750
Year 3	Machine	6,000	1,875	4,125

(2) Reducing balance method

		£
Cost		6,000
Year 1	Depreciation 20% × £6,000	1,200
		4,800
Year 2	Depreciation 20% × £4,800	960
		3,840
Year 3	Depreciation 20% × £3,840	768
Net book value		3,072

Workbook Activity 10

Hillton

(a)

Workings:		*Chopper*	*Mincer*	*Stuffer*	*Total*
		£	£	£	£
Cost		4,000	6,000	8,000	18,000
Depreciation	20X6 – 25%	(1,000)			(1,000)
Depreciation	20X7 – 25%	(1,000)	(1,500)		(2,500)
Depreciation	20X8 – 25%	(1,000)	(1,500)	(2,000)	(4,500)
Net book value at 31 Dec 20X8		1,000	3,000	6,000	10,000

Machinery

	£		£
20X6		20X6	
Cash – chopper	4,000	Balance c/d	4,000
20X7		20X7	
Balance b/d	4,000		
Cash – mincer	6,000	Balance c/d	10,000
	10,000		10,000
20X8		20X8	
Balance b/d	10,000		
Cash – stuffer	8,000	Balance c/d	18,000
	18,000		18,000
20X9			
Balance b/d	18,000		

Accumulated depreciation (machinery)

	£		£
20X6		20X6	
Balance c/d	1,000	Depreciation expense	
		(25% × £4,000)	1,000
20X7		20X7	
Balance c/d	3,500	Balance b/d	1,000
		Depreciation expense	
		(25% × £10,000)	2,500
	3,500		3,500

	£		£
20X8		20X8	
Balance c/d	8,000	Balance b/d	3,500
		Depreciation expense (25% × £18,000)	4,500
	8,000		8,000
		20X9	
		Balance b/d	8,000

Depreciation expense (machinery)

	£		£
20X6		20X6	
Accumulated depreciation	1,000	Profit and loss account	1,000
20X7		20X7	
Accumulated depreciation	2,500	Profit and loss account	2,500
20X8		20X8	
Accumulated depreciation	4,500	Profit and loss account	4,500

(b)

Workings:

	Metro	*Transit*	*Astra*	*Total*
	£	£	£	£
Cost	3,200	6,000	4,200	13,400
Depreciation 20X6 – 40%	(1,280)			(1,280)
NBV 31.12.X6	1,920			
Depreciation 20X7 – 40%	(768)	(2,400)		(3,168)
NBV 31.12.X7	1,152	3,600		
Depreciation 20X8 – 40%	(461)	(1,440)	(1,680)	(3,581)
Net book value at 31 Dec 20X8	691	2,160	2,520	5,371

Motor vehicles

	£		£
20X6		20X6	
Cash – Metro	3,200	Balance c/d	3,200
20X7		20X7	
Balance b/d	3,200		
Cash – Transit	6,000	Balance c/d	9,200
	9,200		9,200
20X8		20X8	
Balance b/d	9,200		
Cash – Astra	4,200	Balance c/d	13,400
	13,400		13,400
20X9			
Balance b/d	13,400		

Accumulated depreciation (machinery)

	£		£
20X6		20X6	
Balance c/d	1,280	Depreciation charge	1,280
	1,280		1,280
20X7		20X7	
		Balance b/d	1,280
Balance c/d	4,448	Depreciation charge	3,168
	4,448		4,448
20X8		20X8	
		Balance b/d	4,448
Balance c/d	8,029	Depreciation charge	3,581
	8,029		8,029
		Balance b/d	8,029

Depreciation expense (motor vehicles)

	£		£
20X6		20X6	
Accumulated depreciation	1,280	Profit and loss account	1,280
20X7		20X7	
Accumulated depreciation	3,168	Profit and loss account	3,168
20X8		20X8	
Accumulated depreciation	3,581	Profit and loss account	3,581

Workbook Activity 11

Depreciation for vehicle sold 1 March 20X3 (18,000 × 20% × 3/12)	900
Depreciation for vehicle purchased 1 June 20X3 (10,000 × 20% × 6/12)	1,000
Depreciation for vehicle purchased 1 September 20X3 (12,000 × 20% × 3/12)	600
Depreciation for other vehicles owned during the year ((28,400 – 18,000) × 20%)	2,080
Total depreciation for the year ended 30 November 20X3	4,580

9 Disposal of fixed assets

Workbook Activity 4

(a) Profit or loss on disposal

	£
Cost	12,000
Depreciation	(5,000)
CV	7,000

Comparing the carrying value of £7,000 with the sale proceeds of £4,000, there is a loss of (7,000 – 4,000) = £3,000.

(b) Ledger account entries

Disposal of fixed assets account

	£		£
Car cost	12,000	Accumulated depreciation	5,000
		Cash at bank a/c (sales proceeds)	4,000
		Loss on disposal	3,000
	12,000		12,000

Car account

	£		£
Balance b/d	12,000	Disposal a/c	12,000

Car accumulated depreciation account

	£		£
Disposal a/c	5,000	Balance b/d	5,000

Cash at bank account

	£		£
Disposal a/c	4,000		

Workbook Activity 5

Machinery

	£		£
20X7		20X7	
Cash	2,700	Balance c/d	2,700
20X8		20X8	
Balance b/d	2,700	Balance c/d	2,700
20X9		20X9	
Balance b/d	2,700	Disposals account	2,700

Accumulated depreciation (machinery)

	£		£
20X7		20X7	
Balance c/d	675	Depreciation expense (25% × £2,700)	675
20X8		20X8	
		Balance b/d	675
Balance c/d	1,181	Depreciation expense (25% × (£2,700 – £675))	506
20X9		20X9	
Disposals account	1,181	Balance b/d	1,181

Depreciation expense (machinery)

	£		£
20X7		20X7	
Accumulated depreciation	675	P & L A/C	675
20X8		20X8	
Accumulated depreciation	506	P & L A/C	506

Disposals

	£		£
20X9		20X9	
Machinery – cost	2,700	Accumulated depreciation	1,181
		Cash	1,300
		P & L A/C – loss on disposal	219
	2,700		2,700

Workbook Activity 6

Keith

1 Calculate the Balance b/d position at 1 January 20X7:

		Cost	*Accumulated depreciation*		*Accumulated depreciation at 1 Jan 20X7*
		£		£	£
Piece machine	(1 June 20X5)	10,000	$\frac{£10,000}{5}$	2,000	4,000
Acrylic machine	(1 Jan 20X6)	5,000	$\frac{£5,000 - £1,000}{5}$	800	800
Heat seal machine	(1 June 20X6)	6,000	$\frac{£6,000}{5}$	1,200	1,200
		21,000		4,000	6,000

2 Calculate the annual depreciation on the new assets:

	Cost	Annual depreciation	
	£		£
20X7			
Lathe machine (1 Jan 20X7)	10,000	$\frac{£10,000}{4}$	2,500
Cutting machine (1 Apr 20X7)	12,000	$\frac{£12,000 - £1,000}{5}$	2,200
Assets b/d at 1 January 20X7	(calc from part 1)		4,000
Charge for the year (20X7)			8,700
20X8			
Lathe machine			2,500
Cutting machine			2,200
Laser machine (1 Jun 20X8)	28,000	$\frac{£28,000 - £2,800}{7}$	3,600
Assets b/d at 1 January 20X7			4,000
Charge for the year (20X8)			12,300
20X9			
Lathe machine			2,500
Cutting machine – disposed of			–
Laser machine			3,600
Micro-cutter (1 Apr 20X9)	20,000		
Add: Installation	1,500		
	21,500	$\frac{£21,500 - 3,000}{5}$	3,700
Assets b/d at 1 January 20X7			4,000
Charge for the year (20X9)			13,800

3 Show the ledger accounts

Plant and machinery account

		£		£
20X7				
Assets Balance b/d		21,000		
Lathe machine		10,000		
Cutting machine		12,000	Balance c/d 31.12.X7	43,000
		43,000		43,000
20X8				
Assets Balance b/d		43,000		
Laser machine		28,000	Balance c/d 31.12.X8	71,000
		71,000		71,000
20X9				
Assets Balance b/d		71,000	Disposal account	12,000
Micro-cutter				
Disposal	3,000			
Bank account	17,000			
Installation costs	1,500	21,500	Balance c/d 31.12.X9	80,500
		92,500		92,500

Accumulated depreciation

	£		£
20X7		20X7	
		Balance b/d (1)	6,000
Balance c/d	14,700	Depreciation account (2)	8,700
	14,700		14,700
		20X8	
		Balance b/d	14,700
Balance c/d	27,000	Depreciation account	12,300
	27,000		27,000
		20X9	
Disposal account (4)	4,400	Balance b/d	27,000
Balance c/d	36,400	Depreciation account	13,800
	40,800		40,800

4 Calculate the accumulated depreciation on the cutting machine disposed of:

Cutting machine	purchased	1 April 20X7
	disposed	1 March 20X9

Therefore depreciation should have been charged for 20X7 and 20X8 and none in 20X9, the year of sale.

Accumulated depreciation is £2,200 × 2 = £4,400.

Debit	Accumulated depreciation account	£4,400	
Credit	Disposal account		£4,400

Depreciation expense

	£		£
20X7		20X7	
Accumulated depreciation	8,700	P & L A/C	8,700
20X8		20X8	
Accumulated depreciation	12,300	P & L A/C	12,300
20X9		20X9	
Accumulated depreciation	13,800	P & L A/C	13,800

Disposals

	£		£
20X9			
Plant and machinery cost	12,000	Accumulated depreciation	4,400
		Part exchange – plant and machinery account	3,000
		Loss on disposal (bal fig)	4,600
	12,000		12,000

5 Disposal journal entries for part exchange:

Debit	Plant and machinery account		£3,000	
Credit	Disposal account			£3,000

Part exchange allowance.

Debit	P & L A/C	£4,600		
Credit	Disposal account			£4,600

Loss on sale

Debit	Plant and machinery			
Cost	(£20,000 – £3,000)	£17,000		
Installation		£1,500		
			£18,500	
Credit	Bank account			£18,500

Balance on cost of new machine – micro-cutter

---

6 Show extracts from financial statements:

Profit and Loss Account extracts

	20X7	*20X8*	*2009*
	£	£	£
Depreciation	8,700	12,300	13,800
Loss on disposal	–	–	4,600

Balance Sheet extracts

		Cost	*Accumulated depreciation*	*Carrying value*
		£	£	£
Fixed assets				
20X7	Plant and machinery	43,000	14,700	28,300
20X8	Plant and machinery	71,000	27,000	44,000
20X9	Plant and machinery	80,500	36,400	44,100

Workbook Activity 7

Disposals account

	£		£
Motor vehicles	12,000	Accumulated depreciation	3,800
Profit on disposal	1,800	Motor vehicles (part ex)	10,000
	13,800		13,800

Accumulated depreciation = £12,000 × 20% × 19/12 = 3,800

Workbook Activity 8

Motor van account

	£		£
Old van	16,400	Disposal account	16,400
Payables (21,000 – 5,500)	15,500		
Disposal account – trade in value	5,500	Balance c/d	21,000
	37,400		37,400
Balance b/d	21,000		

Accumulated depreciation

	£		£
Disposal account	9,840	Balance b/d (16,400 × 15% × 4)	9,840

Disposal account

	£		£
Cost	16,400	Accumulated depreciation	9,840
		Trade in value	5,500
		Loss on disposal	1,060
	16,400		16,400

10 Accounting for stock

Workbook Activity 4

The stock should be valued at the lower of its cost and net realisable value (NRV).

The NRV is calculated as the actual or estimated selling price less any future costs that will be incurred before the product can be sold.

The cost of each PC is £500.

Its NRV less costs to sell is £580 – £100 = £480.

Therefore each PC will be valued at the lower amount of £480: as there are 10 PCs in stock, the value of the closing stock will be
10 × £480 = £4,800.

Workbook Activity 5

Ledger Account	**DR** **£**	**CR** **£**
Closing stock (Balance Sheet)	5,000	
Closing stock (Trading A/C)		5,000

11 Accruals and prepayments

Workbook Activity 8

Rent payable

	£		£
Cash paid	15,000	P&L account	12,000
		Balance c/d (prepayment)	3,000
	15,000		15,000
Balance b/d (prepayment)	3,000		

Gas

	£		£
Gas paid	840	P&L account	1,440
Balance c/d (840 × 5/7) (accrual)	600		
	1,440		1,440
		Balance b/d (accrual)	600

Advertising

	£		£
Cash	3,850	P&L account	3,350
		Balance c/d (prepayment)	500
	3,850		3,850
Balance b/d (prepayment)	500		

Bank interest

	£		£
Cash	28	P&L account	96
Cash	45		
Balance c/d ($^1/_3$ × 69) (accrual)	23		
	96		96
		Balance b/d (accrual)	23

Rates

	£		£
Balance b/d (prepayment $^3/_6 \times 4,800$)	2,400	P&L account	11,300
Cash	5,600		
Balance c/d ($^3/_6 \times 6,600$) (accrual)	3,300		
	11,300		11,300
		Balance b/d (accrual)	3,300

Rent receivable

	£		£
Balance b/d (250 × 3/6) (debtor = accrued income)	125	Cash	250
P&L account (W)	575	Cash	600
Balance c/d (3/12 × 600) (deferred income)	150		
	850		850
		Balance b/d (creditor = deferred income)	150

***Working:* Profit and loss account credit for rent receivable**

	£
1 January 20X4 – 31 March 20X4 ($^3/_6 \times 250$)	125
1 April 20X4 – 31 December 20X4 ($^9/_{12} \times 600$)	450
	575

Workbook Activity 9

A Crew

Stationery

	£		£
31 Dec Balance per trial balance	560	31 Dec P&L account	545
		31 Dec Balance c/d (prepayment)	15
	560		560
1 Jan Balance b/d (prepayment)	15		

Rent

	£		£
31 Dec Balance per trial balance	900	31 Dec P&L account	1,200
31 Dec Balance c/d (accrual)	300		
	1,200		1,200
		1 Jan Balance b/d (accrual)	300

Rates

	£		£
31 Dec Balance per trial balance	380	31 Dec P&L account	310
		31 Dec Balance c/d (prepayment (280 × 3/12)	70
	380		380
1 Jan Balance b/d (prepayment)	70		

Lighting and heating

	£		£
31 Dec Balance per trial balance	590	31 Dec P&L account	605
31 Dec Balance c/d (accrual)	15		
	605		605
		1 Jan Balance b/d (accrual)	15

Insurance

	£		£
31 Dec Balance per trial balance	260	31 Dec P&L account	190
		31 Dec Balance c/d (prepayment)	70
	260		260
1 Jan Balance b/d (prepayment)	70		

Wages and salaries

	£		£
31 Dec Balance per trial balance	2,970	31 Dec P&L account	2,970

Workbook Activity 10

A Metro

Motor tax and insurance

	£		£
Balance b/d (prepayment)	570	P&L account (W2)	2,205
Cash		Balance c/d (W1)	
		(prepayment)	835
1 April	420		
1 May	1,770		
1 July	280		
	3,040		3,040
Balance b/d (prepayment)	835		

Workings:

1 *Prepayment at the end of the year*

	£
Motor tax on six vans paid 1 April 20X0 ($\frac{3}{12}$ × 420)	105
Insurance on ten vans paid 1 May 20X0 ($\frac{4}{12}$ × 1,770)	590
Motor tax on four vans paid 1 July 20X0 ($\frac{6}{12}$ × 280)	140
Total prepayment	835

2 *Profit and loss charge for the year*

There is no need to calculate this as it is the balancing figure, but it could be calculated as follows.

	£
Prepayment b/d	570
Motor tax ($\frac{9}{12}$ × 420)	315
Insurance ($\frac{8}{12}$ × 1,770)	1,180
Motor tax ($\frac{6}{12}$ × 280)	140
Profit and loss charge	2,205

12 Accounting for bad and doubtful debts

Workbook Activity 5

Step 1

Write up the sales ledger control account showing the opening balance, the credit sales for the year and the cash received.

Sales ledger control account

20X6		£	20X6		£
1 Jan	Bal b/d	68,000	31 Dec	Cash	340,000
31 Dec	Sales	354,000			

Step 2

Write off the bad debts for the period:

Dr Bad debt expense account

Cr Sales ledger control account

Bad debt expense

20X6		£	20X6		£
31 Dec	SLCA	2,000			

Sales ledger control account

20X6		£	20X6		£
1 Jan	Balance b/d	68,000	31 Dec	Cash	340,000
31 Dec	Sales	354,000	31 Dec	Bad debt expense	2,000

Step 3

Balance off the SLCA account to find the closing balance against which the provision is required.

SLCA

20X6		£	20X6		£
1 Jan	Balance b/d	68,000	31 Dec	Cash	340,000
31 Dec	Sales	354,000	31 Dec	Bad debt expense	2,000
			31 Dec	Balance c/d	80,000
		422,000			422,000
20X7					
1 Jan	Balance b/d	80,000			

Step 4

Set up the provision required of 5% of £80,000 = £4,000. Remember that there is already an opening balance on provision for doubtful debts account of £3,400 therefore only the increase in provision required of £600 is credited to the provision account and debited to the bad debt expense account.

Bad debt expense account

20X6	£	20X6	£
Provision for doubtful debts	600	31 Dec P & L A/C	600
	600		600

Provision for doubtful debts

20X6	£	20X6	£
		1 Jan Balance b/d	3,400
31 Dec Balance c/d	4,000	31 Dec Bad debt expense	600
	4,000		4,000
		20X7	
		1 Jan Balance b/d	4,000

Step 5

The relevant extract from the Balance Sheet at 31 December 20X6 would be as follows:

	£	£
Current assets	80,000	
Trade debtors		
Less: Provision for doubtful debts	(4,000)	
		76,000

Workbook Activity 6

Angola

Provision for doubtful debts

	£		£
Balance c/d	530	Bad debt expense account	530
	530		530
		Balance b/d	530

Bad debt expense

	£		£
Debts written off			
Cuba	46	P & L A/C	711
Kenya	29		
Peru	106		
Provision account	530		
	711		711

Working – Provision carried down

Specific:	£110 + £240	£350
General:	4% × (£5,031 – £46 – £29 – £106 – £350)	£180
		530

Workbook Activity 7

Zambia

Provision for doubtful debts

	£		£
		Balance b/d	530
Balance c/d (W1)	601	Bad debt expense account extra charge required (W2)	71
	601		601
		Balance b/d	601

Working

1 **Provision carried down**

		£
Specific:		
General:	5% × (£12,500 – £125 – £362)	601
		601

2 **Extra charge required**

	£
Provision required at end of year	601
Provision brought down and available	530
Increase required in provision	71

Bad debt expense

		£		£
Debts written off	Fiji	125	Cash	54
	Mexico	362	P & L A/C	504
Provision account		71		
		558		558

Workbook Activity 8

The accounting concept here is that of prudence.

13 Preparation of final accounts for a sole trader

Workbook Activity 7

David Pedley

Profit and loss account for the year ended 31 December 20X8

	£	£
Sales		28,400
Less: Returns		(200)
		28,200
Opening stock	–	
Purchases	16,100	
Less: Closing stock	(2,050)	
Cost of sales		(14,050)
Gross profit		14,150
Salaries	4,162	
Rent and rates	2,130	
Insurance	174	
General expenses	1,596	
Total expenses		(8,062)
Net profit		6,088

Balance sheet as at 31 December 20X8

	£	£
Fixed assets		
Motor van		1,700
Current assets		
Closing stock	2,050	
Trade Debtors	5,060	
Cash at bank	2,628	
Cash in hand	50	
	9,788	

Current Liabilities		
Trade creditors	(6,400)	
Net current assets		3,388
Net assets		5,088
Capital account		
Capital introduced		4,100
Profit for the year (per trading and profit and loss account)		6,088
Less: Drawings		(5,100)
Proprietor's funds		5,088

Workbook Activity 8

Karen Finch

Profit and loss account for the year ended 31 March 20X8

	£	£
Sales (£17,314 + £4,256)		21,570
Purchases (£10,350 + £5,672)	16,022	
Closing stock	(4,257)	
		(11,765)
Gross profit		9,805
Assistant's salary plus bonus (£2,000 + £400)	2,400	
Electricity (£560 + £170)	730	
Rent and rates	1,100	
Postage and stationery	350	
Depreciation	1,000	
Total expenses		(5,580)
Net profit		4,225

Balance sheet at 31 March 20X8

	£	£
Fixed assets		
Motor van at cost		4,000
Accumulated Depreciation		(1,000)
Net book value		3,000
Current assets		
Stocks	4,257	
Trade debtors	4,256	
Cash (W1)	6,554	
	15,067	
Current liabilities		
Trade creditors	5,672	
Accruals (400 + 170)	570	
	6,242	
Net current assets		8,825
Net assets		11,825
Capital		
Capital introduced at 1 April 20X7		10,000
Profit for the year		4,225
Less Drawings		2,400
Proprietor's funds		11,825

Working:

1	**Cash balance at 31 March 20X8**	£	£
	Capital introduced at 1 April 20X7		10,000
	Amounts received from customers		17,314
			27,314
	Salary of assistant	2,000	
	Cash paid to suppliers	10,350	
	Purchase of motor van	4,000	
	Drawings	2,400	
	Electricity	560	
	Rent and rates	1,100	
	Postage and stationery	350	
			20,760
	Cash balance at 31 March 20X8		6,554

Workbook Activity 9

(a) **Ledger accounts**

Closing stock (profit and loss)

	£		£
Balance to profit and loss account	3,060	Closing stock balance sheet	3,060

Closing stock (balance sheet)

Closing stock profit and loss account	3,060	Balance c/d	3,060
	3,060		3,060
Balance b/d	3,060		

Rates

	£		£
Per trial balance	1,490	Profit and loss	1,175
		Balance c/d (1,260 × 3/12)	315
	1,490		1,490
Balance b/d	315		

Electricity

	£		£
Per trial balance	379	Profit and loss	423
Balance c/d (132/3)	44		
	423		423
		Balance b/d	44

Points to note:

- As regards electricity the accrual of £44 is shown on the balance sheet as a current liability, the effect of it being to increase the charge to profit and loss for electricity.
- With rates the prepayment of £315 is shown on the balance sheet as a current asset (being included between debtors and cash), the effect of it being to reduce the charge to profit and loss for rates.

- In the case of trading and profit and loss account items; income should be debited out of the relevant income account and credited to the trading and profit and loss account; expense should be credit out of the relevant expense account and debited to the trading and profit and loss account.
- Balance sheet items are carried down at the end of the year and included on the balance sheet and are consequently brought down in the ledger accounts as the opening balances at the beginning of the next period.

(b)

Elmdale

Trading and profit and loss account for the year ended 31 December 20X8

	£	£
Sales		21,417
Opening stock	2,700	
Purchases	9,856	
	12,556	
Closing stock	(3,060)	
Cost of sales		9,496
Gross profit		11,921
Rates	1,175	
Electricity	423	
Wages and salaries	3,704	
Sundry expenses	2,100	
Total expenses		7,402
Net profit		4,519

14 Suspense accounts and errors

Workbook Activity 4

(a) Error NOT disclosed by the trial balance

(b) Error NOT disclosed by the trial balance

(c) Error NOT disclosed by the trial balance

(d) Error NOT disclosed by the trial balance

(e) Error disclosed by the trial balance

(f) Error disclosed by the trial balance

Workbook Activity 5

Debit Suspense £109,868

Workbook Activity 6

	Balances at 1 July	
	Debit £	*Credit* £
Motor vehicles	24,200	
Plant and Equipment	22,350	
Stock	9,000	
Cash at Bank	11,217	
Cash	150	
Sales ledger control	131,275	
Purchases ledger control		75,336
VAT owing to HMRC		15,127
Capital		26,247
Bank Loan		12,500
Sales		276,132
Purchases	152,476	
Wages	35,465	
Motor expenses	3,617	
Repairs and Renewals	2,103	
Rent and rates	3,283	
Light and Heat	4,012	
Insurance	4,874	
Sundry Expenses	1,320	
Suspense account (credit balance)		
Total	405,342	405,342

15 Professional ethics

Workbook Activity 5

James needs to safeguard the fundamental principle of objectivity.

His friendship may colour his judgement in favour of his friend.

Workbook Activity 6

(1) Potential conflict with professional behaviour – bookkeepers observe the same standards, therefore implying that a rival has lower standards suggests that a firm is not complying with professional standards.

(2) This is an issue of integrity. Bookkeepers must not be associated with any form of communication or report that they know to be either materially false or misleading.

(3) Ethics involves avoiding negative impacts on the environment that the company operates in. Even though legal, the decision to dump pollution into a river is unethical due to the impact on marine life. Should a bookkeeper be complicit in such an action, it is likely to bring the profession into disrepute.

Workbook Activity 7

Objectivity and confidentiality.

16 Legal considerations

Workbook Activity 7

(a) **C** – If you suspect money laundering is occurring, you should disclose the issue to your MLRO.

(b) **C** – If you are involved in money laundering, you face 14 years imprisonment, and/or an unlimited fine.

Workbook Activity 8

As part of his customer due diligence process, David must undertake the following:

- Verify the client's identity on the basis of documents, data or other reliable information.
- Obtain information on the purpose and intended nature of the client relationship.

Workbook Activity 9

(a) **B** – Customer due diligence refers to Verifying your client's identity.

(b) **B** – Customer due diligence is performed to comply with Money laundering legislation.

17 Partnership accounts

Workbook Activity 3

Current accounts

	Owen	*Griffiths*		*Owen*	*Griffiths*
	£	£		£	£
Drawings	6,500	5,500	Balance b/d	1,000	2,000
			Interest on capital	900	1,000
			Salary	5,000	
Balance c/d	1,950		Profit (see below)	1,550	1,550
			Balance c/d		950
	8,450	5,500		8,450	5,500

Allocation of net profit of £10,000

	Owen	*Griffiths*	*Total*
	£	£	£
Interest on capital	900	1,000	1,900
Salary	5,000	–	5,000
Balance of profit £10,000– £1,900 - £5,000 = £3,100 to be shared 1:1	1,550	1,550	3,100
Totals	7,450	2,550	10,000

Note The interest on the 10% loan accounts is an expense of the partnership and so is not shown in the appropriation account but as an expense in the Profit and Loss Account.

18 Not for profit organisations

Workbook Activity 2

a) Using a membership fee account, we can see that fees of £3,610 will be shown in the Income and Expenditure Account.

Membership fees

	£		£
I & E account	3,610	1.1.X5 Balance b/d	30
31.12.X5 Balance c/d	20	Cash	3,600
	3,630		**3,630**

b) The membership fees paid in advance at 31.12.X5 will be shown as part of liabilities in the balance sheet as this these represent income that will be recognised in a future period in the Income and Expenditure Account

INDEX

S

T

U

V